About the author

Manfred Liebel is Professor of Sociology at the Technical University (TU) of Berlin. He works mainly on international and intercultural research on childhood and youth. He is also a member of the University's Centre for Global Education and International Cooperation and a consultant on working children and youth movements in Latin America and Africa. He is co-editor of *NATs – Working Children and Adolescents International Review/Revista Internacional desde los Niños y Adolescentes Trabajadores* (in both its English and Spanish editions).

He is the author of numerous monographs and books in German, Spanish and English on the subject of children and young people. His main publications since 1990 include:

'Wir wollen nicht überleben, sondern leben.' *Jugend in Lateinamerika.* Frankfurt: IKO, 1990.

Mala Onda. La Juventud Popular en América Latina. Managua: Ediciones Nicarao, 1992.

Protagonismo Infantil. Managua: Editorial Nueva Nicaragua, 1994.

'Wir sind die Gegenwart.' *Kinderarbeit und Kinderbewegungen in Lateinamerika.* Frankfurt: IKO, 1994.

Somos NATRAS. Testimonios de Niños Trabajadores de Nicaragua. Managua: Editorial Nueva Nicaragua, 1996.

'Bis vor kurzem wusste ich nicht, dass ein O rund ist.' *Nicaraguanische Kindheiten* (co-author). Münster: LIT, 1997.

Arbeitende Kinder stärken. Plädoyers für einen subjektorientierten Umgang mit Kinderarbeit (co-editor). Frankfurt: IKO, 1998.

Was Kinder könn(t)en. Handlungsperspektiven von und mit arbeitenden Kindern (co-editor). Frankfurt: IKO, 1999.

La Otra Infancia. Niñez trabajadora y accion social. Lima: Editorial Ifejant, 2000.

Working Children's Protagonism. Social Movements and Empowerment in Latin America, Africa and India (co-editor). Frankfurt & London: IKO, 2001.

Kindheit und Arbeit. Wege zum besseren Verständnis arbeitender Kinder in verschiedenen Kulturen und Kontinenten. Frankfurt & London: IKO, 2001.

Infancia y Trabajo. Para una mejor comprensión de los niños y niñas trabajadores de diferentes culturas y continentes. Lima : Editorial Ifejant, 2003.

Entre Fronteras - Grenzgänge. Jugendkulturen in Mexiko. Berlin: Archiv der Jugendkulturen Verlag, 2004.

About this book

Children's work is neither simply a relic of bygone times nor a feature of so-called backward societies. It is, in fact, currently on the increase – in a number of different ways – in all parts of the world, including the affluent countries of Europe and North America, and is closely linked to the processes of globalization.

This book shows how children's work can take on widely differing forms; how it can harm children, but also benefit them.

The approach of the book differs from most other publications in this field. Beyond being an attempt to define the great variety of children's work much more precisely, it endeavours to understand working children, and their ways of living and acting, from their own perspective. Particular attention is paid to children's own experiences and hopes, especially their attempts to articulate themselves in public and to fight together against exploitation and discrimination.

In this way the book shows that children frequently see and evaluate their work differently from adults. And that measures directed against children's work are not always in the interests of the children.

The author puts forward a plea to pursue a new 'subject-oriented' approach to dealing with children's work, and to take account of socio-cultural contexts, both in theory and practice. It shows that, in doing so, a dialogue between different societies, cultures and continents is indispensible and will contribute to finding viable solutions.

MANFRED LIEBEL

A Will of Their Own

Cross-cultural perspectives on working children

Zed Books

LONDON · NEW YORK

A Will of Their Own: Cross-cultural perspectives on working children was first published by Zed Books Ltd, 7 Cynthia Street, London N1 9JF, UK and Room 400, 175 Fifth Avenue, New York, NY 10010, USA in 2004.

www.zedbooks.co.uk

Cover designed by Andrew Corbett
Set in Monotype Dante and Gill Sans Heavy by Ewan Smith, London
Printed and bound in Malaysia

Distributed in the USA exclusively by Palgrave Macmillan, a division of St Martin's Press, LLC, 175 Fifth Avenue, New York, NY 10010.

A catalogue record for this book is available from the British Library
Library of Congress cataloging-in-publication data: available

ISBN 1 84277 348 8 cased
ISBN 1 84277 349 6 limp

Contents

Preface

This book represents an attempt to discuss the controversial and emotive topic of 'children's work' from a subject-oriented perspective. The focus is on working children themselves, and their work is principally considered from the point of view of the meanings that it has for them. This aspect has been neglected hitherto, despite the frequent invocation of children's rights. Neither in sociological research nor in political debate has the necessary attention been paid to it.

Considering the working child as an active subject and as the focus of attention renders necessary a consideration of the ideology and institutionalization of childhood that arose with bourgeois society in Europe, and spread and continues to spread throughout the world. I am concerned to make clear that the notion that work and the condition of being a child are mutually exclusive, or can only be combined to the detriment of children, which came into existence together with the bourgeois pattern of childhood, has become questionable, both in the case of the societies of the South, held as they are in poverty and dependence, and in that of the comparatively affluent societies of the North, if for different reasons.

In the course of the book, I take up experiences, ideas and proposals that have been articulated for a number of years by the movements and organizations of working children and adolescents in Latin America, Africa and Asia, and connect these with the discussion of recent theoretical drafts and sociological research findings from Latin America, the USA and a number of European countries, in which working children are seen as 'actors' or 'subjects'.

With this book I pursue further the subject-oriented train of thought on children's work and working children initiated in the publications *Wir sind die Gegenwart. Kinderarbeit und Kinderbewegungen in Lateinamerika* (Frankfurt: IKO, 1994; Spanish version: *Protagonismo Infantil. Movimientos de Niños Trabajadores en América Latina*, Managua: Editorial Nueva Nicaragua, 1994) and *La Otra Infancia. Niñez trabajadora y acción social* (Lima: Editorial IFEJANT, 2000), as well as in contributions to three volumes of collected essays (Liebel et al. 1998, 1999, 2001).

From the second half of the 1980s onwards, I was able to have direct experience of dealing with working children in Latin America, and also sporadically in Africa. This experience has changed the orientation of my thinking on children's work from a theoretical to a practical one, and helped me to see the work of children in the context of their lives and from their point of view. In particular, I believe I have gained an idea of the great psychological energy and the cognitive and practical skills that the children possess, and how important it is for them to gain trust and to strengthen their self-confidence in order to allow this energy and these skills to bear fruit.

I have repeatedly had the opportunity to find out in personal conversations and at specialist conferences that I share similar ideas with a number of fellow social researchers and social workers in countries of both the South and the North. I found particularly stimulating the discussions and exchange of ideas with Alejandro Cussiánovich (Peru), Jorge Domic (Bolivia), Carlos Arana, Maritza Cisne and Carlos González (all Nicaragua), Libertad Hernández, Luis Rodríguez Gabarrón and Gerardo Sauri (Mexico), Fabrizio Terenzio (Senegal), Antonella Invernizzi (Switzerland/Great Britain), Giangi Schibotto (Italy), Olga Nieuwenhuys (Netherlands) and in Germany with Sabine Broscheit, Heinz Hengst, Dieter Kirchhöfer, Bernd Overwien, Albert Recknagel, Ursula Velten, Anne Wihstutz, Gisela Wuttke and Helga Zeiher.

Libertad Hernández was the victim of an assassination on 6 August 1998 in Mexico City, which was very probably an act of revenge for her persistent activity in support of human rights, and which has still not been solved by the Mexican authorities.

Bernd Overwien and Anne Wihstutz have commented critically on the typescript of the book, which was first written in German, and have helped me to rethink a number of passages and formulate them more clearly.

I have made some cuts and additions since the first German edition, *Verlag für interkulturelle Kommunikation* (Frankfurt and London: IKO, 2001). The translation from German into English was undertaken by Colin Boone, to whom I express my thanks here. Jess Rothenburger collaborated on the translation of part of Chapter 11, first written in Spanish.

The translation and publication were made possible by financial grants from the German foundation Menschenwürde und Arbeitswelt (Human Dignity and the World of Work) and the Max-Traeger foundation of the German trade union of academic school and college staff (Gewerkschaft Erziehung und Wissenschaft – GEW).

I should be glad to receive questions, criticism and comments at the following address: Technische Universität Berlin, Fakultät I, Institut für Gesellschaftswissenschaften und historisch-politische Bildung – Centre for Global Education and International Cooperation, Sekr. FR 3–7, Franklinstrasse 28/29, D-10785 Berlin, Germany; e-mail: <manfred.liebel@tu-berlin.de>.

Manfred Liebel
Berlin, February 2003

Introduction

Since child labour became a 'social problem' a century and a half ago in the capitalist societies of Europe and North America, and the 'struggle against child labour' began, working children as a social category have paradoxically lost their profile and disappeared as actors on the world stage. Reference was no longer made to working children, only to child labour. Until quite recently, working children were perceived at best as pitiable, helpless victims, or even as an embarrassing blot on the landscape, and were accounted relics of a bygone age.

Voices of working children in the societies of the South

It was to fall to the lot of the working children of the South to prepare the way for a new perspective. With their movements and organizations, which have come into being in Latin America, Africa and Asia since the 1980s, working children have once again given themselves a voice and a face. Thereby they have also called in question many supposed certainties concerning children's work and the struggle for its abolition.

In this book, it is my concern to question habitual reflexes and supposed certainties and judgements on the work of children. In doing so, it is not my intention to minimize the various forms of exploitation and abuse of children that are still widespread and proliferating in the world today, but to open the reader's eyes to the variety of forms and meanings that work has and can have for children. Above all, I wish to make clear that through their work children make an important contribution to their families and societies, recognition of which up to now has largely been lacking, and to show how in a frequently impressive way they are intervening in public affairs and in matters that remain hidden from the public gaze, and developing their own visions of a better life and of work from which they will themselves benefit. In the countries of the South, at least, working children have shown themselves to be, across national borders, protagonists of a society in which the dignity of children is respected like that of its other members.

When, in May 1998, some working children from Nicaragua were visiting Germany at the invitation of the children's aid organization terre des hommes, one twelve-year-old girl took the wind out of the sails of a woman journalist. In answer to her question as to whether she would not give up working if her mother alone brought home enough money, the girl answered: 'Why should I? It makes me proud to earn something myself. I learn how to look after money. It gives me independence.' And the other children supported her: 'We want to work, but we want our work and our human dignity to be respected.'

From seven years of experience with children working and living in the streets in Latin America, and from some sporadic experience in Africa, I have learned that these children have ideas about their lives and their work of which adults as a rule have no idea, and which are far removed from common notions about children's work.[1] When, like the girl from Nicaragua, children say they want to earn money by working, they are aware that in societies whose economy is governed by capitalism even the basic necessities have their price. For instance, they say: 'If we earn no money, we cannot look after our teeth, and we can forget about attending school.' Those who perceive only the dangers and the negative consequences of work for children's health and education fail to take into account the price that the children would have to pay if they did not work. They themselves say: 'If we were not to work, we would remain illiterate, would have to run around in our underwear, succumb to misery and starve to death.'

The working children of the South remind us that we cannot understand and evaluate children's work without considering the specific conditions under which the children live. Many work not only because there is no other solution for them or because they feel responsible for their families, but also because, by means of working, they can overcome their impotence and gain a new self-confidence. The children realize that their work gives them more social weight. Although in many cases they do not see their work as being properly recognized, they feel that they are doing something indispensable for their families and for society. Not a few of the children have a comprehensive view of the significance and value of their work: 'If we did not work,' they say, 'we would live in an economic crisis that would be worse than the one we are experiencing today.'

The children see in their work not merely a burden or a necessity, but also a chance to learn things that school does not offer them. They say: 'Our work helps us to educate ourselves'; it serves 'to take up the experience of adults, to learn to defend ourselves, to make ourselves more independent, to master life, to prepare to be someone in life'. What many working children like is not always the work itself, but the fact that it enables them 'to be together with others'. The children who work in the street frequently say: 'We find friends and can play with one another.' They also like 'sharing work with others'. For many children in the countries of the South, work is an opportunity to get together in groups, either to help each other with their work, or to defend their interests and rights.

It is the children themselves who principally and perhaps also most convincingly call into question the supposed certainties concerning children's work. One of the most important tenets of the movements of working children in the South is that it is not the work itself which causes problems, but the conditions under which they often have to perform it. They are aware that in a situation less marked by poverty and the 'rule of money' they would have a better chance to find work they liked and which gave them something. But there is hardly a working child anywhere who wishes to be kept in a kind of reservation for children, away from work, in which it counts for nothing and is completely at the mercy of the adults. If there are laws governing their situation, then they expect these to allow both children and adults the right to work, and to mean they are better protected and have more say in their work (see Liebel 2001f).

Many children work in Northern societies too

For some years now, the European and North American public has been aware that children's work is not confined to the 'poor' countries of the South. Some studies have made it clear that in the 'rich' Northern countries too many children have paid jobs, as a rule in addition to attending school. This has given rise to a number of concerned commentaries in which the fear is expressed that the health and the school achievements of the children are threatened. Hardly any attention has been paid to what the children themselves have to say on this.

When some students of the Children's Work Project Group at the Technical University of Berlin investigated the reasons why children in Germany work and what they think about their work, they received answers such as the following:

- 'I also chop wood ... Now we want to see if we can sell the wood, because there are a number of old houses in this area that must need it for heating' (boy, ten)
- 'I have specialized in beans and peas, and my beans have grown really well' (girl, thirteen)
- ' ... so now I mean to do babysitting again; I like very small children' (girl, fifteen)
- 'If I was given a newborn baby, I could bring it up by myself – that is what I did with my little brother' (girl, fifteen)
- ' ... what working is ... You learn how to use your time and how to deal with people' (girl, fifteen)

- ' ... you learn a lot about how to do different things' (boy, ten)
- 'I hate just sitting in school' (girl, ten)
- 'You do typical schoolkids' jobs for money too. Of course, it should be some kind of fun, and something you can use later' (boy, fourteen)
- ' ... experience. I get no money for it, but I still help' (girl, fifteen)
- 'It's cool being able to help. It's a kind of ... challenge' (boy, ten)
- 'Boys also should learn to do jobs about the house. It's not just girls' work to do the cooking' (girl, thirteen)
- ' ... when I earn my own money, I can also say: "Yes, I can afford to buy this and that with it"' (girl, fourteen)
- ' ... when I'm older I won't go to my parents saying: "I want money for this or that" – I must work for it myself' (girl, fifteen)
- 'If you just need money ... I wouldn't be stopped by the fear of not being allowed to go to work. I would just do it' (boy, fourteen).[2]

Children's work in Germany, as in other Northern countries, is considerably different from that of children in the countries of the South. As a rule, it is not undertaken to ensure survival, nor does it endanger or put a strain on the children to the same extent. However, despite the differences, it is striking how many similarities there are in the way the children think of their work. It is notable that hardly any children experience their work as something that is forced on them or is unpleasant, but rather as an opportunity to do something serious and useful, of which they can be proud, to earn money of their own that they can dispose of as they like, to stand on their own feet and to learn something useful.[3] In the course of this book there will be more accounts of studies from various countries and continents which support and give more details of these impressions.

A new look at children's work

The perspective on children's work that has predominated hitherto obscures perception of such aspects. It is marked by a conception of work that sees it only as burdensome, a strain and a sacrifice. In particular children's work is thought of only as involving dangers and risks which are bound to hinder children's development and rob them of their freedom. On the other hand, there is a general lack of 'perspectives in which work is one of those human activities with which people grasp life, transform it and produce new aspects of it. In short, the *creative* side of work is absent. Nor is attention paid to the dimension which to the workers themselves opens up the path to a "learning involvement" with their environment' (Lüdtke 1999: 99; emphasis in the original).

As long as such perspectives are lacking, children's work must seem a kind of unfortunate accident of history or fate, which children are at the mercy of. And as such it is difficult to conceive that children could be capable of and interested in acting in a manner that is of significance for their environment, is taken seriously, and has some useful effect. Typical of this lack of imagination is the way in which children's work appears quite separate from the kind of 'performance' they are seen as capable of and which is expected of them. Performance is accepted only as something children are capable of in school, or at best also in sport, where it has nothing to do with production important for subsistence and planning life. Accordingly, the recognition awarded them for this is merely symbolic in nature – a grade, a certificate or at best a shining silver cup.

In our latitudes, the work of children is generally seen as a phenomenon from distant parts of the world or from our own distant past. A clear indication of this is given by a glance at a popular German encyclopaedia (*Meyers Enzyklopädisches Lexikon*, vol. 13). Here, under the heading *Kinderarbeit* (children's work/child labour), we read that this is a phenomenon of the eighteenth and nineteenth centuries, now consigned to history. At that time, it became an 'inhuman cycle' in the course of which both children and parents desperately sought survival, and in doing so had to accept long hours of work and both wearing and risky working procedures.

Public discourse on children's work today is marked by a high moral tone. When the media, or politicians of whatever persuasion, deal with the topic, they express unified indignation that such a thing still exists. Children's work is regarded as backward, barbaric, something that robs children of their childhood and in addition damages the economy.

This leaves a number of things out of the account.

One of these is that children's work – in both the North and the South – covers a wide spectrum, ranging from forms of forced labour to self-determined and need-oriented forms of work. At any rate, the United Nations Children's Fund (UNICEF) finds it important 'to distinguish between beneficial and intolerable work and to recognize that much child labour falls into a grey area between these two extremes' (UNICEF 1997: 24). And: 'In every country, rich or poor, it is the nature of the work children do that determines whether or not they are harmed by it – not the plain fact of their working' (ibid.: 18).

It is left out of the account that the forms of work that damage children's dignity most, and frequently threaten their health or lives, are by no means a result of cultural backwardness, but have been produced by capitalist globalization, whether because an increasing proportion of humanity is being plunged into hopeless poverty, or because the flexible and cheap labour potential of children helps them at least to gain a small advantage in the increasingly tough competition on the world markets (see Seabrook 2001).

It is left out of the account that 'our' moral judgement and the 'measures against child labour' that are demanded are based on a view and a cultural model of childhood that arose under particular circumstances in Europe and cannot simply be transferred to other societies and cultures. Furthermore, a number of problems of this model of childhood are (again) becoming apparent at present in the supposedly developed world. Thus the German educationist Hartmut von Hentig notes: 'When a society does not need its young people up to the age of 25, and shows this to them by interning them in schools, places from which nothing emerges, and makes sure to exclude them from all the tasks that adults carry out and are paid for as an indication and measure of their importance, then it is nurturing its own destroyers' (Hentig 1993: 120f).

Finally, it is left out of the account that working children are also subjects who cope with their own situation and develop their own ideas about their work and their lives. If, for instance, most of the organizations of working children in the South insist on a 'right to work' and social recognition of their work, this is accompanied by massive criticism both of capitalist exploitation and of the Eurocentric arrogance of those who can only imagine 'proper' childhood without work.

A new view of childhood

The fact that in Northern countries too a sense of the limitations and problems implicit in this view of childhood is making itself felt is given by a text by the psychologist Heinz-Rolf Lückert, which was included in the above-named encyclopaedia as a 'special article' on 'children in a changing world', and which undertakes a 'revision of our view of the child'. The article criticizes the way in which in our culture we 'artificially exclude children from our world of work'. Meanwhile, it would far better serve the development of their 'sleeping talents' if we were to 'urge and persuade them to work and stick to their work. The argument that young children are neither prepared for this nor have the necessary concentration is easily refuted. Children have the will to achieve, and show from an early age remarkable persistence, providing that a task appeals to them, and when their activity is noticed and respected' (Lückert 1980: 680). From their very birth, they evidence not only 'the need for contact and tenderness' but also 'the need for orientation and recognition'. This is a matter of achievement – that is, behaviour – which clearly combines strain and satisfaction. This, Lückert states, is meaningful and necessary for children's proper development.

Such a perspective 'places the focus on the *activity itself* as well as its product' (Lüdtke 1999: 101; emphasis in the original). This may be baking a cake that smells delicious and tastes good to friends, parents and siblings, or making a pair of polished shoes whose appearance causes pleasure to oneself or others, or action on behalf of a child that has had an accident in the road, to get medical treatment. These are examples from 'different worlds'. They make it clear that children's work is or can be more than work in the sense of earning money or the means of subsistence. It can be understood as a variety of everyday connections between various activities and their aspects of meaning, for which the concepts at our disposal – not least those of work and play, which are thought of as contraries – always impose a limitation. Pointing out such connections is one object of this book.

From such a perspective, finally, not only work but also childhood appears in a different light from that which became habitual in Western bourgeois society over the past two centuries. In this book, childhood is regarded not as a special sphere in which as yet immature and un-developed creatures have to be protected and promoted, but as a sphere in which children too count as people of equal value, having the right and the ability to be supported, to have their say, and to take part in decisions as to when they wish to begin working, and at what.

Work can be a form of social participation that serves the children, and gives them considerably greater weight in the 'world of grown-ups' than was accorded them in the hitherto dominant paternalistic societies and cultures. Such a perspective does not relieve adults of their respon-sibilities for the next and future generations; on the contrary, it obliges them to no longer make arbitrary decisions over the heads of the 'little ones', but to respect the children's own thoughts and actions.

Subject-oriented approaches to children's work

In recent years, under the influence of the children's movements and the campaigns for children's rights, there have been changes in the debates on children's work. Numerous NGOs, parts of UNICEF and a number of social scientists nowadays oppose an exclusively negative evaluation and general prohibition of children's work. They demand and practise a more varied analysis of the forms, conditions and cultural contexts of children's work. In addition, they speak out for giving children more attention both in scholarly research and in practical politics, and for letting them participate in all decisions that affect them. They do not judge political decisions and measures affecting children's work according to whether they come closer to the long unquestioned goal of abolishing children's work, but according to whether they really bring advantages for the children and their families.

Representatives of this so-called *child-centred approach*[4] largely orient themselves by the maxims of the International Convention on the Rights of the Child (CRC) that was passed by the UN General Assembly in 1989. In the CRC, children's work was evaluated according to whether it was detrimental to children's physical, moral, intellectual or social development. The idea of 'childish development', as represented in the context of the child-centred approach, is oriented to a concept of socialization that sees children not only as passive objects of external influences, but as subjects who actively cooperate in their own development. This gives scope for the social recognition and participation of working children. But in so far as children's working experience is considered only with regard to their own 'development', scant attention is paid to the importance for them of their social status and their opportunities to influence the development of society as a whole, as individuals or as a social group with its own specific interests.

The question of participation is almost exclusively considered from an educational or technical/pragmatic point of view. It is seen as important, because the children learn to trust their abilities and take on responsibility, and because measures only promise success when they are not imposed on those concerned. Children are seen as individuals whose abilities have so far been underestimated and ought now to be more often taken into account by adults. In the child-centred approach, however, working children are not thought of as a social group acting or able to act in an organized manner as *protagonists*.[5] They are neither thought able nor permitted to play an independent and important part in society or to exert an essential influence on political decisions or measures concerning children's work. In this view, working children have rights of their own, but are not seen as having equal rights.

By contrast, the *subject-oriented approach*, which underlies my thesis in this book, not only sees children as 'children', who complement and 'enrich' the acts of adults and the institutions dominated by them, but attempts to see them – in the social and economic sense – as *subjects* who, precisely because they are different from adults and have their own specific interests and needs, must be able to decide themselves about their affairs, and should be supported in this. In this context, special attention must be paid to the social movements and organizations of working children and the experience, insights and perspectives for action that they represent.

Approaching children's work from a subject-oriented perspective means perceiving working children as 'social actors' who through their activity contribute to the preservation and further development of human life and the society in which they live, and merit recognition for this. Their economic contribution and social recognition are of equal importance for children's development as subjects. This also requires seeing the work of children in an open and comprehensive manner, and not reducing the 'value' of their activity to such forms of work as are 'paid'. This also includes not devaluing children's work as 'help'. Recognizing it as an essential activity can, for instance, mean insisting on working conditions appropriate to human dignity and 'just' financial rewards.

By a subject-oriented approach, I also mean seeing children's work from the children's perspective and finding answers to the question of what work means to the children and in what way it is experienced and judged by the children. This means assessing one's own value standards in a self-critical manner, and accepting that children may feel and see their work in quite a different way from that which our habitual way of thinking suggests. This includes allowing children's perspective and judgment their own rightful existence, taking them seriously, and recognizing them as at least of equal status.

The question as to what extent or under what conditions work can become a 'free expression of life' for children is also important. By this I mean considering a way in which children are able to take part in the life of society by means of a freely chosen activity and to exert an influence on their living conditions. This is based on the assumption that work enriches children's lives, and is able to support and reinforce their status as subjects. Children's work is not unavoidably synonymous either with 'exploitation' or 'abuse' of children, nor is it a relic of a past age. Like the course of childhood in history in general, it has been constantly changing, and it now seems that it will in future once again assume a more important place in children's lives, and render it easier for children to be the subjects of their own lives and history.

A subject-oriented approach in this sense is not without its dangers. It runs the risk of playing down 'objective' or 'structural' impulses that become dominant behind children's backs, beyond the reach of their judgement and competence for action. It could also be used by 'interested circles' in 'society' as a whole to shrug off responsibility for children and leave it to their own 'strength' or 'initiative'. This happens, for instance, when in the neo-liberal state needy people are redefined as 'sovereign customers', or those who must rely on their labour power as 'labour power entrepreneurs'.

But such risks cannot be avoided by simply regarding working children as victims who have to be protected in general and preserved from any kind of risk. This would cement the children's position as that of objects, would amount to disenfranchising them, and above all would clash with the demand now being raised by children throughout the world to be able to act independently and have a say in matters that concern them. As is shown in this book, these growing demands also relate to work: an increasing number of children see their own work not primarily as a burden but as a legitimate right and an opportunity to play a more active and important part in society than is provided for by the traditional bourgeois model of childhood.

A subject-oriented approach to children's work requires an awareness that working children too are 'children of the society' in which they live. Their perspectives, judgements and wishes do not develop in some area outside society, and are influenced by the ideologies and norms that belong to this society. Thus, for example, many working children do not see their work primarily as work, or do not want it seen as such, because society suggests to them that children's activities cannot count as work, just because they are performed by children. Or they at first find their lesser remuneration in comparison with that of adults appropriate because they are still children. A collective process of rethinking must clearly first take place on the 'value' of one's own work and the practical relevance of one's own rights, in order to cause children to insist on a comprehensive recognition of their activities, essential as these may be.

In all societies, the assertion of subjectivity is confronted with more or less well-defined structural, cultural and social limitations, and is formed by confronting these. I therefore see it as an indispensable component of a subject-oriented approach to children's work to tackle these limitations. Among them is the fact that children are frequently unable to decide what kind of work they wish to do, or the fact that they have to work under conditions that allow little or no scope for their personal interests or development requirements. Then it is important to enquire how these limitations come about, for instance to what extent they are to be attributed to extreme poverty, relations of dependence caused by dominance, hierarchies of age, ideologies of childhood and/or a particular mode of production. These questions are discussed in the book with a view to possible theoretical explanations of the economic exploitation of children.

But also, and precisely in view of the given limitations of subjectivity, the question remains central as to the role that working children themselves (can) play in dealing with these conditions. A theoretical analysis must also take into account the children's (possible) judgements and actions. This is more than merely a question of scientific method. It has to do with the question as to who is most interested in overcoming the limitations of subjectivity and how theoretical reflection and empirical research can best contribute to achieving this in fact.

In a study called *Wege zum Subjekt* (Approaches to the Subject), the German educationist Erhard Meueler draws attention to how 'the desire to become the subject of one's own actions develops particularly from the situation of the subordinated, suppressed and subjected' (Meueler 1993: 76). He sees this not as a kind of automatic or linear process, but a dialectic one. The greater the suppression, the deeper the resignation, but also the more urgent 'the need for freedom' becomes. According to him,

> pre-existing conditions, unconscious, non-influenceable and not yet freely alterable, form a contradictory unity that the individual must face up to in his practical everyday behaviour. Marked by his history, highly dependent on a multiplicity of life-preserving conditions of modern living, the individual is not wholly congruent with them. He is not autonomous, but with his self-aware, resistant and renewing actions he resists the pressing world of the pre-existing. The freedom that he takes by acting is not absolute. Claiming this freedom is the consequence of his self-reflection and the education that determines it. (ibid.: 81)

When children begin to work, whether because of a situation of urgent material need or from dissatisfaction with their passive status as children, they take up a position as practical actors. The self-reflection and education referred to by Meueler have a better chance to develop if the children are able to express themselves to others and be heard. It is therefore indispensable for their development as subjects to 'give them a voice', and to stress the legitimacy of their own point of view and judgements. It is no less important to stress their acting competence and strengths and to insist on their participation.[6]

But working children's 'own voice' and 'strengths' must be placed in the context of their actual disadvantaging and discrimination and linked to a critique of the system-specific lack of responsibility towards working children. And we need to ensure that working children, with their voices and points of view, do not merely function as an ornament to a society dominated by adults, but are given the opportunity to make themselves felt in this as well. This includes making it possible for working children to articulate themselves in a collective and organized manner and also to be formally and legally represented in decision-making institutions and organizations.

Finally, subject orientation also means determining the 'objective' social tendencies that point beyond the 'object status' of working children and favour their subjectivity. These may entail expanding children's ability to make their own decisions so that new opportunities and forms of work come into being in which they have more space to act according to their own judgement and on their own responsibility. Such forms and opportunities for work go together, for instance, with the relativization of wage labour as the hitherto dominant form of work, with the removal of the borders between the spheres of work and life, between work and leisure time, with the emergence of new forms of responsibility in the home and the community, and perhaps also with the spread of new communication technologies. Here it is important to discover the particular 'innovative' strengths of children and the potential for learning and participation that comes with the various forms of work and technologies.

The forms of work that favour children's subjectivity cannot, of course, come to prevail by means of a natural process, and are not necessarily open to children. In the context of capitalist society, they frequently remain marked by exploitative interests and tend to instrumentalize the children's subjectivity and 'innovative strength'. From a subject-oriented perspective it is therefore indispensable to make children sensitive to subtle mechanisms of instrumentalization and to reinforce their self-confidence and 'negotiating power' wherever they have to defend themselves against unacceptable working and living conditions. One widespread form of collective self-awareness and resistance in various regions of the South is the independent networks of working children and adolescents, some of which have taken on the form of children's movements and trade unions. In the North, hardly any such networks have as yet come into being.

Some concepts used in the book

Where 'children' are referred to in this book, what is meant as a rule is not young children, but children from an age at which they are able to take on practical and productive tasks. The age at which this takes place varies from culture to culture and society to society. In non-Western cultures, it can sometimes be as young as four years of age, for instance when children carry younger siblings on their backs, even if the latter are already able to walk (see Schildkrout 1981: 98). In other societies of the South, children's work does not begin until the age of seven or eight, and this is not always voluntary. In contemporary societies of central Europe, children begin as a rule from the age of twelve to seek jobs and earn 'money of their own', but one may encounter children of eight or nine selling their old books or toys in the street.

In many countries, laws have been passed laying down a minimum age for involvement in an 'occupation'. In Peru, for instance, it is twelve years; in Germany it is linked to the conclusion of compulsory schooling. Convention No. 138 of the International Labour Organization (ILO), passed in 1973, urges governments to make children's work dependent on attaining a minimum age, envisaged as fifteen, and in the case of 'heavy work' eighteen. But these legal stipulations are scarcely observed in any societies, either in the North or the South. They meet with resistance, not only on the part of employers who may wish to keep the cheap labour of children available, but also of parents, who see in this an unrealistic intervention in cultural traditions; or again on the part of children, who see their striving for independence obstructed. The working children in the South who have joined together in movements of their own even demand for themselves an express right to work, by which they mean that children should be able to decide from what age they want to work (see Liebel 2001f).

In writing this book, I was faced with the question of how to describe or name the various societies and cultures to which I refer and which relate to the central problem. It has never been unproblematic to speak of the 'Third World', but since the dissolution of the Soviet power bloc this term has become completely obsolete. When, with a view to the South and now also the East of the globe, reference is made to 'developing countries' or 'developing societies', this creates the incorrect impression that the societies of central Europe and North America are in every respect 'developed' and may serve as models. And when reference is made to 'primitive', 'traditional' or 'pre-modern' cultures, 'modern' Western cultures are also taken as a positive yardstick, by which the other societies are accounted 'retarded' or 'out of date'. The criteria by which development and progress are measured – among other places in experts' reports of the United Nations organizations – originate on the one hand from societies that think of themselves as developed and progressive – a tautological circle in which the non-Western societies always come off worst. There is no general term for any of the societies or cultures to which I refer in this book that is free of ideological implications.

In order to avoid as far as possible these one-sided ascriptions, I shall simply refer for purposes of distinction to societies and countries of the 'North' and 'South', or to 'Western' or 'non-Western' societies, and occasionally to 'foreign' cultures. These distinctions are not to be understood in a strictly geographical sense: Australia or Japan, for instance, can be placed together with the North of the world from an economic viewpoint. Where I group several societies and cultures under the headings 'non-Western' or 'South', I by no means intend to ignore the frequently very great differences between these societies and cultures, but merely to stress the differences from 'Western' or 'Northern' societies. I wish to express the fact that in their important life patterns and practices they diverge from the life patterns and practices familiar to 'us', and that these are often inadequately understood from a Western standpoint. Frequently these are societies that have not assumed the political form of a national state, but possess cultural features in common within such states or across borders which are mostly based on local or group-specific traditions that have remained alive until today.

When I refer to *cultures*, I have in mind above all modes of living, customs, social relations and forms of expression and communication. When I speak of *societies*, I am thinking of social structures, forms of the division of labour, modes and relationships of production, and the power and dominance relationships that are embedded in them. The terms society and culture are not always clearly distinguishable. When I also occasionally refer to capitalist, industrial, post-industrial, bourgeois or affluent societies, I wish in each case to stress structural, economic or cultural particularities that are not subsumed in the distinction between 'Western' or 'non-Western', or 'North' and 'South'.

With regard to the life patterns and practices to which we commonly refer with the concepts of 'work' or 'childhood', it needs to be asked whether these are semantic universals which, without distorting perception and representation, are applicable at all to the extra-European or non-Western societies and cultures dealt with here. In many of these societies, reference is not made in an abstract and generalizing manner to 'work' or 'childhood' as is usual today in Western societies; instead, concrete activities or periods of life are named and distinguished according to their particular social functions and significance. Where general terms are used that correspond or come close to concepts in linguistic logic such as 'work' or 'childhood', they usually do not mean the same as is understood by them in Western societies.

If the terms 'work' and 'childhood' are used in the following despite these differerences, this is based on the consideration that in all societies people act to preserve and improve their lives (that is, they 'work'), and have produced particular patterns of living that distinguish various stages of life and determine their relation to each other. It is necessary, however, to use the concepts 'work' and 'childhood' in a manner that is open to culture-specific forms and meanings, and the attempt must be made to understand and interpret them 'from within', that is, within their own social contexts.

When referring to work performed by children, I talk as a rule of 'children's work'. In contrast to the practice of the ILO and numerous publications on the topic, I use the term 'child labour' only to refer to kinds of work performed by children which are clearly detrimental and disadvantageous to them. In this I follow the view of Boyden et al. (1998) that account must be also be taken of the conceptual level of the multifarious forms and meanings of children's work. In contrast to the expression 'child labour', the expression 'children's work' avoids a hasty evaluation and renders possible the necessary openness.

The abbreviations NGO, ILO and UNICEF occur frequently in the book. NGO stands for non-governmental organization. This refers to non-state organizations which, for instance, fight against globalization or racism, or for human rights, support the interests of minorities, including children, and in this case frequently run social or educational projects of their own. As a rule, they are to be distinguished from *social movements* in which certain population groups combine to support their *own* interests. ILO stands for International Labour Organization, a sub-organization of the United Nations that works for the humane regulation of working conditions and, in this connection, also deals with children's work. UNICEF is the United Nations Children's Fund, which champions the rights of children and plays an important part in putting into effect the UN Convention on the Rights of the Child. Like other UN organizations, the ILO and UNICEF are also referred to as inter-government organizations (IGOs).

The structure of the book

In Chapter 1, I give a survey of the movements and organizations of working children that have come into existence since the 1980s, and make it clear what they have in common and what their significance is for the societies and the children themselves. At the same time, I see the children's movements as a manifestation and pre-condition for the development of the 'social subjectivity' of working children. The question of the subject, which is discussed here with reference to an important publication by the French sociologist Alain Touraine, is discussed in greater detail at the end of the book, and related to the forms of existence of working children.

In Chapter 2, I give a survey of the international trends in socio-logical research into children's work since the 1970s. In doing so, I give a brief account of the most important paradigms and viewpoints and compare them.

In Chapter 3, I introduce several recent empirical studies on the topic of the thinking and action of working children in Latin America, attempt-ing to see and understand them in their life contexts. They come close, to some extent at least, to the view of subject orientation presented in this book, and not by chance employ a qualitative and participative methodology.

In Chapter 4, I attempt to reconstruct the relationship betwen child-hood and work in non-Western societies and cultures from various viewpoints. In doing so, I refer to research in ethnology and cultural anthropology from several decades, which predominantly deals with agricultural societies and cultures in which to some extent subsistence-oriented modes of production determine people's everyday lives and relations. In this section, I wish to stimulate the social imagination as to the multifarious ways in which work can be integrated in the lives of children, and children in the life of society, without robbing children of their childhood.

In Chapter 5, I devote myself to the work of children and adoles-cents in present-day Europe. I take up recent empirical research, and discuss how far it contributes to a more precise understanding of the significance of the work of children for the social and cultural forms of children in these societies now and in the future. In order to show possible perspectives of further research, I will also critically reconstruct various theoretical models of children's work that have been published in German-speaking countries in recent years. I will draw attention to the mainly unexpressed implications of these models, and attempt to formulate a conception that appears to me best suited to understanding and investigating the current tendencies of development and the social significance of children's work in post-industrial capitalist societies.

In Chapter 6, I discuss the results of US social research into the work of children and adolescents in the United States, beginning with an account of the extent and fields of work undertaken by children, with brief refer-ence to the concepts of children's work and its historical development. In the section that follows, I pursue the question of the reasons and motives for which children work, and the extent to which connections can be observed between social situation, gender and ethnic contexts on the one hand, and the specific characteristics of the work of children and adolescents on the other. After this, I discuss the extensive and partly controversial statements to be found in studies on the effects of work on children. In conclusion, I deal with some problematic aspects of social research on children's work and part-time work done by school students in the USA.

In Chapter 7, I take up the relationship between work and play in the lives of children, as one essential topic related to this question. Using material from various societies and cultures, I investigate the variations in this relationship and enquire whether the separation of these two forms of activity, which appears to be taken for granted in Western societies, is in the interests of children, and whether it will last.

In Chapter 8, I examine the social conditions under which children's work becomes exploitation, and discuss the most important typological and theoretical approaches to this problem. I then attempt to understand the effects of exploitative experience of work on children, and how they cope with this. Finally, I ask how the economic exploitation of children can be be combated.

In Chapter 9, I pursue the question of how working children deal with the working conditions they are exposed to, and how they attempt in everyday life to shape work in accordance with their own ideas, producing new forms of work determined by themselves. In doing so, I cite examples of the resistance of working children from the late nineteenth century up to the 1950s. I examine current initiatives on the part of working children in favour of self-determined and cooperative forms of work in countries both in the North and the South.

In Chapter 10, I reconstruct recent proposals and initiatives made by adults in the context of educational projects and institutions to make children's work a positive experience of living and learning. In doing so, I adduce experiences in the South and the North. At the end of the chapter I discuss some pitfalls.

In Chapter 11, I sum up the findings of the studies and ideas contained in the book, and bring them together to consider what the essential content of a subject-oriented theory of working children could involve, particulary in the present-day globalized world.

Notes

1. The following statements are taken from conversations and investigations with working children in El Salvador, Guatemala and Nicaragua (see Liebel 2001a).

2. More information about our ongoing research project, including the results of a children's meeting (Kids aktiv) held in Berlin in November 2001

with seventy-four ten- to fourteen-year-old working children, can be accessed at the following website: <www.kinder-arbeit.de>.

3. It should also be borne in mind that, with globalization, and consequently the values and needs of children spreading throughout the world, a 'new kind of child labour' is coming into existence which no longer results from material distress but is undertaken because children 'simply decide that they need to earn money' (White 1996: 831).

4. See a comprehensive account of this approach in Boyden et al. 1998.

5. On the question of the 'protagonism' of working children, see various articles in Liebel et al. 2001.

6. This aspect is totally omitted in so-called 'objective' analyses of the 'problems of child labour' and policies that degrade children by reducing them to objects of measures, however well meant.

1 | Working children's movements in Africa, Latin America and Asia[1]

§ FROM the 1980s onwards, social movements and organizations of working children have come into being in various regions of the southern hemisphere. They have made it plain that working children are able to be articulate and show knowledge of the matters that affect them, and have managed to convince a number of previously very self-assured adult 'children's work experts' that their voices can no longer be ignored. The Norwegian sociologist Per Miljesteig, for example, is attempting to persuade the World Bank to regard working children as partners and to allow them to participate in its decisions (Miljesteig 2000). Or again, the French sociologist Michel Bonnet, who played a decisive part from 1991 to 1996 in the International Programme for the Elimination of Child Labour (IPEC) of the International Labour Organization (ILO), noted thoughtfully in March 1999 that 'one should not be hypnotised by the problem of child labour, but instead should open up one's awareness for working children and listen to what they have to say to us' (Bonnet 1999: 11). But just what do working children have to say to us, and what influence can they in fact exert? Are there, beyond the great cultural and social differences, common factors in thought and action between the working children of the South?

In support of my remarks, I quote declarations passed at a number of regional and international meetings of delegates of children's organizations since 1994,[2] (mainly unpublished) minutes of children's conferences, autobiographical records of active members of children's organizations (Grillo and Schibotto 1992; Liebel 1996 and 2001a; Enda 1997; IWGCL 1998: 61–9; Enda 2001a), and some documentary and evaluative reports by adult interpreters. Such reports exist on India (Swift 2001),[3] West Africa (Coly 2001; Tolfree 1998; Touré 1998; Swift 1999: 25–30, Terenzio 2001) and some Latin American countries (Schibotto 1990 and 2001a; Cussiánovich 2001a; Ifejant 1996, 1997 and 1998; Swift 1999: 12–24; among others). In the case of Latin America, I can additionally refer to my own experiences and investigations (Liebel 1994, 2000 and 2001a).

In order to grasp significant aspects of the movements and organizations of working children, all the interpretations known to me refer to the category of the 'social subject'. This term is seldom used in the children's own statements, but we can examine them with a view to elucidating whether the children's expressed view of themselves can be adequately interpreted with the use of this category.

First, I will enquire into the common ground in the self-image of working children themselves and that of their organizations. Following this, I will discuss the extent to which the category of the 'social subject' is expressed in this, but also to what specific social and cultural conditions the notion of the social subject is linked. Finally, I will enquire into the possible effects that the children's movements have or may be expected to have on the children involved or on the society in which they live and share.

Common ground between working children's organizations

Working children's organizations consist mainly of children between the ages of twelve and sixteen. Most of them work in the so-called informal sector of the economy, in large cities, on the streets and in open places, but also as domestic servants of affluent families. Many have migrated from the country to the city with their parents, brothers and sisters or alone, or were born in the city as children of migrants. The great majority live and work under conditions that violate their human dignity and threaten their personal development.

Most children's organizations came about with the ideal and material support of adult humanitarian organizations and adults are involved. Not infrequently, the initiative came from adults, but the *raison d'être* of the organizations lies in the fact that they are run by the children themselves, have their own structures and norms, and develop their own ideas, demands and forms of action, which result from the living and working situation of their actors. The organizations are not always on a national scale; in Africa and India they are mostly groups formed in certain cities. In some cases, children belonging to particular 'occupational groups' (e.g. shoe cleaners, porters) and form associations whose radius of action is concentrated on their own type of work. In West Africa, children from the same village or country of origin often join together.

Despite the differences in the forms of organization, origins and cultural contexts of organized working children, various features in common can be found.

1. The children's organizations cite in support of their demands the worldwide validity of human rights, especially those set out in the UN Convention on the Rights of the Child (1989). To some extent, these rights are rephrased and adapted to their own situation, and to some extent they are supplemented by further rights. An example of this is

the '12 rights' formulated jointly by African children's organizations in 1994, whose realization is examined at yearly meetings:

- the right to vocational training in order to learn a trade;
- the right to stay in the village and not move away;
- the right to carry out our activities safely;
- the right to access to justice;
- the right to sick leave;
- the right to be respected;
- the right to be listened to;
- the right to light and limited types of work, adapted to our ages and abilities;
- the right to healthcare;
- the right to learn to read and write;
- the right to have fun and to play;
- the right to express ourselves and organize ourselves. (quoted in Liebel 2001e: 205; with partly differing wording, also to be found in Enda 2001a)

In a statement of the working children of Madagascar (1996), the following rights were demanded:

- to be able to work freely without being harassed or subjected to force;
- to be allowed to live our life fully and move around freely;
- to be treated like other people. (quoted in Liebel 2001e: 216)

In Latin America, the children's organizations specifically emphasize the rights that concern their participation in society. At their fifth meeting, in Lima in 1997, attended by delegates from fourteen countries, the fact that the rights to participation provided by the UN Children's Rights Convention 'are not adequate, because they are not respected in practice' was criticized (quoted in ibid.: 172). In both Latin America and Africa, another right is demanded over and over again in various formulations, one that is not included in the UN convention: children's right to work (see Liebel 2001f).

These examples, which could easily be complemented by others, make clear that it has become natural for the children who organize themselves to see themselves as 'subjects of rights', that is, as owners of certain rights to whose application they are entitled. They also show how the children's organizations interpret, prioritize, concretize and complement the rights decided on for them by adults in order to be better able to deal with and apply them in their own interests; also that they do not mean to leave the application of the rights granted them to the benevolence of adults, but to take it into their own hands.

2. The working children who join together in their own organizations are convinced that they not only have their own rights but also the ability to apply these rights under their own responsibility. They see themselves not only as profiting from or as objects of the goodwill or the concern of adults or of the institutions created by them, but as independent individuals who can judge and design their lives themselves and can contribute something to society. The statement of the fifth meeting of the working children of Latin America and the Caribbean (1997) can be taken as an example. It contains the passage: 'Our organisations are fighting day by day for better working and living conditions, for our rights to suitable education of good quality, for better health conditions, for opportunities to meet in order to carry out common actions, to be the protagonists in our lives ourselves and to be recognised as social subjects in our societies' (quoted in Liebel 2001d: 172).

The discussion of the 'social subject' goes beyond the discussion of the 'possessor of rights' in so far as it also stresses the ability of the children as individuals and of the organizations created and maintained by them to play an independent role in life and society, based on their own judgement and capacity to act. This self-conception is not specific to the children's organizations of Latin America, but is also found in those of Africa and India.

3. In the statements of working children's organizations, it is repeatedly emphasized that they deserve social recognition for their achievements. Thus, in the statement of the first worldwide meeting of working children in Kundapur, India (1996), we read: 'We want respect and security for ourselves and the work that we do' (quoted in Liebel et al. 2001: 351). The 'work' referred to in the statement applies both to the working children as people accomplishing a job that is useful to their families and society, and to the children's organizations carrying out the socially important task of contributing to the improvement of social relationships and to more justice. Now and then in this context the children are spoken of as 'economic subjects' and the children's organizations as (collective) 'political subjects'.

Not all children's organizations claim the 'right to work' with reference to the economic contribution of the children to society, but all agree that their actual work can no longer be undervalued and discriminated against, but must be socially acknowledged.[4] In the current practice of viewing work by children only in terms of its damaging effects, forbidding it and attempting its general elimination ('abolitionism'), they see their own existence as subjects and their human dignity violated. At the same time, they endeavour to bring about regulations that improve their working conditions and make it easier for them to work in dignity. The Kundapur statement ends with the sentence: 'We are against exploitation at work; but we are in favour of work with dignity and appropriate hours, so that we have time for education and leisure' (ibid.: 351). The statement of the fifth meeting of the Latin American working children culminates in the appeal: 'YES to work – NO to exploitation! YES to dignified work – NO to undignified conditions! YES to work – NO to marginalisation! YES to work – NO to discrimination!' (ibid.: 353). In the statement of the '2nd mini-world summit of working children' in Dakar (1998) are the words: 'We want all the world's children to be able one day to decide whether to work or not' (ibid.: 354).

4. The organizations of working children on all continents call for equal rights as between children and adults. They defend themselves against being undervalued, subordinated and hindered in making their own decisions with reference to their youth (being 'minors'). They want to be taken seriously as persons, listened to and paid attention to. They insist on being allowed to question the supremacy of adults, and expect the latter to explain and give reasons for their actions and decisions in so far as they concern the children's present and future. Their claim to their own independence and making their own decisions is substantiated by the fact that children are people with their 'own rights', are entitled to live with human dignity, have specific needs and skills, and best know their own situation. Finally, too, there is the fact that this corresponds to democratic conditions; only in this way will they learn to act responsibly. A particular point is how they as working children have already taken on economic responsibility and contribute to the development of their societies.

The independence claimed relates both to the individual child and to the children's organizations. The Kundapur statement begins with the words: 'We want recognition of our problems, initiatives, proposals and our process of organization' (ibid.: 351). The final statement of the '1st mini-worldsummit of working children' from Huampaní (Lima) (1997) says: 'Up to now, we have been listened to, but our opinions have not been taken into account. We have the right to organise ourselves, but our organisations have not been legally recognised' (ibid.: 352). In the same statement, the reason for this demand is given, namely that only if it is acceded to can working children 'sign contracts, open bank accounts, set up cooperatives, have social security' (ibid.: 353).

5. The organizations of working children do not confine themselves to demanding independent spheres of action ('autonomy'), but also insist on

being given participation in society and being able to exert influence. In the Kundapur declaration, this is formulated as follows: 'We want to be consulted on all decisions concerning us, at the local, national and international level' (ibid.: 351). In the statement of the second mini-summit of Dakar this participation is expressly demanded for their own organizations: 'Working children's movements should be consulted before any decisions are taken about their work. If decisions are to be made, let them be made jointly by all concerned' (ibid.: 354). In the final declaration of the fifth meeting of the working children of Latin America, the claim to participation refers especially to education policy, labour policy, social security and community development. The fact that, although the children are 'protected', they are not allowed to take part in the development of such 'protection' programmes is also criticized (see Liebel 2001d: 172).

The claim to participation shows that self-organized working children do not see themselves as being on the fringe of society, but rather as a legitimate and equal part of it. In this they reflect their experience of double marginalization, on the one hand as workers whose labour potential may be claimed by society but whose effort is not recognized, but instead is denigrated and negated, and on the other as children who, solely because they have not yet reached a given age (decided by adults), are denied judgement and (political) participation in the shaping of society. This double marginalization is particularly explosive in view of an economic and political practice that risks the lives of children along with the lives of people in general. At the end of the statement of the fifth meeting of the working children of Latin America is the passage: 'We NAT's [working children and adolescents] from Latin America and the Caribbean, like our friends in Africa and Asia, see ourselves as producers of life, opposed to the culture of death which refuses us any rights and our complete integration in society. Not to recognise this means excluding us still more than hitherto. To speak at the time of civil rights is mockery' (quoted in ibid.: 172).

6. Working children see their organizations as a way of gaining more influence in their societies and bringing about a better life. In the statement of the children of Latin America, this is expressed as follows: 'Our organisations have shown themselves to be the best way of protecting us from exploitation, mistreatment and disparagement by society. Within our organisations, we feel ourselves to be dignified, able and fully-fledged persons who take pride in our work. Here we educate and train ourselves, and find a place for solidarity and for the working out of proposals for alternatives to the existing system of poverty and violence, which is unacceptable to us' (ibid.: 172).

More, perhaps, than in the case of adult organizations, children's organizations are a social field in which the children can have new experiences of equal and respectful relationships and become aware of their skills and options. This not only enables them to get to know and learn to value themselves better, but also better to judge their situation and their scope for action. The children's organizations are a social area in which the children can experience themselves as social subjects and improve themselves. They thus become a cultural project that holds a mirror to society (that of adults), bringing new visions and practical approaches for a better life.

The children's organizations' view of the 'subject'

The debate on the 'social subject' indicates that children – no matter what age – are people both with their 'own rights' ('subjects of rights') and with specific characteristics and abilities, to be appreciated and respected by their fellow (adult) human beings. This vision of the child is opposed to a view and a social practice that regard and treat children solely as 'objects', whether to serve adults in whatever way (i.e. by being exploited or manipulated), or to protect them (i.e. by keeping them apart from the supposedly dangerous world of adults). Considering children as social subjects does not negate the necessity of offering children protection under certain circumstances, but insists that this must not happen at the cost of their right to power-sharing and participation. Children have rights on principle, and are able to take part in all decisions that concern them and ultimately to determine their own lives.

In this, the working children's movements and organizations have a paradigmatic meaning. They are, for one thing, proof that children can take their interests and rights into their own hands even under difficult conditions, and at the same time show how under favourable conditions children can develop as social subjects.

Meanwhile, the discussion of the 'social subject' and the manner in which its nature manifests itself in the children's organizations depend on certain social and cultural conditions. The working children's organizations generally come into being in an urban context and under the influence of the spread (in the media and in education) of 'new' ideas about individual and social 'human rights' in general and about such rights for children in particular. At the same time they react to conditions that first came about with the spread of capitalism and led to new forms of the 'survival economy' in the 'peripheral' societies of the Third World, in which children play an important part.

This survival economy, like the roles of the children within it, has different aspects. On the one hand, it is marked by the new kind of poverty and the necessity to survive by one's own efforts; that is, it is distinguished by competition, isolation, violence and the exploitation of the weaker. However, it also contains many elements derived from experience of life and trade under non-capitalist conditions, and which are perhaps also to be counted among the basic elements of human existence, i.e. mutual help, consideration for the weak (whether old, very young or sick), respect for the economic contribution of children and for their (age-) specific needs and attributes.

It is not surprising that these various aspects are also reflected in the thought and actions of working children. It is equally evident, however, that the working children's organizations above all embody ways of thinking and maxims for action aimed at social and collective solutions to problems, such as mutual help and mutual respect. With regard to their self-image as subjects, this could mean that elements of the bourgeois view of the subject are combined with elements of traditional cultures and economic activity, resulting in ways of thinking and practical expressions of the role of the subject that in no way coincide with the bourgeois Western model. Further, this could result in specific characteristics and forms of action of children's organizations in the various countries and regions under the influence of traditional cultures and attitudes to life, besides the features in common mentioned above.

In order to approach these questions more closely, I will proceed in three stages. First, with recourse to the reflections of Alain Touraine (1994), I will critically reconstruct the 'original' concept of the subject, and investigate to what extent the children's organizations implicitly identify with it. Second, I will enquire whether a new kind of childhood is developing within the working children's organizations which is no longer compatible with the 'original' bourgeois or modern Western view of the subject and of childhood, or which might even point beyond this. Third, I will examine to what extent and how the children's movements' view of the subject is linked with regional cultures and traditions, and whether specifically new and different conceptions and practices of the subject emerge from this.

The category of the 'subject' is a legacy of the Enlightenment and the French Revolution. It came into being and was first put to the test in the context of Western bourgeois society. It marks a view of the individual and his position in the world that has not, or only in modified form, been accepted in other, extra-European cultures up to the present. According to this view, human life centres on the individual, who is destined and able to understand and master it. Being a subject in this sense means no longer being at the mercy of forces outside oneself, but being free to shape one's own environment and life. This is accompanied by a view that sees each person as a self-assured individual, the possessor of individual rights applicable equally to all. Accordingly, pre-existent traditions and hierarchies, however they may be justified, in principle lose validity and are subject to a critical, rationally based way of thinking and practical measures aiming at equal rights for all.

Working children's movements embody to a degree this modern Western way of thinking, and contribute to its spread in the non-Western world by, for example, calling into question outdated age hierarchies and establishing new, more egalitarian relationships between the generations. But they also involve harsh criticism of various aspects of Western bourgeois thought and behaviour, and pave the way for a view of the subject hitherto unknown or not accepted in the Western world.[5]

In agreement with other social movements of repressed and excluded population groups in the South, the working children's organizations demand and practise a view of the subject and a practical application of this view based on respect for human dignity and human life. In doing this, they reject an attitude and mode of behaviour that stress the freedom of the individual but ignore the economic and social conditions on which it is based, or what becomes of the life and human dignity of those excluded from economic and political power. The promise of bourgeois society to make 'liberty, equality and fraternity' possible for *all* through the freedom of the individual has been in practice emptied of meaning and perverted. It has even contributed to producing social relationships based on rape, exploitation and contempt for the greater part of mankind by a privileged minority.

Alain Touraine (1994), without explicitly referring to the social movements of the South, has critically reconstructed the Western bourgeois concept of the subject in a way that comes close to the working children's movements' view of the subject and their criticism of its perversion in today's world. He sees human life in the 'modern age' as 'fragmented' into many elements, which makes it hard for people to have a comprehensive view of themselves, their relations to other people and their situation in life. According to Touraine, human existence is split up into, for example, life as consumer, as producer, as owner, as a holder of rights, as member of a nation, an ethnic group, a community, a business enterprise, etc. Although the subject cannot be seen as a means of reuniting the fragmented elements of modern life, it is the subject 'that does connect them by weaving a dense web of relations of complementarity and opposition' (ibid.: 220). The 'idea of the subject' runs counter to the tendency 'to be identified with any of the shattered fragments of modernity'; above all, the subject must not simply be confused 'with the freedom of a consumer in a well-supplied market' (ibid.: 220).

Touraine also rejects a purely contemplative view of the subject, in the sense of a simple 'condition of the soul'. The idea of the subject cannot be separated from that of the social actor. 'The subject is an individual's will to act and to be recognized as an actor' (ibid.: 207). He states that the expressions *individual, subject* and *actor* are to be seen in a mutual relationship. They can move apart in social reality, but if they do so this indicates a 'civilisation's new discontent' characterized by 'narcissistic individualism' (ibid.: 209). 'The Subject is not a soul as distinct from a body, but the meaning the soul gives to the body, as opposed to the representations and norms imposed by the social and cultural order' (ibid.: 210).

It is thus consistent that Touraine links the subject with the social movement, and even speaks of the subject as identical with the movement in society. He sees a social movement as 'a collective actor whose primary goal is the defence of the subject' (ibid.: 240). It represents 'at once a social conflict and a cultural project' (ibid.: 240).

The social movements of working children correspond to this description. They can be regarded as collective attempts to overcome exclusion and contempt and to achieve the social recognition of working children as active and productive subjects, and at the same time as attempts to establish new kinds of social relationships that contradict the predominant individualism and the corresponding competitive mentality. This is, in my view, the reason why various interpreters of these movements expressly employ the category of the *social* subject. The movements are thus – like other social movements of repressed and excluded population groups of the South – not to be seen as merely illustrating bourgeois Western ideas, but represent a view of human existence that has either never been achieved or has been abandoned by the bourgeois capitalist societies of the West.

The view and practice of the subject in the context of working children's organizations also go beyond the modern Western view of *childhood*. According to this view, children are granted a certain autonomy and given protection from risks, but these concessions are made at the cost of an active and responsible role for children in society. Children are practically excluded from adult life and assigned to special reservations in which they are 'educated', 'developed' and prepared for the future. Their possible influence on this future is confined to each individual's personal 'qualification', but does not extend to decisions about social relationships. These remain reserved for the adults or their power elites.

With the UN Convention on the Rights of the Child, children are for the first time granted the right to express their opinion and organize themselves to champion their interests, but these new rights offer them no guarantee of actually playing an equal part in society. The diverse models of child participation that have since been worked out and practised in various parts of the world are almost always restricted to relatively marginal questions of social action, for example the planning of children's playgrounds and other institutions specially designed for children, or exhaust themselves in the formal imitation or simulation of adult political formations, for example children's parliaments or child mayors. A real influence on life and on the decisions of adults remains completely denied to them.

The claim to equal rights and participation, as made by the organizations of working children in different parts of the Third World, is incompatible with the bourgeois Western view of childhood, and also goes beyond the individual elements that have meanwhile been conceded. The children's organizations insist not only on being heard on all questions concerning them but also on being able to actively take part in decisions.[6] They demand, for example, to be represented at international level with seats and votes in the committees of the ILO on the same basis as governments, labour unions and employers' organizations. How radically this claim, which also refers to influence on their countries and their own immediate environments, departs from the dominant views of the social role and status of childhood is shown by how considerable difficulties and resistance are repeatedly found even in institutions and with people that are in favour of the idea of rights for children and act in support of them (see Sanz 1997).

The reason why resistance is so strong is presumably not only that the children demand more participation and influence as *children*, but also that they explicitly present themselves as *working* children and insist that their work should be recognized by society and be open as an option to all children ('the right to work in dignity'). In doing so, they contradict a further essential element of the bourgeois Western view of childhood, which aims at a strict separation of childhood and work, and therefore strives to abolish all forms of children's work. In the children's organizations' view of the subject, therefore, work is as important as participation, since they see the child not only as a 'contemplative' and 'private' subject concerned only about his or her personal future, but rather as a responsibly acting social subject, who is an integrated part of society and marks this with his or her daily actions, just as society would not be able to maintain itself and develop without children.

The view of the subject represented by the children's organizations not only results from the fact that the children already work and with their work produce 'social value', but is in my opinion also influenced by cultural traditions that are ignored by the bourgeois Western picture of childhood. It is normal in Amerindian cultures and many African cultures to give children responsibility at an early age, entrusting them with tasks that are important for the community. These activities can be strenuous and involve risks, but they are chosen or restricted in such a way that the children are not over-taxed, and can become acquainted with them gradually and arrange them at their own discretion. The work done is not only important for the community, but gives the children the opportunity to learn essential life skills. Furthermore, they are not strictly separated from playful forms of activity, but rather give the children the chance to try out their strength and mobility, and live out their fantasies and ideas (for examples, see Chapters 4 and 7).

Although the children live within ritualized age structures in which the older are given precedence over the younger, they often already enjoy rights that do not figure at all in modern Western views of children's rights. It is a widespread practice among Amerindian and African peoples to entrust to children animals and arable land which they are able to use according to their own judgement and for which they are responsible. Or they are entitled to a share of the milk or the newborn animals. In some cases, children have to guarantee to make up for damage that arises in connection with their domestic pets. In this way, the children are taken seriously and receive recognition for the responsibilities they take on and the work they perform. In a study originating in Bolivia on 'childhood in rural areas' (*niñez campesina*), these and similar practices are seen as 'a specific form of action to make concrete and define the place of children as subjects and owners of rights' (Molina Barrios and Rojas Lizarazu 1995: 89). They have an importance that cannot be overestimated for the autonomy and participation of children in social life.

My assumption that the view of the subject implicitly held by working children's organizations is influenced by this and similar experiences and memories has not hitherto been supported by research findings. It is based on the fact that the majority of the children who are active in the organizations come from migrant families or have themselves migrated from the country, and that in the poor urban districts in which the children grow up the rural traditions are maintained and influence the structures of the survival economy. In Africa at least, one of the basic tenets of the children's organizations is to maintain connections with their villages of origin and to keep open the option of return there.

The 'right to stay in the village' claimed by them (see the '12 Rights') is illustrated with the words: 'We want to remain in our villages to develop the activities that allow us to be responsible for our own future. To do this, we must organise ourselves on the level of village assemblies' (quoted in Liebel 2001e: 208). In Latin America, many clues can be found in the notes and records of working children attesting to the fact that the memory of the Indian traditions is still alive. At many meetings of children's organizations, the memory of the pre-colonial epoch of their continent is taken as a reason for considering alternatives to the social misery of the present.

The children's organizations' view of the subject cannot, however, simply be seen in terms of a revival of traditions. It also results from experiences of an entirely new kind. The cited expectation of African children to develop activities to assure their own maintenance refers to life in the village, but would presumably not have been thus formulated without the new 'urban' experiences and living conditions. The idea of children organizing themselves in order to support themselves pre-supposes that the children are left to themselves, whether because the traditional supporting communities have broken down or because an 'autonomous life' and 'making their own decisions' become desirable goals in life for the children.

The ways of thinking, viewing things and acting represented by the children's organizations are creative answers to hardships and experiences in life that are mostly new to the children, on the one hand because they as children are beginning their lives, and on the other because the societies in which they grow up are in a situation of social and cultural change. To understand and solve their problems, the children have re-course on the one hand to the cultural traditions of their communities and ethnic groups, and on the other hand to the 'modern' international discussion of human rights, which has reached them through the media and through humanitarian or educational aid projects. Using these not infrequently contradictory 'models', the children generate their own answers. In doing so, their organizations take on tasks that no one in their societies relieves them of. I will illustrate this with the example of recent developments in southern Africa, taking up considerations formulated by Kurt Madörin for the project work of terre des hommes (Switzerland) in Tanzania.

In Zimbabwe, Zambia, Uganda, Tanzania and other countries of southern Africa the number of children who have to care for them-selves and their brothers and sisters ('children-headed households') has considerably increased as a result of growing poverty and not least the spread of AIDS. In Tanzania it has been estimated that by the year 2010 about a quarter of all children under fifteen will have lost one or both parents. The traditional system of the 'extended family' has certainly shown a remarkable capacity of absorption, but has in the meantime reached its limits and is no longer able to integrate the children. In many cases the 'extended family' consists only of grandparents, who will die before long. The orphaned children become a new type of working children. They no longer carry out particular restricted functions within the family, but must search on their own initiative for any kind of work in order to survive. Many of these children migrate to the cities and try to make a living in the streets.

In the countries mentioned – in contrast to West Africa and Latin America – working children's organizations have hitherto played only a small part.[7] However, under the impact of the rapidly growing number of children who are earning their own living and thus taking on an important position in society, the need for and functions of interest groups representing the children themselves are being rethought. For instance, during the '1999 World AIDS Campaign with Children and Young People: Listen, Learn, Live – Key Issues and Ideas for Action', UNAIDS concluded that it is necessary 'to have young people represented in the governing bodies of various organisations such as NGOs for the combating of AIDS or youth promotion organisations ... to bring out the perspective of young people in these groups'. Doubt is growing as to whether it makes sense to regard children only as victims. This way of seeing things, which often coincides with the view of children as dependants, blocks 'perception of what orphans perform in the fields of work, care, family support, psychological adaptation, etc. They attend school under difficult conditions. Girls ... manage whole families, boys help out with the field work and take on unfamiliar domestic chores. From this viewpoint the children and adolescents are not "needy victims", but people with equal rights, specific interests and needs, and their own initiatives' (Madörin 1999).

The initiatives of the children, born from necessity, are the germ cells of their organizations. However, they develop only when the children find a certain measure of acknowledgement for their efforts and their new kind of independence, and when there are adults in their respective societies who are ready 'to accompany the initiatives coming from the children and adolescents with advice, criticism and support, and thus help them to open up perspectives of their own' (ibid.). This makes it possible for the children to see themselves not as incomplete people but as successful survivors.

Social transformations through children's organizations?

What so far is only a possible perspective for action in Tanzania and other countries of southern Africa is a living reality in many countries of West Africa and Latin America, although one that is always under threat. I will attempt here to sketch what to me are the most important aspects of the achievements in synthesis and transformation of the local organizations of working children. Some of these are hypothetical ideas that require closer empirical study.

The children's organizations represent a kind of 'independent childhood' that has not previously existed in this form. It supersedes both traditional age hierarchies and the kind of 'autonomous' childhood enclosed in reservations according to the bourgeois Western pattern. What is new about this independence is the demand for equal social status and effective social participation. The demand for participation and the practice of the children's organizations are not confined to 'children's affairs', but include all aspects of life that are of 'existential' significance for their personal and social development. The daily life of working children is still far removed from the satisfaction of these demands, but the public actions of the children's organizations and their example of 'lived participation' show their demands as legitimate and plausible and pave the way for a change of cultural perspectives on childhood.

It thus becomes easier to see that children can have their own ideas, make proposals and give their societies fresh impetus. The conventional idea that children are only 'empty vessels', and because of their age completely lacking in skills, is called into question by the actions of the children's organizations. It becomes harder to justify the notion that children have only to obey and may not question the actions of adults. The actors of the children's organizations repeatedly record that they are treated in their environment with more respect and see themselves taken seriously. An example of this is the Final Declaration of the 5th Meeting of the African Movement of Working Children and Youth (2000), which states: 'In those places where we are organised, our 12 Rights have considerably progressed for us and for other Working Children and Youth. We can now learn to read and write, we benefit from better healthcare, we can express ourselves, we are respected by everyone as well as by the Judiciary, we are well treated and can work in safer environments, working in a manner in line with our capacities and can rest sometimes' (quoted in Liebel et al. 2001: 355). Or organized working children report that they receive more appreciation and support from their parents, because they are proud of their children and are impressed that they are able to express themselves better and are listened to more often.

That research methods and political forms in which working children figure only as objects are increasingly being called in question may no doubt be attributed to the work of the children's organizations. For example, in the mid-1990s the Colombian sociologist María Cristina Salazar criticized the fact that 'very few studies on children's work have used participatory techniques in which the voices of the children themselves are heard, despite the fact that this is a minimum requirement for understanding the reality of these children' (Salazar 1995: 76). Or the International Working Group on Child Labour, under the impact of the practical work and the demands for participation of the children's organizations, asked 'Have we asked the children?' (IWGCL 1997), and names 'encouraging and facilitating the participation of children in debates about their work' (IWGCL 1998: Executive Summary)[8] as one of its 'most important objectives'. This goal has not so far been achieved in political decision-making bodies (i.e. in governments or the ILO), but the demand for participation of the children's organizations has found so many prominent supporters (see for example Boyden et al. 1998) that it is no longer so easy to banish it from the public stage.

The degree of influence of the organizations of working children in their own countries varies. They do not amount to a power factor that could directly cause the political and economic elites to take particular decisions. Their role has more of a symbolic nature, and their influence depends to a great extent on whether in their countries there are political structures and a social climate favourable to participatory processes. Whether there are social movements and initiatives continually working to achieve respect for human rights and the realization of the UN Convention on the Rights of the Child is equally important. If this is the case, then it is also more likely that the children's organizations will find support from adults, especially from NGOs.

In some countries the children's organizations are explicitly acknowledged by governments, local administrations and social organizations as representatives of the working children and as partners for negotiation. In Nicaragua some agreements with the health ministry and the national police have been successfully arrived at which above all benefited working children in the streets. In Lima, the capital of Peru, a contract with the city authorities was concluded giving paid work under dignified conditions to a few hundred children over twelve years old. In Dakar, the capital of Senegal, the police recognize the membership identification card of the children's organizations and treat working children with more respect. In Bolivia, the central trade union organization accepted the local associations of shoe cleaners, salespersons and other child workers as member organizations, and agreed to press for better working conditions.

Only in a few cases can the influence of the children's organizations be traced in formal agreements, but it does lead to improvements in the daily life of the children which are not very conspicuous but have a noticeable effect for the children. In Dakar, for example, children working as domestic servants are to some extent treated with more respect, and can meet other young people in their free time. Working children are no longer discriminated against in public health institutions, but are treated without reservation. In some countries in which children's organizations are active, the tone with which the media treat working children has changed. Children are less often regarded as layabouts or potential thieves, but expressly appreciated as working children who support their families, or their work is described as a positive alternative to begging and stealing. In other cases, the children's organizations have persuaded local authorities to repair bridges and streets that are often used by the children. Or they have persuaded school directors and administrators to show consideration for working children and take their experiences seriously in their teaching, and in a few cases even to develop curricula especially for working children. In some urban districts the organized children also actively take part in neighbourhood drives for the improvement of living conditions and are accepted as helpful partners who are to be taken seriously, despite initial reservations.

In some countries, children's organizations have been able to gain substantial influence on legislation relating to children and adolescents. For example, in Brazil, considerable participation rights, and in Peru the explicit right of children over twelve to work under dignified conditions, have been enacted. Overall, the children's organizations have given new momentum to the debate on children's rights, filled it with life and, above all, furthered awareness within society that children must be involved in the legal regulation of their concerns and that their organizations must be legally recognized.

The contribution of children's organizations to social transformation not only takes the form of publicly proclaimed proposals and demands. At least as important is the fact that children's organizations contribute by means of their own initiatives and projects to the improvement of the living conditions of working children. Mutual support in emergencies is widespread, for example when a child is seriously ill and urgently needs money for medical treatment, or when a child finds itself alone and in need of a new home after the sudden death of his or her mother. Some organizations have 'community funds' into which the children pay small contributions or the profits from donation drives, in order to have a re-serve for emergencies or common projects. On a self-help basis, training courses are organized to find better opportunities for earning, or even the rudiments of an economy of their own ('self-sustaining economic projects'), making it possible for the children to work and earn money under conditions decided by themselves (more examples are to be found in Chapter 8).

The children's organizations cannot completely alter the living conditions of working children with such initiatives and projects. Nor can they neutralize the structural causes of exploitation and poverty inherent in the capitalist economy. They often 'only' make the children's lives easier and reduce their risks a little. However, in view of the permanent threat of death, this should not be underestimated.[9] Moreover, these initiatives not only promote the solution of the daily existential problems of working children, but can also give them more weight in the community, and promote their social acknowledgement by influencing awareness of the status and role of children in society. It becomes easier to imagine that children should take on tasks essential to survival under their own responsibility and in an organized way, and that the children's work can take on completely different forms and meanings from those usually associated with 'child labour'.[10] The children's organizations demonstrate through their own 'economic' practice that work does not have to be equated with exploitation, that it is not inevitably in conflict with the need of children for play and learning, and that it can even contribute to promoting children's personality development (see Overwien 2001). In this way, they also stimulate the social imagination in respect of alternatives to an economic and social system that is essentially based on the exploitation of human labour potential.

Notes

1. The chapter is based on a paper for the international conference 'Rethinking Childhood – Working Children's Challenge to the Social Sciences', which took place in 2000 at the Institut de Recherche pour le Développement (IRD) at Bondy, near Paris.

2. Explicitly I refer to the official reports and final declarations of the following meetings: 1st World Meeting, Kundapur, India, 24 November–8 December 1996; World Meeting (1st Mini-World Summit), Huampaní, Peru, 10–15 August 1997; World Meeting (2nd Mini-World Summit), Dakar, Senegal, 1–4 March 1998; 5th Latin American and Caribbean Meeting, Lima, Peru, 6–9 August 1997; 6th Latin American Meeting, La Asunción, Paraguay, 12–18 August 2001; 1st African Meeting, Bouaké, Ivory Coast, 18–23 July 1994; 2nd African Meeting, Bouaké, Ivory Coast, 30 October–3 November 1995; 3rd African Meeting, Ouagadougou, Burkina Faso, 14–20 October 1996; 4th African Meeting,

Popenguine, Senegal, 17–27 February 1998; 5th African Meeting, Bamako, Mali, 31 October–14 November 2000; 6th Latin American and Caribbean Meeting, La Asunción, Paraguay, 12–26 August 2001; Mini-World Meeting ('Premundialito'), Milan, Italy, 25 November–2 December 2002. These declarations and other manifestions of working children can also be accessed on the following websites: <www.pronats.de; www.italianats.org; www.workingchild.org; www.enda.sn/eja; www.ifejants.org>.

3. References to the organized actions of working children in other Asian countries (Philippines, Bangladesh, Nepal, Thailand and Indonesia) are to be found in Camacho 1999a and b; IWGCL 1998; Boyden et al. 1998.

4. Some organizations – such as the National Movement of Street Children in Brazil and the groups affiliated to the Global March against Child Labour – demand the complete and unconditional elimination of child labour. However, these organizations and groups are dominated and led mostly by adults.

5. In the West, too, there have been various trends and social movements that have taken up the individualist view of the subject. However, up to now they have not arrived at a view of the *child* as a 'social subject' with a capacity for 'protagonism' (see Cussiánovich 2001b; Liebel 2001g).

6. This view of participation is more than 'giving working children a voice', as demanded by some NGOs. Anyone who takes a close look at the statements of working children's organizations will realize that they by no means 'isolate the issue of child labour from the wider social setting', as feared by Lavalette (1999: 13).

7. The IWGCL reported on an organization of 'parking boys' in Zimbabwe (IWGCL 1998: 62). For initiatives for a movement of working children in Zimbabwe, see also Bourdillon (2000: 194).

8. 'Adults, however well intentioned they may be, cannot unquestionably identify what is good and bad about employment, as seen from the child's point of view. This is not to say that children always "know best" any more than adults always "know best". Rather, it is to say that the views of children are a necessary component of anything that claims to give a full account of child labour in all of its forms and with all of its implications' (IWGCL 1998: 44).

9. Their meaning for working children is not impaired by the fact that children's movements are always in danger of failing in capitalist terms or of being instrumentalized as cheap and useful solutions for social problems for which the state or society in general should be responsible. Usually, children's organizations are aware of these problems and try to tackle them.

10. It would be worth examining to what extent these are comparable to the tasks and social role of the 'autonomous children's groups' that are still not uncommon among many Amerindian, African and South Pacific peoples in country regions (see Chapter 4).

2 | Children's work from the perspective of social research: an international stock-taking

§ IN this chapter I shall give a survey of the international trends in research on children's work since the 1970s. In doing so, I shall present the most important paradigms and viewpoints briefly, and relate them to one another.

The ILO and the NGOs as pioneers

Up to the 1980s, little interest was shown by social scientists in research on children's work in its present forms. Since then, it has rapidly increased in extent and intensity. The great majority of studies concern themselves with children's work in countries of the South. In the 1990s, social scientists took an increasing, although still comparatively small, interest in children's work in the North. So far there have been no comparative studies on children's work in different parts of the world.

Most research publications were published under the aegis of the International Labour Organization (ILO) or in its name. Since 1979, the ILO has conducted a programme of its own on child labour research. The first studies sought to cover the whole panorama of children's work worldwide – legislation, forms of work, work sectors, working conditions – without being able to deal with each of these aspects in the necessary depth (see Mendelievich 1979). The focus was also mainly on the formal sector.

A remarkable theoretical and methodological contribution to research into children's work is that edited by Rodgers and Standing (1981b) for the ILO. Here for the first time an attempt was made to classify the economic activities of children, and attention was paid to the difficulty of this task. In particular the introductory essay by Rodgers and Standing, together with the articles in the volume by Bekombo (1981) and Schildkrout (1981) on Africa and that by Dube (1981) on India, emphasize the necessity of studying and evaluating children's work in its socio-cultural context. I quote Rodgers and Standing's concluding remarks in detail:

> Many forms of child work are a source of interest and possibly creative activity for the children concerned, and contribute significantly to family incomes or to family subsistence. Conventional views of the normal duration of childhood, or of the desirability of formal schooling, tend

to obscure these points. ... Where child labour does have adverse effects ... they can usually be traced to the socio-economic framework within which children work, as much as to the work itself. Thus the suppression of child wage labour opportunities is unlikely to increase the welfare of the children concerned unless substitute income sources and alternative possibilities for personal development are developed at the same time. ... Action towards child work must be sympathetically oriented towards the needs and perceptions of the children themselves. It must also be based on a thorough understanding of the motivations behind child work, its functions, and the individual gains from it, whether for the children themselves or for others who benefit from their work. (Rodgers and Standing 1981a: 42–3)

Without taking particular account of the findings of this publication, in the following years the ILO concentrated above all on compiling statistical data on children's work in various countries and regions as well as worldwide, and refining the instruments for collecting them. This was to serve to set up national action programmes to combat children's work (see Bequele and Boyden 1988). This led to the foundation of the International Programme on the Elimination of Child Labour (IPEC) in 1992 (see ILO 1996 and 2002; Liebel 2001b).[1] Important criteria for orientation are the 'Guidelines for a Project Design' developed by Alec Fyfe (1993) for the ILO. Apart from the ILO, other inter-governmental organizations (IGOs) such as UNICEF, the World Health Organization (WHO) and the World Bank have commissioned studies on children's work.

Whereas the WHO paid attention above all to risks to health (see, e.g., WHO 1987) and the World Bank devoted attention to the connections between child labour and poverty (most recently Fallon and Tzannatos 1998; Grootaert and Patrinos 1999), UNICEF put the emphasis of its studies on the so-called street children. UNICEF made an important contribution to research with the stipulation that a situation analysis was to be carried out in every country in which it is represented. These analyses were to produce comparable information on the living conditions of 'minors in particularly difficult circumstances of life' (UNICEF), which also included working children. The analyses were to be based on guidelines set out in a *Methodological Guide*. A successful example of this is the study by Espinoza and Glauser et al. (1987), which was able to acquire important data on the living conditions of working children with its situation analysis.

A new joint initiative of the ILO, UNICEF and the World Bank – called 'Developing New Strategies for Understanding Children's Work and Its

Impact' – aims to improve child labour research, data collection and analysis, to enhance local and national capacity for research and to improve the evaluation of interventions. This inter-agency project, launched in December 2000, is coordinated from the UNICEF Innocenti Research Centre in Florence, Italy.

Numerous publications on children's work also originate in non-governmental organizations (NGOs). These were written either to support their efforts in the enforcing of children's rights, or to direct attention in general to the living conditions of the children to whom their social and educational work is devoted. The authors were, to begin with, mostly activists of the organization, with little experience in the application of research methods. At first there were local or country-specific situation descriptions, which incorporated the experience of the activists with working children and their endeavours to improve the children's living conditions. The main point of criticism of these reports is that they used secondary literature, above all from the media, indiscriminately and without including findings from research of their own, or stating what methods of investigation they were based on. This made these reports of little use in the development of indicators for situation analysis of working children and almost no use for comparative study projects.

Despite their methodological weakness, the NGOs' publications contributed to bringing the living conditions of working children to the notice of the aid organizations, governments and research institutions and the general public. Some reports had a ground-breaking effect, for instance depictions of the working conditions of children in the carpet industry or the textile industry, in the streets of big cities, in servitude and prostitution.[2] One example is the eight reports of Anti-Slavery International for the standing committee of the United Nations against modern forms of slavery, which deals with children's work in various branches of industry and activity.[3]

In recent years, the studies carried out or commissioned by NGOs have gained considerably in quality. Above all the International Save the Children Alliance (ISCA) has initiated field research in several countries, some of it intensive, which was also methodologically innovative.[4] The foundation of the International Working Group on Child Labour (IWGCL), which was supported by several NGOs, was also important. It has carried out surveys in numerous countries in the South and North which have promoted a differentiated view of children's work taking into account the cultural context (see IWGCL 1998).

A particular variant of research is the studies that have been made in recent years in the context of the organizations of working children.[5]

They mainly apply ethnographic methods and are based on the individual and collective statements of the working children themselves. Contrary to common supposition, research by independent scientists has so far been relatively rare. In the South, universities and research institutions do not as a rule have the necessary resources to carry out studies of their own. Thus it is not surprising that the existing independent studies are almost exclusively by scholars from the North. This includes above all ethnologists, anthropologists and economists, and more recently sociologists.

In ethnological and anthropological research, the main interest is in the influence of children's work on the socialization process, which is regarded as a preparatory process for a useful and fulfilled life as an adult. From the social perspective, work is considered with regard to its implications for the acquisition of skills, the development of working morale, class consciousness and the social division of labour. The focus of research tends to be on socialization by work rather than on the economic importance of children's work.

With few exceptions, the studies are devoted to rural areas. Children's work has been considered with a view to population policy, above all in the context of fertility and large families, and less as part of the rural economy. Michael Cain and Enid Schildkrout are regarded as pioneers in this field. Cain (1980) studied children's work in a village in Bangladesh. For the measurement of the participation of children in work, he used the *time-budget* approach.[6] Schildkrout (1978, 1980 and 1981) analysed the relationship between children's work and women's work in northern Nigeria. The ethnological and anthropological research is characterized by the use of innovative methods.[7]

Although research into children's work does not have a high status among economists, some economic studies have been made. An early contribution which remains important is the study by Tienda (1979) on the economic activities of children in Peru. Recent contributions come particularly from research projects on the economics of development, and are mainly concerned with the connections between poverty and various forms of gainful employment of children (e.g. Hemmer et al. 1997). One remarkable recent theoretical study regards the inadequate credit systems in the countries of the South as being particularly responsible for the extent of children's work, and formulates alternatives in economic policy (Ranjan 1999).

In recent years, the interest of sociologists in children's work has grown considerably. It was inspired and provoked by the 'deconstructivist' approaches in sociological childhood research, according to which childhood is an interest-governed 'social construct' of society, which is dominated by adults, and may prevent children from shaping their lives independently as 'social actors'. The systematic exclusion of children from economic processes is thought to be a component of the social construction. On the basis of this approach, some studies have been made in recent years on children's work in the USA, Great Britain and Scandinavian countries.[8]

Three of the few independent sociological research studies on children's work in the South are by a Dutch anthropologist (Nieuwenhuys 1994), a Swiss sociologist (Lucchini 1998) and a Swedish social geographer (Aragão-Lagergren 1997). However, some studies have been made by native sociologists that can be deemed independent, for instance in Colombia (Salazar 1990), Zimbabwe (Reynolds 1991; Bourdillon 2000), the Philippines (Camacho 1999a and b) and Bolivia (Domic Ruiz 1999). New lines of investigation are developed in two collections edited by Schlemmer (1996 in French and 2000 in English) and by Lieten and White (2001). An indication of the growing interest of sociologists is also to be seen in the fact that the international journal *Childhood* has recently · published articles on children's work more frequently.

The influence of political interests

Research on children's work is particularly influenced by political, ideological or cultural interests. As it is often financed by organizations that pursue specific interests, as a rule the problems and questions that predominate in the studies at any given moment are the main topical themes of policy or of programmes of the IGOs or NGOs. As a rule, this research deals only with the aspects that are of interest to the actors involved. So far the children, who are the main actors in the world of children's work, have had little influence on the questions posed in research or the decision as to what should be researched. Mostly, they are simply not asked.

For a long time the predominant interest was in regarding and studying children's work as an offence against existing laws. Children's work was seen as a relic of past times, and frequently even as an indicator of cultural backwardness. Research was to contribute to pushing forward the 'modernization' of society and to activating the prohibition of children's work laid down in legislation.[9]

Given the lack of success of these efforts and the rapid worldwide increase in diverse forms of children's work, the assumption gained ground that a more differentiated approach was required. Now there was a demand to differentiate between forms of work that are really harmful to children's development and those that contribute to improving their living conditions or are even beneficial to the development of their personalities. Instead of building on the general prohibition of children's work, the question was posed as to how children could be protected from work that is hazardous or may damage their development, and the significance that children's work has within the poverty-governed strategies for the survival of their families.[10] The question of what moves the children themselves to take up a particular kind of work, and the significance that they themselves attach to their work, also gained in importance.

With regard to the causes of children's work, simple explanation models based either on 'poverty' or 'orientation to traditional values' ('cultural backwardness') were called into question. 'Complex' explanatory models were demanded or designed, combining objective and subjective or economic and cultural factors, taking into account that the work of children has widely differing forms and can be performed under varying conditions and for varying motives (see IWGCL 1998; ILO 2002).

Meanwhile, two main trends of research interest have developed. In the context of the ILO, the dominant interest is to examine the comprehensive causes of children's work and to enquire what effects the inclusion of children in economic processes at an early age has for the development potential of national societies (see ILO 1996). In the context of UNICEF and most of the large internationally active NGOs, the primary interest is to research into not only the causes but also above all the effects of the various forms of children's work on the rights and opportunities for development of the children affected (see UNICEF 1997). Whereas the ILO directs its attention predominantly to the 'particularly bad forms of child labour', in independent reseach and in the context of the NGOs the necessity of taking account of the whole spectrum of children's work in its current and predictable forms is stressed (see IWGCL 1998: 22ff; Boyden et al. 1998).

Definitions and evaluations of children's work

Here it becomes clear that there is no consensus on the basic definitions. Even within the organizations (e.g. the ILO or UNICEF) the concept of 'children's work' has various meanings according to programme, author or topic. There is no agreement as to what work is. That which is work to some is not work to others. Frequently, the definition of work is marked by moral attitudes, which determine which activities should or should not count as work. For instance, begging, according to UNICEF, is not work, but is nevertheless included in a number of programmes as 'illegal work'. Another tendency is not to take the economic value of activities seriously or recognize them, because they are carried out only by children or only a few adults are involved in them. One problem arises from the fact that the ILO sees work as an economic activity that contributes to the gross national product. This excludes a number of forms of children's work, for instance domestic work, which is mainly performed by girls. This becomes clear in an example contained in Boyden et al. (1998: 20f). The authors depict a young African girl helping her family in various typical ways.

When she gets up an hour before sunrise to help clean the house, fetch water, and make breakfast, she is not working, according to official definitions. That is because these activities are not considered to contribute to the national economy. But when she goes outside to help her mother tend the garden from which they sell products in the local market, she now begins to work, as indeed she still does when they go together to the market to sell some produce. However, when she takes vegetables from the same garden inside and prepares the midday meal from them, she is no longer working. Later she goes out to fetch firewood, which is heavy to carry and must be brought from over a mile away, but she is not working. Then she goes back out to gather fodder to feed the farm animals which are used for traction, and is now working again. She is also officially working when she helps her family in the fields. When she goes back inside to clean up in the kitchen and to help bed down her younger brother and sister, singing them to sleep long after sundown, she is not working. And, of course, she was not working during the three hours she spent in school.

According to the definitions usually used by governments in compiling their statistics, this girl worked only for a small part of the day. In many statistics, she would not register as working at all, for children are frequently not registered as working if they also attend school, even if work takes up more time than school. The conclusion one draws from this is that, when looking at the statistics, work and attending school appear mutually exclusive (for similar examples in South Asia, see Nieuwenhuys 1994; Krishna 1996).

Another problem arises from the fact that what is recorded as work is sometimes part-time work and sometimes full-time work on the part of the children. Since even a child who works only sporadically is counted in the national statistics, almost the whole world has become accustomed to imagining, when children's work or child workers are mentioned, that all these children work all day every day, whereas in fact the vast majority of children do not do so.

The situation is made even more unclear by the fact that in many countries children who have not yet attained the minimum age to work legally – which, according to country, may vary from age twelve to fifteen – are not counted at all, in order not to create the impression that international agreements or the country's own laws are being flouted.

A further confusing factor is that it frequently does not emerge from statistics and surveys whether the figures relate to a particular point in time or a particular period. A number of surveys merely count the children who were working on the day or in the week of the survey, so that children working seasonally or sporadically are ignored.

Above and beyond the problems of statistical coverage, there is no consensus on what is to be understood by 'children's work'. Some see children's work more from the viewpoint of the national economy, others rather from that of the subsistence economy. Some see it rather in terms of the 'modernizing' or 'civilizing' of supposedly backward societies, others rather in terms of its significance for individual development, personal freedom or status in society. According to whichever viewpoint is predominant, different criteria are chosen to delimit children's work from other activities and evaluate it in a specific manner.

At any rate, it seems to me essential not to burden the concept of children's work with moral valuations. I agree, for instance, with Boyden et al. (1998: 22; see also Myers 1999) that the concept must not remain limited to activities and forms of activity that are normally accounted 'negative', 'harmful', 'bad', etc. Further, it seems to me essential that the notion should not be narrowed down to the 'economic', but rather should do justice as far as possible to the wide range of activities and forms of activity performed by children in various parts of the world. Thus it should not be limited to paid activities or activities that increase the 'national product' according to common conceptions. At the same time, I am aware that there is little sense in allowing the notion of 'work' quite simply to mean any kind of activity; even a general definition of 'being active' would be tied to particular assumptions and would be debatable (see Chapter 5: 128ff).

Furthermore, I believe there is little sense in subsuming under 'work' everything that may be 'generally considered' work. Apart from the fact that there is no worldwide consensus on this, this attempt at a solution would involve us in a tautological circle. That which is predominantly understood as 'work' in a given society or culture (assuming that it entertains at all the notion to which we are accustomed of work as distinct from other activities) only reflects certain cultural patterns, of course, which mostly bear the stamp of the dominant classes in their own interests, and are reproduced by them.

This also applies to children's view of work. At least in the affluent countries and individualist cultures of the North, they often see work as something that appears forced upon them and therefore unpleasant, while they associate certain activities that are strenuous and take much time with 'pleasure' rather than 'work', if they have chosen them freely.[11] In many countries of the South, the activity with which they contribute to the subsistence of their families appears burdensome and strenuous, but they would term it 'help' rather than work, since 'proper' work is thought to be exclusively a matter for adults. Or children who collect leftovers or garbage in a market to ensure their own survival would, on being questioned, probably deny that this was work, because they are ashamed. Given the double ideology that work can only be an unpleasant burden and that it is not proper or suitable for children, a process of rethinking is clearly needed precisely among the children themselves as to the value and the social significance of their own activities, in order for them themselves to evaluate them as work and to make them a source of self-esteem.

Every definition of children's work implies certain prior decisions and reflects certain interests. The definition also includes as a rule culture-specific assumptions that are not always considered. My interest is in seeing as work, as comprehensively as possible, all activities carried out by children – of any age – that result from an objective and/or subjectively felt necessity of individual and social reproduction. This is admittedly a very general definition that demands further detail and clarification. But it is sufficiently specific to distinguish the work of children from their other activities, and at the same time sufficiently open to cover the wide spectrum of forms of work and to take account of culture-specific peculiarities and subjective valuations and ascriptions of significance.

Differentiating analyses of children's work

In the 1990s, the ILO took up the distinction between *labour* and *work*, in order to separate the 'harmful' forms of children's work from the 'tolerable'. This distinction has been criticized by independent researchers and in the context of the NGOs as being too coarse and theoretically implausible (see White 1994, 1996 and 1999; James et al. 1998: 110ff; Liebel 2001c). Instead, an attempt is made to cover the spectrum of the forms of children's work within a 'continuum' ranging from negatively to positively evaluated forms of children's work (White 1994). A similar attempt to describe and evaluate children's work in a differentiated manner is the so-called *balance model*, which relates the harmful and advantageous components of the various forms of children's work to each other and evaluates them (Mortimer and Finch 1996; Hobbs and McKechnie 1997; IWGCL 1998: 37ff). On the negative side (costs), possible criteria such as dangers to health and security, limitation of leisure, obstruction of education, instrumentalistic orientations and limiting of contact with parents and peers are named. On the positive side (benefits) promotion of autonomy and trust in one's own strength, acquisition of business knowledge and work experience are mentioned.

Boyden et al. (1998) insist that there has been no success so far in establishing the actual effects of the various forms of work on the lives and development of children. Many studies are based on the unthinking adoption of the 'modern' western European concept of childhood, without taking account of the actual cultural contexts, and for this reason alone arrive at conclusions on the negative consequences of children's work for the children's mental and physical development and their social integration in adulthood. This viewpoint is more influenced by notions of 'childhood' than calculated to grasp the reality of the lives of working children.

In order to avoid these 'fundamental conceptional errors' in understanding children and the meaning that work has for them, Myers and Boyden (1998) propose replacing the narrow view of children's work as exploitation by a wider view that takes account of its multifarious influences on children's growth and development. In order to properly grasp the physical and psychological effects on the well-being and development of children, it needs, they state, to be noted that children 'are not merely passive recipients of an experience, but contribute actively to its development' (ibid.: 11). Precisely for this reason, it is possible that children 'seek and value work as a source of learning, social acceptance, independence, feelings of accomplishment and self-worth, or other personal benefits beyond strictly economic considerations' (ibid.: 11). Myers and Boyden point out that the role and importance of work for children's development are strongly influenced by their particular 'cultural system'. For instance, the view of solidarity within the family and the assumption by children of vital tasks as a matter of course are of great importance. In a culture more strongly marked by an individualized lifestyle, children's work is seen rather as a way of becoming independent and living a life of one's own at an earlier age.[12] Even when work is performed under traumatic or highly stressful circumstances, children frequently show a remarkable power of resistance and make use of the advantages of their work.

At least, in recent research into children's work, a more judicious and cautious attitude has developed with regard to the important part that work can play in the lives and conditions of development of children. This is shown by various conferences at which research scholars, together with experts from NGOs and IGOs, reflect on the conceptional and methodological inadequacies of previous studies, and introduce new proposals.[13] At such conferences, two questions have been granted pride of place: the controversial connections between children's work and education, and research methodology.

New approaches in research are no longer content to trace the negative consequences of certain forms of children's work for attendance and success at school, and they adopt a critical stance towards the view favoured by UNICEF and the ILO that work and education are incompatible for children (see Salazar and Alarcón Glasínovich 1996; Recknagel 2001a). Instead, they ask how the relationship between education and work 'can be made to effectively serve children's best interests' (Myers and Boyden 1998: 15). Education is understood not only as education in school, especially as it is becoming increasingly clear that the typical experience of school contributes little or nothing to the personal development of working children, and even undermines their ability to maintain their position in the growing urban-industrial societies. On the one hand, the question is asked as to how school ('formal education') can be reformed in the interests of the children and the processes of 'informal education' rooted in everyday life can be exploited and strengthened. On the other hand, it is asked what work 'suitable for children' that helps to 'build children's social and economic skills, confidence, self-esteem, and integration into family and community' should be like and how it can be promoted (ibid.: 17).

At present there is a general consensus that methodology has been too little considered in research on children's work hitherto. In many studies there was not even any mention of the approaches used. A look at studies that do indicate their research methods shows that questionnaire surveys remain the most frequently used method, and that they glean their information almost exclusively from adults, i.e. employers, parents, carers, etc. In contrast, at present a participative methodology oriented to everyday life is proposed (though still very rarely practised), which is to include the perspective of working children themselves. Generally speaking, the trend in research on children's work has changed from an adult-centred perspective to a more child-centred approach. This means that there is an increasing tendency to regard children as the subjects rather than the objects of study (see Boyden et al. 1998: 145 ff; IWGCL 1998: 44ff; Liebel et al. 2001).

Notes

1. Recent research outputs by IPEC can be accessed on the following website: <www.ilo.org/public/english/standards/ipec/>.

2. See reports by Anti-Slavery International, Save the Children, Rädda Barnen.

3. Between 1979 and 1987 Anti-Slavery International (London) published a number of reports on children's work in Morocco, India, Thailand, South Africa, Spain, Italy, Jamaica and Great Britain.

4. A particularly successful recent example is the study by Martin Woodhead (1998), which was carried out by the Swedish branch of ISCA, Rädda Barnen, and published in Stockholm (see Chapter 3).

5. These are to be found above all in the journal *NATs – Working Children and Adolescents International Review*, which has been published in English and Spanish, with an Italian regional edition, since 1995. From the same context are the articles in the two German-language collected volumes Liebel et al. 1998 and 1999, and in the English-language volume Liebel et al. 2001.

6. The time-budget approach is also used in the study by Molina Barrios and Rojas Lizarazu (1995) on rural childhood in Bolivia.

7. Loo and Reinhart (1993) provide an interesting German-language survey of ethnological studies on children.

8. See for instance the collections of James and Prout 1990; Coninck-Smith et al. 1997; Hengst and Zeiher 2000; Mizen et al. 2001; as a coherent theoretical essay James et al. 1998; and as a critique Lavalette 1999.

9. This is, for instance, the approach of the studies on children's work carried out between 1989 and 1999 in a number of German federal states (See Ingenhorst 2001).

10. Ground-breaking in this field was Bequele and Myers 1995.

11. One example is competitive sport (see Sack 1977; Kirchhöfer 1999).

12. This aspect has recently also been stressed by German sociologists and educationists with regard to children's work in the North (see Hengst 1998; Kirchhöfer 1998).

13. Examples are the Urban Childhood Conference (1977) in Trondheim, Norway; the IREWOC workshop 'Children, Work and Education' (1999) in Amsterdam; and the international conference 'Rethinking Childhood. Working Children's Challenge to the Social Sciences', which took place in November 2000 in Bondy, near Paris. Several contributions to the Trondheim conference were published in the review *Childhood*, 6(1), 1999.

3 | The working child has a will of its own: subject-oriented and participative research on children's work in Latin America

§ IN Latin America, as in other parts of the world, research into children's work and working children is marked by two contrary paradigms. Some research is oriented towards a picture of childhood that arose with bourgeois society in Europe and sees the work of children as a relic of past times, 'hostile to children' and thus finally to be abolished. According to this approach, working children are frequently considered as 'legal subjects', but are not taken seriously as subjects with their own views on life and their own abilities. This research direction is above all interested in data and documentation that underline the harmful and negative consequences of work for children.[1]

Together with this, there is an increasing body of research that does not automatically regard the relationship of childhood and work as negative, but as an open relationship that needs to be examined in a differentiated manner, and above all taking into account the viewpoint of the working children themselves. This approach attempts to see and treat the working children in a comprehensive sense as subjects. In this chapter I shall discuss some studies of this kind which appear to me particularly important, partly from a conceptual viewpoint, partly from a methodological point of view.

By the conceptual viewpoint, I mean one governed by the 'image' of the child or childhood, either in the way it estimates the (potential) abilities of children to express and present themselves, or in what ideals or visions it has of children and childhood. It is important for a subject-oriented view to picture children not only as articulate, but as people who are sometimes silent, but always take action to cope with their situation and their lives, and who in doing so always 'make sense of their situation' in a way that serves to orient their actions. That is to say, subject-oriented research faces the task of deciphering the children's 'own will', even when it is not always in language, or is concealed behind the child's words.

In terms of the methodological aspect, the question as to how the children can present themselves is of interest. It is not enough merely to pay heed to the 'voice of the children', for instance by interviewing children rather than adults. Also in terms of this aspect, it is equally important how children, in the various stages of a study, can influence the categories or indicators on which it is based and the decisions to be made, and whether techniques are applied that really make it possible for the children to behave and express themselves 'uninhibitedly' and 'independently', and put across their view of things.

In relation to working children, it is particularly important to bring out the children's own will and self-interpretation, and to consider these independently of the normal, usually negative, interpretation patterns of what the children are able to do and do (especially their work). An attempt must be made to 'read' the positive, alternative possibilities from children's (observable) actions and (linguistic) statements, not in order to idealize them, but to help them assert their rights in the face of the dominant viewpoints. Here social research can also contribute to making it possible and easier for children, in a world that mainly responds to them with incomprehension or even hostility, to find self-confidence, to take a stand, to feel their worth, to have a better negotiating position. That is, the attempt must be made to trace how, in spite of all the difficulties, children attempt to master their lives, even when they do not always succeed. The enquiry should primarily be directed towards their possibilities, their potential, not their failures.

In the first part of this chapter, I will consider from the conceptual viewpoint three studies undertaken in Brazil (Da Silva Telles and Abramo 1987), Uruguay (Lucchini 1998) and Bolivia (Domic Ruiz 1999). Since these studies are wholly or partly based on the theory of *social representations*, I will begin by outlining this before discussing the studies themselves.[2] In the second part, two studies that were carried out in Central America claiming to use a participative methodology will be critically analysed and compared (Pineda and Guerra 1998; Woodhead 1998).

Discovering working children as subjects
On the theory of social representations

This theory proceeds from the assumption that reality, as soon as it becomes the object of human communication (meaning as a rule that it is couched in words, concepts or images), assumes certain meanings. By social representation, Jodelet understands the totality 'of informative, cognitive, ideological, normative elements, articles of faith, values, attitudes, opinions, etc. ... These elements always structure in a specific manner knowledge about the state of reality' (Jodelet 1989: 36). The representations are expressed in 'discourses'.[3]

The theory of social representations is above all an interest in the knowledge that serves people to orient themselves in their everyday lives, or to shape these according to particular wishes or interests. It sees knowledge in a comprehensive sense in its cognitive, affective and symbolic content and in its individual and collective forms. According to this, knowledge manifests itself not only in words, but also in movements, gestures ('body language'), sounds, images, etc. And it is not only articulated and 'charged' with meaning by the individual in a particular way, but comes about and is expressed also as the common knowledge of social collectives, whether these are particular social groups or whole societies, cultures or civilizations, which secure their common features through this common knowledge and the interpretations it involves, or are fixed 'ideologically' in the interests of power elites to particular viewpoints. 'The content of representations is to a large extent culturally defined by myths, ideologies, and in a general way by the symbolic universe of the various groups.' (Lucchini 1998: 152). Reference to social representations can relate both to the reasons for and the process of genesis of this knowledge and to the modes of its appropriation and social consequences.

Social representations do not come about and reproduce themselves by chance. In their individual forms is reflected the need peculiar to man to make his way and assert himself in life. In their collective forms are reflected the interests of social groups, whether of dominant social classes, sexes, ethnic groups, age groups or power elites, or population groups that are excluded from power, subjected to it or socially marginalized.

Domic Ruiz (1999) and Lucchini (1998)[4] demonstrate by the example of the social representations of the child, childhood, children's work and the metaphor of the street child[5] how in Western bourgeois societies certain normative 'discourses' come about and are institutionalized, which as it were place an ideological stamp on these social phenomena. Thus, for instance, something is ascribed to the child, children, or childhood that is supposed to be appropriate to him/her/it, for example particular qualities, skills or a lack of skills legitimizing a particular social status or even exclusion from society.[6] In this way, reality is not simply measured and judged, but the perception and representation of that which counts as 'reality' is already marked by it.

Domic Ruiz points out, however, rightly, that the social representations are neither a 'pure reflection of the external world or the passive reproduction of the external in the internal' (Domic Ruiz 1999: 13), nor a monopoly of the power elites or dominant groups. They are always also interpretations of everyday experience in which the power of imagination of human individuals is expressed. In this sense, for instance, in working children or members of the dispossessed classes there are conceptions and images of 'childhood' or 'children's work' that are fundamentally different from the Western bourgeois ideal image of the child or the Western myth of childhood, and which influence their self-image and behaviour (see Lucchini 1998: 158f).

The three studies discussed below are governed by this comprehensive concept of social representations and use it in order to bring out and to comprehend the frequently hidden and concealed aspects of the reality and the views of working children. I shall begin by giving an account of the findings, and then discuss them comparatively, including an assessment of methodological aspects.

Working children in São Paulo

In the study by Da Silva Telles and Abramo (1987), carried out in the early 1980s, the fact that working children 'never figure as having had significant experiences, although these could possibly cast light on and help to decipher the multifarious and various practices by which workers cope with the conditions under which they live' is criticized (ibid.: 198). For this reason, children's work must be considered in a different manner from usual.

Data on children's work must be seen as 'lived situations', 'which are thought and worked out inside the symbolic universe and linked with values and representations; in this manner the men, women and children interpret the conditions forced upon them, translate them into their everyday experience and repeatedly give new meaning to their lives and the world in which they share' (ibid.: 198).

The picture of the child as a 'state-protected creature' that is dominant and laid down in legislation, and the legal non-recognition of the working child as a worker and citizen with rights of his own, prevent the 'lived reality' of the working children from being visible and perceived. Working children 'live in a position of double illegality' (ibid.: 202); on the one hand, because of their age they are described as 'minors', and on the other they are pushed into the so-called 'informal labour market', in which they can only carry out activities 'not recognised by the law' (ibid.: 202). Thus they are subjected doubly to a power model that falsifies their lived reality and their experience. In addition, their activities, because of their illegal and clandestine character, are approximated to the 'world of crime', and seen as coming under the aegis of the police and the state institutions of welfare and repression.

They have to work in an area 'in which the borderline between petty crime and "honest work" is blurred; and in the case of the children the borderline is still less clear, as in this sphere of work children who still have connections with their families share their lives with abandoned children that live in the streets and "delinquent" children that pass through the welfare institutions of the state' (ibid.: 203).

The situation is made worse by the fact that only so-called 'regular employment' is socially and legally accepted, and this is denied to the children. 'The legally defined transition to the age of majority and the acquisition of the right to work connected with this appear as the necessary precondition to belonging to society' (ibid.: 206). The children's daily experience of work thus remains caught up in a 'double negativity' without any 'positive meanings' and 'without the means required for recognition in the social and public sphere' (ibid.: 206).

'The drama experienced by these children has neither a social nor a legal basis on which to achieve a socially recognised identity in a positive manner. The children are prevented from communicating the experiences they live through with others, and are unable to enter into the "common world of experience" that helps to give workers self-assurance. By living in the underground of society, the children can find neither a name nor recognition for their wishes and demands, their rebellion and their discontent' (ibid.: 205).

Faced with this 'negative block' (Da Silva Telles and Abramo 1987), scholars are faced with the task of making visible and deciphering the meanings that the children give to their work implicitly or explicitly. In my view, we can understand them as an expression of the 'power' and the 'success in integration' of the subject who withstands the imposed patterns of interpretation, which are 'ideological' and determined by power interests, and who interprets his experience from the point of view of *his own* interests and context of life in terms of his own meaning.[7] The authors of the study discussed here remark only briefly on this (although the date of origin of the study, at a time when the debate on children's work from the perspective of the children had hardly begun, has to be taken into account).

From the words of the children, the authors derive 'a double appreciation of work'.

On the one hand, it is based on their own sociability (meeting people, making new friendships, getting to know the world) and some chances to lead their own lives and help earn their own living, thanks to remuneration that permits them 'to buy things of their own', and access to a pleasurable experience which as a rule is hard to come by in view of the limited and controlled family budget. On the other hand, their work, as a contribution to the living costs, gives them greater legitimacy within the family, and relativises the relations of authority that normally obtain in the families. (ibid.: 208)[8]

The authors find it remarkable that working children see the positive meanings of their working experience above all in attaining a 'greater degree of recognition, freedom and autonomy' (ibid.: 208) – remarkable above all because 'none of this is fully realised' (ibid.: 208). They pass on the greater part of their income to their parents, the disposal of their time remains under the strict control of the family, attainable 'sociability' is largely limited to the time when the children are among themselves, and the work available to children is to a great extent marked by discipline, control and subjection. Therefore there is more than a mere description of reality to be seen in the statements of working children. The ideas of autonomy and freedom can be seen as a critique of their subjection within the family and as expression of the hope of expanding their own scope for freedom and action through work. To some extent, the criticism is also directed against the conditions of a kind of work in which 'everything must be accepted' – as one office boy expressed it (ibid.: 210).

'Between the sphere of the family and the sphere of work, between minority and majority, the existing world does not open up many paths to them. In view of the isolation of their experience, they have few opportunities to express themselves and to structure areas of recognition in which their claims and wishes could achieve positive meanings' (ibid.: 214). The question arises as to whether and to what extent they can 'structure themselves in collective intentions and identities' (ibid.: 214). To find an answer to this, the diverse, more or less organized forms of expression and comradeship of the young people ('youth cultures') and the messages contained in them must be more closely studied. 'Perhaps we would find paths there that would permit us to decipher the various, discontinuous ways by which these children and adolescents secure for themselves a place in society, outside of the pre-arranged places in the world to which they are subjected' (ibid.: 214).

Working children in Montevideo

Riccardo Lucchini's study (1998) is devoted to male children aged from twelve to fifteen who work in the streets of Montevideo (Uruguay).[9] It examines the forms of work and the meanings that they have for the children. The study regards the children who work in the street as 'actors', and attempts to understand their interpretations of their situation and their action strategies from their own viewpoint and logic.

Lucchini terms the children's working conditions in most cases 'precarious'; they are characterized by 'great instability and a frequent change of activity. The children are constantly changing their occupations, employers and working relationships' (ibid.: 38). As a rule, 'periods of activity alternate with periods without work' (ibid.: 39), partly caused by obligations at school, the decisions being made by the children. Most of the children in the study work 'on their own account'. 'The absence of an employer is no accident, but the result of an intentional practice' (ibid.: 39).

The children prefer working to begging. 'Selling something gives the children the feeling of being useful and possessing a certain skill. Even if trade does not function as the child might wish, it knows that it is performing an activity that is not suppressed or merely tolerated. When it begs, the child plays the role of a victim lacking the autonomy to do anything else. The begging child also feels condemned by other children who are also on the street but do not beg. The stigmatisation by his peers is felt strongly by the begging child' (ibid.: 41). Other than financial income, the two most important positive aspects of work that give the children satisfaction are thus 'feeling useful' and the idea of acting themselves and not being dependent upon the benevolence of others. The question of the social recognition that the activity brings with it is also of significance. It is important to stress this, because not only begging but also 'working' in the street often leads to discrimination and suspicion.

Many children prefer not always to work at the same place (e.g. a bus station), but to move from place to place and to combine the sale of various articles (e.g. flowers, sweets, greetings cards): 'This allows the child to expand the sources of his income and to spread the risks better' (ibid.: 42).

Although children frequently begin their gainful employment by imitating other children, 'independence in the street is an important value to them, even when a child forms part of a group' (ibid.: 42). This independence is also sought when a child recognizes that there are numerous difficulties in life in the street. A child who works for a third party implicitly admits that his own skills are insufficient, and above all that he lacks the necessary cunning. Cunning and artfulness are among the most highly esteemed skills. On the other hand, a child is by no means stigmatized by other children if he works with a member of his family or combines with other children and shares the income with them. 'In the former case, the work of the child is not seen as an expression of dependence: it brings in no income, but is an expression of solidarity within the family despite the material difficulties. In this case, the child has no boss, and the other children do not expect him to show independence' (ibid.: 42f).

There are nevertheless children who opt for an 'independent kind of work'. This depends above all on the conditions set by the employer. 'If he allows the child to dispose of that part of his income that belongs to him, the dependence is not felt to be irksome' (ibid.: 43). Some children see an advantage in this kind of work, because they are able to dispose of their whole income, and do not have to reinvest it. 'Accordingly, the child can give dependence not felt to be irksome preference over irksome independence. In the former case, the immediate availability of profit compensates for the contractual dependence. The ability to spend money gives the child a certain autonomy, particularly since the profit is directly available to him, not only through the employer' (ibid.: 43).

With respect to working conditions in the street, Lucchini distinguishes two 'ideal types' of children: on the one hand, the 'innovative' type, who invests and takes risks, and delays gratification for the sake of a higher income; and on the other the 'immediate' type, for whom immediate consumption is more important than other considerations. These two types form two poles at the ends of a continuum within which the individual cases are to be found.

Lucchini interprets these two basic tendencies with reference to several fundamental assumptions about the 'social personality'. This includes four basic dimensions: 'self-regulation' ('the ability to define goals in order to be autonomous'), 'adaptability' ('the ability to expose oneself to external difficulties and to adapt the means to goals that are not self-chosen'), 'cooperation' ('the ability to cooperate with others and show reliability and solidarity'), and 'sensitivity' ('the ability to imagine, to invent, to feel, to have an ideal'). 'The totality of the relations between the roles that the individual knows and presents constitutes the structure of his social personality' (ibid.: 44). These roles are defined according to the four basic dimensions named, which for their part come into existence during the process of socialization and from the concrete social context.

Lucchini now specifies the two 'ideal types', according to the four basic dimensions of the social personality, in the following manner: 'The two first dimensions [self-regulation, adaptability] are easier to deal with than the others. The innovative type can in fact be characterised by self-regulation, and the immediate type by adaptability. It can also be shown that the innovative type accentuates sensitivity more than the immediate type. The ability to cooperate also appears to be more important. In this way, we can say that the innovative type is characterised by autonomy, the definition of personal goals, imagination and inventiveness' (ibid.: 44). In contrast, Lucchini sees the immediate type characterized by yielding to external difficulties, and limiting himself to episodic cooperation with others.

Lucchini observes how children who work as itenerant vendors frequently change from the state of 'immediacy' to that of 'innovation'. The contrary development is rare.

> The innovative child is a person who finds new goals at the same time as he pursues the goals of his group. This form of active adaptation contrasts with the conformism of the immediacy-oriented child, which uses the means that happen to be at his disposal. At the same time, immediacy-orientation does not necessarily mean that the child is in the service of third parties. It may well be that he works for himself. That which characterises him is his mimeticism: he imitates the model or normal behaviour. (ibid.: 44)

According to Lucchini, the children sometimes work in groups of two or three, but this is not the rule. From an economic standpoint there are no decisive advantages that would further the collective organization. The temporary character of the work and easy access to the objects to be sold do not stimulate the associative forms (ibid.: 44f).

Another observation that Lucchini makes among the itinerant vendors is that of an autonomy that grows over time. He thinks it possible to distinguish three stages. When the child begins his work in the street, he gives the greater part of his earnings to his parents. In the second stage, the child takes care of his income and keeps the greater part for himself. 'He uses the street as a sphere of learning, and gains from this more security and autonomy. He knows the street better than his parents. On the other hand, he has new needs that are generated by daily observation of the shop windows in the centre of town. He needs more money' (ibid.: 46). In the third stage, the child retains all the money he earns for himself, and confines himself to occasionally giving his parents presents. 'These stages constitute a course of development through which the children pass in various rhythms and sometimes incompletely' (ibid.: 46).

For the children, the street is not a goal in itself, but the means to certain ends. Lucchini names these goals as work ('calle-trabajo'), protest ('calle-protesta') and play ('calle-lúdica') (ibid.: 55). For the children work turns the street into a legitimate place, and makes it possible for them to be accepted there. But their presence in the street is always also linked to the other goals. The use of the street as a place of protest aims at more independence. Equally, work and play in the street are 'closely linked to one another' (ibid.: 46). According to Lucchini, a pre-condition for this is that work in the case in point is not an obligation but was chosen by the children themselves. The various goals of the street are in a complementary interrelation with one another – that is, they are not mutually exclusive. The change from one goal to the other is easier and more fluid when the children are in the street of their own free will. In the case of children who are not able to choose their work freely, however, work and play are not wholly separated. The difference between the two categories of children results chiefly from the economic situation of their families, which is brittle in both cases. They belong to the same social stratum. A given child can very quickly move from one category to the other.

According to this study, the children are not content in the street when they are not able to pursue some particular concrete activity. 'The child is ashamed of being in the street with nothing to do' (ibid.: 47). 'Being without a particular activity causes boredom, the need for diversion, and the feeling of being condemned' (ibid.: 47). 'For all children, the street is a place of learning, and most of them express this in a spontaneous manner. This learning relates above all to getting to know people and their behaviour. It primarily affects the modes of social interaction' (ibid.: 48).

In order to master life in the street, children develop various forms of 'social organization': gangs, networks, groups of two or three. A child can belong to several forms of group simultaneously. Among children who are in the street primarily to work, the most common form is the loose network. This is characterized by a low degree of formalization and structuring, is hardly visible, and soon adapts to the changing conditions in the children's environment (ibid.: 83).

Working children in La Paz and El Alto

The study by Domic Ruiz (1999) is devoted to male children aged between ten and fourteen who earn their living in the streets of La Paz and El Alto (Bolivia). He is interested in the question of the way in which the children's work is 'represented' in the thoughts and feelings of the children on the one hand and their parents on the other, and the effect these 'social representations' have on the children's actions and ability to act. The various representations are weighted and depicted in their relationship with each other.

According to Domic Ruiz's study, the children and their parents agree that children's work is important above all because it brings in (money) income and serves to support the family and to enable the children to maintain themselves. One difference between children and parents is that children additionally (in second place in order of importance) find their work significant in that it allows them 'productive action', by which they understand both the carrying out of the work and the product resulting from their work. So while in the thinking of the parents the children's work is regarded almost exclusively in its 'economic' or pecuniary aspect, 'the attitude of the children to their work goes beyond the fact of payment, that is, they evalute the activity in itself as something which creates a product or result' (ibid.: 138f).

Apart from the aspects mentioned, both children and their parents also attribute to work – although with less emphasis – significance for learning; here they have in mind above all the fact that the income connected with the work makes it possible to afford the expenditure necessary for the children to attend school. Furthermore, children connect their work with the negative experience of maltreatment and discrimination, and in general with problems, incidents and difficulties. The fathers – not the mothers – on the other hand express fears that the children's work may be accompanied by neglect, thus threatening their education and development. The fathers' fears are stated in a general form, without concrete reference to the work situation of their own children, and are evaluated by Domic Ruiz as an expression of the fact that the fathers regard the children's work with ambivalent feelings, since it calls into question their dominant position as the family 'bread-winners'. The mothers, on the other hand, show themselves much more strongly emotionally tied to their children, and trust them to cope even with difficult situations.

The central significance of the income in the context of work shows that not every kind of work done by children meets with recognition either in the thinking of the children or that of their parents. Thus work done in the household without payment is perceived only as 'helping', and regarded particularly by the parents as a kind of natural obligation on the part of the children. The study does not deal explicitly with the work of girls, but allows the conclusion that the results of their work above all are devalued and made invisible in this way.

From the viewpoint of working children, the income that accompanies work has three kinds of meaning: '*Earning* money, *having* money, and *dealing with* money' (ibid.: 144; emphasis in the original). 'Earning money' means for the children both receiving an income for work realized and attaining a goal and being successful; this is closely connected with the notion that the mobilization of energy and attention, together with certain skills, is required in order to achieve a particular result. 'Having money' means for the children being an important factor in the family economy (they contribute up to 30 per cent to the maintenance of the family) and having a feeling of security, being able to acquire and enjoy themselves things that correspond to their own needs. 'Those who have and possess things can decide on their own wishes, needs and relationships with others. In the case of the children, this is still more evident, as having their own money procures them *power*, which is normally not granted to them in view of their age and stage of development. This strengthens their feeling of security' (ibid.: 147). 'Dealing with money' means for the children having access to objects and being able to do things that are as a rule not accessible to them, that is, expanding their options and scope for decision. This demands from them, and also gives them the experience of, being in control of their actions, making priorities, and finding independent answers to their everyday needs and to unforeseen situations.

When the children emphasize that their work is important to them to earn their living, they have in mind primarily the fact that they have to look after themselves, and are forced or able to make decisions of their own, i.e. to act autonomously. 'The absence of parents or the lack of external control and protection place the working child in a position that cancels out the "natural" subordination to the adult world' (ibid.: 155) and thus dissipates notions suggested by the conventional image of childhood. This is a central factor in their socialization process. The children are obliged to acquire the faculty of finding their own practical solutions to fundamental requirements, and to react suitably to situations or conflicts. Domic Ruiz found in working children 'a well-developed social competence and a very good knowledge of their social surroundings; they are able to encounter conflict situations, and react appropriately to new social events and states of affairs. They are able to make use in the optimum manner of opportunities that offer themselves by chance; that is, they have structured strategies of behaviour that permit them to give effective and creative answers to the situations that their lives present them with' (ibid.: 156).

The monetary contribution to the maintenance of the family gives the children in many cases a privileged position in the family, where their work is accepted, recognized and appreciated. At least the child who earns money with his work is thus able to leave behind him the status of an 'invisible child' and 'show himself as a subject able to take on responsibility, whose words carry weight and who has the power to influence decisions' (ibid.: 164). In the case of family households run by mothers without partners above all, working children occupy a strong position and enjoy such respect that the social relations between the generations hardly have hierarchical traits any longer.[10] From the viewpoint of the children, their work is not significant only because of the money that is earned through it. It is rather regarded as of 'great social value', as it goes together with 'responsibility, devotion and a positive attitude to life' (ibid.: 170), and even more so with an attitude 'motivated by mutual help' (ibid.: 170). Domic Ruiz sees in the thinking of children about their work many elements 'that exceed the limits of money (income) and again bring out the nature of work as a productive activity which transforms them, and as a repository of social values' (ibid.: 170).

The position promulgated by UNICEF and numerous NGOs and governments that school is more important for children than work, and must have priority, is not confirmed in the study by Domic Ruiz. According to him, 'children find in work more and better advantages than in formal learning ("*estudio*"), for one thing because of the short-term results, and for another because without the work they could not attend school at all' (ibid.: 172). In a case of conflict, they therefore prefer work to school, which does not mean, however, that they have no interest in 'learning'. Their interest in learning is, however, closely interwoven with the idea that it must contribute in a palpable way to mastering their lives, improving their work, or finding better work opportunities.

As already indicated, the children studied by Ruiz do not only see advantages in their work, but also criticize maltreatment, discrimination and other problems and difficulties experienced in the course of it. The children connect the negative aspects of their work with their living conditions in poverty, their situation as 'minors', their ethnic-cultural origin, social prejudices and the specific working conditions that are imposed upon them or are available to them as children. With regard to their working conditions, the children refer explicitly to the exploitation of their labour potential. They criticize the fact 'that they are paid too little, that their overtime is not recognised, that the wage agreed on is not paid them, that they have no access to social benefits, that they are not given the food the employer is supposed to supply, and that they have no access at all to medical treatment' (ibid.: 174). According to Domic Ruiz, the discourse of working children on their socio-cultural origins, their place within the social spectrum in which they find themselves, and their interpretation of reality as they experience it shows 'a surprising amount of awareness and knowledge' (ibid.: 175). In their critical comments, they refer not only to the more evident and obvious aspects of the social structures in which they live, but also bring in socio-linguistic elements, modes of behaviour, forms of expression and dress 'that are constitutive for collective identities and express their class situation' (ibid.: 175).

Domic Ruiz comes to the conclusion that the wide knowledge of the working children, their 'reading' of reality, their 'representations' and their consciousness

> are the answers to a long process of experience that results from their situation within the social context and their dynamic inclusion in the world of work. This process makes working children's social behaviour and communication richer, more comprehensive and in some respects also more autonomous. The discourse of the children on socio-economic conditions shows that they perceive not merely these as such, but also the mutual relations between actions, which permits them to create a system of relations themselves. Their interpretation of reality is related to a totality from which each part derives its meaning. (ibid.: 176)

Comparative discussion and summary evaluation

The studies described have set new standards for the empirical investigation of children's work which are relevant beyond Latin America. Other studies had been undertaken which demonstrate the way of thinking and the perspective of working children,[11] but these were essentially ethnographic stock-takings confined to the collection, classification and intuitive interpretation of statements (*testimonios*) made by the children. In contrast, the studies described here are distinguished by the fact that they open up and interpret the way of thinking of working children in their socio-economic and socio-cultural contexts. Both the collection and the interpretation of the data are based on the systematic methodological application of a subject-oriented theoretical conception.

This is particularly true of the study by Domic Ruiz, which approaches the various meanings that children's work has for them and for their mothers and fathers in a procedure involving several stages. This begins with explorative conversations with children and parents, and a group discussion with children, in which in an associative manner the aspects of the meaning of 'being a child' and its compatibility or non-compatibility with work are investigated. Further questions are aimed at the significance of the child within the family, its 'participation', the satisfaction of its needs and – in the adults – the ideas, customs and rites relating to death, burial and above all the pain of the loss of a child. On the basis of these conversations, it was established in more strongly structured conversations with ten children and five parents what meanings attach to the children's work and to what extent these meanings are interrelated. The result was represented graphically as a tree with branches of varying thickness ('*arbol máximo*') and integrated into a questionnaire consisting of open questions, incomplete sentences and keywords which those questioned were to complete and comment on. Sixty children and thirty mothers and fathers were involved in this questionnaire. In addition, in the case of some of the children questioned, projective techniques ('*laminas inductoras*') were used, in which drawings showing children in various situations in life were to be commented on.

Finally, the main interrogation was carried out with 120 children aged from ten to fourteen, and sixty mothers and fathers. This was based on a partly structured questionnaire in which the various meanings given by children and their parents to the children's work were represented, partly in graphic form and partly in words. Based on this interrogation, matrices were drawn up showing the most frequently named meanings and the relations between them in their various degrees of strength. 'The elements with the strongest relations constitute the central nucleus (*nucleo central*) of the social representation' (ibid.: 226). In order to understand better still the meaning of the social representations, intensive interviews and group discussions were carried out with some children and parents, and the content of the resulting notes analytically evaluated. Photo-stories (*técnica de fotolenguaje*) related to certain ethno-cultural aspects were added, designed to prompt the children to think about the relevance of their ethnic origin to their social situation and their experiences in everyday life. At all stages of the study, attention was paid to the fact that the children working in the streets of La Paz and El Alto are almost all of Amerindian origin, and that many aspects of meaning of their work result from this ethno-cultural context or can only be understood in view of it. Where this was desired by those questioned, or was unavoidable for the understanding of aspects of meaning, they had the opportunity to express themselves in their maternal language, Aymara. In all, 360 children and adults were involved in the study, the collection phase of which extended over eleven months.

Lucchini's study is based essentially on empathetic observation in the streets of Montevideo, where the children spent most of their time, and above all pursued the various activities essential for their living. Wherever possible, conversations were carried out with the children in which they depicted and commented on their biographies and everyday experiences. From the transcripts of the conversations, reports in the children's own words (*testimonios*) were drawn up. The goal was not to judge these personal reports as to the truth of their content, but to 'understand' them, and in particular 'to understand how the social processes function'

(Lucchini 1998: xvi). Correspondingly, no personal report was used to contradict or relativize another. Nor were the reports used to verify or contradict hypotheses; rather they were considered and interpreted in their various social contexts, as far as these could be deduced from the observations and other documents.

The central topics of the study were not laid down in advance, but resulted step by step from the combination of various methods, above all the observations of the daily actions of, and from conversations with, the children. It does not always emerge unambiguously from Lucchini's presentation how the process of the gradual focusing of topics and contexts took place, and to what the interpretations were oriented. However, it seems to me important that this was an open procedure which offered the children sufficient scope for their own interpretations, and that the researchers saw themselves obliged 'to recognise and accept the plural character of reality' (ibid.: xvii). In all, forty children aged from twelve to fifteen were involved in the study, whose collection phase lasted six months.

Da Silva Telles and Abramo's study was available only in the form of a 'first draft', which the authors themselves describe as a 'discussion proposal' (Da Silva Telles and Abramo 1987: 197). It gives no information regarding the age, sex or number of the children involved in the study. Nor are the methods used described in detail. I have nevertheless included this study in my account, since it represents a comparatively early attempt to understand the reality of the lives of working children from their own perspective, without being restricted to a stock-taking. The 'lived reality' (ibid.: 202) of the children is related, in a manner that can be termed programmatic, to the material and ideological reality forced upon them, and ways are shown in which the statements of the children concerning their lives can be interpreted and understood.

The three studies described are devoted to working children who earn their living in the urban context in the street. This definition does not by any means cover all the groups of children working today in Latin America. Since furthermore the studies of Domic Ruiz and Lucchini deal only with male children, it may be assumed that the perspectives and aspects of meaning of work do not apply in the same way to all working children. However, these studies are so rich in theoretical considerations and methodological experience that they are able to stimulate and facilitate subject-oriented access to the 'lived reality' of working children in other social and cultural contexts as well.

In the following section, two studies will be discussed which, like those described above, deal with the way of thinking of working children. The special point in their case is that they came about within the practical context of two internationally active NGOs, and are calculated to give new orientations to educational and social work with children. For this reason, the question of participation is central, both with regard to research methodology and to educational practice. Accordingly, in my account of the two studies I shall concentrate on the question of what view of participation the studies are based on, and to what extent they are successful in bringing out children's viewpoints and interpretations of their lives.

Participative research on working children

The two studies in question (Pineda and Guerra 1998; Woodhead 1998) were carried out in Central America in the second half of the 1990s under the aegis of one Norwegian and one Swedish children's aid organization (Redd Barna and Rädda Barnen). In the preface to the first study, which is devoted to children in Nicaragua, the local representative of the Norwegian aid organization shows herself convinced that she is contributing to 'including the children in our own work not merely as target groups but as partners, collaborators, and friends' (Pineda and Guerra 1998: 7). The coordinator and author of the second study, which deals with working children in El Salvador, Guatemala and Nicaragua,[12] justifies his approach with the 'conviction that the participation of the children is the fundamental point of departure in order to understand the problem of child labour more comprehensively and to intervene more effectively' (Woodhead 1998: 16).

The studies will be discussed here in the light of the question of whether the inclusion of children in research studies is in fact a guarantee that the children's perspective also receives due attention, and thus has a better chance of being taken account of in the practical work of the aid organizations. Since this is as a rule research carried out by adults, despite their best intentions it is by no means automatic that they are in fact able to do justice to the children's way of thinking and feeling. This is not merely a methodological problem, susceptible of solution by cunningly devised 'participative' investigation techniques and the research workers' own cerebrations, but also has an aspect related to research policy. Studies on children's work in particular operate within a field of conflict which is to a high degree political, in which contrary views about what is appropriate to children and may best contribute to the solution of their problems collide. At a time when 'children's participation' is in fashion and the hitherto dominant policy of technocratic measures is under considerable pressure to show its success and legitimacy, it is at least possible that the inclusion of children in research projects may be misused, precisely when children are able to make detailed statements, to legitimize and establish in a subtle manner the monopoly of interpretation and action of interested groups of adults.

Participation as dispossession

The study by Pineda and Guerra (1998) is devoted to various aspects of the reality of children's lives. It examines how children see and judge their families, school, their work, their future and themselves. In conclusion it enquires into how children cope with stressful situations and what their ideas are about the relative roles of the sexes.

In contrast to most other NGO publications, this study provides information on the methods and techniques used, and gives an account of the theoretical background. Pineda and Guerra – both of whom are psychologists – stress that they see children as subjects in the sense that 'every person provides his/her own subjective universe, which is not merely a reflection, but rather a construction of life as they experience it. This process of construction is an active process, which is determined both by the subject and by reality' (ibid.: 35).

For the study, three groups of children were selected with the intention of a comparative examination: thirty-eight working children who were involved in educational social projects, forty-one working children involved in no project, and forty-one children who were not working but only attending school. The children are between seven and twelve years of age, approximately half boys and half girls. They all live in Managua. With regard to the socio-structural characteristics, from the selection it emerged that all the working children live in conditions of poverty, while all the non-working children come from relatively affluent families. As 'work', activities were considered 'which create income and have a vital importance for the living of the individual or his/her family' (ibid.: 22).

In order to grasp the children's perspective, together with the semi-standardized interviews that were undertaken with all the children (the questionnaires were unfortunately not published), open group interviews were carried out with ten children from each socio-structural group, centring on questions on their work and families. In addition, self-evaluation scales were used. At the end of the process, the biographies of three selected children were reconstructed in order better to understand the quantitative data. In contrast to the prejudices of adults towards children, which the authors term 'adultisation of the child' or 'infantilisation of the child', they claim that they themselves 'understand the children as they are, according to their age, individuality, and from inside the child, that is, their subjectivity' (ibid.: 33).

In my critical consideration of the study, I shall concentrate on the remarks on the children's view of their work and the way they cope with stressful situations.

Pineda and Guerra themselves show surprise that working children in general have a positive attitude to their work;[13] 55 per cent expressly state that they like to work, 27 per cent say that their work makes them feel useful and important. Three out of four children state that their lives would be worse if they did not work. It emerges from the group discussions that most children would still work even if they had no financial problems in their families and their parents were able to give them all they need.

As in other studies, in this study too it was confirmed that the positive attitude of working children to work is not to be seen as a lack of a capacity to criticize. It goes together with a clear critique of their working conditions. In the study, 70 per cent of the children name negative aspects, such as that work does not leave them enough time for school or to play, that they are maltreated in the street, or insulted as 'glue-sniffers' or 'layabouts', or that they are exploited at work.

Meanwhile, Pineda and Guerra's readiness to take the children's statements seriously comes up against an imaginary limit as soon as they attempt to interpret them as 'mental representations' and in their 'meaning structures'.[14] According to them, the reason the children have a positive attitude to work is that they are bored at home, have no toys, or are not allowed to play. 'Many children see in their working situations an opportunity to play, with greater freedom, away from their parents' control' (ibid.: 91). Or elsewhere: 'According to what the children say, work seems to them to be a sphere where they can play, interact with their peers, and enjoy a certain amount of freedom. It is an opportunity for entertainment that they find nowhere else, since they have no toys, no television, and no sports or games are organised for them' (ibid.: 160).

The study by no means covers all the reasons given by children in other studies for why they work.[15] It seems that Pineda and Guerra were above all interested in finding out why children so rarely spend their time and energy at home, and so frequently in the street and other places that are usually the province of adults. In the part of the study that deals with the family, it appears that working children are confronted at home with many limitations and conflicts, and are to a high degree regimented and frequently also maltreated by their parents. The interest shown by children in linking work and play, in appropriating a social sphere through and at work, and in making possible free social communication with their peers alone deserves a more precise interpretation than is given here.

This, however, is not taken seriously. Instead of casting light on its various aspects, it is without ceremony devalued to the status of a substitute act and even declared a 'phenomenon of social alienation'. 'These children are doubtless alienated. Work has become an important part of their lives, as is usual for adults, and they see it as something of vital importance. But behind this, the alienation has a double meaning, as they have internalised work not only as a key element of their identity, but it has also become something most attractive to them. This means an obstacle to break through the circle of poverty; the children prolong and reinforce their poverty by aiming at little more than the performance of marginal work' (ibid.: 160).

Thus merely because they cannot accept what they do not allow to be possible, the two researchers see children's wish to work, either to be more independent, to lead less controlled lives, or with whatever other expectations, as a social catastrophe. Instead of accepting the wishes and fantasies contained in the children's conceptions of work (and to ask themselves how these would be supported and realized), the researchers' imagination is limited to the question as to how the children can be purged of the 'cult of work' (ibid.: 160) and persuaded to find pleasure again in family life (by means of more toys? More TV? Better parents?).

In this study, then, the patient elucidation of the children's attitudes and motives with regard to work has the sole goal of developing more effective strategies of 'reduction of children's work'. It serves only to better imagine how all the elements that the children find 'interesting and attractive' in their work might be diverted to other spheres and activities.

In order to bring children to spend more time on other activities relevant to their development, we must transform these into attractive and interesting activities – that is, more attractive and interesting than the work the children perform. At this age, activities do not have a hierarchy that is steered by conscious reflection or judgments on things that are more or less important for each child. Furthermore, the hierarchies of activities take shape according to that which is seen as attractive and/or interesting in them. For this reason, children cannot be convinced by words alone. What is needed is a new organisation of children's lives with the possibility of spending their time on activities that are more attractive to children. Extra-school activities such as sport are a good idea, but it remains a challenge to transform the school itself into an attractive place for working children. (ibid.: 161)

How seldom children are finally trusted to judge and shape their lives becomes apparent in the evaluation of the children's strategies in dealing with stress. The authors gain the impression that working children act less than non-working children in a manner directly aimed at the solution of their problems, in the sense of solving their problems themselves, seeking social support, or consciously waiting for a better moment. Instead, they tend to 'ineffectual and pointless actions and reactions' (ibid.: 144). Under this heading are grouped such reactions as feeling sad, tired, bored, uncertain, at someone's mercy or alone, being nervous, dreaming, not going to school any more, or wishing to die. Such remarks, made in the course of interviews or group discussions, may have very different meanings and relate to quite different occasions. Being sad can, for instance, represent the beginning of a process of reflection; feeling alone can be the first step towards ending this unsatisfactory state; not wanting to go to school any more can be the result of a conscious decision. The interpretations made in the study exclusively stress the possible negative aspects, without taking account of the circumstances or the kinds of stress to which the children's remarks relate, and without establishing whether these are stable personality traits.

From 'snapshots' like those presented in the study, there is no way one can conclude how children actually behave in their everyday lives or how they would behave under different circumstances. Countless examples, and in particular the processes in the independent organizations of working children, show that children who, for instance, appear sad, speechless or uncertain can in no time become glowing and eloquent examplars of children's rights, and that they are very well able to approach the solution of their problems directly, and even in an organized manner. By reason of its methodological approach, this study does not grasp the behaviour of the children, but merely their feelings and ideas, or rather their linguistic ability to express these. Furthermore, an action structure is evaluated as 'effective' only when it is based on the rational weighing up of goals and means, and has taken shape beforehand in the children's heads (or language). By contrast, behaviour that follows spontaneously from a situation (of need), and may render it possible for a child to relieve stress, 'catch its breath' or 'get on a firm footing', is devalued by Pineda and Guerra as 'emotional' and 'ineffective'.

It is therefore no wonder that children from affluent families, who as a rule have no precarious situations to cope with and in whose lives 'trial' action or action for learning purposes is typical, come off better in the study than working children. The decisive defect of the study is that, with the claim of examining the children's 'world-view' and 'acting capacity' from their own evidence, it in fact reproduces age-old bourgeois prejudices about the lack of rationality and the 'cultural backwardness' of the 'lower strata' and their children.[16] The view of the subject presented by Pineda and Guerra in the theoretical preamble to their study, according to which people do not reflect, but construct, reality, is not applied to working children. They remain unimaginable to them as independent actors who may even act in an organized manner.

Participation as an opportunity for development

The other study to be discussed here (Woodhead 1998), which was carried out under the aegis of the Swedish children's aid organization Rädda Barnen, also claims to explore various aspects of the reality of life of working children from their own perspective. It enquires what meanings work has in children's lives, how children judge their work and their experience of school, and how they estimate their own competences and scope for action comparatively and in relation to their parents.

The participative approach of the study is supported in detail by stating that the children have the right to be heard in all matters that affect them, and that they are able to express their feelings, views and expectations, where they find a context that respects their specific possibilities of expression, interests and forms of communication. The children's views are accounted an important indicator in particular of the psycho-social effects of work. 'Children are not passively affected by their work – too young and innocent to understand what is going on. They are active contributors to their social world, trying to make sense of their present circumstances, the constraints and the opportunities available to them. Seeking children's perspectives on their present lives is a first step towards their participation in shaping their future lives' (ibid.: 21).

An essential feature of the study is that in the selection of children and the design of the investigation process it has recourse to the experiences of adults involved with the children on the spot (local fieldworkers) and to local particularities. In the selection, not only the age range of the children (ten to fourteen) and the inclusion of the same number of boys and girls was decided on, but also spheres and forms of work performed by children particularly common in the country concerned (including rural areas). Furthermore, attention was paid to including above all children who were not already involved in educational projects and therefore had little opportunity for or experience of speaking for themselves and making their views known.

Thirty-six children in Guatemala, forty-five in Nicaragua and thirty-six in El Salvador took part in the study. They worked in workshops for the manufacture of fireworks, in lead mines, in agricultural export plantations and family firms, in markets and supermarkets, and as itinerant street vendors.

The study expressly refrained from using individual interviews or written questionnaires, because these otherwise widely used methods would not have corresponded to the experiences and possibilities of expression of the working children. Instead, a 'participatory group procedure' was developed, centring on the 'Children's Perspectives Protocol', a kind of guideline for structuring the group discussion and the notes of the two (adult) discussion leaders according to topic areas. The groups were made up according to spheres of work.

The children were invited to describe their daily lives and the circumstances and details of their work, special attention being paid to their 'social networks', the 'good and bad things' about their work and at school, and their various preferences in situations in which there was a conflict between work and attending school. The children were also asked to draw up rankings of their preferred activities, explain them, and state to what extent they thought them appropriate to their ages. Finally, the children were invited to give an account of how they behaved in everyday conflict situations in which they had to make decisions, and what possible solutions they could imagine. In all these questions, the children were 'encouraged to represent their feelings and beliefs in the ways that are most meaningful to them, including drawings, mapping, role play as well as group discussion' (ibid.: 25). With one child from each discussion group, a biography was composed which served to complement the details from the group discussions.

The study arrives at the conclusion that the children have their own ideas about their work and that they are mainly conscious of the limitations that result from their living conditions: poverty, family traditions and expectations, the unequal distribution of power between adults and children, the meaning of their age, gender and position in the family, the significance attached to schooling, and the problems in attending school and using it for themselves. Although many children do not like the work and the way they are treated, they are able to appreciate the living conditions of their families which make the work necessary, and are for many also a source of pride. The working children also show themselves able to consider their work with a view to their future lives and recognize the advantages and disavantages that result for them. 'In many cases they are also able to make complex judgments about the appropriateness of work for different ages, for girls and for boys, and explain the reasons why' (ibid.: 41).

It emerges from the present study, as also from other investigations that give children the opportunity to express themselves freely and without restrictive instructions about their conditions of living and working (see Lucchini 1998; Domic Ruiz 1999; Liebel 2001a), that the children judge their work in a discriminating manner. They frequently criticize working conditions that threaten their health or even their lives, or offend against their human dignity. In the same breath, however, they may mention numerous advantages that their work brings with it; here many children have in mind not only the profit or the utility that their working income has for their families or for school attendance, but also the fact that they felt 'pride in their work and valued the friendships and solidarity of working alongside others. [They] also referred to the skills they learn, the way work prepares them for the future ... ' (ibid.: 62).

In contrast to current views, most children do not see attending school as an alternative that is clearly suitable in terms of solving their problems. 'Nor do they condemn their work and idealise their schooling in the dramatic terms of much of the rhetoric about child labour' (ibid.: 75). By far the majority of children prefer to combine working with school attendance, and wish for better conditions at both work and school to render this possible.

In the children's judgement on the advantages and disadvantages of work and school, relations with parents, teachers, employers and fellow workers play a particular part. The children largely accept the expectations of the adults that they should behave well and treat them with obedience and respect. But 'at the same time they are highly sensitive about perceived humiliation, unfair or abusive treatment ... These feelings are most strongly expressed in situations (such as domestic work by girls) where young people feel their lives are controlled by an employer. These experiences contribute to a sense of shame and worthlessness, as well as feelings about being stigmatised by their poverty and the necessity of their work' (ibid.: 105). The children expect from adults above all praise and recognition for their activities and achievements. They also attach great importance to the friendships that arise among them, together with comradeship and mutual support in their common activities, either at work or in school.

A legal prohibition on work for children under fifteen is regarded by few children as helpful. Most children react 'with a mixture of mockery and disbelief' (ibid.: 88) to this idea, which is after all the official legal position in many countries of the North, and ought, according to the will of the UNICEF, ILO and many governments, to be implemented in the countries of the South. Their greatest worry is what would happen to them and their families if the income from their work were no longer available. In this case, not a few children would see the only solution to be flouting the law or going 'underground', which would make it 'still harder to regulate exploitative child labour and to give the children the support they seek' (ibid.: 88).

The study makes clear, and terms it 'a clear lesson' (ibid.: 62), that working children as 'insiders' do not always judge their work in the same manner as adults, who are regarded as 'outsiders'. This applies, not least, to those adults who have for years dealt with the phenomenon of children's work and acquired the reputation of experts. Thus the study underlines not only the necessity to give the 'children's perspective' more attention in further research, but also issues a challenge to a number of dogmas that up to the present have constituted a large part of sociological research on children.

One of these is the idea that it is in the children's interests for scholars to achieve an ever more precise coverage of the 'worst', 'exploitative', etc., forms of children's work, in order for them to be better combated. Another is the notion that the 'effects' of children's work can be derived from an increasingly precise cataloguing of the forms of work performed by children. These two ideas obscure perception not only of the divergent views and feelings of the children affected, but also miss the decisive circumstance that children – whether voluntarily or not – play an important part in their own development. 'How far a hazard actually harms a child's development depends on children's vulnerability, the significance of work in the wider context of their lives, as well as the value attached to their work by those on whom they depend for support and self-esteem' (ibid.: 107; see also Boyden et al. 1998).

A comparative evaluation of the two studies

Both of these studies claim to represent children's work from the perspective of working children, and make use of participative research methods to find out about the children's voice and views. The statements by children recorded in the two studies make it clear that working children do not see or judge their work in the same way as adult interpreters. At the same time, the two studies arrive at different or even contrary conclusions. The reason for this lies in the differences in their attitudes towards children's capacity for self-expression.

In Pineda and Guerra's study, the statements of the children themselves are not taken seriously, but merely taken as a kind of interpretation material. This runs counter to the theoretical claim raised by the study itself to see the children as active constructors of their own reality. Their statements are thus utilized to legitimize already fixed views, either on the fundamentally harmful effects of children's work, or on the inability of working children to judge and cope suitably with their situation.

In Woodhead's study, by contrast, the children's statements are taken literally and seen as evidence that the children do indeed possess marked abilities to cope with their situation, mentally and in their actions. The children's statements are furthermore taken as an occasion to question current dogmas of research into children's work, and to demand that more attention be paid to the children's perspective. The study also draws attention to the fact that the view of 'development', 'health' and 'education' contained in the International Convention on Children's Rights cannot claim universal validity in all societies and cultures.

However, in the case of Woodhead's study it must be asked whether its perspective on children's 'development' is not still too restricted. In my view, in future studies on children's work 'from the children's perspective', it will be important to see children in a more comprehensive sense as 'social subjects', who do not merely influence the 'effects' of their work and their own 'development', but can also play an important part in their societies, and to ask what significance their experience of work has in this context.

Notes

1. The study by Alarcón Glasínovich (1991) on children's work in Lima can be taken as an example of this approach (see also Alarcón Glasínovich 1998).

2. The following remarks refer chiefly to Jodelet 1989 and Wagner and Elejabarrieta 1994.

3. This is in the sense proposed by Michel Foucault, who sees in (linguistic) discourses a kind of filter which already subjects perception of reality to censorship and distorts it. He demonstrates this, among other things, by considering bourgeois society's linguistic treatment of sexuality, which he terms 'the discursivation of sex'. He considers it important not only to examine discourses from all sides, 'but also the will that supports them and the strategic intention that underlies them' (Foucault 1976: 16).

4. The part of the study related to this was written in collaboration with Antonella Invernizzi.

5. In Lucchini's treatment of 'representations' and 'discourses' on children in the street, which are dominant within the aid institutions and among social workers, it becomes clear to what extent perception and dealing with the children is marked by the 'social representations' and 'discourses' that are dominant in

a society or culture. On the discourses of the 'street child' in Latin America and Germany, see also Liebel 2000c.

6. These processes are dealt with critically also in the 'constructivistic' approaches of recent European sociology of childhood (see James and Prout 1990; James et al. 1998; Zeiher et al. 1996), and recently also in relation to 'children's work' (see Hengst and Zeiher 2000).

7. On this, see my ideas in Chapter 1, developed following Touraine (1994).

8. See also the study by Pineda and Guerra (1998) discussed in the second part of the chapter; although they tend basically to reproduce the 'negative block', they cannot avoid confirming some positive meanings that the children connect with their work. Their interpretations, however, finish by regarding the children's perception as a kind of substitute action according to which the children ascribe positive meanings (more freedom, less control, a social sphere of their own, social communication) because they cannot find and enjoy these at the places (family, school) that are actually designed and 'suitable' for these.

9. The published book also contains a special section on 'street girls' in Buenos Aires, examined with an eye to prostitution, family relations and drug use; I do not deal with this section.

10. It must be noted that this study deals only with male children.

11. Particularly worthy of mention is the study carried out by Schibotto in Peru (1990); as a survey see also the study reports contained in Liebel et al. (2001).

12. The study also relates to working children in Ethiopia, Bangladesh and the Philippines.

13. 'The facts reveal that the children are more attached to their work than we foresaw' (Pineda and Guerra 1998: 160).

14. By 'mental representations', the authors understand 'processes that cover images and ideas about things, events or actions that are not perceived at the moment' (ibid.: 35). By 'meaning structures', they understand 'more or less stable patterns that ascribe meanings to objects, events or actions and take shape in stable forms of perception, interpretation and evaluation' (ibid.: 35).

15. See for example the studies of Invernizzi, López de Castilla and Liebel reported in Liebel et al. (2001), or the study by Woodhead (1998) discussed below.

16. It is no accident that Pineda and Guerra, in their conclusions, refer to the theoretical construct attributed to US ethnologist Oscar Lewis of the 'culture of poverty', according to which 'one of the characteristics of poor children is the absence of childhood as a more or less extended, protected stage. On the individual level, this culture is characterised by feelings of impotence, uncertainty, dependence, inferiority, marginality, lack of expectations for the future and fatalism' (Pineda and Guerra 1998: 161).

4 | Childhood and work in non-Western cultures: the fruits of ethnological and anthropological research

§ ACCORDING to the Western pattern of childhood that developed in the industrial societies of Europe from the eighteenth century onwards, it is accounted progress if children do not work. Childhood and work are seen as mutually exclusive contraries. Work by children is accepted at best as part of an educational process. In this case, work is localized in institutions intended for children and serves only purposes of learning or the creation of certain, as a rule rigid, patterns of behaviour. No significance for the creative development of human life is attributed to this kind of work; it is thus rather a kind of simulation of work.

The Western pattern of childhood is widespread in the world today, and is also the unspoken basis of the policy of international organizations such as UNICEF or ILO, which is aimed at the complete abolition of children's work. It has, however, by no means achieved universal validity in the world. In many societies that in the Western view are 'underdeveloped', and in particular among the dispossessed and marginalized classes, quite different notions and forms of life in childhood remain widespread.[1] In these, work has an important place.

Children's work provides evidence that the phase of life that we refer to as childhood is not only regarded as a still immature stage of preparation for adult life, but that it already involves important tasks for the reproduction and development of society. The work of children, which occurs in a variety of forms, draws our attention to the fact that the view of 'child labour' dominant in the West and within the international agencies (ILO, UNICEF) is extremely restricted. It shows that children's work cannot only be regarded as 'exploitation' or 'deprivation of childhood', but can be of positive significance for the children's social recognition, independence, 'rights', participation and personality development. I also see the representation of the various forms and meanings of children's work in these societies and their structural contexts as a plea against the 'underestimation of the child in its ability to perceive social connections and to react to them' (Renner et al. 1997: 180f)[2] that is normal in 'modern' Western societies.

In the present chapter I shall first deal with the various forms in which the relation of the age groups to one another is regulated, and examine the relevance that the economic activities of children have for this. I shall then consider in greater detail the specific work tasks that are allotted to children, and enquire into the learning processes at work. In doing so, I shall also deal with conflicts that arise with the introduction of school according to the European pattern. In a further step, I will then examine how the development of autonomous groups of working children takes place, and enquire into the different ways in which property and rights of their own are assigned to children.

So as not to create the impression that the allotting of working tasks takes place in all non-Western societies as it were naturally, together with social recognition and equal rights for children, I will also examine the ethnological and autobiographical sources available to me for contrary statements. The indications found of the enslaving of children in some pre-colonial African societies are, if correct, a sign of how great the differences were and still are between non-Western societies and cultures. For the present and future development of the relationship of children and work, however, those processes that accompanied colonialization, the introduction of the capitalist mode of production, and the 'Western' school system, and which continue to be virulent, have greater relevance. They lead to numerous conflicts and contradictions, and make it almost impossible to make unambiguous statements about the future relation of childhood and work in the societies and cultures referred to here. However, I believe that the estimations attempted in this chapter at least make a contribution to stimulating the imagination as to what was possible and may also be possible in the future. In order to facilitate assessment of the sources that I adduce, at the end of the chapter I shall offer some considerations on problems of ethnological research on and with children.

Age categories and economic responsibilities

All human societies divide the process of ageing into phases to which as a rule they give particular names. However, that which in the West is summed up under the concept of 'childhood' is not seen as a rule in other societies and cultures as a homogeneous block, but is in turn 'divided into phases each of which is characterised by various skills and susceptibilities, and in which certain codes of behaviour or clothing, rights and responsibilities apply' (Boyden et al. 1998: 33). The stages implicitly assumed or explicitly marked ('rites of passage') express major changes in social status.

The chronological exactitude familiar to us in the determination of different ages is alien to the rites of passage in many other societies. Frequently, dates of birth are not known or are not considered important.

Hausa mothers in Nigeria, for instance, take exact note of the age of their babies in the first few months after birth, because at this time they have to observe certain rituals and rules important for their survival; but later less importance is attached to determining their age exactly (see Schildkrout 1978).

There are certain points in common between the cultures concerning the most important changes in the course of growing older. As as rule, it is assumed that significant changes or progress in physical strength and mobility, cognitive and social competence occur during the second year of life, then around the sixth or seventh year, and in puberty. There is agreement that the first year of life is the most vulnerable age.

In some cases, children are not recognized as proper human beings until their survival is to some extent ensured by their having reached the age of one year. 'In many traditional societies, a child must have survived for a certain time after birth before being recognized as "living". Naming ceremonies and other rituals that mark the arrival of a new life are intentionally delayed because of the usual high rate of infant mortality' (Boyden et al. 1998: 33).

Another agreement between cultures consists in the fact that early childhood is seen as a time of unreason (see Rogoff et al. 1975). The Gonja in northern Ghana, for instance, see 'lack of understanding' as the most important trait of small children, and assume that 'understanding' is achieved by the age of six or seven (cf. Goody 1970). The Baining in Papua New Guinea say about a baby 'its eye is not clear', meaning that the little child does not know or understand yet, or is in darkness – the same thing (see Fajans 1997: 86).

In many cultures, however, despite the assumption of unreason in small children, the competences of the children are not regarded as simply a gift of nature. In Bangladesh, for instance. they are connected with the assumption of economic responsibilities.

> The word *shishu* does not relate merely to the age or stage of physical development of a child. It is a stage that is determined by the circum stances of life. ... A child that 'knows too much', a child that can look after itself, is no longer at all regarded as *shishu*. On the other hand, a child that is well provided for and looked after, and kept from responsibility, remains *shishu* until the age of about 12. Under no circumstances is the term *shishu* still used for adolescents in puberty. (Aziz and Maloney 1985: 16, cited in Blanchet 1996: 14)

Whereas intercultural agreement relating to early childhood is relatively great, differences predominate in relation to mid-childhood and adolescence. This becomes apparent above all in the question of economic responsibilities.

In Mola, Zimbabwe, children of both sexes take part in agricultural work from the age of ten. They not only work, but also own the land allotted to them and domestic animals, mainly fowl, sometimes also goats. It is expected of a ten-year-old boy that he build his own house, while a girl should additionally be able, in the case of the absence or sickness of the older women, to make an essential contribution to the daily domestic chores, for example collecting wild plants to spice the food, grinding or pulverizing them, and finally boiling them (see Reynolds 1985 and 1991).

Outside the modern societies of the North, work in the period of life between six and twelve years of age is attributed great importance for personal development. 'Starting work is often the most important sign of the beginning of mid-childhood and the most important strategy for the socialisation of the child during this period. Children over the age of 6 are not only deemed physically and mentally capable of working, but they also benefit from it. In many places, work is essential for the acquisition of knowledge and skills, for the children's social integration, and their own estimation of their abilities' (Boyden et al. 1998: 34f).

Among the Gamo in southern Ethiopia, the social status of the child is closely connected with the economic tasks that it performs. Children up to the age of about five are called *Gesho Noyta*; they are not yet given any tasks. Children from five to ten are called *Não*; at this age, the children begin to assist their fathers and mothers with their work. In the following age group, called *Wet'te Não*, girls and boys already assume full responsibility in domestic and agricultural activities (Melaku 2000: 32). In general in the cultures of Ethiopia, the delimitation of age between childhood and adulthood is 'not very important. No-one asks children their age when they perform various tasks. In the countries of the North, when required to identify himself, a person will give his name and date of birth, but in Ethiopia this question is usually answered with the name of the grandfather and his ethnic group' (ibid.: 61).

The performance of specific productive tasks is as a rule adapted to the particular skills attributed to the child's age and gender, and in turn contributes to producing skills accounted typical of a given age or gender. Work is at first mostly limited to lighter jobs in the home, errands or the collecting of fodder and firewood. Smaller children are as a rule allowed to combine work and play. At this age, adults have few expectations of the children's productivity, and see to it that they are nor over-stretched.

In the middle period of childhood, i.e. from the age of about seven, the child is given considerably more complex and demanding tasks. For instance, on the asparagus farms on the northern coast of Peru, the work of children below the age of seven is restricted to collecting and pulling up weeds. But when they are between seven and ten they are more intensively occupied, especially in digging up weeds, harvesting or spreading fertilizer. Young children are allowed to make mistakes, but from the age of seven they are more commonly punished for failure to carry out tasks given. From about the age of eleven they assume the same tasks as adults (see Mendoza 1993).

In the culture of the Incas, ten to twelve age groups were distinguished between birth and death. In the first five categories were the children. The newborn were followed by the age group of the one- to five-year-olds; these were considered not only as playful, but also to some extent suited to looking after smaller children. The group of five- to nine-year-olds were considered able to assist their parents and, for instance, harvest fruit. The nine- to twelve-year-olds were entrusted with driving birds out of the cornfields, hunting them and collecting the feathers, and to some extent also looking after the cattle. The twelve- to eighteen-year-olds looked after the llamas and other animals, or worked as apprentice craftsmen (see Rostowrowski 1988; Schibotto 1990: 36). However, the tasks set, the various stages in the life of each individual, and the entitlement to manage work processes were not simply derived from age, but were oriented to 'the ability to fulfil these responsibilities, i.e. to be suited or not suited for this' (Portocarrero Grados 1998: 16). Up to the present, in the Inca culture age is not calculated in years, and people are not classified according to age but by their physical condition and ability to perform certain kinds of work. The children's participation in agricultural or craft work serves, in addition to its material usefulness, to give them at an early age 'a feeling of responsibility for the work, so that they will learn better later on to deal with more complex tasks' (ibid.: 21).

Today, there are in the Andean region various versions of a division according to age. Magdalena Machaca Mendieta refers to María Nuñez, a twenty-eight-year-old woman from a village in the Peruvian province of Ayacucho, who, like many people in this area, is rooted in the Andean culture. She thinks that each phase of life is like a particular kind of flower that has a particular kind of blossom.

The *Llulla Wawas*, the babies, the *Tiyaqña*, those who can eat alone – between about 6 and 8 months; the *Tawanpaq*, the crawlers between eight and nine months; the *Puriq* and *Sacaña*, from that age up to about one and a half years old, and the *Iqu* up to a good two and a half years, who can already help by bringing firewood or driving dogs away. The *Warma* from the age of 3 then help, for instance, by looking after sheep and guarding the house. From about the age of 11, different terms are used for girls and boys. *Maptacha* and *Pasñacha* do not work independently, and from about the age of 12 the *Llawimaqta* and *Llawirimuq* perform the same tasks as the *Maqta* and *Cepas* (from 16) and the *Machu Maqta* and *Takyasqa*, as those over 20 are called, according to Doña María. (Machaca Mendieta 2000: 11f)

Children sow seeds, look after cattle, prepare food and medicines, or help to look after the sick, and do a number of other things. In this way they acquire at an early age much knowledge about their environment. 'They know the animals they look after intimately. They know the particular qualities of their fields, and about the climate, the role of the village authorities and the problems of the community' (ibid.: 12).

The Baining in Papua New Guinea use mode of locomotion as a means of delineating physical age. A newborn baby is carried in an adult's arms or in a cloth tied across the chest. In answer to the question 'How old is he (or she)?' a child of this age is described as *ta tal ka/ki* (they carry him/her). After the age of five to six months, parents begin to carry their children on their shoulders. Children of this age are described as *ka/ki kalak* (he/she sits on the shoulders). An older child is identified by the phrase *ka/ki tit* (he/she walks). Of an older child that has become even more independent (e.g. boys and girls in the seven-to-nine range) it is said *ka/ki tit mas* (he/she goes fully), meaning that he or she goes for water, firewood, gathering, travelling in the bush, etc. (see Fajans 1997: 86f).

In the non-Western societies considered by me, the tasks allotted, the various stages in the life of each individual and the entitlement to be in charge of work processes are not, as in Western societies, based on age, but on the ability to fulfil the responsibilities concerned, that is, aptitude or lack of aptitude to do so. The stages of life are not counted in years, nor are people classified according to chronological age, but according to their physical condition and their ability to perform certain tasks. The participation of children in work in agriculture or other trades serves, apart from its material benefit, to generate in them at an early stage a feeling of reponsibility for their work, so that they will later learn to master more complex tasks.

Allotting of tasks and recognition of work

Among the Iatmul in Papua New Guinea, the children share in the work of adults or older children at a very early age. This begins in a playful manner:

> They carry out only the simplest work phases until they have mastered a work process independently. Over a relatively long period of time, a successive increase in the repertoire of kinds of work takes place. Pressure is not exerted on them, in so far as they do not have to master particular work processes by a particular time. The content of the work does not basically change, i.e. children do the same work as the adults. Only fetching and carrying and errands are typical activities of children, and most important for the smallest. Further analysis shows that children of four or five are already able to perform tasks that are important for the community. A girl of twelve to fourteen already masters the whole repertoire of tasks that women have to perform. The comparison with the boys is interesting, as these do not have to be able to perform all the tasks allotted to males before the age of eighteen. (Weiss 1993: 116f)

Whereas Iatmul adults work on average forty hours a week, the children's working time is considerably less. A twelve-year-old girl works on average three hours a day, a seventeen-year-old four and a half. The children devote about half of their working time to themselves and the other half to family members and other persons. Weiss attributes the relatively short working time not to the generosity of the adults, or to a belief that the time of childhood ought to be unburdened by work, but to recognition of the children's independence and the circumstance that this society does not depend on fully exploiting their skills and labour potential. In addition, the children are enabled by their autonomous economic activities 'to independently build up close relations with various people – relations marked by the principle of mutuality. Even the smallest kinds of assistance or presents play an important part for the maintenance and cementing of this network of relations. When a six-year-old girl gives her aunt some of the fruit she has collected, the aunt is not only pleased, but will support the girl when she needs help in anything' (ibid.: 119). The children's ability and willingness to work 'increases both their standing and their independence' (ibid.: 119).

It is also reported of the Tonga, who live in the south-west Pacific region, that for them children's work is, like that of the adults, connected with high esteem. 'The cultural significance of work is accompanied by positive and emotional relations, and the exchange of products is to be understood as the expression of a tie. Work in childhood, adolescence and adulthood has a personal, emotional and cultural meaning. It is mainly performed in a group or within the family, and is highly charged with libido' (Meiser 1997: 219; in greater detail in Meiser 1995: 126f). Children's work among the Tonga has always been regarded and appreciated as culturally valuable. In earlier times, a girl's first bed-mat and a boy's first harvested fruit were presented to the chief, an occasion marked by great ceremony (see Bott 1958; Kavapalu 1991: 96). Nowadays the children's first products are presented to the local nobles or a high-ranking family member (see Meiser 1997: 213).

Among the Fulbe, who practise cattle-raising predominantly in Mali and Benin, both boys and girls are entrusted with a herd of cattle from the age of about ten or eleven. Boys may find themselves alone in the bush with their father's herd for years on end, but as a rule they go to pasture accompanied by siblings, and are regularly relieved. Although the hardships of the pastoral life can be very variedly experienced, the young Fulbe have only praise for the bare and frequently very lonely existence in the bush. As pastors, they have the experience 'of being able to act with complete autonomy, mastering life independently of social instances' (Boesen 1996: 197), and are permitted to 'express their high self-esteem without restraint. The whistling of young Fulbe, which on occasion has virtuoso quality, and their exuberant yodelling, can only be heard in the bush. These moments of intensive self-certainty are linked in the pastor with his relation to the cattle' (ibid.: 197).

From earliest childhood, they get to know their herd as an interesting community resembling a human one in many respects.

> Its members, each of which has a name, are very different; each one has its own particular characteristics and has, besides, a personal star that guides it and determines its individual fate. The animals also manifest needs and preferences resembling those of humans. In the Fulbe's view, for instance, each cow has a preferred friend in the herd that it tries to keep close to. Furthermore, cattle also belong to distinct lines of descent, which the Fulbe are able to trace back over several generations. In their animals, for instance in the descendants of a cow from the family of the mother, they have before their eyes direct witnesses of their own origin. (ibid.: 197f)

When young herdsmen return to the village in the evening or when encountered in the pasture, they are entitled to the greeting 'an e durande' ('you and the pasture') – a more or less obligatory recognition of their activity, which is not given in the case of other work, except, for instance, the equally obligatory greeting on meeting a woman carrying water ('an *e gooru'* = 'you and the stream') (see ibid.: 199). The strict division of labour between young and old is not to be understood as the exploitation and repression of the young by the old, but 'as a special bond with the cattle conceded to the young, that is, as forms of the experience of individual independence and freedom' (ibid.: 206).

Among the nomadic people of Kel Adagh, who live predominantly in the north of Mali on the border with Algeria, it is said that 'children have twelve tasks'. This is not meant literally, but expresses the fact that the children take on a variety of jobs.

> Apart from looking after young animals, they collect firewood, fetch and carry, help with preparing and cooking meals, take the donkey to water, work at the drinking-trough, and do milking; sensible girls or boys are entrusted with herds of small animals by the day or the week. Even if children do not match the strength and endurance of adults ... looking after the herds and performing the domestic work of the Kel Adagh would be unthinkable without them. The many and varied tasks of the children by no means mean that children are regarded as miniature adults; a clear distinction is made between the work of children and that of adults. (Klute 1996: 216)

The primary task of children is looking after the herds of young animals, with which they are also frequently compared. Children are considered particularly suitable for this task as they are more light footed and agile than the heavier adults. 'Like the young animals, the children however stay close to the camp, where they work under the guidance and supervision of the adults. The routine of pasture is precisely prescribed, and in the case of difficulties, the adults can intervene in the children's work. During this phase, the allotting of tasks takes place between girls and boys, with virtually no difference' (ibid.: 217). Only at puberty do the rules of a gender-specific division of labour begin to take effect. Whereas the girls orient themselves by adult women and chiefly perform their tasks, pastoral work is now reserved for the boys. 'The transition takes place, however, gradually and differently from one child to another; it is initiated by puberty, but is not marked by any particular event. When a girl can take on the difficult tasks of the adult woman or when a boy is regarded as a proper herdsman is decided not by their physical maturity and still less their age, but by the question "whether they have acquired sense"' (ibid.: 217).

Among other peoples of Africa, too, a wealth of inventiveness is visible in their dealings with children and their inclusion in work processes. Children are not only 'valued because of the variety of their talents and the possibilities that develop from these' (Cooper 1998: 222), but forms of work are practised with and by the children that take account of their particular abilities and needs and which benefit them (see Eckert 1999).

It was reported from a village in Borneo in the 1960s and 1970s that children at the age of five or six were not yet accounted really sensible, but that tasks in the household and childcare were already entrusted to them. It was expected of boys and girls alike that they take care of younger siblings, swing the babies' hammock, and take care that small children did not fall in the river. Nine-year-old children had already acquired the basic knowledge required for social and mental survival, and were broadly able to care for themselves. 'The boys increasingly collected firewood with their mothers, the girls rather learned to cook, but the basic activities were not gender-specific: at the age of nine, both boys and girls could cook rice and prepare a simple side dish' (Köpping 1993: 269).

Rigoberta Menchú, winner of the Nobel Peace Prize, born in 1959 and raised in a Maya village in the highlands of Guatemala, reports in her autobiography how at the age of five she already had to help with the work on the plantations on the coast, where her parents worked as hired labourers during the harvest.

> I took care of my little brother, so that my mother could fulfil her workload. My little brother was perhaps two at the time and still being breast-fed, because we Indios do this as long as possible in order to save on food. For this reason, my mother often had to interrupt her work to feed my little brother. During that time I did her work, so that she lost no time, and afterwards continued to look after the baby. My work complemented my mother's but was not paid. ... I felt very useless, because there was nothing I could do for my mother except look after my little brother. During this period, consciousness of my situation awoke. I wanted to work properly and also earn money, in order to be more help to her. (Burgos 1985: 54f)

At the age of eight, Rigoberta earned her first money as a coffee-picker on the plantation. Although she felt herself 'treated like cattle' while working, she was 'proud that I could now make a palpable contribution to the living of the family, and felt like a grown-up. I slaved every day anew to make life a little easier for my parents' (ibid.: 56f).

At home in the highlands, she was responsible for looking after the dogs from her seventh year onwards. From the time she was nine, she helped her father hoeing in the fields. 'I worked almost like a little man.

I cut firewood with the axe or the machete and fetched water. There was no drinking water close to our hut, and you had to walk four kilometres to fetch it. But we were content, sowed our bit of maize, and sometimes the harvest was enough to live on' (ibid.: 65). Although life in the mountains was hard and they often had nothing warm to put on to protect themselves from wind and rain, she found 'life much happier' here than on the plantation. When she was ten, she was accepted into the circle of adults. 'My parents called me over and explained adult life to me. They did not need to tell me much, as it was the same life I had been leading for some time' (ibid.: 71).

In the non-Western societies considered here, it is part of the basic repertoire of the culture to entrust children from an early age with tasks that are of vital importance for the community. The work is not infrequently physically demanding, but is experienced positively by the children, as it is accompanied by respect for them as individuals and by social recognition.

Learning while working

In many non-Western societies, the early inclusion of children in work processes is intended to provide the children with skills necessary to master life, based on the principle that children learn adult activities best through observation, their own experience, and in some cases imitation. This does not mean mere exercises or simulation; the children's work already has concrete 'value', either for the extended family or the village community, or for the children themselves.

It is reported of the Kung Bushmen in southern Africa 'that girls as young as two years of age grasp their little digging-sticks to help the women in the search for wild onions and bulbs. The little boys go "hunting" at first with a toy bow and arrow, and later are given proper equipment and by the age of ten should be able to catch something that can be eaten' (Paul 1997: 196, with reference to Wilhelm 1953). In the societies based on agriculture, even the babies observe the cultivation process from the backs of their mothers and so later quickly learn 'all the techniques and phases of planting, care and harvesting of the crops by means of fetching and carrying and practice on small fields of their own' (ibid.: 197). By the time the girls reach the age for marriage, they have mastered the basics of agriculture. Where work in the fields is done by men, for example among the Gbande in Liberia (see Germann 1933) or in the oases of the Sahara (see Bellin 1963), the small boys proceed like their fathers in their fields or gardens. 'The children are used from an early age as field watchers, to scare birds, and prevent wild pigs and other animals from destroying the harvest with shouts and by throwing stones' (Paul 1997: 197, referring to Janira 1956).

In areas where cattle-raising is practised, the boys, and less commonly the girls, take on watching duties at an early age, at first with the small animals. 'Because the men's conversation frequently has to do with the number, strength, size, looks and utility of the animals in their herds, the boys also take pride in acquiring a competent knowledge of cattle' (ibid.: 197). Telipit Ole Saitoti, who was born in 1940 and passed through the traditional age phases of the Masai as a child and adolescent, and later, having studied ecology, worked in nature protection projects in Kenya, reports from his own experience what precise knowledge the children acquire by taking on concrete tasks essential for survival at an early age.

The boys make an important contribution to the preservation and care of the herds of cattle. As a real Masai, a young person is accustomed from an early age to regard the cattle not only as material wealth, but as it were also as an expansion of himself. He realizes how essential it is to learn everything about the animals. Thus, when he has sharp eyes, he can recognize a sick cow by the look of its hide. Then, by certain symptoms, he can diagnose the nature of the sickness; for instance, a swelling of the lymph glands announces the dreaded east coast fever. He will then separate this animal from the rest of the herd, to prevent the disease from spreading, and take measures to heal it. A young Masai must also notice if any members of the herd are missing, not by simply counting them, but by feeling the absence of a particular animal, as one feels the absence of a friend. Drawing on his own rich pastoral experience, his father has explained the structure of the herd to him, explaining which animals always take up the rear, which prefer the flanks and which always remain in front. When the herdsman is looking for missing animals, he must above all observe the sides and the end of the herd, because the cattle grazing there are more likely to remain behind and get lost than the others; they are also more exposed to attacks by beasts of prey. A boy also learns how important it is to remain watchful; in the bush, one can lose the whole herd by falling asleep. When a boy is watchful, he can also say exactly when he saw which animal last, and thus help others who are searching for a missing animal. ... A father will ensure that his son is able to recognize enemies of the cattle such as hyenas, leopards and of course lions in time. He must be able to read their tracks and also interpret their voices, and know how he can approach them without being discovered. (Ole Saitoti and Beckwith 1981: 57f)

Among the Rarámuri, an American people in the south-west of the Mexican federal state of Chihuahua, the work of looking after cattle, which the children carry out from the age of six,[3] goes together with a particular kind of learning: for instance, the children get to know and distinguish which wild plants are edible and have healing properties. When looking after goats, they also gather wild grass which they bind as brooms, or long pine needles from which small baskets are woven. The children have to look after the animals and prevent them being savaged by coyotes, getting lost, or damaging crops. If such things happen, the children may be called to account. As a rule, the children that look after the animals have domestic animals themselves, which could be used to replace any damaged. The children are rewarded for their work. They have a right to a share in the milk and some of the newborn animals (see Lewis 1963: 256f).

In the Mayan culture, too, children's work is regarded as an opportunity and a process during which the boys and girls acquire certain skills and abilities. Lorenza Laines, who comes from a Mayan village in Guatemala, describes the learning process using the example of agricultural work, with reference to her own experience in childhood:

> The small boy accompanies his father and begins by observing him. Later on he is given concrete tasks such as looking for firewood or preparing the tools for working the soil, and gradually he moves on to performing a task in the field or helping to raise the animals. The working and learning process of the girls consists in helping their mothers with the housework or making material for their clothing, this too being a process of gradually taking on more complex tasks. According to age, the girl is given tools for the performance of the task concerned. The places where the children learn a given job are as a rule their own home, the farmyard, sometimes also communal facilities, or the field where the father carries out agricultural work. Through their work, the children also acquire values such as respect, honesty, responsibility and with especial emphasis a love for their work, for it is important to the Maya people to impress upon the children that work conveys dignity. (Laines and Fundación Rigoberta Menchú 1999: 2)

In a number of autobiographical statements collected by Renner and Seidenfaden (1997), it becomes clear how varied the children's work experience was, and the great importance attached to it for learning and the children's later lives. 'Learning to work was like a game,' a member of the Hopi from the south-west of the USA, who was born in 1890, remembers.

We children were always with our parents, imitating what they did. We followed our fathers out into the fields, and helped to plant and weed the crops. The old men went for walks with us and taught us the use of the wild plants and how to collect them. We joined the women when they went looking for plants for weaving, and accompanied them when they dug up clay to make pots. We too tasted the clay – as the women did to test it. We watched the fields to drive away birds and rodents, helped to pick peaches, which were to be dried in the sun, and harvest melons that were to be carried up to the *mesa* [plateau]. We rode the donkeys to the maize harvest, to fetch fuel and to look after the sheep. We helped in house-building at least by carrying up the adobe that was used to cover the roofs. Thus we grew up being useful. (Talayesva 1964, cited in Renner and Seidenfaden 1997, vol. 2: 165)

The Amerindians attribute great importance to children's work in teaching them to fend for themselves, and support them in this. A woman born around 1875 belonging to the Fox tribe in the Great Lakes area[4] reported how she began at the age of seven to make clothes for her dolls, and helped her mother from the age of nine.

When sowing began in the spring, someone said to me: 'Why don't you plant something for yourself?' I sure did want to cultivate something for myself! When all the women were weeding in the plantation, someone else said to me: 'Listen, you need to weed in your field as well!' To do this, I was even given a little hoe. In the end the toil was over, and we were all glad. ... When what we had planted had ripened, someone said to me: 'But now you have to cook what you have grown.' I did not mind trying. When my dish was finished, my parents tasted it. 'It tastes really good, what she has grown, and she has cooked it with great care.' Of course, I was proud at being praised like this. In fact they had only said it to make me like cooking. But I thought to myself: 'Maybe there is some truth in it after all.' ... When my mother woke up in the morning, she told me: 'Get up and go and fetch some water! And bring a few dry branches so that we can make a fire.' If I did not feel like obeying her, she made me. That is how she always treated me. But later on she took out a little axe and gave it to me with the words: 'From today that is your wood chopper.' From then on we went to collect wood together, and I carried home all I had gathered on my back. She tied it up for me and showed me how to bundle it properly. Soon I also went out by myself to fetch wood. When I was eleven, I watched her weaving. 'You try,' she told me. She made a little bag and showed me how to do it. I almost got it right the first time, but the result was kind of poor. But she reassured me: 'Just try again.' This time the bag turned out rather larger, and was rather better.

Later on, the girl learned to make reed mats and moccasins. 'My mother was very proud of me when I could make everything myself. "You see, now you can look after yourself all alone, because you can make everything yourself. That is why I have always been on at you, not to annoy you. I have got you used to working so that you can learn something for yourself. When you can do everything easily, you will never be in need, when I am no longer living. You will be able to make all you need yourself"' (cited in Renner and Seidenfaden 1997: 46f).

In the traditional Javanese culture of Indonesia, children acquire 'the necessary knowledge and skills by watching and joining in' (Hadar 1998: 60). From the age of five or six, the children are expected to recognize their own position in society and control their feelings and behaviour accordingly. When the process of separation from its mother has been completed, the Javanese child is 'accepted into the circle of siblings and peers, and gradually introduced by this group and the family to economic, political, and cultural-religious activities. … This happens to a large extent by observation and imitation, taking part in the various activities' (ibid.: 79). A special part is played in the lives of the girls by the women, into whose world the girls grow 'relatively seamlessly' and 'are accepted as soon as they can do the relevant work' (ibid.: 79).

Among the Kel Adagh in northern Mali, small children are given fetching and carrying and small errands to do, and praised when they have understood the instructions and carried them out properly. The dominant educational principles are not punishment or the threat of punishment, but praise and positive feedback. Adults observe their children not only to note when or whether they become 'sensible', but also to explain their tasks, various work processes and techniques. Knowledge and skills are transmitted not in school-type lessons but by practical examples.

> After a child has been taken several times searching for camels and catching them for riding, has been shown the technique of stalking, and how the reins are to be put on, it will be sent off alone and its return to the camp awaited with excitement. If the child is unsuccessful, an adult will go and help him. But in any case it will be observed, to see how adroitly it behaves, whether it finds animal tracks, or shows a talent for dealing with animals and 'animal understanding'. These tests are not so much concerned with teaching the children something, or if possible everything, but rather to find out their peculiarities. Children are still accounted malleable, and are taught, for example, to accustom

themselves to deprivation, hunger and thirst and to learn perseverance, but the Kel Adagh accept the individualities of both humans and animals rather than striving to change them. (Klute 1996: 219f)

This kind of learning is essentially different from the kind of acquisition of knowledge that is imposed in 'modern' schools. The 'equation of knowledge with that which can be cast in words and can be captured "in black and white" that characterizes school 'is a problematic restriction' (Elwert 2000: 185). It does not do justice to and ignores the non-verbal knowledge that children acquire during work. In addition, the official, usually centralistically oriented, school system 'takes no note of the potential of local knowledge' (ibid.: 185).[5] Nor does it take note of the specific forms of living in which children take on responsibility for their families while of 'school age' or even earlier, and tends to discriminate against and exclude these children. This can be made clearer by the example of a Quechua girl in Bolivia, who on starting school had to combine work at home with school attendance.

So I carried the smallest on my back and held the hand of the other, and Marina carried the bottles and nappies, and my fourth little sister carried the school exercise books. So we all went to school. In one corner we had a cardboard box into which we placed the smallest child while the rest of us were learning. When she cried we gave her a bottle. ... Two years later the teacher would not let me bring my little sisters any more, because they made a noise. ... Well, as the teacher had given me this order, I then went to school alone. I locked the house up, and the small children had to stay in the street, because the hut had no windows and was dark inside, so they were afraid if they were locked in. ... Then my father told me to leave school, because I was able to read and now could learn other things by reading. But I did not want to leave, and insisted and continued to go to school. ... Of course, I always lacked study material. Some teachers understood this, others did not. And so they beat me, beat me terribly, because I was not a good learner. (all quotations from the notes of Viezzer 1981)

In more recent studies on the Andean region, too, it is pointed out that children's work in the country is not sufficiently noticed and appreciated, and that this gives rise to almost insoluble conflicts for girls in particular (see Molina Barrios and Rojas Lizarazu 1995: 168ff; Machaca Mendieta 2000: 13). In Peru, these conflicts have become further intensified, since in the course of the 'constructivist educational reform' of 1999 group work and extra-school activities, some of which take place at weekends, were integrated into the obligatory school programme.

The extent to which school is experienced as compulsion emerges from the autobiography of Archie Fire Lame Deer, a member of the Sioux-Lakota in North America. In the mission school, the native American children were forbidden to speak their language or talk about their religion. Moreover, it was a 'great shock' to him to be beaten, 'for Indians do not beat their children'.

> I only went to this school for two or three days. They did not want to keep me, because I was too wild for them. They said I was a creature from the mountains and forests, untamed and obstinate. 'This boy is not civilized; he cannot conform' were their words. 'He is one of these children that were raised in a teepee or a hut without a proper floor by people who have gone back to the old way of living. They are little savages; nothing can be done with them.' So I stayed away, and that was quite all right with me. My grandfather and my uncle, Philip Quick Bear, a tribal policeman, thought it was quite OK. 'You have the best teacher there is, your grandfather Henry,' my uncle told me. 'You don't need to go to school; school may make you someone that is neither red nor white. You can learn nothing from a piece of paper.' [Archie Fire learned some English at second hand] But my real school was the forests, the mountains, streams and animals. ... Nature was my teacher and the prairie was my classroom. (Lame Deer and Erdoes 1992: 80, 43f)

The forms of 'learning while working' or 'learning in everyday life' usual in non-Western societies are not tied to archaic, pre-industrial modes of production. Together with Marx's ideas on 'polytechnic instruction' in post-capitalist society, they also play a central part in numerous recent concepts and projects in progressive education related to current post-industrial societies. As a rule they see themselves as alternatives to the Western school system, which continues to be based on a separation of learning and work.

Autonomous children's groups

One of the 'modern' Western conceptions of childhood is that children have a sphere of relative freedom, reserved for play and largely free of social responsibility. The freedom of the children is based on the fact that the adults take care of them, and thus is dependent on this. The actions of the children have virtually no relevance in the life of the adults, and are not taken particularly seriously by them. Where children act in groups, these are largely under the control of the adults, or are even constituted by them for specific purposes, as a rule to play and/or to learn what the adults think important.

In many non-Western societies, it is also taken for granted that children have their own social sphere. The children's groups that come about here, however, differ from the Western patterns of childhood and group practices. They do not exist in an area free of work or responsibility, and the actions of the children in this context are immediately relevant to social life. They are bound by certain systems of ritual within whose framework the children have a large degree of autonomy. The adults hardly intervene, and the actions of the children are taken seriously.

Florence Weiss calls the 'most important discovery' of her studies among the Iatmul in Papua New Guinea 'that the children spend several hours a day in autonomous children's groups' (Weiss 1993: 111). She was surprised at their 'great freedom' and evident presence. Day by day she encountered such groups: some children had gathered in front of a house and played a particular game (e.g. the 'clay shard game'); others were active outside the village, hunting birds, or again were occupied preparing food. When older children, usually girls, have to look after a baby, they rarely stay at home, but take it with them to the group. This means that even babies are with other children for several hours a day. 'The children are clever at combining their task of looking after the little ones with their own interests, e.g. going on an excursion' (ibid.: 120).

At the age of four or five, the children form groups of their own. 'Up to the age of about fourteen, the groups are mixed, and thereafter they separate into girls and boys. The children's activities are numerous, ranging from games, picnics, or working together to excursions to other villages' (ibid.: 120).[6] The children's groups are a part of the social organization of the Iatmul village and are recognized by the adults. The children organize themselves independently and are not supervised by the adults when they are together. In their groups, they learn 'social behaviour and craft skills, acquire knowledge, not from their parents but among themselves and from older children' (ibid.: 124) and practise co-operation. In Weiss's view, the children's groups contribute to improving their relations with the grown-ups and reducing their dependence on them. She sees an 'independent children's culture' coming about in them which differs from the 'culture for children' usual in Western societies. She sees the economic pre-condition for this in the fact that the children not only have time for their own activities, but also have 'free access to the means of production'.[7] She finds it equally important that the adults are not intent on the 'development' of the children and do not constantly intervene to preserve or insist on qualities ascribed to children.

Ute Meiser, too, discovered in the studies that she carried out in 1991 and 1992 among the Tonga in the south-west Pacific that the groups formed by children 'have a central importance for their social and emotional development' (Meiser 1997: 208; in more detail in Meiser 1995). From its first year of life, a child is urged to find its own way into the children's groups. 'Further socialization takes place to a large extent in the groups. In a process of mutual identification the children develop, work, play, seek food and cook together. They quarrel, throw stones at one another, wrestle, and then make up. The parents rarely intervene in the "internal" disputes' (Meiser 1997: 215). In the children's groups of the Tonga, Meiser sees a social institution relatively independent of the parents and recognized, in which mutual processes of development and learning take place. They are 'an autonomous and culturally recognized sphere of life of the children in which they are allowed active and uncontrolled behaviour and to try out their own role relations' (ibid.: 223). She arrived at the conviction 'that Tongan children are able to claim their own world or "children's culture" and are equally integrated into the world of the adults. They are recognized by them and make important contributions to the family economy. In a certain way they are independent of the adults, but never independent of the group, which forms the basis of their material and emotional provision' (ibid.: 223).

Autonomous children's groups are also found among the Andean peoples of South America. They are formed from groups of siblings from the age of three to six, of both sexes, which expand as they get older to form larger groups of children from different families. In one study on the Peruvian Andes, they are described as groups of friends of a similar age 'who come together to play and to accompany each other at work' (Ortiz Rescaniere 1994: 45). Combining takes place at the children's own initiative and follows their own needs. The group meets almost every day and is active near the houses or at the workplaces of the children, especially looking after cattle or in the fields at and after the harvest. Market days, village festivals and the frequently long journey to school offer opportunities to meet.[8]

The children's group is not given any special tasks by the adults, but apart from allowing them to play together it serves the children to coordinate their working tasks and to help each other. It is generally accepted by the adults and regarded as a natural part of the children's lives. The children's group is not hierarchically structured either by age or gender. However, there is always a leader who coordinates the group and encourages particular activities. This function is nor formalized or lasting, but can result from any given situation. Those boys and girls become leaders 'who are able to suggest a game that suits the occasion and is accepted by all, who have the gift of organizing, are jovial and able to transmit their good humour to the other children. It appears that leadership of the group depends rather on personality, social attitude and the circumstances than on any special knowledge' (ibid.: 48).

In contrast to adult society, in the children's group there are hardly any gender- or age-specific role differences. The members feel themselves equal among equals. Although rivalries and conflicts among the children in a group cannot be excluded, 'solidarity and cordiality' (ibid.: 49)[9] predominate. The largely unhierarchic forms of relationship correspond to the characteristics of Andean culture. 'Rural Andean society has no marked hierarchical tradition. Competence for decision-making and positions of prestige, which exist within any social community, fluctuate and can change in the course of a lifetime' (ibid.: 50). There are power differences between the communities of the adults, however, for example in knowledge or possessions. The fluid borders of work and play that are to be observed in the children's group correspond to the general self-image and practices of Andean society. Here, play and the playful element in work activities are more clearly marked than in urban society. When the children's group plays at working, or combines work with play, 'it is doing this not only to learn to work, but behaving in a similar way to the adults' (ibid.: 34).

Among the Ayizo in southern Benin, children and adolescents join together in largely autonomously acting groups. The groups have 'self-organization with self-given rules and elected representatives' (Elwert 2000: 179). The groups and movements of working children that have come into existence in Latin America and Africa since the 1970s largely operate in the urban areas, but are also influenced in their self-image and forms of action by traditions that have their origin in the childhood practices of local peoples and cultures.

The conveyance of property and the rights of children

Among the indigenous peoples of America, Africa and the southwest Pacific region, the practice of giving girls and boys cattle and arable land for their own use is also widespread. The children are given these at various times in their lives in a manner laid down by culture and ritual. Among the Fulbe in northern Benin, all children are given a cow or a heifer at birth by their father. 'When this animal produces offspring, that shows whether the child – boy or girl – has talent as a cattle-raiser'[10] (Boesen 1996: 203). Young herdsmen also give each other 'friendship cows'; this transaction, which involves much ceremony and expensive feasting, permits them 'to celebrate themselves as cattle-owners and herdsmen in front of everybody' (ibid.: 199). Among the Kel Adagh in the north of Mali, the children are given animals on the day when their naming is celebrated, as also on other occasions in the course of their youth (see Klute 1996: 220).

In an autobiographical document, a member of the Hopi tribe in the south-western USA remembers how his father promised him and his brother 'to give us a couple of sheep of our own if we did not quarrel. ... He gave my brother five animals, and me four, two sheep and two goats. When I asked him why we did not both get the same number, he replied: "You are not such a good shepherd as your brother!" Thereupon I cried until he handed over another sheep to balance up the numbers. My little flock made me very happy, and from then on I tended them with more devotion than hitherto' (Talayesva 1964, cited in Renner and Seidenfaden 1997, vol. 2: 174).

Among peoples in East and West Africa, each age group, as a rule covering eight years, has specific tasks and rights, particularly property rights. Among the Ayizo, for instance, who live in the south of the republic of Benin, the age group of young men is

> responsible for defence, staging jokes, and especially the hard work of clearing the fields. During clearing, the trees and bushes must be cut down before being burned. When the primeval forest is transformed into fields in this way, this work is metaphorically described as *ahwán* [war]. Physical strength and skill are required. They form the dominant parameters of achievement. The dances are also subordinated to these. The movements of the dances strongly resemble those of the various kinds of work in the fields. Particularly intensive drumming challenges pairs of dancers to compete. Those who demonstrate strength and agility reap applause. (Elwert 2000: 178f)

At an early age, the adolescents are given property of which they can dispose freely. Among the Xulanu of West Africa, the village community or the relatives are responsible for the expensive investment of the purchase of the dugout canoe for the young collective of fishermen, so that they can operate independently.

In some rural areas in Ethiopia, 'children are given little fields to motivate them to work and to render it possible for them to develop an economically sound basis for their lives as adults' (Melaku 2000: 7). The children are given the task of cultivating the land in their keeping during a particular period of the year. Sometimes children are given plants, a calf or a cow to care for on their own (ibid.: 46). In the coffee-growing regions of Ethiopia, it is usual to leave to the children the coffee beans that are left over after the harvest. 'Coffee beans are allowed to fall to the ground, or not picked on purpose, so that the children can collect them later. The coffee collected by the children is either kept in a particular vessel with the agreement of the children and their families, or is sold soon after it has been collected. The money is used, regardless of the amount, to buy a hen, a sheep or any other kind of domestic animal' (ibid.: 46), which is then at the children's disposal. Sometimes the money is also used to cover the costs of attending school or to buy clothing. 'As a rule the parents advise the children how to spend the money' (ibid.: 47).

Among the Iatmul in Papua New Guinea, children, like adults, have the right, in accordance with their belonging to a clan, to use land and water. 'This free access, that is, independent of the parents or other adults, to the means of production permits the children to acquire products quite independently, or to produce them from raw materials and use them for their own purposes. This means autonomy and independence for the children' (Weiss 1993: 116). In addition, most of the children among the Iatmul possess their own working tools, and are able to dispose freely of the products they make. 'The Iatmul are quite concerned to regard a person and everything that belongs to him or her as an independent whole. Even babies are given their own spoons and plates that no one may take away from them. Even when a woman has caught no fish, but her daughter brings fish home, she will not take any without asking, to cook it for the family. Parents expect children to share their products, but the decision is left to the children; nothing may be taken away from them' (ibid.: 118).

Among the Tonga, who live in the south-west Pacific, not only is appropriate participation in the process of production expected; they also have access to the resources and means of production. Thus the children gather food independently or catch fish, pick Pandanus leaves that are used to make mats, or use the plantation area of the extended family. Children have specific areas of work to deal with in which they are able to act independently and creatively. Meiser (1997: 212) reports how one boy, who was responsible for looking after domestic animals such as hens and pigs, proudly showed her a chicken-house made of bamboo that he had made together with his friend. Through their independent dealing with resources, and the responsibility that is granted them, the children 'have a high degree of autonomy and an especially significant sphere of freedom at their disposal' (ibid.: 212).

In the cultural area of the Aymara- and Quechua-speaking peoples of the Andean region of South America, it has been usual for centuries not only to organize work according to age groups, but also to give children of both sexes property, as a rule animals, but also arable areas, for their own use. They have 'their own fields and their animals, which the parents of the village community have allotted to them according to the age and the skills of the children' (Machaca Mendieta 2000: 12). This usually means that the boy or girl can use the animals or the land to pay for some of his/her expenses, so as not to be wholly dependent on adults (see Molina Barrios and Rojas Lizarazu 1995: 89). These practices can also be seen as a 'recognition of their work, and a way of allowing them to share in the results of their productive work' (ibid.: 89). In addition, they are 'a specific way in which to concretize and define the place of children as subjects and owners of rights' (ibid.: 89), and have an almost inestimable significance for the autonomy and participation of the children in social life.

In the non-Western societies described, children are not only regarded as part of the labour force, but quite naturally share in the fruits of their labours. The various forms of early transference of property show that there exists a marked awareness of the fact that children grow into responsible members of society only when they too have access to means of production and the material basis of life. Transferred property in this sense, however, is not to be confused with the forms of 'private property' predominant in Western societies, but is rather a kind of 'social property', the use of which is embedded in a usually locally oriented mode of production that primarily serves to satisfy the requirements of the community for survival.

Enslavement and exploitation of children

Even in the non-Western societies described above, the relation between children and work is a contradictory phenomenon. On the one hand, taking on jobs of work means for the children that they receive social recognition, more rights and a social status that can go far beyond what is accorded children in Western societies. On the other hand, not infrequently children are engaged by adults to such a degree that they hardly have any time left for themselves and for playful activities. Or they must expect corporal punishment if they do not fulfil the tasks imposed upon them.[11]

In pre-colonial societies in which slavery was practised, children also had to work as slaves. In the internal African slave market,[12] together with women, children were particularly sought after, and as a rule fetched high prices. 'Children were attractive to slave-owners, because they could more easily be acculturated in the different societies and households' (Eckert 1999: 133). There is only scattered evidence of the specific work of children and their (relative) freedom within the context of slavery. As a rule, the work involved activities in agriculture and the household. In the trading towns on the River Zaire in central Africa, for instance, a female slave would begin as a small girl to work every day in the fields of her owner (see Harms 1981). Boys sometimes worked in trade and craft, but were, like the girls, frequently active in the fields or in the house (see Wright 1993: 2).

Under the colonial regime, too – for instance in Cameroon up to the 1920s – many children worked as slaves on plantations or in the households of Africans (see Eckert 1998). In northern Nigeria, a lively trade with child slaves flourished in the early decades of the twentieth century, many boys being used for tending cattle (see Lovejoy and Hogendorn 1993). The practice of 'pawning' women and children was also widespread. This was often 'the answer to a crisis such as hunger or disease, but could also be the reaction to a fine or tax demands imposed by the colonial state. Not infrequently, however, it was also a means of accumulation, when, for instance, men gave their children as security for business deals. The creditor disposed of the labour power of the pawned person' (Eckert 1999: 133; see also Falola and Lovejoy 1994).

In some African societies, children's work is still occasionally compared with that of slaves, i.e. it has a totally subordinate character and is far removed from giving the children more autonomy or participation.[13] On the Indian subcontinent, it is mainly children belonging to the lower castes or the Muslim religious minority who are induced or forced to work (see Gupta and Voll 1999: 86). Between non-Western societies there are accordingly large differences in the manner in which children's work is regarded and practised. It does not automatically result from the fact that children work that they acquire a social status with equal rights, or are recognized and treated as subjects.

The negative aspects for children of their inclusion in work processes in non-Western societies and cultures are often due to 'alien' influences or the changes in social structures and relations that came about with colonialization and finally with the introduction of the capitalist mode of production, or at least they are made more acute by these (Balagopalan 2002). Colonial subjection and unrestrained exploitation of whole peoples have made it difficult or quite impossible for them to maintain the previously practised cautious forms of inclusion of children in work processes and the processes of learning and development connected with these. 'Under the harsh conditions of colonialisation, children's work does not vanish. It has its place in colonial exploitation, taking on traits of feudal serfdom and in many cases real slavery' (Schibotto 1990: 39).

In many colonies, the establishment of agrarian export industries, for example for coffee, cocoa or cotton, was accompanied by a great demand for the labour potential of children. In the former British colony of the Gold Coast, the Ghana of today, from the 1930s onwards more and more children were recruited directly by the white cocoa farmers. These were usually ten- to fourteen-year-old boys who had migrated from the impoverished north of the Gold Coast to the south of the colony in search of paid work (see Van Hear 1982). Similar developments are documented for Kenya (see Clayton and Savage 1974). In the Kilimanjaro region of present-day Tanzania, African and European producers of agrarian export goods often competed for children as workers (see Moore 1986: 122). In southern Africa, especially in the British colony of Southern Rhodesia (the modern Zimbabwe), many children also had to labour in the gold, asbestos and muscovite mines (see Van Onselen 1976).

A further large sphere of children's work in the African colonies was the household. 'Parents sent their young daughters to the towns as servant girls. In return, the girls were sometimes enabled to attend school, but more commonly the parents received money' (Eckert 1999: 134). In 1950 the colonial administration in the Nigerian metropolis of Lagos counted approximately 1,500 employed children below the age of nine, two-thirds of them girls, who worked mostly as domestic servants (see Iliffe 1987: 186). The African sociologist and later president of Ghana, Kofi A. Busia, reported in the same year on the hard working day of children employed in households in Accra: 'They are badly fed, hardly any clothing is placed at their disposal, they sleep without covers frequently on the bare floor, in the kitchen or on the veranda; they often have to work from 4 in the morning until late evening' (Busia 1950: 36, cited in Eckert 1999: 134). Many children were also employed in petty trade, especially selling food – about one-fifth of children of school age in Accra in the 1950s (Iliffe 1987: 186).

The efforts to implement compulsory school attendance that were intensified in Africa after the end of the colonial era had effects on the division of labour among the generations in many families. 'School attendance deprived many households at least partially of the labour power of children and adolescents. Women were particularly affected by this, because it was not least the sharing in the housework by girls and young women that had rendered it possible for the mothers to work on a farm or elsewhere' (Eckert 1999: 134; see also Moore and Vaughan 1994: 230f). This could lead to greater poverty and weakened the social status of the women, since they were now dependent on the income of the men (see Schildkrout 1981: 106). Additionally, schoolgirls and schoolboys now often took on 'occasional jobs to be able to buy paper and other utensils for school' (Eckert 1999: 134).

In the post-colonial societies of the South, it is above all the system of wage labour – often in tandem with racial discrimination and disadvantaging – which degrades the children of the native population groups, together with their families, to the status of factors of production, counting no longer as human beings with their own needs and rights, but only as useful and easily managed cheap labour power. The autobiography of Rigoberta Menchú shows impressively by the example of work on the export plantations (*fincas* in Spanish) in Guatemala how children were forced with their parents into a regime of exploitation that stopped at nothing.

> Work on the *fincas* was not only hard, the workers were also cheated. There is an office on the *finca* in which the amount [of coffee beans] that each worker has harvested during the day is weighed and noted. My brothers – clever as they were – had discovered that all the weights were falsified. They showed much less than had actually been picked. This happens everywhere. The señores who check our work get rich at our expense. From the first day the agents come to the villages and hire people, we are treated like cattle. On the lorries or on the farm – every trifle and every move has to be paid for. Up to the last day, when the account is paid in the cantina, they rob the workers. (Burgos 1985: 63)

> We had only been on the *finca* two weeks when my little brother died of undernourishment. My mother had to stay off work for a few days to bury him. Two of my brothers died on the *finca*. I never knew my eldest brother, Felipe. He died when the coffee plantation was sprayed from the air while the people were still working. He was susceptible to the substance sprayed, and died from poisoning. I was eight years old when my brother Nicolás died, and I saw him die. He was the youngest of us, and had just turned two. He cried and cried and cried, and my mother did not know what to do. His stomach was very swollen because he was so undernourished. He had been very unwell from the first day on the *finca*. My mother could not look after him the whole time, because otherwise she would have lost her job. We were not allowed to leave work. My little brother managed to survive for two weeks in this state, and then the death throes began. We did not know what to do with him. Apart from us, there were only two from our village on the *finca*; the rest were working on different plantations. There was thus a lack

of cohesion. We were working in groups, but with people from other villages, whom we did not understand because they spoke a different language.[14] We did not understand Spanish either. We could not make ourselves understood, but we needed help. Who could we turn to? There was no one we could tell of our plight. Least of all the overseer. He would presumably have dismissed us immediately. As for the owner, we did not even know him. My mother was desperate. (ibid.: 59f)

From that time on, I – how shall I put it? – raged against life. I was afraid of life, too, because I said to myself: 'This is the kind of life that is awaiting you: you have a lot of children, and then they die.' It is not easy for a mother to see her child die without being able to help it. I have not forgotten these two weeks on the *finca* up to now. It is a memory full of hatred ... a time which I still remember full of hatred. (ibid.: 62f)

The people from the native villages are forced to go into service together with their children as hired labourers, and to leave their villages for a time or permanently, because since the colonial conquest large parts of their land have been taken away from them, thus removing their basis of survival. A new form of poverty comes about which is quite different from their previous life, hard though that was. The forms of children's work practised hitherto, which took account of their peculiarities and processes of development, and promoted their capacities, independence and participation in the community, can be maintained only with great difficulty. The same applies to the practice of the transference of property, as less land and fewer animals become available for this. The new form of poverty, which obliges people to earn money by selling their labour, necessarily influences people's dealings with their own children. The latter are now needed as labourers who contribute directly or indirectly to the earning of the money necessary for survival. They can therefore hardly be perceived and treated any more as people with their own needs and as a guarantee for the future of their own culture, but almost only as available labour and a source of income. The children frequently begin to see themselves in this way as well, and at the latest in adolescence leave their traditional environment to seek their 'fortune' somewhere else, where they hope to find someone who will buy their labour.

This can be illustrated by a further personal report, by a boy born in 1932 in a Hindu village in the north-east of India as a member of the caste of the Bauri ('untouchables'). As the Bauri possess no land of their own, they earn their living as agricultural and unskilled labourers. Although the children are set to work as soon as possible, the family income is often inadequate to satisfy even the most basic needs.

When the rainy season ended, the harvest began. After the harvest, father worked in the quarry, where he broke up and processed rocks with his pickaxe. When I was six, father took me on his shoulders to the quarry and the places he worked at as a labourer. At the age of six I helped with the building of a house for pilgrims in the temple town near our village. I earned half the sum of two annas. Because we were hungry, we worked from early morning to evening with a one-hour break at midday. We ate watered rice that we had brought from home. If we had none, we bought a small amount of pressed rice in the bazaar. ...

The next morning, I had to go with my father to the quarry. For a month I helped him removing the rubble that resulted from working the rock. Then he gave me a little pickaxe. I tried to break the rocks, but my hands got full of blisters and hurt badly. After two weeks, I refused to break rocks any more, and stayed in the club-house and played with other children. Hunger drove me back to the pilgrims' house that was being built. There I worked for four months, until the walls were so high that the men forbade us children to work on them any more, being afraid that we might fall and injure ourselves. So once again I played with others in the club-house. Sometimes I went fishing, or gathered leaves. After four further months, I managed to break three rocks a day. Father was very pleased at this, and brought me pressed rice and fried rice, of which he took none for himself. When I was twelve, the government began to build an airfield near the temple town. For this big project workers were needed from many villages. For five months, we were put to cutting down a big forest on the site of which the airfield was to be built. Everybody from my part of the village worked there: men for 16 annas (1 rupee) a day, women for 14 annas, children 12 annas. Small children from 5–6 years of age took small branches home as firewood; the government kept the trunks. When the forest had been removed, we built the landing strips. One day, we saw an aeroplane above our heads. In surprise and fright, we children ran away with shouts of desperation and hid behind trees until it disappeared in the distance. ...

Our working group consisted of two trained masons from higher castes, seven Bauri men from other villages, and seven Bauri women from our village. We Bauris were the unskilled labourers. ... One of the masons, named Benu, took a liking to me, but at the time I did not realise why. He would send me on small errands to the bazaar, where I bought tea, rice, vegetables and bidi [cheap village cigarettes of strong tobacco wrapped in tobacco leaves] for him. He would buy me things to eat. Thus I stayed on the building site all week. At pay-day each week,

I went home for a day to give up my earnings. (Freeman 1979, cited in Renner and Seidenfaden 1997, vol. 1: 388ff)

The inclusion of children in wage labour and their abuse as cheap and malleable labour in non-Western societies is not only the consequence of colonialization and the introduction of the capitalist mode of production. It also goes back partly to traditional structures of rule, often with a religious basis; for instance, the caste system in India utilizes these and intensifies them. In African societies since the colonial era, rivalries and mutual mistrust between groups with different languages and religions have been intentionally stirred up in order to weaken the people and make them docile. A particularly striking and tragic example is the relationship between Tutsi and Hutu in Ruanda, Burundi and the Congo region. From Ruanda comes the following personal report of a Hutu girl born in 1920, who had to take employment in a Tutsi household out of poverty.

As a 12-year-old girl, I still lived with my parents, and up to that time I remained naked, because we were poor then and had few European clothes. When I turned 13, I began to wear a goatskin. Tutsi girls do not wear goatskins, but cowhide, because it looks better. This is because the Tutsi are more affluent than we are, and there are many more cattle-breeders among them than among the Hutu. They are judged by their wealth. But I was living in such poverty that I had nothing to wear but a goatskin, which marked me off as poor. ...

A Hutu girl's day was very hard at that time. There was a school, but my father did not want me to attend it. He told me the Tutsi were given preference over the Hutu by the white people, and said: 'Why do you want to bother yourself with learning, and become unpopular with the Tutsi as well?' These were my father's reasons why I should not go to school. I looked after the goats that belonged to my parents, and did nothing else until I was 15. ... When I was 15, my father proposed sending me to the house of his feudal master as a maid. The master's wife had demanded this, saying she did not have a girl to help her in the house, particularly to look after her baby. I agreed, although I really wanted to reject the idea, because my mother warned me that I would never be able to marry, because when a Hutu girl had been a servant of Tutsis she was regarded as a slave and had difficulty in finding a husband. For this reason, my mother opposed my father, but he was intransigent, and there was nothing more she could say. The real reason, however, was that when a girl lives there all kinds of misunderstandings take place. People say she sleeps with the boys, or the male servants try to establish sexual relations with her. In fact, this did not happen to me, but I knew of such cases. I did not want to go, but my father forced me, saying: 'It is only for a week, so that our cow does not get taken away. If you go, this shows that I am not refusing his demands.' Hardly had I arrived when the woman said to me: 'A maid is not a guest.' I saw what she meant by this, and began at once to sweep and do other things. ... We only ate once a day, in the evening – bananas, peas prepared with butter and spices. There was nothing to eat during the day. I drank milk, which was enough for me. (Codere 1973, cited in Renner and Seidenfaden 1997, vol. 1: 158ff)

There are structural reasons for what forms children's work takes and its significance for their development and position in society. The need to give children tasks important for survival does not necessarily lead to their being exploited and maltreated. Only when structures of marked social inequality and dominance take shape does the probability increase that children's work changes from a medium of personal development and social participation to a medium of subjection and exploitation. Although today the great majority of non-Western societies and cultures hardly exist any more in their traditional form, and are penetrated by structures of dominance and exploitation that are mostly of a racist nature, cultural traditions often persist, and are even gaining new strength. These are far more friendly to children and render possible a social position for them that in some cases goes far beyond the extent that is normal in so-called developed Western societies.

Problems of ethnological childhood research and conclusions

The literature on ethnology and cultural anthropology known to me unfortunately contains little information on structural contexts of children's work, and is restricted to recounting details from their daily lives. This restriction derives partly from a justified caution against prematurely forcing the details of life observed into Western moulds. But up to a certain point, the observations themselves are marked by these. Florence Weiss is one of the few ethnologists who point out that children's work is only very selectively perceived and one-sidedly interpreted by ethnologists, because they covertly orient themselves to the notions of childhood and children's work that predominate in Western countries.

It seems generally to be the case that ethnologists take an interest in the relation between economic conditions and children's lives above all when children have to work hard and long, which in the case of the Iatmul does not apply to the adults, let alone the children. And so we do not find in the writings of any ethnologists that have researched among the Iatmul an indication that children's work is a striking feature of life.[15] But also the fact that adults and children in this society do not work much, yet have enough to eat, is in a direct relation to the totality of the economic system. The freedom that Iatmul children have to pursue other activities than work is also economically conditioned. In other words, without a knowledge of the economic context we do not have a framework within which childhood takes place.[16] (Weiss 1993: 115)

Thus she points out that among the Iatmul in Papua New Guinea studied by her, economic activities develop as an 'expression of necessity and need', 'but correspondingly to the circumstance that they consume little themselves and so need to produce only little, they do not need to work much even despite their primitive technology' (ibid.: 115). This means for the children too, despite a basic need for work, much more freedom in the running of their daily lives, and their work is far removed from burdening their lives in an inappropriate way, let alone being hazardous for them. Accordingly, it is possible for the requirements of an individual or a group to determine 'whether someone works and for how long. This results in an alternation of the most varied activities, especially among the children' (ibid.: 115).

Another problem of ethnological and anthropological research consists in the fact that it 'has hitherto hardly not dealt at all with the age-specific division of labour – by contrast with the gender-specific' (Eckert 1999: 135). When it does deal with children, it hardly ever lets them speak for themselves, and rarely endeavours to bring out the children's perspective.[17] When anthropologists dealt with childhood, they were ultimately investigating questions of adult cultures and not the children's ideas or expectations. Children were regarded more or less 'as passive objects, as helpless spectators in a pressing environment which effects and produces their every behaviour ... as continually assimilating, learning and responding to the adult, having little autonomy, contributing nothing to social values or behaviour except the latent outpourings of earlier acquired experiences' (Hardman 1973: 87). Like Hardman, Weiss points out that in ethnological research childhood is 'seen primarily with a view to future adulthood. Our view is directed to development. Childhood is degraded to the position of a phase with no value of its own' (Weiss 1993: 100).

Such a viewpoint, in which the conception of childhood predominant today in Western society is reproduced, is highly significant for the consideration of childhood in non-Western societies and cultures. It distorts perception and obstructs understanding – which is already difficult – of the frequently quite different courses and practices of childhood in these societies, especially the meaning of the inclusion of children in economic processes for themselves and their status in society. Only when we ask what children think about society, how they classify animals, human beings and foodstuffs, whether and how their conceptions, systems of concepts and world-view differ from those of the adults (see Hardman 1973), does it become possible to appreciate even approximately the special nature of childhood in other societies alien to us. 'Children blend into society as a whole, contribute to it, are integrated into it, and yet the culture simply does not represent them. For this reason it is necessary to gain knowledge of how children see life to a great extent from their behaviour and statements' (Reynolds 1989: 2). Only in this way can we suitably appreciate the experiences connected with 'alien' children in terms also of their possible significance for the shaping of childhood in our world.[18]

The point is not to see in the childhoods of non-Western cultures and children's inclusion in work processes presented here simply models for childhood in Western societies. These are themselves linked to certain structural and technological pre-conditions and dependent on the economic practices of these societies. Nor do they exist in 'pure' form, but are always to a certain extent 'hybrid' products of controversial social and cultural influences (see, e.g., Balagopalan 2002). However, studying them helps us better to recognize the limits and problems of the forms of childhood familiar to us and to stimulate our imagination as to the possible nature of an improved childhood.

All the 'positive' examples of children's work presented here come from societies that are based on agrarian production, and in which work serves the extended family's own requirements and those of the local community. Even where the beginnings of wage labour are to be seen, these are subordinated to the laws of the subsistence economy and local barter. The gradual inclusion of children in work processes is based on the way in which the children are able to directly experience and observe the work of adults, and the simple technology used permits the children to carry out socially essential work and take on economic responsibility without long preparation.

As soon as wage labour becomes more widespread and marginalizes the self-determined forms of local economy, the forms in which children's labour potential is used also change, and it becomes considerably harder for children to perform economic tasks independently. Children tend to be reduced to the function of exploitable labour potential, or are excluded from the work process and handed over to the school, which is constructed according to the European pattern. Independent children bearing economic responsibility are turned into children who now need to be protected, supervised and educated. The autonomous children's groups lose their supporting significance and become, where they do not disappear completely, a marginal location of childish pastimes.[19]

But such processes do not render the positive approaches and experiences of children's work presented here pointless. On the one hand, they continue to exist in many societies in the South, and are to some extent being revived. On the other hand, the exclusive dominance of wage labour has also been called into question in the post-industrial societies of the North, and forms of economy and work are being sought that are need-oriented, self-determined and related to the local area.[20] With them new possibilities also arise for children to gain experience of work and take on socially relevant tasks that benefit themselves.

Notes

1. The examples presented in this chapter come mainly from Africa, America and the Melanesian islands. Most of the ethnological and cultural-anthropological studies to which I refer relate to these regions.

2. Renner refers to Mary Ellen Goodman, who, in her study *The Culture of Childhood* (1970), attempts to expose the false conclusions of US educational theory and upbringing, with the use of intercultural material.

3. See also the autobiographical account of Pedro Martinez, who was born in 1889 and grew up in an Indian mountain village in the south-west of Mexico, as reported by Oscar Lewis: 'I was seven when my uncle Augustin one day asked me whether I would like to go with him and look after the oxen. ... I rose at five in the morning, fetched some water from the well and watered the plum trees. Then I had to drive the oxen to pasture, a long way, as far as Cuicuixtlán' (Lewis 1963: 51f).

4. Nowadays the Fox live scattered in three reservations in the US federal states of Iowa, Kansas and Oklahoma.

5. Paul (1997: 205) also points out that the 'high degree of social and cultural competence' achieved by children and adolescents in 'old Africa' through 'play and collaboration' 'was in many respects reduced by the introduction of schools according to the European pattern'.

6. Weiss quotes an observation made by the American ethnologist Gregory Bateson in the 1920s among the Iatmul: 'During their time of independence, the children form a proper republic of their own. I know very little about this organisation. They may spend the whole time in the bush, play there, gather food, join together in large groups and make a picnic. I have never gone out with such a group, but I have come across one once or twice when I was hunting near a village in the bush. The whole children's society is closely-knit, and I saw one or two couples – boy and girl – who had built themselves a

protective hut and sat in it, obviously running a household. There are also nocturnal expeditions, on which they go looking for frogs. Not infrequently, a group will wander around close to the village the whole night. I have always visited them in the early hours of the morning and brought them biscuits ...' (Bateson 1932: 274, cited in Weiss 1993: 120).

7. See the following section of this chapter.

8. Seidenfaden (1997: 192) assumes that an important condition of the autonomy of the children's groups is the independence that the children 'have in their socially recognized activity of caring for and guarding the cattle, which also places them at some geographical distance from the village'. In the mechanisms of social distance and autonomy of children's groups he sees a promising object of investigation for a comparative cultural anthropology of childhood.

9. The Australian ethnologist Kavapalu, who has written a comprehensive ethnography on childhood in Tonga (1991), also points out that all the authorities and orders of rank that are determined in Tongan families and society by age and gender are of no significance in the children's groups and are there spontaneously suspended. By contrast, children are well aware how to behave towards siblings and other relatives of higher rank in formal situations, e.g. at family and other celebrations. The play researcher Schwartz (1992: 217) describes the children's groups as an 'area broadly free of repression' within Tongan society, in which the child can create and realize its own ideas.

10. The Fulbe speak in this connection of *riiku* or *risku* (cf. Arabic *rizq* = 'living, daily bread, gift of God').

11. For instance, we read in the childhood memoirs of Pedro José Gonzalez, born in 1885, who grew up as a member of the Guajiro in the north-west of Venezuela: 'Most of the time I was not able to play, because I had the hard job of pasturing the sheep, goats, asses, horses and cattle. I even had to feed the pigs. I also had to fetch enough water for all the animals to be able to drink. So my mother was always giving me instructions. She wanted to make it clear that I was not to fool around with anyone, because those who played were idlers, no-goods, who did not look after their parents' animals. A real man would have no desire to play around, she said. The only important thing for him was to tend the animals' (Watson 1970, cited in Renner and Seidenfaden 1997, vol. 2: 284). The Baining in Papua New Guinea also suppress spontaneous play by children, because it expresses their 'asociality', meaning lack of control over bodily functions and inability to work (see Fajans 1997: 168).

12. In Africa, the slave trade began on a large scale in the mid-fifteenth century, due mostly to the European conquerors. It is estimated that between 15 and 30 million people were abducted and taken across the Atlantic under the worst possible conditions, where they were exploited on sugar cane and cotton plantations in Brazil, the Caribbean and the United States. The Polish journalist Ryszard Kapuscinski (2001: 85) writes about the consequences: 'Africa has still not yet recovered from this tragedy, this nightmare. ... The slave trade ... poisoned interhuman relations among the inhabitants of Africa, aroused mutual hatred, frequently started wars. The stronger strove to overpower the weak and sell them on the market; kings traded with their subjects, victors with defeated, judges with the condemned.'

13. The Kel Adagh say: 'The children are our slaves,' by which they mean that children's work has (partly) replaced that of slaves (see Klute 1996: 218). The children among the Kel Ewey Tuareg also have to do the work of the pre-colonial slaves (see Spittler 1990: 190).

14. More than twenty indigenous languages are spoken in Guatemala (M.L.).

15. Thus Gregory Bateson (1932, 1965) nowhere mentions that the children work. Margaret Mead (1950: 71) merely remarks that the children imitate adults in their play.

16. Weiss criticizes the fact that neither Bateson nor Mead examined the socio-economic system of the Iatmul. Moreover, Mead put forward the viewpoint that the children's living conditions were determined by the attitudes of the adults. Thus she interprets the behaviour of adults towards children on the level of pure attitudes, without connecting these with the simplest material conditions of life (see Weiss 1981: 12f).

17. Eckert (1999: 135) notes that in the ethnological specialist literature 'personal reports or observations by the children are hardly documented'.

18. It is for this reason that I have, wherever possible, adduced and quoted at length personal documents by children and their childhood memories.

19. In a study dealing with the consequences of country–town migration among the Iatmul in Papua New Guinea, Weiss (1999: 321) notes: 'Patterns of behaviour and attitudes that made sense in the village have to be given up and replaced by control and discipline. … With regard to the children, under the new economic conditions what we call the invention of childhood comes about, a processs that began in Europe in the eighteenth century. Children became creatures that had to be educated, in which process the mothers played an important part. That which in the village had been supported by the group and the social structures, like the institution of autonomous children's groups, is transferred in the town to the family, above all the mothers.'

20. These approaches have been practised and discussed for years under headings such as 'community economy', 'the economics of solidarity' or 'local economy'.

5 | Working children in Europe – loss or new perspectives of childhood?

§ THE phenomenon of working children has been regarded in the contemporary societies of Europe predominantly as a kind of deficiency or regression in social development. It is accounted as the anachronistic expression of an erroneous development that threatens the childhood project of the modern era, hampers children in their personal development and prevents them from living their childhood appropriately. Occasionally, children's work is seen as a problematic sign that poverty is returning, and that the children will become victims of deteriorating living conditions.

On the other hand, there is an increasing number of voices that call the growing number of children who work or wish to work an indication 'that in the most highly developed Western industry and service societies a return to more subjectivity and productivity of children is beginning to become apparent' (Wintersberger 2000: 171) and that the work of children today – far removed from the early capitalist practices of the exploitation of children – is an integral part of their 'emancipation and becoming social subjects' (Benes 2000: 130).

In order to arrive at a convincing evaluation of the development tendencies of children's work and its meanings in the lives of children of today, the perspective of 'childhood' and of 'children's work' must be detached from outdated ideological patterns, and opened up for a more wide-ranging consideration of the course of childhood and the forms of children's work that are becoming evident today.

This has been happening for some years in the sociological research of several European countries, especially Great Britain and Scandinavia. An important element in this is that children are seen as actors participating in the 'social construction' of their societies, and that an attempt is being made to observe the thinking and acting of children from their own perspective. In contrast to most of the studies carried out in other European countries (see Council of Europe 1996; Cecchetti 1998),[1] the interests pursued with this research into children's work are also broader. For one thing, not all studies are restricted to gainful employment; for another, they do not merely record the extent of offences against the law, but also attempt to explain the extent and the various conditions of children's work, and cast more and precise light on the positive and negative meanings that the various types of work have for children.

I shall begin by giving a survey of the research that sets out to cover the extent and the areas of children's work, together with its forms and conditions, in the countries concerned. Then I shall pursue the reasons and motives that are given as causing children to work, and enquire into how and with what results the meanings of work for the children were studied. A further part of the chapter will be devoted to studies that explicitly view the children as 'social actors' and attempt to see their work 'with fresh eyes'. Then, in order to show possible perspectives of further research, I shall critically reconstruct various theoretical models of children's work that have been published in German-speaking countries in recent years. I will draw attention to the mainly unexpressed implications of these models, and attempt to formulate a conception that appears to me best suited to understanding and investigating the current tendencies of development and the social significance of children's work in post-industrial capitalist societies. Finally, I shall discuss on an international basis the question of whether and for what reasons childhood patterns can be discerned among working children in Europe which point beyond the bourgeois model of childhood and are historically new.

The extent and areas of children's work

Statements concerning the extent of work by children are usually related to gainful employment. In Germany it was established that in the course of a school year 42 to 51.8 per cent of pupils in the seventh to ninth or eighth to tenth grades (age twelve to sixteen) were working while attending school. In the German federal state of Hesse, as many of 34 per cent of pupils have worked before concluding their sixth year of school, i.e. before the age of eleven (Ingenhorst 2001). For Great Britain it emerges from several investigations carried out during the past fifteen years that between a third and half the children of an age for compulsory school attendance (or between the ages of eleven and fifteen) were performing paid work at the time of interview. When the pupils leave school, in Germany 80 per cent and in Britain two-thirds to three-quarters of them have already had experience of paid work (Ingenhorst 2001; Mizen et al. 1999: 424f; see also Mizen et al. 2001a; Hobbs and McKechnie 1997: 24ff). The number of children who have jobs as well as attending school from the age of eleven is thus larger than the number of those who do not. It has presumably increased in the past two decades and is increasing further. If we add other forms of work, whose extent among children has hitherto hardly been investigated, the number of working children would presumably be still higher.

One reason why statements on the extent of children's work are usually restricted to gainful employment is certainly that this form of work can most easily be conceptualized and thus statistically covered. However, in a few studies with a claim to being representative, other forms of children's work are included. Morrow (1994 and 2000) gives an example, expressly basing her study in two cities in Great Britain on an 'open' concept of work. She left it up to the children interviewed to name all extra-school activities, whether or not they were paid and whether or not the children viewed them as work. Only subsequently was an attempt made to place the statements in particular categories, in order thus to arrive at statements about the various forms of the children's work.

In contrast to the authors of most other studies, Morrow did not work with standardized questionnaires, but had the children write essays, which were complemented by group discussions. With this procedure, she hoped to cover aspects of the children's lives

> which a questionnaire might not have included, or might indeed have excluded because of the form of the questionnaire. For example, in the case of direct questions about 'working', the children might not relate their informal activity to the question because the concept 'work' tends to be constructed as formal wage labour. Indeed, other 'adult categories' imposed on children's experiences may preclude children from describing them. The children were asked to describe all the things they do, not just work, outside school hours, and they were 'prompted' by being told that by writing the essay they would be helping with some research into the work that children do, such as part-time or holiday jobs, and also helping at home, doing the shopping, baby-sitting, and so on. (Morrow 1994: 129f)

The activities described by the children were coded and statistically evaluated. Morrow proceeded from four main categories: wage labour, marginal economic activity, non-domestic family labour and domestic family labour.[2]

In her report on the study, Morrow dispenses with giving absolute figures, because the activities described by the children frequently cover several categories at the same time. Wage labour, understood as regular part-time work in an employment situation, was performed by 226 of the children covered by the sample; 12 per cent of the children were active in marginal economic activities, among which Morrow also included 'self-employment'. This category coveres a broad spectrum of activities 'which do not fit clearly into other categories of work: activities which were typified by their irregularity and short-time nature, though some of the children described undertaking these activities on a regular, long-term basis. These included baby-sitting for non-family, car-washing, and other odd jobs that are performed on a kind of self-employed basis' (ibid.: 131). Ten per cent of the children who reported on their work named work in the family firm. About 30 per cent of boys and 50 per cent of girls named domestic labour. Morrow includes in this category daily routine activities, caring for small children and other caring jobs, supply, maintenance or repair work in the home, on the car, etc.

A survey of studies carried out in Germany and Great Britain shows that in the course of paid work – as in other central European countries – most children are occupied with delivering newspapers. The spectrum of other relatively frequently performed jobs ranges from babysitting, car-washing, serving in shops and restaurants, door-to-door selling, errands, cleaning work and simple office work to more rarely performed jobs on building sites or in factories. Most of the children are employed illegally[3] and are rarely registered. Boys begin paid work earlier than girls. Most of the activities involve manual work requiring no training. The employment is as a rule not secured by contract and is relatively poorly rewarded (see Ingenhorst 2001; Mizen et al. 1999: 425).[4]

In Germany only a tenth of children in work are paid with due observation of the formalities (a tax card) (Ingenhorst 2001). According to a recent study in the German federal state of Thüringen, only 23 per cent stated that they had concluded a contract for their work, boys more commonly than girls, and high school pupils more commonly than junior high school pupils. In 16 per cent of all cases, thirteen-year-olds had a contractual agreement, fourteen-year-olds in 22 per cent, and fifteen-year-olds in 27 per cent. Among the pupils who delivered newspapers or advertising matter, 40 per cent reported a contractual agreement, while in the field of catering only 10 per cent did. Most children (80 per cent) had found their jobs through the agency of their parents, friends or personal connections. Only in 5–8 per cent of cases was direct application via the labour market involved or successful. The labour exchange had no significant part in arranging the work of the pupils (Thüringen 2000).

Forms and conditions of children's work

Gainful employment of children is no longer necessarily to be equated with 'dependent' employment, but also covers forms of 'independent' and 'self-employed' activity. Together with kinds of work from which an 'employer' profits (e.g. delivering newspapers), there are forms from which the employer gains an advantage but no financial profit (e.g. baby-sitting). In addition to various forms of paid work, children perform a variety of 'unpaid' activities that are important for survival and the satisfaction of the needs of others. This includes, for example, help in the parental household or the family firm, or performing tasks in the context of social services, neighbourhood assistance or environmental conservation. In the case of domestic work, it is assumed that 'jobs of new kinds and differently distributed in time are coming into being', in the undertaking of which the children are no longer 'the recipients of individual commissions and instructions' but are independent actors (Zeiher 2000: 63).[5]

The work done by the great majority of children is 'part-time work' undertaken in addition to school attendance, sometimes after school, sometimes in the school holidays. In Germany, according to the federal state, between 36 and 46 per cent work several times a week, and be-tween 6 and 8 per cent daily, including weekends. Some work only during the school holidays, while others work year round. In the federal states of North Rhine-Westphalia and Hesse, the average daily work actually performed amounts to between 2.9 and 3.9 hours (see Liebel 1998). In British studies it was found that most children perform paid work for between five and eight hours a week (Mizen 1992; Hibbett and Bateson 1995; Hobbs and McKechnie 1997: 45; O'Donnell and White 1998: 14). With an average of nine hours a week, girls as a rule work longer than boys (average seven hours), and the number of working hours increases with age (ibid.: 17). Most children work after school on weekdays or on Saturdays (ibid.: 17). A third of the children in the region of Tyneside, England, have more than one job (ibid.: 8); according to another study representative of Great Britain, the figure is 17 per cent (Middleton et al. 1998: 46).

In contrast to Britain and Germany, in southern and eastern Euro-pean areas, especially among migrants and children particularly affected by poverty, paid work is undertaken more frequently at the expense of school attendance (for Portugal, see Eaton and Pereira da Silva 1998; PEETI 2001; Sarmento et al. 2000: 78ff; for Spain, see Comité Español del UNICEF and IUNDIA 2000: 66ff; for Greece and Italy, see Cecchetti 1998: 87ff). A Russian study found that interest in school attendance as a rule diminishes among children who work, above all because they regard it as 'worthless' to them (Mansurov 2001: 163). This is also connected with the fact that 'the moral value of education in Russian society has decreased' (ibid.: 165). For Italy, on the other hand, a 'clear change in the time pattern of work' has been observed: 'Whereas in the past work was chiefly full-time and collided with school attendance, it is now increasingly part-time or seasonal work, which makes school attendance possible for the children' (Benes 2000: 126).

Paid work performed by children has assumed very different forms and is undertaken under varying conditions. On the one hand, children are used as cheap and flexible labour, and have to work under circumstances that have to be termed exploitative and which expose the children to arbitrary and unacceptable conditions. This kind of children's work is on the increase above all in southern and eastern Europe, in the economic sectors that are striving to remain internationally competitive at a relatively low technological level. In the Portuguese textile, clothing and shoe industry, mainly fourteen- to eighteen-year-olds are employed because they have a claim to only 75 per cent of the legal minimum wage (Eaton and Pereira da Silva 1998: 331). In Spain many children of immigrants from North Africa work in extreme conditions in export-oriented agriculture, others in restaurants and tourism (Grupo de trabajo infantil 1996: v; Cecchetti 1998: 20). In small subcontracting businesses in the shoe industry, and in the area of home work for the textile industry, too, numerous children work under questionable conditions (Cecchetti 1998: 28f; Council of Europe 1996: 57 and 1997). In Italy, especially in the south, many children work in small industrial workshops and in agriculture in unhealthy and unsafe conditions (Cecchetti 1998: 26). For Russia, it is stressed that economic necessity or the strong wish of a growing number of children to earn money and make themselves independent is 'crudely exploited by adults through the criminal gangs' (Mansurov 2001: 161f).

On the other hand, children today frequently perform 'jobs' that leave room for their own initiative, and in doing which they can combine fun with earning money. Frequently, these are even activities in which the children are no longer confronted by an 'employer', but themselves act in an 'entrepreneurial' fashion. Examples of this are private services in the neighbourhood such as gardening, help with homework, babysitting, etc. A number of studies stress that the extent of 'self-employment' has grown considerably. At the same time, the question arises in connection with these jobs as to whether they are not restricted to marginal areas of the economy, while the central areas remain closed to children or are open to them only under conditions that disadvantage them as hitherto by comparison with adult workers (see Kirchhöfer 2000).

The working conditions of employed children have hitherto been examined only in isolated cases and partially. What is mostly to be found are figures on the amount of payment and the dangers of accident or health risks. On payment, Ingenhorst (2001: 140) remarks that children in Germany on average receive DM10 (= €5.11) an hour. A recent study in the federal state of Thuringia registered average earnings by boys of DM9.41 (€4.81), compared with only DM8.72 (€4.46) in the case of girls. With pupils over fifteen years of age, there were average hourly earnings of DM9.44 (€4.83), while younger children earned DM8.75 (€4.47) (Thüringen 2000). Hobbs and McKechnie noted (1997: 40) for the four regions of Great Britain studied that the children earned between £1.80 and £2.34 (€2.90–3.80) per hour and between £11.85 and £13.97 (€19.25–22.70) per week. For the region of Tyneside, O'Donnell and White (1998: 18ff) found that the majority of children received less than £3 (€4.80) an hour and had an average weekly wage of £14.03 (€22.80). According to them, girls obtain higher hourly and weekly earnings than boys, which is partly attributable to the fact that girls predominantly work in retail sales together with adults (babysitting was not included in the study), where payment is as a rule better than in other 'children's jobs'. Hobbs and McKechnie (1997: 54), in contrast, arrived at the finding that there were more girls in the lower income groups and more boys in the higher. The finding, representative for Great Britain, is also remarkable for the fact that children of single parents (mainly mothers) and from families dependent on state assistance work more hours for less money than other children (Middleton et al. 1998: 53).

Children's average incomes are without doubt lower than those of employed adults, which shows that they are disadvantaged compared with the latter. Most working children are also of this opinion when asked. In a study carried out in Belfast (Leonard 1999: 26), 79 per cent of the children stated that their employer profited particularly from employing children. They commented on their work situation with the words: 'He [the employer] is happy because I am working for low wages,' 'He is ripping me off and he knows it,' thus showing that 'they are aware that they are likely to be paid lower wages than adults' (ibid.: 26).

On the other hand, the 'value' of the work of children and adults cannot be simply compared, as it usually consists of differing tasks which often presuppose differing qualifications. However, the differential also partly reflects the fact that the labour potential of children is more cheaply available on the labour market, especially when the work is legally prohibited and the children thus cannot appeal to employment rights or minimum standards. The empirical studies contain hardly any reflections on the 'justice' of the judgement of children's labour potential or the reasons for its being undervalued. In Great Britain, at least, there has been since the 1980s a well-founded theoretical debate on how the 'disadvantaging' of working children and the 'unequal' evaluation of their work is influenced by social-structural, economic and cultural determinants, and how this may be combated (see Elson 1982; James et al. 1998; Lavalette 1999).

As well as remuneration, most studies refer to the risks to children in relation to their work. This has to do both with the 'hardness' of the work and whether the children are adequately protected from possible hazards or are in a position to refuse unacceptable requirements. It is not surprising that reference is made most to accidents and injuries, as these are more easily identified than other risks and strains which might have consequences only after a longer period of time. According to the study by Hobbs and McKechnie (1997: 58), in the five regions examined by them accident or injury occurred once or more often to 18–23 per cent of the children. Other British studies give figures of between 31 and 36 per cent (MacLennan et al. 1985; Pond and Searle 1991). Hobbs and McKechnie attribute these differences partly to the fact that many studies did not include babysitting, during which accidents rarely take place. Most of the accidents happen during the delivery of newspapers or advertising matter, and do not as a rule differ from the kinds of accidents or risks to which children are in general exposed in their leisure time, on the way to or from school, or at school.

With regard to health hazards during work undertaken by children which go beyond individual accidents and injuries, I was not able to find any studies relating to countries in central Europe. For Germany, Ingen-horst (2001: 147) observes: 'For the vast majority of working children, the dangers and risks to health are minor. Only in a few cases do children experience serious injury or health-related problems at work.' Hobbs and McKechnie (1997: 61) call for epidemiological studies on the effects of work on children, demanding that they should consider comprehensively 'the impact of work on the development of the child'. This would also entail taking account of the social and cultural contexts in which children work, since the effects of work are not only the result of the types and conditions of work, but also of the way in which society evaluates and regulates children's work (see Boyden et al. 1998: 75ff).

Reasons and motives for working

The reasons and motives that cause children to work are as many and varied as the forms and conditions of their work. In Europe it has become rare for children to be forced to work by their parents or other adults. Children's scope for decisions has increased, and they are able today 'to choose the progression of their working lives from a relatively early age' (Eaton and Pereira da Silva 1998: 329). The question of whether economic distress or poverty plays a decisive part in the increase in children's work in Europe – comparable with that of the countries of the South – is controversial, and can hardly be anwered in the same way for all children or all forms of children's work.

All recent studies on work by children in central and northern Europe, at any rate, are agreed that it is largely not undertaken owing to coercion or from material need.

> Today the phenomenon of children's work appears an expression of young people's values, and as a component of a new culture of work that competes with school, which achieves less and less. It is becoming increasingly clear that there are reasons for children's work other than economic compulsion. Among them are interest in their own development and well-being, in an expansion of possibilities of consumption, in the strengthening of their own motives and expectations, as well as the desire for individual emancipation. (Benes 2000: 125)

This statement, relating to Italy, can be confirmed in relation to other European countries and the USA as well.

In Great Britain, children's work is distributed among children of all income groups in similar proportions. This also applies where only gainful employment is taken into account. Morrow (1994: 139) draws the conclusion from her study: 'The contemporary relationship between children's employment and family income is by no means straightforward.' Hobbs and McKechnie (1997: 92) come to the conclusion that 'many children work without any obvious economic need', and describe it as 'simplistic to assume that poverty drives children to work' (ibid.: 50). Lavalette, too, who is most critical of children's work, states 'that some children may work because of poverty but many child workers come from affluent families' (Lavalette 2000: 120). He arrives at this conclusion after perusal of all available empirical studies and on the basis of his own investigation (Lavelette 1994).

Mansurov (2001: 160) notes in relation to Russia that children frequently take on paid work because the material plight of their family obliges them to, but that children 'as a rule' do not work to secure their livelihood but to be able to buy certain items for themselves such as a football, a bicycle, shoes, toys or particular clothing. Mansurov also points out that in many parts of Russia it is customary among relatively well-off families to include children in the work of the family firm from an early age (ibid.: 159).

In the case of Great Britain, Hobbs and McKechnie (1997: 91f) even found that the proportion of working children was higher in 'less deprived schools' than in 'schools with high indicators of deprivation' Morrow too observed that children worked more commonly in the more affluent areas of the city examined by her than in the poorer areas. She supposes one reason for this to be that there are more jobs for children in the wealthier areas.

> People may be able to afford to have their newspapers delivered, hire baby-sitters, pay for their cars to be washed and lawns mowed. Shops may be busier on Saturdays in a prosperous district, and there may be a higher demand for traditional services which demand cheap, unskilled workers. ... There may be correspondingly fewer such jobs available in deprived inner-city areas, or the jobs that are available may be filled by other members of the labour market, women or young people, for example, who have no alternative but to accept low pay and poor working conditions. (Morrow 1994: 140)

Morrow sees further reasons for the lower rate of children's work among children from poorer families in the fact that they are a 'relatively immobile labour force' and are not able simply to travel to the town centre, where jobs are available. 'One girl in my sample who had a very busy schedule at week-ends and worked on Sundays in a riding stables described her mother as "a taxi driver" for herself and her sister' (ibid.: 140). Morrow also supposes that more affluent children have better connections and social networks that are useful to them when seeking jobs. Finally, she sees the taking on of a job by children as also influenced by the varying class and culture-dependent values of the parents. She points to the example of girls of South Asian origin who are not allowed to sell newspapers in the street and do not wish to. And in working-class families 'there may be some ignominy attached to one's children working, a notion that "they shouldn't need to", and conversely a certain amount of prestige to be gained by not having one's children working in the family shop, for example. Affluent families can afford to buy their children almost everything , but the point is that they may choose not to, and instead encourage (or allow) the child to have a job as an educational experience to "learn" the value of hard work and money' (ibid.: 140).

It would be premature to conclude from such observations that a lack of material resources may not also be a reason for taking on paid work. Mizen and co-workers gained the impression that in low-income families the money earned by their children was considered an important contribution to the domestic budget. Many children, by buying food with the money they earn themselves, relieve the family budget (Mizen 1992; Mizen et al. 1998; similarly Leonard 1998: 86f). In two other studies, 6 per cent of the working children questioned stated that they placed their earnings at the disposal of the family (O'Donnell and White 1998: 26; Middleton et al. 1998: 54; Middleton and Loumidis 2001: 31f; figures for Germany are similiar: see Ingenhorst 2001). In two other British studies, 6 per cent of the working children questioned said that they handed over their earnings to the family (O'Donnell and White 1998: 26; Middleton et al. 1998: 54; Middleton and Loumidis 2001: 31f). This percentage is certainly not high, but it indicates that in many families the income of the children from their work is counted on, and that the children feel responsible for contributing to the living of their families. This applies above all to single-parent families and families dependent on state support (see Middleton et al. 1998: 53f).

Further, it needs to be considered that the requirements of children have expanded, and cost an increasing quantity of money. What is involved is no longer only the food and clothing necessary for survival; children want to consume certain items and pursue activities in their leisure time which give them recognition in the peer group and the feeling of 'counting'.[6] In this sense, the decision to pursue paid work can no longer be seen 'as the simple choice to consume but rather represents a necessary act on the part of many children to merely participate in many of the "normal" routines of childhood' (Mizen et al. 1999: 433). In this, the children are doubtless under the influence of the growing power of global commercial interests. Their leisure requirements are hardly covered any longer by free community provisions, and can be met only when the children have money. 'For those children for whom money is something difficult to come by, the search for some sort of wage is one of the few viable alternatives' (ibid.: 433).

Even where a lack of material resources is seen as a reason why children pursue paid work, it is not assumed that they are forced to do so. The search for paid work is today an expression of children's own wishes, and is almost always based on their own decisions. It shows that it is part of a widespread attitude on the part of children today not to leave the possibility of working to adults, but also to claim it for themselves. This applies all the more to work that is not performed primarily for the sake of the income, but in order to have the feeling of doing something 'important' or 'serious', to gain practical experience and to have a say in the world of the grown-ups.

A new look at children's work

Only when working children cease to be regarded solely from the viewpoint of what they may become or what they lack to become competent adults is it possible to see the 'value' and the meaning of the various kinds of work in their full complexity both for society and for the children. This approach has been favoured by some European sociologists during the past few years. This is partly accompanied by the problematic restriction of children's work to gainful employment or wage labour made by almost all studies hitherto. In the following, the findings of a Norwegian study, together with two British studies and one from Northern Ireland, which pursue new directions in this sense in research into children's work in the respective countries, are presented and discussed.[7]

In an essay published in 1997, the Norwegian sociologist Anne Solberg describes how, by perceiving children as actors, she acquired a sense of the various kinds of work they do and began to understand its numerous meanings for the children. In the context of a qualitatively oriented community study on the north coast of Norway in the mid-1970s, she had 'discovered' forms and aspects of the work of children that were far removed from the usual perception of children's work as exploitation and a social problem (see Solberg 1997: 188ff; Solberg 2001).[8]

In these communities, which live predominantly from fishing, she found that from the age of eight or nine children take on specific tasks such as cutting out fish tongues, peeling shrimps or baiting fish with long lines. This work is not given to the children for educational reasons, so that they might do 'something useful', but because 'all hands are needed' (Solberg 1997: 192), and the work contributes to the production of food that is consumed inside and outside the community. Meanwhile, the children are not forced to work, but can decide themselves whether and how long they want to work. Hours of work and the course of their work are largely in their hands. As a rule, the children relieve their mothers on coming home from school in the afternoon. The financial reward is in accordance with the quantity produced, and is no different from that given to adults for comparable work. The children learn the requisite skills gradually during their work, usually accompanied and supported by their mothers to begin with. As soon as the children are ten to twelve years old, they prefer to work in groups with other children of their age.

The work is to some extent divided differently between boys and girls, and is also regarded differently by them. The work of fish-baiting is done by both sexes. Shrimp-peeling, on the other hand, is thought to be women's work, while the cutting out of tongues is done by the boys. Solberg also notes a difference in the way boys and girls speak of their work. 'The girls emphasized the value of having "something to do" and stressed the importance of the social relations of work. On the other hand, the boys, in particular the big cutters among them, talked about their work with enthusiasm. They showed great pride in their own work capacity and endurance, and pointed to the high financial outcome as "proof" of their virtues' (ibid.: 194). It was important to the tongue-cutters that they themselves owned their working tools and that they did not just receive their 'pay' from an employer, but had to sell their own products. Girls wishing to work as tongue-cutters do not find it easy to penetrate this male domain.

Solberg also rejects the tendency to regard the children's work she investigated as simply a matter of the past which is disappearing with technological progress. Examination of the kinds of work undertaken showed that there was 'no simple and direct connection between the level of technology and the integration of children' (ibid.: 198). In the forms of work examined by her, the technology was simple and most of the manual jobs such as peeling and baiting could have been made superfluous by using technological innovations. But the fact that such innovations are not used and the organization of work (for instance the regularization of working hours) has not been 'modernized' up to now is in her eyes to be viewed not as backwardness but as a conscious 'strategic adaptation' to the available resources and a decision in favour of self-determined forms of work. At the same time, new technological methods were certainly used in fishing (e.g. larger boats and more complex tools), as they made the work easier and increased the yield.

According to her account, Solberg's investigations on the north coast of Norway gave her a 'new look' at the multifarious activities of children in other places too, and caused her to rethink the relationship between childhood and work. In the district of Oslo where she lived, her attention was drawn to numerous working activities performed by children which she had not noticed before (see ibid.: 200). She now noticed many children selling flowers, 'snowballs', magazines or lottery tickets, putting advertising leaflets in letter-boxes or delivering newspapers. In one shop she noticed a girl of about ten helping the shop-owner. 'She was allowed to weigh the goods and also to receive payment and to give back change. It was obvious to me that she enjoyed what she was doing – looking seriously engaged in making the calculations correctly. From time to time her supervisor nodded to her, discreeetly but undoubtedly with appreciation. I had great pleasure observing them. The shopkeeper showed an admirable patience in guiding without interfering, and it seemed to be a very good experience to be allowed to pretend to be a shop assistant in this realistic manner' (ibid.: 201).

In carrying out further investigations in the urban environment, Solberg arrives at the conclusion that the work of children forms an important part of the local economy by no means only in rural or fishing communities. 'Children in all parts of Norway turned out to make contributions within their own neighbourhood. Running errands was the task category that was most frequently reported. Housework in other people's homes, childminding and outdoor work, like gardening and snow shovelling, formed part of the work life also of the 11–12 year olds. ... A significant part of the childhood population reported having been involved in door-to-door selling of lottery tickets and other items' (ibid.: 203). Many activities brought the children in the urban environment and in 'modern occupations' as well into contact with the workplaces of their parents or were carried on in conjunction with one or other parent, for instance shopkeeping, cleaning work, carpeting, errands or various kinds of caring.

At the conclusion of her studies, Solberg is convinced that the forms of work performed by children both in the fishing communities and in urban centres are not exotic exceptions, but are to be regarded as part of 'contemporary childhood'; that is, in 'modern societies' too childhood does not necessarily have to be separate from working life. She regards the work of children, precisely when it forms an important part of the local or household economy, as a form of 'actual participation' by the children in social life.

Working children as actors

The studies from Great Britain and Northern Ireland to be discussed in the following also perceive the children as 'responsible actors' (Morrow 1994), and attempt to understand and display children's work motivation and experience from their own viewpoint and 'standpoint' (Mayall 2002). In this way Morrow, in her above-quoted study on children from eleven to sixteen in two British cities, comes to the conclusion 'that children do not work merely in order to consume, but in order to give themselves a feeling of being responsible and more "grown-up" generally, which accords with other aspirations they may have towards greater emotional/sexual maturity, besides "material" maturity' (ibid.: 142). Work for the sake of money was only one of the forms of work she came across, thanks to her open conception of work and her methodical approach.

Of the children who wished primarily to earn money with their work, some spent it on consumer goods, while others wanted to save it in order to be able to go away in the holidays, to buy themselves a TV later on, or to acquire fish. Other children stated that work gave them self-confidence and independence. Others again saw in their work an opportunity to gather useful experience for the future. Some children gave as the reason for their work that they wanted to help others. With part of her earnings, one girl supported a child in Ruanda. The children who engaged in domestic work primarily did this because their parents were 'out at work' or because they had been urged to by their parents. Some girls criticized the fact that this work was expected of them but not of their brothers. Work in the family firm, on the other hand, was described without evaluation as a fact, and was felt to be natural, because their 'own business' or their 'own firm' was involved.

Her conception and approach permit Morrow to recognize that the work of children represents a broad spectrum of differing experiences that cannot be reduced to a common denominator. In this sense, she warns against the hasty assumption that children work only for the sake of consumption. Instead, she proposes paying more attention to which responsibilities children take on in their work and not to lose sight of the fact that at work there are often 'reciprocal relations between family members' (ibid.: 138f).

Meanwhile, other recent studies in Great Britain also attach greater importance to children's self-estimation, and take it more seriously. These studies continue to be limited to gainful employment, but work with qualitative procedures that allow more scope to the words and viewpoints of the children (see Middleton et al. 1998; Leonard 1998 and 1999; Save the Children 1998). On the basis of the consideration that, despite a number of studies of the extent and types of work by children, little was still known about 'what the children think of the work they do, how important it is to them, and what role it plays in their lives' (Save the Children 1998: 59),[9] the children's aid organization Save the Children carried out semi-structured interviews with eleven- to sixteen-year-old children in five regions of Great Britain.

From these resulted, across borders of ethnic and gender differences, great similarities in the attitudes to work and the motives that cause children to undertake paid work.

Work plays a key part in their lives. The money [earned by working] is a way of gaining independence, enabling them to participate socially with their friends, to buy clothes, eat out and buy leisure equipment. Many of these young people come from low income areas, and some children were contributing both directly and indirectly to the household income. That is, they were either handing over some of their earnings to their parents, or they were buying essential items for themselves or for their school work. Many young people were saving their earnings. For the majority the work represented more than just having the money. It was a way of meeting new people, being with their friends and getting away from home. In some cases it was a key to alleviating boredom. For others it was a way of gaining experience and confidence. (ibid.: 79)

In some cases, the children also complained of not being fairly treated, especially by comparison with their grown-up fellow workers. A few also criticized the fact that they were not paid fairly for extra work, and were exposed to hazardous or unpleasant situations. Most considered it necessary for children to be better protected against hazardous work, but found the existing regulations inadequate; they particularly criticized the general prohibition of work in the evenings and on Sundays. Finally, they wished for better regulations and information on their rights as workers, particularly an official right of complaint (see ibid.: 79).

In a pilot study carried out in the Northern Ireland capital, Belfast, by Madeleine Leonard (1999) with thirteen- to fifteen-year-old pupils, quantitative and qualitative procedures were combined, with the intention of coming as close as possible to the complexity of the work experience and the biographies of the children. The attempt was made via group discussions, part-structured interviews and case studies 'to explore the many different contexts in which children work and their varying social and economic circumstances', and to present the everyday reality of working children from their own point of view (ibid.: 33).

Here, a great discrepancy becomes evident between the wishes and estimates of the children regarding their work and the legal regulations intended for their protection. The great majority of children showed themselves convinced that they had a legitimate right to work, contrary to the existing legal restrictions (see ibid.: 56). As the report on the investigation quotes the children extensively, we will give some of their comments here: 'There should be more variety of jobs for young people. Young people are more mature these days and I think we should be given more chances of employment'; 'Young people should have the right to work any hours they want to. It is as if they are being controlled by adults. They are near sixteen and have limited hours to work. I don't believe in it. I work whatever hours I want'; 'Young people have the right to stand on their own two feet without the government butting in. They have a right to work for independence'; 'I think that there should be a wide range of jobs available to people of our age as not everyone wants to babysit. We should have a chance to try and do more experienced jobs'; 'I believe everybody has a right to earn money provided the job is something they enjoy doing, doesn't interfere with school and gives them a fair wage for the tasks set' (ibid.: 57f).

The children who claim a right to work are by no means uncritical of the conditions under which they frequently perform their jobs. They even make concrete proposals as to how their working conditions could be improved: 'There should be details on wage slips, containing hours, payment etc., and this would stop employers taking advantage of young inexperienced people. Working conditions should be up to standard and schools should clearly inform their pupils of their rights concerning work and employment'; 'Young people should be treated as equals and have the same rights and working conditions as everyone else. There should be a minimum wage and a proper system for complaints etc. People should not discriminate against adolescents simply because they are young'; 'Children should not be generalised. Some children are capable of holding a job and some are not. Age discrimination is taken very seriously when older people are in the spotlight. I find it very unfair that someone who works for the same amount of time and puts the same amount of effort into a job can be paid twice the amount just because they are older'; 'Adults seem to have rights when working while young people don't. This should be changed so that there are equal rights for all workers and a minimum wage paid to young workers' (ibid.: 63f).

From her study, Leonard draws the conclusion that legal regulations and measures for the protection of working children are only meaningful when they are created with the participation of the children and adolescents affected and take account of their views and proposals. She requires the trade unions to recognize that many children under the age of sixteen work, and to represent their interests, for instance by negotiating a minimum wage for working children.[10] She expects the schools to take up the real work experience of the children in their teaching, to inform the children of their rights, and support them in reinforcing the skills acquired at work (see ibid.: 68f).

Theoretical conceptions of children's work

At present, in European countries[11] four basic theoretical conceptions of children's work are put forward:

- children's work is seen as gainful employment;
- children's work is seen as school work;

- children's work is seen as a mixture of social and cultural activities the lowest common denominator of which consists in the fact that the children play an active part in society;
- children's work is seen as an activity with definite goals and a recognizable relevance for the satisfaction of human needs, which in this sense is socially necessary.

Children's work as gainful employment

When children's work is seen as gainful employment, the image as a rule arises from the exploitation of juvenile labour potential that came about with the capitalist mode of production. In nearly all historical studies, the focus of interest is on 'industrial' or 'factory' work, including mining, while forms of 'domestic' and 'agricultural' work are neglected, not to mention the forms of children's work that had long existed and did not serve the purpose of immediate earnings. In present-day studies based on the concept of gainful employment, attention is directed to the 'informal' employment of children, as a rule summed up under the term 'odd jobs'.

Seeing children's work as gainful employment follows the traditional notion that children represent a specific embodiment of labour potential, calculated to produce monetary values. In this view, the goal of children's work is seen on the one hand in making a profit, and on the other to receive a wage. According to this, children's work is to be equated with wage labour or 'dependent' employment. In a study on 'Children's work in the Federal Republic of Germany' published in 1980, children's work is seen in this sense as 'the gainful employment of children with the aim of profit-making on the part of the entrepreneur, regardless of how long the children's work lasts, how often it takes place, or whether it is prohibited or not' (Stark-von der Haar and von der Haar 1980: 10). It is expressly noted that 'working in the parental household (washing up, shopping, help with gardening)' is not to be accounted children's work, 'nor is polytechnical instruction or *Arbeitslehre* (as an introduction to the world of work)' (ibid.: 10).

This view of children's work is oriented to the forms of children's employment that developed in the course of capitalist industrialization. For various reasons – partly humanitarian, partly utilitarian and determined by competition – from the mid-nineteenth century onwards these led to legal regulations governing youth work protection, and finally a general prohibition of children's work.

Up to the present, all studies carried out in Germany that regard children's work exclusively as wage-earning or gainful employment are oriented to these attitudes. They take it as read that children's work is damaging to children, and set out to discover to what extent the employment of children infringes existing regulations concerning youth work protection, and how this can be opposed. Only gradually is the consideration emerging that present-day forms of children's work are not simply a prolongation of the children's wage labour of the early industrial period, and that more attention must be paid to the reasons and personal motives that induce children to work.

Thus Ingenhorst, purely with regard to the gainful employment of children, comes to the conclusion that 'the structure of children's work in the Federal Republic is highly complex'. It presents itself 'as a broad field of varied activities, intensities and forms that can only with difficulty be subdivided into clear categories'. In the case of the paid employment of children and adolescents, there are 'no normed conditions of work; instead, the field is wide open for necessities, wishes, and opportunities' (Ingenhorst 1998: 61; see also Ingenhorst 2001).

At the present time the realization is growing that even the paid employment of children cannot inevitably be equated with 'dependent' employment, let alone 'exploitation', but that it can also have a meaning in terms of overcoming the normative notions of the parental home (and the school), and the gradual establishment of an independent mode of existence. Even in the studies being carried out in Germany commissioned by the state governments, it is noted that apart from the wish to dispose of self-earned money, having fun at or through work, gaining social recognition, collecting experience for everyday working life, learning more, and feeling socially useful are among the motives of children when they take on paid employment. The fact that earning money through paid employment is mentioned first results from the basic characteristic of this kind of work, that is, of being work that is financially 'gainful'.

Even when the forms of gainful employment of children are seen to be complex, and attention is paid to the reasons and motives of the children, a number of activities that play an increasing part in the lives of the children, and which with good reason can be seen as work too, are ignored. Although, and perhaps precisely because, these are not primarily concerned with earning money, and as a rule there is no 'employer' claiming the children's labour potential, these are significant for the satisfaction of human needs and social development.

No attention, for instance, is paid to housework or any economic activities outside the home that remain unpaid. No attention is paid to the diverse activities that children think up for themselves and carry out to escape the boredom of ready-made children's games or the barrenness of daily family life. These sometimes produce some money, but this is not regarded as the main point of the enterprise (an example is selling old toys or books in the pedestrian zone of a town, or even organizing a children's flea market together with others in aid of the school or the nearest church community). The studies similarly do not cover kinds of work for which children and adolescents seek refuge in the street in order to obtain the necessary income for their living, for lack of alternative means (e.g. begging, stealing or prostitution). The by no means marginal fields of competitive sport or show business where children subject themselves to almost limitless strains and efforts to satisfy their own ambition or the vanity of their parents, or with the tempting hope of getting quick fame, are also not considered.

The broad spectrum of children's work beyond paid employment is, in its various facets and meanings, little known and still less examined. This will be discussed further below, when an attempt is made to formulate another and, it seems to me, more appropriate conception of children's work.

Children's work as school work

One view runs counter to all other conceptions of children's work, namely that compulsory school attendance represents one, or even *the*, modern form of children's work. This view quotes as support the fact that school claims an increasing part of children's daily time budget. Thus Qvortrup contrasts 'school work' with 'children's manual work' and states that the latter has 'gradually lost weight quantitatively. It has changed from being the predominant activity of children to being a residual one, a relic of bygone times, while school work has developed from a rudimentary form to the predominant one' (Qvortrup 2000: 28; see also Qvortrup 2001). Wintersberger (2000: 170), too, demands a revision of the 'historical' view of children's work, to include at least 'the work of children for school'; school is 'a new form of children's work' (ibid.: 177). This change of perspective in the conceptualization of children's work is supported by various arguments.

One argument points out that school and the world of industrial work have similar structures. School is seen as a 'workplace' whose 'forms of contact and structures of relationships ... are determined increasingly clearly by the norms of industrial production' (Hengst 1981: 34). With the thorough rationalization of the organization of schools, an 'industrial time organization' becomes dominant, 'which is not oriented to basic human needs but institutionally pre-arranged dates, periods and timetables' (Eder and Kränzl-Nagl 1998: 216). Analogously to the sphere of work, the pupils are made to perform 'work necessary for the existence of society' (ibid.: 216). The modes of behaviour expected of the pupils, such as discipline, obedience or single-mindedness, are oriented to 'values of the Protestant work ethos or the modern principle of performance and competition' (ibid.: 217). Furthermore, the time spent by children at and on school tends 'to equal and exceed the working time of adults' (ibid.: 245).

Another argument states that 'school work' corresponds to the 'trend from manual to abstract or symbolic activities' (Qvortrup 2000: 28) that marks the 'kind of production' predominant in modern societies. Attending school in these societies has to be regarded as work, since it produces the human capital required for expanded production. The particular feature of children's school work consists in the fact 'that children produce labour power which as such is a product that manifests itself in the equations of supply and demand on the labour market. At the same time, their school work – even if with a delay conditioned by the diachronic nature of the modern economy – is an indispensable precondition for the production of other goods and services in society, and can therefore not be dismissed as useless' (ibid.: 35).

Both of these arguments are governed by the interest in gaining greater social recognition and 'appreciation' for the performance that children are required to achieve at school. Qualifying them as work is aimed at arguing for a 'child-related income' (Eder and Kränzl-Nagl 1998: 215). It is meant 'to enable children and their advocates to negotiate with the state or other public institutions about their just share in social production as a reward for their contribution to the social tissue of society' (Qvortrup 2000: 411).

Declaring children's school attendance simply as one, or even *the* modern, form of 'children's work' raises several problems. Despite the recognition of children as subjects capable of action and having social significance, the argumentation is based on a view of work which – as Qvortrup himself notes – remains 'inherent in the system'. When the school is declared to be a 'workplace' or 'school work' is regarded as the 'production of human capital', 'school work' is connected with *negative* experiences on the part of the children. It counts as work precisely because it does not serve the satisfaction of needs or the creation of 'utility values' but is directed to the production of 'barter values' and is a strain on the children for which they have to be compensated, as it were, by an income of their own. To this extent, the conception of school work remains within the framework of the same logic as the conception of children's work as paid work.

The assumption that 'school work' is the most *modern* form of children's work is also to be questioned. Eder and Kränzl-Nagl themselves note that the structural features and principles of performance are still predominant in the schools of today, which 'continue to be closely oriented to the pattern of industrial work forms', and no longer stand up to the 'rapid developments' in the world of work and on the labour market (Eder and Kränzl-Nagl 1998: 218). Whereas schools are still largely organized according to 'authoritarian patterns', in the adult world of work a 'contrary trend' is rather to be observed; there it is no longer discipline and obedience which are required, but rather 'team spirit, creativity, flexibility, consensual conflict avoidance, independence and responsibility' (ibid.: 217).

In a recent publication, Hengst (2000: 78) points out that 'school as a workplace' claims a considerable proportion of children's time, but is losing weight and importance as a place of learning. Educational biographies are becoming increasingly detached from the school and school learning. Important experience with relevance for the future of the individual is nowadays rather found outside school, above all in the field of 'commercial children's culture', where the children find 'media, materials, information, service providers and committed or like-minded peers' for almost any kind of topic interest. 'These happenings compete with school learning (sometimes even on the barter level). Every twelve-year-old today has at least a vague idea that there are kinds of education whose acquisition gives them more than that obtained at school' (ibid.: 78).

When Qvortrup declares that 'school work' is in fact the sole modern form of children's work, and cites the 'diachronic' character of 'modern' society in support of this, he is overlooking at least two things. On the one hand, the fact that the knowledge required for work (also in its symbolic forms) is no longer acquired in advance and once and for all in the early phases of life, but has become a lifelong task. On the other, the fact that precisely in technologically advanced societies, experience of work that is not congruent with 'school work' is becoming necessary and possible already in childhood. One clear indication of this is the growing wish of many children to at least complement school, which they find out of touch with reality, by 'work of their own' outside school. Similar considerations lie behind the increasing number of initiatives in the context of schools and out-of-school educational establishments to develop work projects that link 'physical' and 'mental' work and enable the children to gain 'real' economic experience (see Chapter 9). In order to be able to judge the forms and meaning of present-day children's work appropriately, it is no longer enough only to consider its function as 'utility' for existing society; it needs also to be asked what it means for the personal lives, development as subjects and social participation of the children.

This aspect is touched on in a recent publication by Wintersberger (2000: 177) in which he demands 'a revision of the view of school work as modern children's work'. According to him, although 'the social recognition of school work as an equivalent to the gainful employment of adults can have positive effects on the distribution of resources between the generations' (ibid.: 180), an appropriate conception of children's work must also consider its possible 'positive' meaning for the children and their identity formation. From this view, Wintersberger draws the conclusion that children in our society 'must be offered more opportunities to experience meaningful work outside of school, but school as a world of work must also be recognized and correspondingly organized as such' (ibid.: 187).

Children's work as cultural and social activity

On the basis of the consideration that children's work can be adequately grasped neither as 'gainful employment' nor as 'school work', Heinz Hengst demands a conception of work 'that accords the cultural and social significance of work greater importance than the economic' (Hengst 1998: 243). He supports this argument by stating that fewer and fewer people 'work for the market' directly, i.e. many no longer sell their labour via the 'labour market' or pursue 'paid work', and that in modern everyday parlance many activities 'outside the market' are termed work. In his attempt to arrive at a 'redefinition', Hengst refers to the 'folk work concept' of US anthropologist Cato Wadel (1979).

On the basis of informal conversations, Wadel noted the following aspects of the everyday conception of work: the use of physical energy, routine and repetitive actions, special workplaces and times, necessary activities, product- and result-oriented activities, and some kind of instruction. According to him, all these criteria are also applied to activities (e.g. sport) that do not count as work. According to an everyday view, a distinction is made between work and leisure – work is connected with the activity being paid, leisure with fun and freedom from obligations – but there is an 'area of overlap'. From this, Wadel concludes that people think it important not to regard activities as something monolithic, but as mixtures, with a greater or smaller proportion of work involved (see ibid.: 368ff).

Drawing attention to empirical investigations on the thinking of working children and adolescents in Germany (Ingenhorst and Wienhold 1992), Hengst states that they see their own work, as does Wadel, 'as widely differing mixtures' (Hengst 1998: 244). Because contemporary children in societies like the German Federal Republic have access to a variety of activities that contain elements of both work and leisure, it may be assumed that they have 'complex, fluid and by no means cut-and-dried conceptions' (ibid.: 244). In view of this, Hengst proposes that the analysis of activities should 'not stop at that which from an economic viewpoint is labelled [children's] work' (ibid.: 244).

Apart from the reference to the everyday perspective of children and adolescents, Hengst adduces two reasons for his proposal. First, the 'erosions of the work society' lead to a massive increase in activities in the 'public benefit sphere' such as 'social services, health service, education, art, research, ecology, nature conservation and the representing of interests' (ibid.: 245). Hengst documents this with the Shell study *Jugend '97* (Youth '97), which noted a new kind of approach by young people to their hobbies: 'Not uncommonly, it is the private hobby that smooths the way to commitments/activity for public benefit. In the fascination with technology and the preference for making and experimenting with things may lie the key that opens the door for young people to a sense of fire precautions and environmental protection. Computer freaks suddenly look beyond their immediate personal sphere when technological know-how is in demand' (Jugendwerk der Deutschen Shell 1997: 88).

Second, it found, the resources used by children and adolescents today for sporting activities, hobbies and various (above all) out-of-school activities are undergoing a 'qualitative change'. Unlike the media and materials of the industrial epoch, they no longer represent the difference between play and learning on the one hand and work on the other, and correspondingly a clear separation between children's and adults' activities. 'With the computer and Internet kids play, learn and work with the same hard- and software as the grown-ups in the world of work. At most, they place the emphasis differently in the field of software' (Hengst 1998: 246). Both in the field of consumption and in non-commercial fields of activity out of school (e.g. the work of environmental organizations or Jugend forscht – the German organization for scientific and technological research by young people) it becomes clear, according to Hengst, 'that the traditional separation of children's and adults' activities, of play, learning and (even scholarly) work have become fluid' (ibid.: 246).

Finally, Hengst points out how the new forms of work and time occupation that are coming about in the course of the 'restructuring of work activity' are breaking up the clear separation of work from life that was hitherto an essential structural feature of industrial and social conditions. Referring to a study by work researcher Günther Voss, Hengst sees forms of the relation between occupational and other activities coming into being 'that may in a number of aspects remind one of pre-industrial conditions of life and work, but quite clearly are precursors of future forms of work and existence' (Voss 1998: 480). This is accompanied, according to Hengst, by 'a pluralization of the meanings of work' (Hengst 2000: 72).

In contrast to the customary talk of 'child labour', the newly created 'work of children' means to Hengst a promise of autonomy. He perceives it above all in the context of the media system, which is linked with the world of consumption. Here, 'the possibilities of control and access by children have expanded in a variety of ways' (ibid.: 79), and from the children's activities a 'children's culture as a second culture of learning' is resulting (ibid.: 73). The cultural and social activities of children not regarded hitherto as work are termed work by Hengst because in them is manifest young people's aspiration to leave the ghetto of childhood and to play a part in the adult world, i.e. to do things previously reserved for adults.

A point in favour of Hengst's conception of 'children's work' is that it is open to historical change and includes the subjective meanings that are contained in various, above all newly created, forms of activity. He points out that the conception of children's work, like that of work itself, is a social construction. This has two consequences for the debate on children's work. On the one hand what is termed children's work consists of a variety of differing activities. For instance, it may be observed that the conception of children's work is becoming less and less restricted to 'wage labour', and that all kinds of activities performed by children, for instance cooperation with adults, or looking after themselves in the parental household, taking on tasks in an ecology group, taking part in wars as soldiers, commerce, stealing, (compulsory) school attendance and much more, are today called children's work. Second, talk of children's work is always accompanied by a particular evaluation which tends either to see children's work in general as 'hostile to children' or as a possible aspect of their daily activities that benefits them. It thus depends considerably to which tendency one's viewpoint belongs as to what activities are subsumed under the label of children's work.

Meanwhile, the question arises as to what the point is of detaching the notion of work entirely from economic contexts. Hengst calls all activities work in which children act independently or on their own initiative in any way at all, whatever relevance these actions may have for society or for the children. When the notion of work is thus treated with cultural ambivalence, what activities are to be viewed as work becomes basically arbitrary. The 'work of children' finally becomes a metaphor for an assumed development in the course of which the differences between children and adults are erased and the children have progressed to being autonomously acting individuals.

Children's work as an activity with definite aims relevant to the satisfaction of human needs

The conception of children's work to be presented here now is still largely theoretical. I will outline its basic elements – partly with reference to the ideas of German educationists Fritz Haunert and Reinhard Lang (1994), and Dieter Kirchhöfer (1998 and 1999). According to this view, all activities of children count as work which have a recognizable relevance for the satisfaction of human needs, and in this sense are aimed at a material substratum. It is also important to enquire into the social and cultural context in which the work of children is located, and the framework within which it is carried out. It is not presupposed that it is either a negative or a positive expression of a tendency of social development. Instead, the conception is intended to make it possible to thematize both negative and positive aspects of children's work experience and to recognize and evaluate the various meanings of work, either for society or for the working children themselves.

The conception takes account of the fact that children today perform a variety of activities that cannot be termed wage-dependent paid work in the strict sense, but nevertheless possess an economic value and are a significant contribution to their livelihood. Even in the case of the jobs with which children today frequently earn money, there is rarely an employer on whom they are directly dependent and who is able to dictate the conditions of their work. Their jobs are much more frequently in the field of private service provision than in firms, and are practised in different locations as required. Together with this, the perception of tasks in the parental household and family firms is increasingly important. Numerous children create odd jobs themselves, either to eke out their pocket money or to do something that appears to them meaningful and useful, and gives them the feeling of playing a part in life that is to be taken seriously.

In a study on the significance of work in youth social work, Haunert and Lang (1994: 89) point out that in young people's 'everyday talk' references to work are acquiring new meanings. On the one hand, more claims of a qualitative kind are made that go beyond the mere gaining of money, and on the other a sense of meaningfulness and identity is expected from activities beyond paid work. 'That which in the modern era used to be connected with the notion of work and in general restricted to paid work now no longer takes place here but in "other kinds of work"'. Haunert and Lang therefore propose splitting up the notion of work into 'consumptional use of time', 'gainful employment' and 'other forms of work' (ibid.: 89).

> Just as fulfilment and the finding of identity are no longer possible today solely in paid work but also in other forms of work, to take it a step farther it may even no longer be possible for this human need to be realized in paid work, because the features attributed to 'work' that are connected with meanings, myths and self-projecting capacities, and in the traditional concept of work in the modern era were reserved for paid work, can for many people no longer be located there. There is no cogent reason why in the foreseeable future people should not call activities meaningful to them 'work', and the work that serves to provide material security only 'paid work' or 'gainful employment', in order by means of this linguistic differentiation to render reality in a manner that satisfies the need for meaningful communication. (ibid.: 89)

Gainful employment would then be 'the less important form' by comparison to 'other kinds of activity that ensure subsistence and promote sociality' (ibid.: 90), which could now be defined as work.

For the work of children, this means taking more seriously precisely those of their activities that do not primarily serve to earn money or are practised in the form of wage-dependent gainful employment. At the same time, the question arises as to whether it is necessary and meaningful to draw such a line between activities of children that are to be termed work and those that are not. In the culturalistic conception developed by Hengst, this question is answered in the negative. I, on the other hand, hold the view that it is meaningful to speak of work in regard to children's activities only when these are deliberately aimed at a 'product' with a recognizable relevance for the preservation and planning of human life, and also with certain chronological limits.

Important modules for such a conception of children's work have been contributed by educationist Dieter Kirchhöfer. He is interested above all in the question of how work for children can become important and a positive experience of life. For this, he has recourse to the general definition of work given by Karl Marx in the first volume of *Das Kapital*: 'Work is to begin with a process between man and nature, a process in which man supplies, regulates and controls his metabolism with nature by means of his own actions' (Marx 1979: 193). In order to delimit the activity of work as against learning and play, Kirchhöfer finds it necessary to go beyond this definition to see 'working' as an 'activity with an aim in view, in which the future result – more or less clearly outlined – is mentally anticipated' (Kirchhöfer 1998: 66). This is not yet the case with the 'spontaneous, affectively ruled or unconscious forms of activity in early childhood' (ibid.: 66). However, as soon as a child is able to control its own actions consciously, it is able to work, and work becomes for it a 'necessary field of development'. Then the child through working has 'an influence on a reality existing outside of itself (objects, circumstances, other people), and seeks to bring about a change in these. It realizes and objectivizes its intentions and its will in these things and thus creates something lasting and at rest, in contrast to the fleeting and restless nature of play. Once produced by the subject, this lasting element has the effect of being both the result of past behaviour and the condition of future actions' (ibid.: 66).

The distinction made by Kirchhöfer between work and play is conceptual and analytic in nature. It does not mean that work and play can always be strictly distinguished in the lives of children; precisely under the conditions of contemporary 'good' societies, 'play' and 'serious matters' in the case of children frequently overlap, or 'links' (Invernizzi 2001) and 'mixtures' of a particular kind come about, as Hengst (1998 and 2000) has plausibly argued. But from an analytical point of view, it is meaningful to concur with Kirchhöfer in terming as work only those aspects and forms of childish action in which an 'activity aimed at the alteration of objective states of affairs' is contained, and with which 'the individual satisfies his own needs or those of others, and thus creates usefulness' (Kirchhöfer 1998: 67).

Kirchhöfer has attained not only a sufficiently 'broad' but also a 'flexible' concept of work, which does not ascribe to a given activity the attribute 'of being work' unalterably and exclusively.

> The characteristic is *fluid*, that is, an activity can lose this quality again or acquire one; for instance, the discipline of juggling with balls (ballwork) can during practice become a non-purposeful relaxing activity (in street-ball). Activities are *non-monolithic*, i.e. they can have features of both learning or play and of work, as for instance high-performance climbing – to stay in the mental world of sport – is capable of displaying pleasurable states of excitement or spontaneous affective actions. The attribution as work is also *relative*, that is, from different perspectives, e.g. that of the player or the onlooker, one and the same activity can be work or play. (ibid.: 67f)

Whether a given activity performed by children is to be seen as work also depends not only on its content, form and subjective aim, but also always on the social and cultural context in which it takes place. Only in this historically variable context can it be decided whether a kind of work is 'necessary' or 'useful', or is relevant for the satisfaction of needs or for the preservation or design of life.

With regard to the 'post-industrial' societies of the North, it is occasionally stated that work whose usefulness or utility value is immediately evident and can thus be experienced by the worker possesses less scope and significance compared with intellectual or mental work, the product of which is not immediately visible nor easily ascribed to individuals (see Wintersberger 1996: 199f). This assumption is central to the conception that perceives in 'school work' the only modern form of children's work, but also in the culturalistic conception of children's work represented by Hengst. To Jens Qvortrup it is only a question of time before 'manual work' disappears totally from the scene in favour of 'symbolic work' (Qvortrup 2000: 27ff). For Hengst, what he calls 'traditional children's work' has long been replaced by the playful and 'productive' appropriation of consumable media items, the contours of which he perceives above all 'in a fluid mixture of activities on widely differing social stages' (Hengst 2000: 94).

In such scenarios, one thing that is ignored is that in post-industrial societies too work performed by children is often connected with physical experience, and that children indeed expressly seek this. Sight is also lost of the fact that it frequently takes place under conditions that make it harder for the children to experience themselves as 'productive subjects' and to see it as an essential part of themselves. The conception put forward here, which sees children's work as an activity with a particular aim with relevance for the preservation and planning of life, keeps these two aspects equally in mind. On the one hand they relate to the technological aspect, and on the other to the social-structural aspect of children's social development and location.

The technological development of a society is a contradictory process involving inequalities, by which the forms of work are never completely determined, and only in one direction. It is by no means inevitable that in particularly technologically 'advanced' societies only 'symbolic' kinds of work that presuppose a comprehensive abstract 'school' qualification and which are therefore inaccessible to or unsuitable for children are possible. Besides continuing 'old' forms of work after the pattern of 'craft work', 'new' forms come into being which are not necessarily more complex or 'more incomprehensible' to children. Both in the context of 'old' and 'new' technologies, sensuous qualities can come about that render it possible for children to play their part, and to test and further develop physical and/or mental abilities – that is, to learn these while working. In technologically advanced societies, too, there are (always) kinds of work that have direct effects (not only in the distant future), and serve to satisfy everyday needs; which can be performed by individuals or in small groups (not only in large units of production organized strictly by division of labour); which are relatively transitory or are learned 'en passant' and in which everyday experience can be utilized; which render possible the expansion of qualifications during the work process itself; and finally which also provide personal satisfaction and render possible satisfying social relations.

On the other hand, it has to be taken into consideration that the work of children frequently takes place, in the affluent and technologically progressive societies of the North as well, under conditions that bring disadvantages rather than advantages for the children. This refers not only to traditional forms of wage-dependent gainful employment, but to all forms of activity in which children are bound up in power relationships that prevent them from acting independently or making decisions or disposing of the fruits of their work themselves. This may be the case in the context of domestic work or so-called assistance in a family firm, but also where the children are forced or induced by their parents or other adults – from whatever motives – to take on activities that over-tax them physically or psychologically. This is also frequently the case with 'school work'.[12]

In the conception of children's work presented here, the following aspects of the work of children are thematized in a connected manner and made accessible to judgement:

- the 'value' of the work in the sense of its relevance for survival and the satisfaction of needs;
- the 'quality' of the work in the sense of the experience and 'informal' learning processes made possible by it;
- the 'relative value' of the work in the sense of the social recognition connected with it and its influence on living conditions and social circumstances ('participation');
- the 'conditions' of the work in the sense of its being embedded in social production and power relations and its corresponding consequences for the organization and perspectives of the children's lives.

In this way, the conception makes it possible to identify and distinguish the various forms of work and 'other' activities more clearly than in the 'culturalistic' conception. It also makes it possible, in contrast to the concepts of 'gainful employment' and 'school work', not only to identify the general usefulness of the work for society or for particular 'beneficiaries', but also to take up the work experience of children and to include those kinds of work that are meaningful for the children themselves in a positive sense.

Children's work and perspectives of childhood in Europe

In the highly industrialized societies of Europe, the work of children seemed to have disappeared with the growing economic affluence following the Second World War. With a few exceptions, even in the social sciences it was not investigated. Especially in research into childhood and adolescence, it was taken as self-evident that the bourgeois pattern of childhood marked by the absence of work was generally accepted in society. Contemporary childhood was essentially seen as consisting of family, school and leisure time.

Michael-Sebastian Honig (1999: 119) states: 'In the twentieth century, the notion of what is suitable for children as developed by the protagonists of progressive education became the normative foundation of the social status of the child, and the prohibition of children's work its institutional foundation. In this sense, the educational conception of childhood was institutionally realized in the "century of the child" (Ellen Key) as a phase of life of learning and play.' In so far as childhood was regarded as 'threatened', its end even imminent, what was envisaged was not the return of children's work but the transformation of children into consumers of goods and media (see Postman 1982).

The studies carried out in European countries in recent years which are concerned with the work of children give a different picture, as demonstrated above. They show that work occupies a natural place in the lives of most children from about the age of twelve. What this means for children and the course of childhood is controversial even among these researchers. Some see in work a danger for children and the 'childhood project of the modern era'. They see children's work primarily as gainful employment and interpret it as a surreptitious form of the instrumentalization, abuse and exploitation of children in the context of the capitalist economic system (see Lavalette 1994; Mellaissoux 2000).

Others see in children's work an indication rather that children are on the way to a new status in society with equal rights and more influence. Without excluding the possibility of problems of the continued subordination and exploitation of children, they see this process as being promoted by fundamental changes in the social organization of the processes of production and reproduction (see Solberg 1996; Morrow 1994; James et al. 1998; Wintersberger 2000; Hengst 2000; Kirchhöfer 2000). Despite the differences in the conceptualization of children's work that are to be found in the recent sociological literature, there is agreement that children's work in the societies of Europe today no longer fits the pattern of childhood that was current in the early capitalist era. Children are no longer to be regarded as part of the 'industrial reserve army' (Marx), their work is mainly no longer 'born of need' and is no longer an essential condition for survival. When children work today, this is largely due to their own decisions, and they are as a rule not forced to work under conditions that run contrary to their own ideas and interests.

The growing number of children who work or wish to work is an indication of 'how in the most developed Western industrial and service societies a return to increased subjectivity and productivity in children is beginning to emerge' (Wintersberger 2000: 171). It is increasingly the children themselves who are pushing themselves into the world of work of the adults and who wish to play an active part there, whether to earn money of their own, or to gain recognition and have a say in the 'adult world'. Children are drawing as it were the 'economic' consequences from their social maturity, which has increased in recent decades, and are claiming a new status as subjects which is not limited to the marginalized and inconsequential arena of childhood after the outdated bourgeois pattern.

It can be seen from the renewed expansion of children's work how the separation of work and school, learning and working, children and adults that took place successively in the capitalist industrial societies is once more being called into question. School as the central sphere of the institutionalization of modern childhood is generally experienced in its present form by children as unsatisfactory and out of touch with real life. This is supported by a Danish study in which 1,200 pupils from the seventh to ninth grades were included: 'About 40 per cent of the pupils do not consider that one is allowed to make use of one's imagination in school, and an equal number say that school does not present any challenges to them. ... A quarter state that school work seldom deals with real life and that the things they are good at do not count in school. Almost half of the pupils say that their interests are difficult to satisfy at school. Half of all the pupils, or even more, want to have the opportunity to work more with their hands' (*Dagens Nyheter*, 15 June 1997, cited in Boyden et al. 1998: 142; see also Frederiksen 1999).

In Germany too attention has been drawn in a number of studies for some years to the fact that children feel school to be out of touch with life and reality. For instance, a qualitative study on 'the dreams, hopes and everyday lives of thirteen- to fifteen-year-olds' in the mid-1980s came to the conclusion 'that school is felt to be meaningless from the point of view of content. In the young people's interpretation, it bears no relation to the current realities of life, neither does it prepare them with concrete knowledge for later [occupational] life. The "lack of meaning" of school becomes apparent in its interpretation by the pupils as a pointless duty: one has to go to school ... without knowing what use the knowledge is that is being laboriously acquired' (Sander and Vollbrecht 1985: 232).

A more recent study by the German Youth Institute (Deutsches Jugendinstitut) on informal learning during leisure time also shows that children attach relatively little importance to school in their daily lives, and that they aspire to 'more serious, goal-oriented activities' in which learning is not the main thing, but 'fun and productive action'. 'As our investigation shows, the main thing is to enjoy the activity. It is also "enjoyable", however, to be responsible for the choice and execution of activities oneself, or to leave the status of child behind one by means of working activities' (Lipski 2001: 105).

But do children have a chance to behave like this in societies in which more and more people have to face being superfluous on the labour market? If we regard children, as is often the case, only as potential labour in the existing capitalist system of paid work, and school only as an institution that prepares them for regulated wage labour, it is super-fluous to pose such a question. It is all too evident that fewer and fewer children will be able to count on such perspectives in life in future. If, however, we see children as subjects who assume tasks that are essential for living and who are already productive in their present phase of life, and help to shape society, the question appears in a different light. Then expanded opportunities for children to play an important and satisfying part in society do indeed become visible.

Children's desire for work and to play an active part in society is to some extent met by restructurings in the 'post-industrial' societies which have been termed 'dismantling of borders in human work' (see Voss 1998). This removal of borders can be observed in the areas of work organization and lifestyle and in the relation between the various forms of work. In the area of work organization, the increasing weight of im-material factors is causing the tying of work to specific chronological and spatial structures to be dissolved, and new 'work roles' are coming into being.

Work is no longer – as in conveyor-belt production – oriented to pro-cesses and goals laid down in detail in advance, but takes place in a relatively unstructured framework of action that has to be structured by the workers acting on their own responsibility. Accordingly, instead of occupational qualifications, subject-centred competences are gaining importance which are neither directed to a particular 'occupation' nor need to, or can, be learned once and for all before entry into the world of work.

The removal of fixed borders in lifestyle becomes apparent in the fact that the separation of work and leisure or gainful employment and private life is being dissolved, so that daily life contains new blends of the hitherto disparate areas.

The elimination of borders between different forms of work can be seen in the way in which the borders between 'dependent' and 'independent' work are becoming blurred, and a variety of transitional forms between exchange-value-oriented paid work and the various forms of utility and community-oriented work are coming into being. The latter forms of work are being upgraded and are being newly experienced and evaluated by many people.

As long as these processes remain within the framework of the capitalist mode of production, they by no means offer a guarantee that the 'owners of the labour capital' (Voss) can now determine their work and lives and use them to their own advantage. On the contrary, they are in danger of merely increasing the availability of 'labour potential' for goals that continue to be determined by others, and of resulting in 'considerably more comprehensive access by employers to people's potential and its use for economic purposes' (Voss 1998: 479). But they also tend to call hierarchical structures and subordination into question, and to strengthen people as subjects.

The development of these processes in their effects on children and the ability of the latter to participate in work that was hitherto the preserve of adults is not yet clearly visible. It can at least be assumed, with Dieter Kirchhöfer, that

- 'the separation of the world of work of the adults will dissolve, and the adult world will open up to or approach children's spheres of life in both time and space;
- occupational qualifications will become less and less a factor as an indicator of separation between childhood and adulthood, cease to be a goal of development separated from the mainstream of life, and thus become questionable in a separate phase of preparation for working life;
- the hitherto separate spheres of work, learning, education and their assignment to particular phases of life will overlap and melt into a

process of learning congruous with the length and breadth of life, and closer to life'. (Kirchhöfer 2000: 221)

It remains open to question whether the restructuring, revaluation and redistribution of work in society will in fact reach the point 'where work activities become increasingly more appropriate to children, or the activities of children become more work-like' (ibid.: 222). But at least the fact that 'the borders between childhood and adulthood are becoming blurred and indistinct' (Jostock 1999: 88) cannot be ignored. The spheres of life and experience of children are no longer thoroughly separated from those of adults, but are becoming blended with them. Educational institutions designed for children have long lost their claim to a monopoly of moulding and shaping the lives of children, and are in – frequently helpless – competition with the world of experience of the media, consumerism and, increasingly, work itself. It is no accident that sociologists today are assigning children a 'right to participation', and countless models are being drafted and tried out to give children the feeling that they can 'have their say' and 'share in running things'. The children's world that has served hitherto in societies of the West as a pattern for a 'happy childhood', cut off from the world of adults and 'smothered with good intentions', appears a thing of the past.

In the early years of the twenty-first century, children's work is 'more suited than almost any other topic to sensitize people to the changed relationship between childhood and adulthood' (Hengst 2000: 73), and the question arises as to the place that children will occupy in the future social and generational division of labour. We certainly cannot take it that a social condition will as it were automatically come about in which children are able to act and gain recognition as independent planners of their present and future lives, possessing equal rights with adults. In order to achieve and guarantee this, it will be necessary that neither children's lives nor those of adults remain tied to and dominated by wage labour under the control of capitalist exploitation interests. A possible way might consist in linking 'the societies of paid work, education, subsistence, domestic work and citizenship' (Böhnisch and Schröer 2001: 190) and integrating the educational institutions into 'social and economic networks of new work' (ibid.: 191). This task cannot fall to the children who are working or seeking work, but is the responsibility of all those who hold the lives of the coming generations as dear as their own.

Notes

1. These two publications give a survey of the extent of children's work and the relevant regulations in several European countries; the second also contains

case studies on Greece, Italy, Portugal and Great Britain. In addition to wage employment, household work and the self-employment of children are dealt with, the two last on a very restricted basis of data, however.

2. These categories follow a suggestion in Rodgers and Standing 1981.

3. Hobbs and McKechnie (1997: 58) see a danger of exploitation of children in the fact that they 'are not recognised as part of the social labour force'.

4. With reference to the following studies: MacLennan et al. 1985; Pond and Searle 1991; Lavalette et al. 1995; TUC 1997; Balding 1997; Hobbs and McKechnie 1997; Rikowski and Neary 1997; O'Donnell and White 1998.

5. 'Domestic work' performed by children was until very recently much neglected in sociological research. There is some coverage in two British and one Australian publication (Brannen 1995; Becker et al. 2001; Goodnow 1988). There is a study from Great Britain dealing with work in family firms, in this case the role of children in businesses run by Chinese immigrants (Song 1996 and 2001).

6. White (1996: 830f) points out that these tendencies are to be encountered worldwide today, and are among the working motives of children in the 'Third World' as well.

7. In addition to the studies discussed below, we may mention another British study in which an attempt was made to relate the perceptions of twelve- to sixteen-year-old children with various characteristics to their work (see McKechnie et al. 1996).

8. The methodological aspects of her journey of discovery are discussed in detail in Solberg 1996.

9. Leonard (1998: 91) notes critically that 'during the major part of the 20th century the perspectives of the children were unmentioned and their contribution to the economy made invisible. The error of this position is increasingly called in question, but it remains the case that much more, above all qualitative research on children's work is urgently required.'

10. In a study of its own on the work of schoolchildren, the British Trades Union Congress comes to the remarkable conclusion: 'school children should be able to work if they want to. But that work needs to be clearly legislated and effectively enforced to protect school children against damage to their health and education and exploitation by unscrupulous bosses' (TUC 1997: 19).

11. Principally, I refer to the discussion in German-speaking countries.

12. From the viewpoint of the position of children within the structure of the generations, of their power or impotence and their disdvantaging, it would be useful to adduce all the conceptions of children's work discussed here. In this sense, Schlemmer (2000: 12f) suggests seeing all activities of children as work from a heuristic angle and asking to what extent they are exploited while performing them.

6 | Working children and adolescents in the USA – juggling school and work[1]

§ IN the USA, in contrast to European countries, children's work undertaken within the country itself is hardly considered a particular problem area. It is largely taken as normal that children do some paid work outside school. 'Amongst adults in the USA ... it is commonly assumed that work is a rewarding experience for the child in that it tells them about the "real world"' (McKechnie 1999: 202). This applies increasingly (again) to forms of non-remunerated work such as domestic work or the performing of tasks within the community.

This relative acceptance of jobs undertaken by one's own children is also reflected in most studies on the topic. They are not so much directed towards warning against the problems of child work and checking that the provisions of the laws relating to the protection of working children are applied,[2] but rather enquire soberly into the advantages and disadvantages that jobs have for children and adolescents. For over twenty years, paid work has been regarded in the scholarly literature too as a 'normal pattern of adolescent development' (Mortimer and Finch 1996).

Most studies concern themselves with the issue of the implications of part-time work undertaken by high school students for social behaviour, success at school, the development of competences and later (working) life. They assume that work can have both positive and negative consequences, and attempt to determine the variables that have an effect in one direction or the other. Their research interest is governed by a kind of balance model that compares the advantages and disadvantages of the work of children and adolescents.[3] The reasons and motives for which children work are rarely enquired into.

Following a survey of the concepts of work employed in US social research, I shall first give an account, in two sections on paid work and household work, of the extent and areas of work undertaken by children, with brief reference to its historical development. In the section that follows, using the scanty existing studies, I shall pursue the issue of the reasons and motives for which children work, and the extent to which connections can be observed between social situation, gender and ethnic contexts on the one hand, and the specific characteristics of the work of children and adolescents on the other. After that, I shall discuss the extensive and partly controversial statements to be found in studies on the effects of work on children. In conclusion, I shall deal with some problematic aspects of social research on children's work and part-time work undertaken by school students in the USA.

What is understood by children's work in US research?

Social research on children's and adolescents' work in the USA concentrates mainly on paid work in the formal labour force. In addition, there are some studies dealing with household work done by children. With one exception, however (Mortimer and Finch 1996, together with partial studies carried out by colleagues), these two forms of work are not thematized coherently. Other forms of work are occasionally mentioned,[4] but not treated as subjects in their own right.

After the Second World War, it took over thirty years before research was initiated into paid work undertaken by children and adolescents. 'Although the emergence of the adolescent student-worker [in the sense of paid work] took place during the 1950s and 1960s, social scientists did not truly discover the phenomenon until the late 1970s' (Steinberg and Cauffman 1995: 132).[5] Studies on the household work of children, on the other hand, had occasionally been carried out before this.

Most of the studies deal – frequently not explicitly – with paid work in the formal labour force. Steinberg and Cauffman (1995: 133) give as a reason for this that 'adolescence has been transformed in modern industrial society from a developmental era defined by production to one mainly of consumption, earning and spending money has become one of the most salient features of the period. For this reason, earning money (and deciding whether and how to spend it) is an extremely significant aspect of the adolescent's work experience, with the potential to affect the young person's attitudes, values, behaviors, and beliefs.' Other forms of work, especially where payment is not involved, are considered, in contrast, as marginal or outdated.

Such reasoning is necessarily accompanied by a limited view of the variety of experience of work of children and adolescents today, and the perspective is largely restricted to instrumental aspects of work experience. Additionally, this research fails to see the fundamental changes that may be taking place in the forms of the course of childhood and adolescence and the generational division of labour. Seeing contemporary US society only as a consumer society in which life is governed by the availability of money, moreover, does not permit aspects going beyond this in the view of·the work of children and adolescents, or thoughts about alternative paths of development.

Up to a point, this problem becomes visible in studies on household work, for instance when the question is posed as to the significance and meaning that this work has or may have for the subjects involved. Thus it is enquired whether this kind of work can be comprehended solely from the points of view of socialization and education, or whether it also – and possibly increasingly – has a meaning in the generational division of labour and the social relation between children and adults (White and Brinkerhoff 1981a). The question as to whether helpfulness is a relevant dimension in this and other forms of the work of children and adolescents (Eberly et al. 1993; Call 1996; Call et al. 1995) also points in this direction.

A further difference in research in both forms of children's and adolescents' work is that they deal with different age groups. Research into household work covers the age range from two to eighteen years, whereas that on paid work is almost wholly restricted to the group of adolescents from sixteen to eighteen years old.[6] Thus this research rarely mentions children's work, child work or child labour, but speaks of teenage work, youth work or youth labour. References to child work and child labour are, with few examples, restricted to some studies on work medicine and social medicine concerned with the accidents, injuries and health hazards of working children.[7]

The authors of the empirical studies do not as a rule take the trouble to give a precise account of their conceptual view of work or children's work, or to provide a theoretical basis for it. Nor do ideas relating to children become apparent on the changing forms of work in post-industrial society or the changing relations between traditional forms of work and activities that were hitherto assigned to 'leisure', the consumer field or educational institutions.[8] Only in studies on household work does a view of children's work become visible which places it in the context of changing relations between the sphere of production and so-called reproduction.

Paid work: its extent and historical development

For some time in the USA, it was assumed that paid work undertaken by children would gradually be displaced by compulsory schooling. And indeed the gainful employment of children did recede step by step up to the mid-twentieth century, interrupted by the years of the First and Second World Wars. It seemed at first as though a form of childhood was becoming established in which work no longer played a part. 'In the 1950s, the primary settings in which adolescent development took place were the family, the peer group, and the school. By the end of the 1970s, the workplace had become a salient and significant context for young people's development, even among those who were enrolled in high school full-time' (Steinberg and Cauffman 1995: 131). The British sociologist Jim McKechnie notes: 'A new pattern emerges which suggests that, while a minority of children combined education and work in the 1940s, it had now become more common for children to combine school and employment' (McKechnie 1999: 200).

According to the data of the US Department of Labor and Bureau of Labor Statistics, in 1980 considerably more children and adolescents were in employment than in the year 1940. Whereas in 1940 the proportion of registered fourteen- to fifteen-year-olds among boys was 3 per cent and among girls 1 per cent of the age group, the corresponding proportions forty years later had risen to 16 and 14.5 per cent respectively. In the case of sixteen-year-olds there is an even greater increase. In this age group 4 and 1 per cent in 1940 contrast with 44 and 41 per cent respectively in 1980 (Greenberger and Steinberg 1986). 'Working while going to school, the exception at the middle of the 20th century, had become the rule as the century drew to a close' (Steinberg and Cauffman 1995: 132).

This 'dramatic rise' (McKechnie) continued during the 1980s, according to an evaluation of official statistical data undertaken by Landrigan et al. (1992).[9] According to this, in 1988 4 million children and adolescents between the ages of twelve and seventeen were registered as employed.[10] Steinberg et al. (1993) talk, with reference to figures of their own for this period, of 'well over 6 million' and explain the discrepancy by stating that only some children and adolescents are statistically covered by the Department of Labor. In addition to these, a considerable number of children are illegally employed.

One of the few studies dealing with the implications of the legal status of working children[11] arrives at the result that, for 1995–97, in an average week an estimated 153,600 children and adolescents were working illegally in the United States, comprising 40,800 sixteen- and seventeen-year-olds, 68,100 fourteen- and fifteen-year-olds, and 44,700 children under fourteen. Most of these young people – 151,000 – were working in non-agricultural employment, with 2,600 in agricultural employment. The total number estimated to have been employed illegally at some point during 1996 is 300,900, of whom 295,800 worked in non-agricultural industries and 5,100 worked in agriculture. In an average week, over 2 million hours of illegal work are estimated to have been performed by these young people, totalling 110 million hours in a year (Kruse and Mahony 2000: 20–1). The authors note that the data probably underestimate the number of illegally employed children in some fields, especially in the apparel, restaurant and meat processing industries ('sweat shops'), and in home-based work for pay.

In more recent studies, which are based on regional surveys of their own and as a rule include boys and girls up to the age of eighteen, it is stressed that 'nearly all the pupils at high schools today work for some time' (Mortimer and Finch 1996: 2). A representative study based on the 1987–88 National Survey of Families and Households found that 70 per cent of sixteen- to eighteen-year-olds had been in paid work during the months preceding the survey, and that 61 per cent of pupils in the tenth grade and 90 per cent of those in the eleventh and twelfth grades had paid jobs at some time during the school year (Manning 1990).

In the mid-1990s, Steinberg and Cauffman (1995: 137) calculated: 'More than 80% of high school students have paying part-time jobs during the school year sometime during their high school career. Approximately 65% of high school students work at some point during any given school year. Approximately 33% of high school students – or more than 2 million American teenagers – are employed at any single moment in time during the school year.'

Similar results were arrived at in a later large-scale survey in Baltimore, Maryland. According to this, at ages thirteen and fourteen, slightly more than half the students worked during the school year, but by age fifteen, employment rates rose to 75 per cent and remained in the 70–80 per cent range thereafter (Entwisle et al. 2000: 283). 'Almost all youths do paid work in high school, and most work during middle school as well' (ibid.: 293; see also Entwisle et al. 1999).[12]

With regard to the demographic characteristics of working children, Kruse and Mahony (2000: 27) conclude that 'white non-Hispanics appear to have been most likely to be working illegally, contrary to popular impressions that illegal employment is concentrated among disadvantaged racial and ethnic minorities. While non-citizens [migrants without US citizenship] were less likely than citizens to be employed, those who were employed were significantly more likely to be working illegally, which may reflect limited mobility and job opportunities among non-citizens.'

The authors properly enquire into the economic consequences resulting from the illegal nature of work. They note that young people working in illegal jobs earned an average of $1.38 less than young adults legally working in those jobs. 'Applied to the total hours figures, the cost savings from all illegal employment of youths was about $2.6 million per week, or $136 million per year; this indicates that legally employed 15–20-year-olds would have been earning about $688 million, or 25% more, in those same jobs' (ibid.: 32–3).

Data from a survey undertaken in 1980 indicate that the average working high school sophomore worked approximately twelve hours per week and the average working senior approximately nineteen hours per week (Steinberg and Cauffman 1995: 138). Comparable figures are reported by Bachman and Schulenberg (1991) for cohorts of employed seniors from 1985 to 1989: the average boy worked between nineteen and twenty hours each week, while the average employed senior girl worked between seventeen and nineteen hours weekly.

Proceeding from the assumption that negative consequences are to be expected for adolescents from a working time of twenty hours a week, several studies investigated how many school students worked more and how many less than twenty hours a week. Amalgating the data this way indicates that approximately one-fifth of employed sophomores, juniors and seniors worked more than twenty hours weekly (Steinberg and Cauffman 1995). A survey of 71,863 high school seniors who work showed that 46 per cent of the boys and 38 per cent of the girls were employed more than twenty hours a week (Bachmann and Schulenberg 1991).

Most studies indicate that the vast majority are employed in the retail and service industries, although there are important differences by region, age and gender. In general, older working students are more likely to hold formal jobs (e.g. retail or food service work) than are younger working students, who are more likely to hold informal jobs (e.g. babysitting, gardening or newspaper delivery). With increasing age, they more commonly work in areas in which adults also work. Working teenagers who live in rural areas are more likely to be employed in agricultural occupations than are their urban or suburban counterparts. Also, boys are more likely to work in manual labour than are girls, who are more likely than boys to work in service positions.

With regard to the areas in which children and adolescents are employed, the existing studies present differing findings. Earlier studies (e.g. Greenberger and Steinberg 1986) reveal that a large proportion of student workers were active in very few kinds of jobs. On the basis of data from the year 1980, it was found that almost half the high school seniors were occupied in two types of job – as restaurant workers and retail store clerks; according to a study from the early 1990s, there were almost 60 per cent in the same jobs (Steinberg et al. 1993). From this, Steinberg and Cauffman (1995: 140) draw the conclusion: 'The nature of work performed by adolescents has changed appreciably over time, with more and more employed adolescents concentrated in fewer and fewer jobs, mainly within the food service and retail service sectors of the economy.'

In contrast to this, recent studies come to the conclusion that there is a 'wide variety and richness of the jobs that students held' (Entwisle et al. 2000: 286). Bidwell et al. (1998: 181) also found a substantial number of adolescents employed in a wide diversity of jobs not usually associated with teenage work. 'The job titles alone span a sizeable portion of the lower white-collar and service sectors of the occupational structure, with blue-collar extensions into the semiskilled realm and white-collar extensions into various kinds of supervisory work, and into media and the arts.' They found that some teenagers are employed in jobs that make serious demands on their talents, skills and self-discipline.

In 'unskilled' jobs, Entwisle et al. (2000: 286–7) found students who worked as 'laborers' on chicken farms, or cut grass, cleaned streets, chopped wood, planted tobacco, paved roads, laid pipes, dug trenches, or loaded freight at the harbour, to name but a few kinds of job. 'Service workers' worked not only in fast-food restaurants,[13] but also as bellmen or housemen at hotels, as deck hands on local ships, at the sports arenas in the city, including the major league baseball park, golf courses, and race tracks. Many service workers had 'artistic' jobs, such as printing T-shirts or painting cars. Substantial percentages of students also worked at 'semiskilled' clerical, sales or craft jobs, even at age thirteen.

Boys and girls are not represented to an equal extent in all fields of work. Up to a point, the traditional gender differences in the division of labour are reproduced in their occupations. But with regard to the rate of student employment as such the gender gap has disappeared. 'Prior to 1950, it was far more likely for male than for female students to hold jobs. By 1980, this was no longer the case. Girls are still just as likely as boys to work' (Steinberg and Cauffman 1995: 140).

Finally, it has to be noted that adolescent employment in the USA has become a more middle-class phenomenon over time. 'Before 1940, the adolescent experience after age 16 was severely bifurcated by social class, with middle-class youngsters focused on school and their less affluent peers in the workforce full-time (Kett 1977). The emergence of the student worker altered this, however, with more and more youngsters of means entering the workplace while remaining enrolled in high school. Today, adolescent employment continues to be a cross-class phenomenon, with middle-class youth in fact slightly more likely to be employed than their poorer peers' (Steinberg and Cauffman 1995: 140–1).

However, other studies point out that, despite the overall reduced number of workers in it, agriculture is a sphere in which work undertaken by children under the age of fourteen is still general. 'Agriculture is also the least regulated sector of the U.S. economy and is one of the few industries where children may engage in work typically performed by adults' (Piotrkowski and Carrubba 1999: 136). With the economic pressures facing many farmers, adolescents and teenage children often fill roles previously held by hired help. As farmers and their spouses take jobs off the farm to supplement income, farm children take on increasing responsibility for farm operations (Pollack et al. 1990: 371; ILO 2002: 26).

A large proportion of the children occupied in agriculture come from families of Latin American origin. It is estimated that about 25,000 children of migrant farmers (aged ten to fifteen) work in the fields (Piotrkowski and Carrubba 1999: 136), some from as young as six years old (Buirski 1994). Migrant and seasonal farmworker families, who have an average annual income of $4,700, are dependent on their children working on the farm (Wilk 1993: 286). Anecdotal evidence suggests that many migrant farmworker children work eight hours per day during the school week, and that many work as many as four hours before the school day starts (Mull 1993). In Florida, 85 per cent of migrant farmworker children do not graduate from high school (Winters-Smith and Larner 1992).

Household work: its extent and significance

As compared with paid work, the household work of children has been little investigated. But today it is generally assumed that children contribute a significant and increasing amount to total household work (see, for example, Lee et al. 2000). White and Brinkerhoff (1981b) found that approximately 86 per cent of boys and 81 per cent of girls between the ages of two and seventeen were regularly required to do chores in the home. Similarly, Cogle and Tasker (1982) found that 88 per cent of children aged six to seventeen performed at least one household chore on a regular basis. All the chores were of a decidedly domestic nature, such as cleaning bathrooms, doing laundry, cleaning dishes, mowing lawns, or food preparation. Another study (Zill and Peterson 1982) reported similar findings. Blair (1992a and b) found in her study that children spend most of their work time on tasks typically associated with the traditional housewife role. Thus meal preparation, washing dishes, cleaning the house and washing and ironing clothes together accounted for 78 per cent of children's work contributions.

Being assigned chores around the house and garden is described by White and Brinkerhoff (1981a: 792) as a developmental process.

In some households it apparently begins very early and, by the time children are 9 or 10, well over 90 percent are involved in regular chores.

Participation tends to fall off slightly in the late teens as adolescents reduce their participation in all family activities, but chores remain a near universal. ... Children begin their involvement in household chores by assuming responsibility for themselves: picking up their own toys, making their own beds, and cleaning up their own rooms. By the time they are 10 years old, however, most children have moved beyond purely self-centered chores and are doing work for their family. As children grow older they move from helping their parents, say by setting the table or folding the clothes, to replacing their parents by assuming full responsibility for some tasks.

The overall amounts of time spent by children on household chores vary considerably from one study to the next. White and Brinkerhoff (ibid.) reported that the median number of hours spent per week on housework was four. Cogle and Tasker (1982) reported an average of 3.5 hours per week. Meanwhile, Sanik (1981) reported that in 1977 children performed an average of 8.4 hours per week of housework, up from a figure of 6.3 for children in 1967. In a piece of rural area research (Lawrence and Wozniak 1987) it was found that the children averaged 7.5 hours per week on household work, mostly on shopping and maintenance of the home, garden, car, and pets.

Blair (1992a) found in her study that children perform approximately 12 per cent of all work done within the home. A children's marketing specialist (McNeal 1999: 71) recently estimates that children in the USA perform 11 per cent of total household work. In an earlier study (Peters and Haldeman 1987) it had been found that school-age children from single-parent families contributed 21.3 per cent of the total time spent on non-physical care in their families, while children in two-parent/one-earner and two-parent/two-earner families contributed 6.1 per cent and 4.7 per cent respectively. The authors conclude: 'The increased relative time spent on household work by children, especially in single-parent families, may foster feelings of shared responsibility among family members' (ibid.: 222). Yet no matter which figure is considered, it illuminates 'the importance of children within the home in regard to household chores' (Blair 1992a: 249).

The distribution of household chores is not entirely equitable. The older children are, the more work they will be assigned, and this is more evident among girls than boys. Girls are likely to perform greater overall amounts of household work than boys (White and Brinkerhoff 1981a and b; Cogle and Tasker 1982; McHale et al. 1990). 'Daughters perform more labor than sons, and their greater labor contributions are disproportionately allocated to those tasks traditionally defined as "women's work"' (Blair 1992b: 201). In Blair's study, it is stated that in those households with only male children, the children's total work is only 4.99 hours per week, which represents only 8 per cent of all work performed in the home, and children average only 3.14 hours per week in female-dominated chores. However, in those households with only female children, the children's total work is 6.70 hours per week and represents 11 per cent of all work, and children average 5.84 hours per week in female-dominated tasks. 'This would seem to indicate a sex-based division of labor is in operation during even the childhood years' (Blair 1992a: 252).

McHale et al. (1990) distinguish in household work between explicitly 'feminine tasks' such as cleaning, washing dishes or cooking and 'masculine tasks', such as home repairs or outdoor work. They arrive at the conclusion that girls were predominantly involved in feminine tasks, but also that boys are involved in these tasks more frequently than in masculine tasks. The authors give as a partial reason for this that the feminine tasks have to be done on a daily basis, whereas 'men's work' is less routine and may have more of a discretionary element. Additionally, the extent of the involvement of boys in feminine tasks depends on the social context: it is particularly high in dual-earner families. At the group level, girls' and boys' patterns of involvement were quite different from those of their mothers and fathers. The relatively high rates of boys' involvement in feminine tasks was in sharp contrast to such task performance by fathers from single-earner families. 'These results suggest that ambiguity about appropriate sex-role behavior, brought about by incongruities between boys' activities and their fathers' sex-role orientations, may be stressful for some boys and may interfere with the sense of competence that normally may arise as a result of sucessfully accomplishing tasks and receiving parental support for doing so' (ibid.: 1,424).

With regard to the rural/urban status of the household, White and Brinkerhoff (1981b) state that rural children exhibit higher levels of involvement in housework than urban children, which may perhaps may be related to the types of work that the children always perform in rural and urban environments respectively. In the study by Blair (1992a), however, it is stated that families living adjacent to metropolitan areas used children to the greatest extent (8.37 hours per week). The author thinks it possible, however, that children in non-metropolitan areas perform more work, but in chores outside the defined boundaries of the measures used in her study. Blair also found that in low-income families the children did a little more work (7.65 hours per week) than in the wealthiest families (6.44 hours per week).

White and Brinkerhoff (1981a) report that approximately 23 per cent of parents surveyed stated that their children assisted them around the home because they needed the help. Other studies have shown that there is a significant increase in children's work in the home when the mother works outside the home (Hedges and Barnett 1972; Propper 1972; Rubin 1983). In particular, Hedges and Barnett (1972: 11) conclude that 'when a mother takes a job, a portion of her chores are shifted to her children rather than to her husband'. Hence, children may represent a greater resource for mothers than fathers. Thrall (1978) concludes that the employment of mothers does, in fact, lead to greater participation by children, as compared to husbands, to make up for the loss of availability of the mother. This result is also confirmed by Blair's study (1992a). She found that in dual-earner families, the number of hours spent outside the home by both parents is associated with an increase in the total work performed by children, as well as an increase in their percentage performance of all work in the home. This is especially true of mothers' employment hours, with children in homes where mothers work forty hours per week or more performing 8.49 hours per week or more of housework, as well as representing 13 per cent or more of all work peformed in the home. 'In a comparison of fathers' and mothers' employment hours, it is readily apparent that children represent a source of potential household labor, in the absence of mothers more so than fathers' (ibid.: 254). The children's household work can be understood more as a source of alleviation for mothers than as a contribution to household chores generally. 'Children are used more when the time of the mother is constrained, as opposed to that of the father' (ibid.: 256; for similar results see recently Greenstein 2000).

Reasons and motives for children's work

Only in a few US studies is attention paid to the reasons and motives for children's work. I shall first present the findings on paid employment, and then those on domestic work.

Landrigan et al. (1992) take the view – not resulting, however, from investigations of their own – that the great increase in the (officially registered) wage labour of children and adolescents since the 1940s is due to the growth in poverty and the increase in the number of immigrants,[14] in connection with the subsequent relaxation of federal enforcement of labour law in the 1980s. Greenberger and Steinberg (1986), on the other hand, see the reason for the large extent of paid work in childhood and adolescence in the fact that these age groups are now targeted as consumers in their own right. Such pressures, coupled with traditional sources of money (e.g. pocket money) not keeping pace with inflation, have resulted in more children looking to employment as a source of money.

Other studies pursue more closely the question of how the paid work of children and adolescents is segmented along socio-demographic lines. Contrary to the widespread assumption that it is primarily children living in poverty and coming from socially disadvantaged families who are engaged in paid work, some large-scale surveys show a lower prevalence of work among minority-group or disadvantaged high schoolers (e.g. D'Amico 1984).

A recent study that traces the children's biographies from starting school in 1982 up to the present comes to the conclusion that employment levels do 'not vary much by family socioenomic status but appear to favor students from the higher-status families' (Entwisle et al. 2000: 283). The rates of employment were significantly higher for whites than for African-Americans. Race was the most consistent predictor of job-holding between the ages of thirteen and seventeen. At age seventeen, students from higher-status families were also more likely to hold jobs (ibid.: 284).

With regard to sixteen- to eighteen-year-old males and females, another study concludes that entry into the labour market is highly dependent on the family resources. However, contrary to theories that suggest that economic need propels youths into the labour force, it is stressed that it is rather factors such as lower household income or unemployment of parents which tend to decrease the odds of youth labour participation. 'The greater the household resources, the more likely a youth is to enter the labor force' (Keithly and Deseran 1995: 486). The fact that the first jobs of young workers are predominantly found in the local economy and are likely to be obtained through family friends is adduced as a reason for this. Thus a higher socio-economic status brings a better range of networks in job searches (ibid.: 486–7; similarly Borman 1991; Campbell et al. 1986). Through such statements, it becomes clear that the debate on paid work by children links up directly with the problem of youth unemployment. The question is no longer whether or for what reasons children have to work, but whether and under what circumstances young people are able to find paid work.

However, caution is necessary in assuming that paid work is of no significance in the case of socially disadvantaged children and adolescents. In the study by Entwisle et al. (2000: 284), 'compared to whites, African Americans reported equal or greater job-seeking effort but lower rates of obtaining the jobs they applied for'. A comparable situation applies to the regularity of work. Among the consistent workers, there were more whites than African-Americans. The majority of the latter worked irregularly (43 per cent) or not at all (11 per cent), which was attributed to the fact that they have to content themselves with less attractive occasional jobs, or encountered greater difficulties in the search for work. 'Lower-status youngsters may not be able to get jobs as easily as higher-status youngsters – fewer lower-status than higher-status youths held jobs at every stage. Lower-status youths "work less" in this sense; but when they do work, they work more intensively. ... Youngsters whose families were most financially stressed worked the greatest number of hours' (ibid.: 292).

The study by Entwisle et al. is distinguished from other studies by its more discriminating perspective. It does not restrict itself to enquiring why children and adolescents work, but investigates possible connections between social status and the nature of the work. In doing so, it arrives at the remarkable conclusion that African-Americans and economically disadvantaged students carry out semi-skilled jobs at an earlier age (thirteen to fourteen) than whites, but that they 'get stuck' predominantly in unskilled jobs with increasing age (from fifteen).

Entwisle et al. not only observe that socio-economic status affects the nature and conditions of work, but also presume that middle-class youngsters are in paid work for quite different reasons to children and adolescents from poor families. In their study, they found that 'students from lower-status families more often than those from higher-status families gave their earnings to the family "to help support the household" or used the money they earned to pay for necessary school supplies' (ibid.: 292). Among seventeen-year-olds, for instance, 58 per cent of the lower-status students stated that they supported their families with their earnings, while the proportion was only 15 per cent among the higher-status youngsters. Therefore, Entwisle et al. concluded, the length of working time must also be seen in relation to the reasons for which the students work.[15] This specific detail has frequently been ignored in research hitherto.

Call (1996), in her study carried out together with Mortimer and Finch, found that among ninth- to twelfth-grade high school students only between 6 and 15 per cent gave their earnings directly to the family. However, substantial minorities of them used their pay in other ways that were helpful to economically hard-pressed parents: between 26 and 54 per cent bought school supplies; 22 to 50 per cent saved their money for their future education; and 27 to 44 per cent saved for other investment purposes. Some parents indicated that they appreciated their employed children's ability to purchase things that they wanted them to have but could not afford. Adolescents were equally likely to give money to their families and to save money for future schooling and other investments.

Revealing findings on the connections between social situation and children's work were also contained in a further study dealing with the reasons for and consequences of illegal child work. According to this, the percentage of all children who worked illegally at some point in 1996 did not vary much (or significantly) over the income categories. But the illegally employed children from poor families made an essential contribution to pulling their families out of poverty. In the absence of illegal child employment, 18.4 per cent of the families would have been at or below the poverty line; with illegal child employment, the percentage was 15.7 per cent, implying that illegally employed children pulled 2.7 per cent of their families out of poverty status. In contrast, legally employed children were less likely to be in poverty before or after their employment, and the income from their employment pulled 1.7 per cent of them out of poverty status. 'In short, poverty does not appear to have been a major factor pushing youths into illegal employment, but illegal employment may have been somewhat more important than legal employment in pulling the families of these youths out of poverty' (Kruse and Mahony 2000: 30).

As in the case of paid work, most research in the area of household work has investigated the impact of work experiences on children's psychological well-being or development, while few attempts have been made to explain their participation. Nevertheless, there are two competing explanations of the participation of children in household work, one proposing that parents assign chores to children as a socializing experience, and the second positing that parents use children as a labour source when an increase in the need for household work arises.

The first explanation, emphasizing the commitment of the parents to the growth and development of their children, is largely related to the general concept of children and childhood in the United States. As Zelizer (1994) describes, children have moved from being seen as 'economically useful' to being seen as 'emotionally priceless'. Given the 'priceless child' imagery, it became more likely that parents would look upon children's assistance with chores in the home as being an essential part of the development of their personal qualities, such as a sense of responsibility, self-esteem or autonomy. Housework performed by children has therefore become more of an instructional or educational tool for parents. Thus, in the study by White and Brinkerhoff (1981a), 72 per cent of the parents questioned supported the contributions of their children in the home in the following terms: 'Work gives them a sense of responsibility. Makes them appreciate what they have. I think it helps them grow into responsible adults.' However, it needs to be asked whether such reasons are perhaps not the whole truth, but also conceal an economic interest in the labour potential of their children.

The competing explanation for children's contribution to household work focuses on those family/structural variables that might alter the demand for household work. It proposes that children are used as a source of work in the home when the household work requirements exceed the available or willingly granted time of the adult members of the home; in other words, children will tend to be used when the time available to parents becomes constrained or limited.

Indeed, a number of studies show that the social situation of the family has effects on taking advantage of the labour potential of children in household work (on previous research see Goodnow 1988). Thus the study of Call et al. (1995: 135) shows 'that adolescents from larger families, with less financial resources, and whose mothers are employed, take on more household responsibilities' and so 'respond to economic and other family need'. White and Brinkerhoff (1981a: 794) suggest: 'Families with working mothers or single parents are more likely to say that they ask their children to work because the work needs to be done and they need the help.' Blair, too, comes to the conclusion in her study (1992a: 257) that the number of wage earners in the home and in particular the number of hours spent weekly by mothers in the paid labour force have an influence on the participation of children in household work. 'Children would appear to be utilized more as a labor source in those situations where the adult members, particularly the mother, are otherwise not available to perform the chores themselves. It would thus seem that children are assigned household labor tasks more for pragmatic reasons by parents rather than for concerns about their development of proper values or the like.'

This is by no means a trivial matter in regard to the implications for children. 'Given the escalating prominence of dual-earner families, children may be increasingly used as a source of "replacement labor" within the home. That is, children may now be used to perform those chores, particularly female-dominated areas of tasks, which adults in the home formerly fulfilled, but now either abandon, postpone, or assign to others' (ibid.: 257). This duality of parental treatment of children seems to result 'in a decrease in the differences between adult and child roles in the family. Hence, childhood itself may be undergoing a transition not unlike that which occurred early in this [the twentieth] century' (ibid.: 257).

However, the question arises as to whether the increased inclusion of children in domestic work can be seen only from the viewpoint of an increase in duties. Neither the assumption that children are involved in housework from motives of upbringing nor the assumption that this derives from structural conditions – that is, from urgent needs – perceives the children as acting subjects. Both explanations are based on the assumption 'that children are assigned to tasks or are, at the very minimum, supervised in their household duties by their parents. Quite simply, children are not looked upon as performing housework for altruistic or individual reasons beyond the desire to comply with the parents or to satisfy them in a direct fashion' (Blair 1992a: 242–3).

An additional perspective on children's work comes from the broader literature on the meanings of work. With reference to adult work, Menninger (1964: xiv) characterized the sociological approach as a recognition that 'work is a method of relating meaningfully to the family and the community – a group process by which the individual becomes an entity, but, at the same time, is identified with the group'. Application of this idea to children's work suggests that the participation of children and adults in household tasks may contribute to increased family solidarity and mutual recognition and respect.

In this respect, two studies that concerned themselves expressly with the issue of the conditions under which the voluntary helpfulness of adolescents in the family context takes place (Eberly et al. 1993) and what implications this may have for the development of competences (Call et al. 1995; Call 1996) show notable findings.

Eberly et al. first observe with reference to two earlier studies (Eisenberg et al. 1991; Skarin and Smoely 1976) that girls are generally observed to be more helpful than boys. In their own study, too, which relates to ten- to fifteen-year-olds, parents reported that daughters helped them more often than did sons. Furthermore, mothers reported that they received more help than did fathers. In general, there was a decrease in helpfulness between late childhood and middle adolescence, with the exception of the mother–daughter relationship, in which no decrease was found. Finally, perhaps the most revealing finding was that there was a positive relationship between perceptions of parental acceptance and reports of adolescent helpfulness. In other words, the readiness of adolescents to assist their parents is not an inherent feature of a particular age, but results from the way in which the parents relate to their children. In this sense, 'adolescent helpfulness toward parents provides another window for viewing changes in parent–adolescent relations' (Eberly et al. 1993: 241).

In their study, Call et al. (1995) pursue the issue of the conditions under which the inclusion of children in the economic activities of the family leads to a 'sense of competence' or 'sense of mastery'. In contrast to former descriptive studies (e.g. White and Brinkerhoff 1981a and b), they offer a theoretical model linking the context of adolescent helpful acts with their meaning for self-perception. They found that performing household chores is related to a lower sense of competence only for white boys, who may view household chores as bothersome and lacking value. For girls, the negative effect of household chores on competence was present only when the father–daughter relationship was not supportive and when the mother's manner of allocating tasks diminished the girl's autonomy. They come to the conclusion that 'whereas helpfulness may be situationally required, its effects depend on the helpful act's meaning, as contextually constructed, as well as the motivation of the actor. ... The person's action may have to be voluntaristic to invoke positive developmental conquences; helping can then be more readily attributed to one's own agency, increasing self-competence' (Call et al. 1995: 136).

Costs and benefits of children's work

In US social research, possible effects of the experience of work by children and adolescents are soberly balanced against each other in terms of cost and benefits.

Following the founding of the National Child Labor Committee (NCLC) in 1904, there were up until the 1950s recurring initiatives such as the back-to-school movement which strove for the abolition of any kind of child work before the end of schooling. Since the 1970s, however, working, at least for the high school age group, has again been regarded positively. Government panels such as the 1974 President's Science Advisory Committee Panel on Youth and the 1980 National Commission on Youth emphasized the benefits of employment and that efforts should be made to combine work and school experiences. 'Work was perceived as a force to socialize the young person into the adult role, developing independence and responsibility, and enhancing positive work attitudes and realism in the choice of career' (McKechnie 1999: 204).

In the 1970s, several publications, such as that of Stephens (1979), proclaimed the developmental benefits of adolescent employment. Some authors (Firestone 1970; Farson 1974; Holt 1974) even demanded a 'right to work' or a 'right to economic power' for children, to promote their independence and equal rights. The psychologist and advocate of children's rights Richard Farson argued that from the income resulting from their own work children 'stand to gain not only financial rewards, but the dignity which derives from work and achievement. With it will come a new measure of respect from the adults, and more importantly, a new measure of respect for themselves' (Farson 1974: 155). John Holt, who was a teacher for many years, criticized the way in which school prevents children from being able 'to make contact with the larger society around them, and, even more, to play any kind of active, responsible, useful part in it' (Holt 1974: 26). In his view, 'if we expected more from children, and they for themselves, they would be able to learn much more about the world around them, much more quickly, than they do now' (ibid.: 97; on the debate on children's rights in the USA at that time, see Liebel 2001g: 331–5).[16]

During the early 1980s warning voices again arose. In particular the research team working with psychologists Ellen Greenberger and Laurence Steinberg voiced concern about the potential costs of school-year employment for youngsters' development and education and suggested that the putative benefits of working for adolescent personality development might have been overstated. These authors argued that working long hours (generally, more than fifteen hours weekly) was associated with diminished school performance, an increase in anti-social activity, including drug and alcohol use and school misconduct, higher levels of deviant behaviour, cynicism towards work, and tolerance of unethical business practices among workers. Finally, they expressed concern about the impact of adolescent employment on parent–adolescent relations, in particular the erosion of parental authority (Greenberger and Steinberg 1980; Steinberg and Greenberger et al. 1981a and b; Steinberg and Greenberger et al. 1982; Greenberger and Steinberg 1986).

As the 1980s drew to a close, 'research on adolescent employment increased in frequency and in sophistication. By 1989, it had become clear that the question of whether adolescents benefit from working or are harmed by it was far too simple. Rather, this question was replaced by a series of questions concerning the conditions under which working was beneficial, harmful, or inconsequential' (Steinberg and Cauffman 1995: 143). These conditions included, for example, the number of hours of weekly employment (work intensiveness), the type of work performed (work quality), and the nature of the link between work and other aspects of the adolescent's life.[17]

Irrespective of their postulate of a more discriminating procedure, however, even in the 1990s Steinberg and his collaborators kept to the view that undertaking jobs, especially if the working hours are long (twenty hours or more per week) and the work involves few qualifications, entails a number of problems for vocational development and psychological adjustment. They admit 'that young people may learn certain practical skills and work habits from employment that might not be so easily acquired in school' (ibid.: 155). Among the most important of these skills they mention interpersonal competences such as how to deal with customers, how to get along with fellow workers, and those involving knowledge about the world of work, including some understanding of such things as how a business works or how to find a job. But, on the other hand, they state that, generally, working leads to undesirable social and work habits, makes young people more individualistic, increases anti-social behaviour, including aggression, negatively affects self-reliance and self-esteem, and has a (modest) negative impact on adolescents' physical health and well-being (Steinberg and Dornbusch 1991; Steinberg et al. 1993; Steinberg and Cauffman 1995; Steinberg and Avenevoli 1998).[18]

In contrast, other authors argue 'that limiting our focus to the quantity of part-time employment provides both a negative and truncated perspective of the nature and the consequences of teenagers' part-time employment. Essentially, this approach casts employment in the role of the villain, inasmuch as only the costs and none of the benefits of part-time employment are emphasized' (Barling et al. 1995: 144). They point out that even the most obvious benefit of an increase in the quantity of employment, increased personal income, has acquired a negative connotation in that only a small minority of teenagers report spending their earnings on living expenses or saving for their future education.

In sharp contrast, these authors suggest that work is not a homogeneous experience for all employed teenagers and that subjective experiences of work are critical in understanding the consequences of work. Assessing subjective experiences enables them to see 'meaningful effects on productivity and psychological well-being, adult development and family and personal functioning' (ibid.: 144). In their study, they come to the conclusion that employment quality significantly moderates the amount of part-time work and is more important than employment quantity alone for predicting its consequences for working adolescents. Particularly, they come to the conclusion that 'employment quantity was positively associated with self-esteem when autonomy and role clarity were high' (ibid.: 151). However, in order to ascertain the quality of the work and to understand its psychological effects, account must also be taken of skill variety, task significance, task identity and feedback.

In one of the few studies dealing with both paid work and household work,[19] it was found that early work experience fosters self-competence, 'when supervisors behave toward adolescents in a manner that is consistent with their desire and need for independence' (Call 1996: 90–1). An important variable turned out to be whether the adolescents were able to see their own work as 'helpful for others'. This was particularly the case when their work had been valued by adults and contributed to the welfare of their family and they were allowed some measure of autonomy in carrying out the tasks.

Today there is a consensus among most of the researchers in the USA that at least a moderate quantity of work hours in relatively light or higher-quality jobs can bring benefits for children. It is assumed that this can contribute to promoting both their self-confidence and their gaining of independence from the family, and produce personalities that act effectively and responsibly and can cope better with difficult situations in life. 'Because of work during the first years at high school, the social self-conception clearly grows, because the power and autonomy that result from money earned by one's own work have grown' (Marsh 1991: 186). Even for less ambitious jobs, it is suggested that they can be a source of practical knowledge relating to real life (Green 1986 and 1990). Job experience in adolescence, particularly when it 'provides an opportunity to use and develop valuable skills', is seen as an important source of human capital that increases the likelihood of employment later on (Stern and Eichorn 1989: 208). 'It enables young people to accumulate personal resources that have value in the labor market' (Entwisle et al. 2000: 280). Particularly for minority and economically disadvantaged urban youth, job experience in adolescence 'can add to human capital and may improve opportunities for employment' (ibid.: 293–4).

Mortimer and Johnson (1998b) arrived at similar conclusions in a recent longitudinal study. They found 'that young people who were employed for relatively long periods of time at low intensity during high school have quite favorable outcomes with respect to schooling (for men) and part-time work (for both genders). Male and female high-intensity high school workers move into the full-time labor force more quickly, and boys have higher earnings. For women, very restricted employment in high school (none or low-duration, low-intensity employment) is associated with more post-secondary unemployment' (ibid.: 471).

In one study on the effects of work on orientations for the future (Stevens et al. 1992), significant differences between boys and girls are found. The longer the work experience, the more positive the effects on the education plans of boys. Boys who have already worked for some time also attach 'greater importance to the future relations to wives and children, as well as to parents and other relatives', tending to give preference to a traditional role distribution between men and women (ibid.: 162). In the case of girls, by contrast, experience of work tends rather to call the traditional distribution of roles into question. They tend to postpone marriage and to reduce the demands made on them by the family. Boys with longer work experience also anticipate playing a more active part in their community.

The authors of a study about the household work of rural children reflect on the relationship between children's experiences of housework and their preparation for the future. They suggest that many of the skills needed in the adult workplace 'can be acquired through participation in household tasks. At the very least, children could benefit from doing more for themselves and perhaps, in the process, help alleviate time pressures at home through a more balanced distribution of the workload among family members' (Lawrence and Wozniak 1987: 936).

In the USA, particular attention is paid to the effects of part-time paid work on children's attainments at school. Some studies have found a relationship between intensive work (fifteen to twenty hours per week) and negative educational outcomes (e.g. Steinberg et al. 1993; Steinberg and Cauffman 1995). But most studies agree that negative effects cannot be ascribed to 'work as such' (Marsh 1991: 86). It is also not considered sufficient to pay attention only to the number of hours worked. More significant is the 'quality of the employment' (Markel and Frone 1998: 285) and whether the school takes account of the work interests and experience of the students.

A further question that is discussed controversially relates to the relation of cause and effect. Some researchers point out that statements about the supposed effect of work on academic performance are based only on simple statistical correlations, and that the other, perhaps more influential variables take too little account of the biographies and the social environment of adolescents. What appears to be the 'effect' of work may be traced back to preceding selection effects (on the debate on 'selection versus socialization', see Steinberg and Cauffman 1995; Mortimer and Johnson 1998a: 201).

In one recent study, for example, it is suspected 'that the predominant causal process linking youth work to poor school performance is that poor-performing students lose interest in school and are more willing to spend long hours on the job' (Entwisle et al. 2000: 293). From study of their biographies, the authors arrived at the conclusion that many students who started working at age thirteen were less strongly attached to school long before they began paid work. In particular in the case of lower-status students, grade failure and early school disengagement seem to lead them 'to channel their energies toward work as an alternative arena for success' (ibid.: 292).

In view of the widespread interest in work, it is also seen as 'unrealistic to limit the employment of high school students' (Markel and Frone 1998: 285). Instead, it is claimed more effort should be made to render school timetables more flexible and to make possible more interesting and varied job experience 'in order to increase the positive consequences of employment and decrease the negative ones during adolescence' (ibid.: 285). For the same reasons, teenagers should be given more access to jobs 'that provide opportunities for autonomy and skill variety' (Barling et al. 1995: 153; similarly Stern and Eichorn 1989: 208–9; Loughlin 1999: 22). Another author finds it necessary 'to integrate work and school experiences more fully, so the work experience is perceived to be a natural extension of school' (Marsh 1991: 186). As the conclusion of a comparative study of adolescents' perceptions of 'school-supervised' and 'non-school supervised' work, it is proposed 'that schools should take a more active role in adolescent employment', facilitating work that is meaningful, and where students can learn responsibility and problem-solving, can make greater use of academic skills and have more contact with adults (Stone et al. 1990: 48).

Mortimer and Johnson (1998a), too, give as the conclusion of a study on the topic of high school students' views of the relationship between school and work: 'Since more than half the seniors (54 per cent) acknowledged that "my job has taught me the importance of getting a good education", it would seem that working students, in fact, do recognize the connection between work and school and may be particularly responsive to teachers' efforts to further integrate these dimensions of their lives by enabling working students to draw on their experiences on the job in class. Such efforts may be especially productive, given criticisms of what goes on in school as not being relevant to "real life"' (ibid.: 203).

In only a few US studies is attention paid to the children's and adolescents' own perceptions and interpretation of their experiences (exceptions to this are the qualitative studies of Green 1986 and 1990; Mortimer and Finch 1996; Mortimer and Johnson 1998a and b). An earlier study by Mortimer and Finch (1996), based on a representative sample of high schools, found that the majority of part-time workers felt that their work was 'almost always' meaningful and that they perceived a value in their work. And even in an earlier study by Greenberger and Steinberg (1986), it was remarked – even if by the way – that the majority of the adolescents felt that they made a satisfying contribution to the production of goods and services.

A critical stock-taking

For thirty years, social research on working children and adolescents in the United States has been marked by the debate as to whether work experience bring costs or benefits for children and adolescents. Meanwhile, research findings are up to a point influenced by political vicissitudes.

During the 1970s, the debate was closely linked with a critique of the existing school system, which was reproached with making children insufficiently familiar with social reality, and with preparing them inadequately for their working lives. Therefore work experience during school attendance was predominantly positively evaluated, and numerous reform proposals – including some by government committees – for the school system were submitted, in which it was suggested that students be given wider working experience. This was also intended to open up hitherto untapped reserves of talent among the lower classes and ethnic minorities, who up until then had been disadvantaged by the school system. In addition, as shown above, the work of children was advocated in terms of their equal rights and emancipation in society.

In the 1980s, a reorientation took place. The interest of most research workers was now more strongly determined by the fear that (excessively) early work experience could lead to negative consequences for success at school and for social behaviour. The background to this was twofold. On the one hand, the number of children and adolescents who were looking for or already performing a job during school time and regarded this as a right had grown rapidly. On the other, the 'political wind' had turned in another, rather conservative, direction, drawing attention to the supposed bad behaviour of the new generation. Instead of rendering new experiences possible for young people and promoting their independence, the predominant social interest was now directed more strongly to adapting children and adolescents to existing institutions and to control them socially.

However, in US social research there were always other voices, and in the 1990s interest increased again in balancing the advantages and disadvantages of work experience for children. The negative evaluations were more intensively called into question (e.g. selection hypothesis against development hypothesis). What was involved was now no longer, or no longer mainly, work as such or the time devoted to work, but the 'quality' of work and the circumstances under which children and adolescents take up and perform a job were more carefully considered.

Scepticism towards generalized views increased, and more discrimination was adopted in research methodology.

Studies on paid and household work ran parallel without being related to each other. Other forms of work were not studied. The investigations relate to very different age groups, and in studies on paid work have a clear emphasis on high school students aged sixteen to eighteen years. Studies on household work, by contrast, relate also to younger age groups. The distinction is rarely made between children and adolescents who are in paid work outside school, and those for whom the paid work – partly because of the precarious economic situation of their families – has become their predominant activity. The few studies on paid work undertaken by younger children remain fixed in a victim perspective and exhaust themselves largely in an anecdotal listing of abuses. Only occasionally does reflection on the subjective conditions of work experience take place with attempts to take account of the perspectives of the children and adolescents, and here in turn almost only in studies on household work.

Even where – as frequently in research on paid work – the costs and benefits of work are drawn up and contrasted with the intention of making distinctions clearer, the children's subjective interpretations are hardly ever taken into consideration (Levison 2000: 126; Zelizer 2002: 377). The criteria on which the evaluations are based are generally derived from theories, or are based on assumptions, that have little or nothing to do with the perspectives and self-interpretations of the children and adolescents themselves.

Most studies in the 1980s, and also a number dating from the 1990s – mostly carried out by psychologists – are implicitly oriented in their evaluations to a development model that sees childhood and adolescence as a 'psychosocial moratorium'. According to this, work in childhood and adolescence is a deviation from the norm, associated with negative consequences. According to this model, 'early' work experience leads necessarily to limitations in development or to unfortunate developments that are, for instance, criticized as 'precociousness'.

In the 1990s, when studies were more frequently carried out by sociologists, and occasionally also by economists, the labour market and human capital perspective gains influence. The question of what effects the work experience of children and adolescents has on their competences which may be relevant for monetary gain, their future status, and their opportunities on the (paid) labour market is asked.

The labour market perspective takes a particular view of children, envisaging them as essentially innocent, ignorant of the world and incompetent to fend off its evils or even to recognise their own best interest. They are depicted as helpless victims, dependent on protection and rescue by adults. This is primarly a modern Western urban, middle-class notion of childhood. This notion is historically and anthropologically unusual, not only for the radical division it draws between childhood and adulthood, but also for valuing children's helpfulness rather than usefulness. (Myers 2001: 31)

The human capital perspective 'focuses more positive attention on working children as unrealised potential for economic development – potential worth investing in – rather than merely as victims, labour law violaters and employment threats' (ibid.: 35). This approach fails, however, to see working children and adolescents as subjects or social actors any more than the labour market approach. Children and adolescents are rather considered as vessels to be filled with suitable contents, with a view to their later use as labour potential.

The children are almost never interviewed themselves, and hardly ever play an active part in the research designs. Even rarer are qualitative studies that attempt to do justice to the perspective of the children. One of the few studies in which this is done is a dissertation (Green 1986), still unpublished but for a brief summary article (Green 1990).

Therefore, most studies, despite their great quantity of data, do justice only to a limited extent to the significance of work in the lives of children. The perspective 'that dominates orthodox accounts of childhood inevitably leads towards a failure to acknowledge that children's actions are meaningful in their own terms or that children are purposeful social actors' (Mizen et al. 1999: 426). Only when working children cease to be regarded solely from the viewpoint of what they may become or what they lack to become competent adults will it be possible to see the 'value' and the meaning of the various kinds of work in their full complexity both for society and for the children.

Only then would it become apparent that working children and adolescents have always resisted, and are able to resist, circumstances that they feel to be unjust. In the highly readable historical study by David Nasaw (1985), many actions and organizational initiatives by newsies, messengers and shoeshine boys in New York and other cities in the USA are described, but the account is restricted to the first twenty years of the past century. One of the rare recent examples mentioned concerns some high school students employed by a chain restaurant in a small West Virginia town. In 1987 they joined together to negotiate with the management – without success, however – to stop keeping them past midnight on school nights, and were supported in this by their parents. However, this example is used by the researchers (Pollack et al. 1990: 366) only to emphasize the misuse of the children.

It is by no means to be denied that there is meaning in investigating the exploitation and abuse of children and taking steps against it. However, this not only requires perceiving working children and adolescents as 'social actors', but also interpreting their working experience in its social, cultural and historical context. And this hardly ever happens in the US studies. The objective causes and subjective motives of the children's and adolescents' work are not sufficiently closely studied, nor are the possible effects of their work related to the conditions of production and the interests that govern the economy. Abuses and practices offending against human dignity are frequently pointed out in the studies, but there are no analyses that investigate the fundamental reasons for the exploitation of children. The only publication known to me that deals explicitly with the problem of exploitation (Piotrkowski and Carrubba 1999) confines itself to reproducing the criteria formulated by the International Labour Organization (ILO) with regard to the Third World (for a critique of these criteria, see Chapter 7). Attention is rarely paid in the studies to the living conditions of the children and adolescents, and when this is done it relates almost exclusively to the socialization and development of the children.

Under these conditions, US social research, despite its great breadth, makes only a limited contribution to understanding the meanings that the various forms of work have in the lives of US children and adolescents today. As in Europe, to what extent the palpable increase in the number of working children and adolescents signifies epoch-making changes in childhood and the relations between the generations still remains to be investigated.

Notes

1. This is the title of an essay by the Canadian labour market researcher Deborah Sunter (1992).

2. Exceptions are some publications in medical and legal specialist journals (e.g. Pollack et al. 1990; Landrigan et al. 1992; Wilk 1993; Moskowitz 2000). In one recent study it is noted: 'No systematic information is available on how many children in the United States work in violation of child labor laws, or on the causes and consequences of illegal child labor' (Kruse and Mahony 2000: 18).

3. The model is discussed in Mortimer and Finch 1996; Hobbs and McKechnie 1997; IWGCL 1998.

4. Steinberg and Cauffman (1995: 133) name as examples 'informal work

in the neighborhood, such as occasional lawn-mowing or babysitting; unpaid volunteer work for community organizations; unpaid work that is connected to an educational program, such as work study or cooperative education; paid work in a family-owned business; paid work in a government-orchestrated employment and training program'. Many further examples, above all in the informal economy, could have been added.

5. Steinberg and Cauffman add in brackets following this sentence: 'Adults' interests often lag behind those of young people', thus admitting – probably unintentionally – that research on the paid work of children and adolescents is almost entirely dictated by the interests of adults.

6. 'Child labor for children under age 15 generally has not been a focus of attention' (Piotrkowski and Carrubba 1999: 135). Exceptions are to be found mostly in longitudinal studies, e.g. in Entwisle et al. (2000), in which the authors pursue the biographies of the children from their thirteenth year at least; or in epidemiological studies tracing the health hazards and injuries to children at work (e.g. Landrigan et al. 1992; Wilk 1993).

7. 'The risks of injury, illness, and toxic exposure associated with child labor appear to pose a significant public health problem, but they have only begun to be explored' (Pollack et al. 1990: 361).

8. On Europe, see the articles by Qvortrup 2001; Hengst 1998 and 2000; Kirchhöfer 1998; and Chapter 5 of the present book. Hengst interestingly makes a link to studies by US work and culture researchers (Wadel 1979; Toffler 1980; Csikszentmihalyi 1979) which, however, have not been taken up in social research about children's and adolescents' work. In the Canadian writer Naomi Klein's account (2000) of the 'global players' there are numerous examples of new forms of children's work within the American school system; however, she too does not identify them as 'work'.

9. Loughlin (1999: 19) too emphasizes: 'The part-time employment of young people has increased significantly since the 1980s, both in relative and absolute terms.' Mihalic and Elliott (1997: 465) speak of an 'explosion in teen-age employment'.

10. Approximately ten years later, there were 4,090,000 (Moskowitz 2000).

11. The Fair Labor Standards Act, enacted in 1938, remains the major federal legislation governing child labour in the USA. It established that no child under the age of sixteen may work during school hours, and a ceiling is set on the number of hours of employment permissible for each school day and each school week. Employment in any hazardous non-agricultural occupation is prohibited for anyone under eighteen years old. Thus, no one under eighteen may work in mining, logging, brick and tile manufacture, roofing or excavating, as a helper on a vehicle or on power-driven machinery. Meat processing machinery, delicatessen slicers and supermarket box-crushers are especially prohibited. In agriculture, where the restrictions are much less stringent, hazardous work is prohibited only until age sixteen, and all work on family farms is totally exempted. According to the law, however, no child under sixteen working on a non-family farm is allowed to drive a tractor or to handle or apply pesticides and herbicides.

12. The conclusion that 'it is therefore feasible to argue that working for

payment is a common experience for children in the USA' (McKechnie 1999: 201) takes too little account of the fact that few US studies include in their data children under the age of sixteen or pre-high school children.

13. This was a widespread assumption in research in the 1980s.

14. 'Vast immigration into the United States over the past decade, much of it illegal, has created large populations of vulnerable children who are all too easily exploited by unscrupulous employers' (Landrigan 1993: 268).

15. Loughlin (1999: 31) draws attention to the difference between 'full-time students working part-time, and individuals who have either completed high school or dropped out of high school without obtaining any postsecondary education. These two groups seek employment for different reasons, work for different amounts of time each week, may well obtain different quality jobs, and probably spend the money they earn differently.'

16. John Holt's thoughts are in the tradition of the American psychologist and educationist John Dewey, who was influential above all in the first half of the twentieth century (see Dewey 1916/1936; Fishman and McCarthy 1998).

17. At the same time, from a recent research review, Frone (1999: 120) draws the conclusion: 'In comparison to other domains of adolescent life (i.e. school, peer group, and family), we know relatively little about the impact of employment on adolescent development.'

18. This is contradicted by other statements in earlier studies by the same authors, e.g. that working by adolescents can have a positive impact on such socio-cognitive skills as awareness of others and the capacity to handle a number of social situations. In their studies working children, at least in more qualified and less routine jobs, have been shown to have a better understanding of social relationships and were able to accommodate the views and roles of others (Steinberg et al. 1981a and b; Steinberg et al. 1982).

19. It was carried out by a research team headed by Jeylan Mortimer (see Mortimer and Finch 1996).

7 | Work and play in the lives of children: reflections on an unfortunate separation and possible connections

§ THE exclusively negative evaluation of children's work customary in 'modern' Western societies includes the idea that children ought to play rather than work. According to this idea, play and work are contrasting forms of human activity. By contrast, we know from ethnological studies of non-Western societies that in them work and play were not separated, any more than children from adults. Under the impact of the negative consequences that the separation of children from the world of adults and of work brings with it, in contemporary Western societies too the dichotomy of work and play is being increasingly questioned, and new relations are being sought.

After surveying and commenting critically on theories of children's play that have come into being in Western bourgeois societies since the Enlightenment, I shall give an account of some findings from ethnological studies on non-Western societies. In conclusion, I shall discuss some aspects of the present-day relation between play and work in contemporary Western societies.

Theories of children's play

In Western theories of play, playing was long thought of as the typical alternative to work appropriate to the child. Children's play is, meanwhile, not necessarily thought of as an expression of the children's own lives and views; what is considered is whether and to what extent it contributes to 'educating' children, 'developing' them, and 'socializing' them for adult society.[1] 'Child's play' is, in this view, accounted a privileged area of 'normalizing' intervention and does not necessarily correspond to the experiences and meanings that the children themselves attach to the activities that are defined by adult theoreticians as 'play'.

Since the Enlightenment, play has been ascribed particular significance in educational processes. In the educational climate of the Enlightenment, play was regarded as the hitherto missing link between nature and culture, passion and reason, primitiveness and civilization. 'It pointed back to the animal origins and at the same time forward to the highest form of development of humanity. It could thus be enlisted for the educational task of freeing children from enslavement by their lower instincts and putting them in a state of moral and spiritual enlightenment that was to be attained through the "higher" power of reason' (Cohen 1994: 54). Playing was thought of as a 'natural' predisposition and particular characteristic of the 'noble savage', which could easily also be ascribed to children, women and the lower orders, who were thought of as 'primitive' or 'unreasonable'. Common to them was thought to be 'the inability to make work out of play, to discipline the capricious lusts of the body in the service of reason and society' (ibid.: 54).[2] To call a particular kind of action play thus meant considering it second rate. Only actions declared to be work were of 'serious' importance.

The most persistent and popular theories today are still those 'that attempt to localize play on a particular "level" of behaviour both in the development of the self and in that of society' (ibid.: 51f). According to the so-called recapitulation theory first presented by the American psychologist Stanley Hall in 1880, the child, in the process of becoming an adult, repeats the historical stages of development of human society, by developing from a Stone Age baby to a modern person. Hall assumed that play had a central importance in this process of civilization. He was the first to put forward the idea that play could be so constructed that children improve their ability to learn by it and cultivate their social and moral adaptability to the urban industrial revolution (see Hall 1905/1969: 202ff).

The child as embodiment of the primitive, and play as the 'mild regression' peculiar to it, are also to be found in various forms in the work of Sigmund Freud and Jean Piaget. Freud sees in children's games aggressive forms of wish fulfilment, in which the emotional conflicts of the first months of life are either lived through or controlled in symbolic form. Going one step farther, he asserts that the 'obsessive rituals' observed by him in children's play and the 'magical thinking' that accompanies them are symptomatic of that which connects children, artists, adult neurotics and primitive 'savages' (see Freud 1912–13/1991 and 1938/1993). Piaget, on the other hand, sees in play an ordered universe of rules and laws that the child learns to master in the course of its cognitive and moral development, in which it passes through phases of increasing complexity. At the child grows older, the early fantasy games lose their attraction and their place is taken by games that are more bound by rules and more highly organized (see Piaget 1978). Cohen comments: 'Freud's child is a poetess or a dreamer who plays Batman or Wondergirl in a family novel, reconciling the daydream of noble origin with the (all too common) fate of subordination. Piaget's young generation gets straight down to business and plays swapping, in order to to learn the laws of barter and the original accumulation' (Cohen 1994: 53).

In child psychology manuals and educational counselling literature, play is propagated today as an essential element of emotional and cognitive development, with the aid of which the aggressive and egocentric impulses regarded as a natural (as it were pre-civilized) feature of children are to be channelled and converted into a socially accepted form. In educational institutions, too, play is frequently included as a way of imparting to children the desired modes of behaviour.

The educational instrumentalization of children's play is accompanied by a 'loss of reality' (Lenzen 1985: 251) in children's lives. It reinforces a process that has separated the lives of children from those of adults and placed them in reservations in which nothing 'serious' happens, no 'useful' results can be achieved, and which function according to the motto: 'Go away and play!' (Ulmann 1979). This criticism can also be sensed in Piaget, when he remarks that play chiefly has a compensatory function that permits the child to show an intellectual reaction in its fantasy which it is not capable of in reality.

However, the question is whether this is ascribed to the inadequate 'development' of the child or to a 'reality' that offers it no opportunities for this. Only when the 'fantasy-related' play activity of children is separated from 'reality-related' activities, which are only loosely to be grasped within the notion of work, can it become the helpless object of educational strategies on a level at which nothing real happens any longer and action is merely symbolic.

From a class theoretical perspective, Cohen points out that the educationalizing of children's play not only exposes its actors to a 'process of patronizing' but has also 'led to still stronger denigration of the games connected with street culture' (Cohen 1994: 70f). These games were and still are, where they still take place in the societies of the West, also always activities in which 'real' life links up with 'fantasy' life. They continue to draw their material from everyday life and the overcoming of the risks of life with which both children and adults have to cope.

Meanwhile, the compensatory functions of play in Western societies are nowadays by no means limited to children and the lower classes. What Cohen notes about the 'rise of the entrepreneurial culture' in Britain in the 1980s can be observed today in other 'post-industrial' societies. 'A leisure industry specialized in the construction of adventure playgrounds for adults grew up. There the yuppies could learn to deal with stress by playing Tarzan or the naked ape. The discovery of play as a natural way to heal the alienation of work at once reconciled enjoyment and profit' (ibid.: 55).

The theories current today use a conception of play that is completely purged of real play and appears to have nothing to do with social structures or production. They nearly all have recourse to the definition by the Dutch philosopher Johan Huizinga, which today is accounted 'classical' and claims universal validity: '[Play is] a free activity standing quite consciously outside "ordinary" life as being "not serious" but at the same time absorbing the player intensely and utterly. It is an activity connected with no material interest and no profit can be gained by it. It proceeds within its own proper boundaries of time and space according to fixed rules and in an orderly manner. It promotes the formation of social groupings which tend to surround themselves with secrecy and to stress their difference from the common world by disguise or other means' (Huizinga 1938/1949: 13). This definition assumes it as a given that a sphere of life separated from 'work' has developed which functions according to social laws other than those of 'ordinary life'. Play is presented as the counter-image and opposite of work.

Possible relations to work are seen only in the sphere of sport and of games and cultural performances (or shows) aimed at an audience. Some authors here bring in a distinction between 'play' and 'games'. In the field of play, it is assumed that there is a fluid transition between play and work. In the case of professional performances of play or sport practised with the goal of earning money or making a profit, it is said that they 'fall far toward the work end of the work–play continuum. The professional ballplayer, even when he enjoys his work, cannot escape the fact that his sport participation is a task, to which he is obliged to submit. If he misses a game or a practice session he may be fined or in some other way sanctioned. This obviously violates the freedom so critical to play' (Sack 1977: 190).

Among modern play researchers, the only controversial point is whether play serves rather for the preservation of the 'cultural heritage' and existing structures by introducing the players to them and reinforcing them by practice, or whether play represents an innovative power calculated to promote social change. Most classical theories of play put forward the thesis that superfluous energy is worked off in play, and that playing serves for relaxation, recreation, recapitulation and compensation. They may be termed apologetic in so far as they accept the dominant social structures and norms as given and regard them as being appropriate to life. They are interested solely in clarifying how the members of a society can be integrated by play into the broader cultural behaviour patterns and norms of this society. According to them, play prepares the child for his place in it by imitating the social structure.

By contrast, the US play researcher Brian Sutton-Smith (1978: 54f) sees in games, especially children's games, an innovative potential. Children's play to him has an 'anticipatory character' which is also calculated 'to reverse' social structures:

> Play is based on democratic behaviour according to which everyone has his turn, and this really reverses the one-sidedness of daily life. ... When we are adolescents, the greater part of our lives is spent being subordinated to others. But in playing we do not merely gain control over our social being, we also increasingly control the roles and reversal of identity. In most early games, reversals are permitted that do not exist in life. In playing, you are allowed both to agree and to reject, hunt and flee, attack and defend.

With reference to animal games, car games, space games or adult games, Sutton-Smith speaks of forms of play 'in which the child anticipates what it cannot master as a child. We may say that its conflict between power and impotence is given a new expression in play, according to which it is no longer impotent but powerful, even though in a simulated form' (ibid.: 61).

The extent to which Sutton-Smith too is caught up in 'Western society' and is uncritical of its specific structures of reproduction and power becomes clear in his following remark: 'The early central person games (hunting, racing, etc.) mainly have something to do with dominance and remain the most important games in the more authoritarian societies. The later competitive games have more to do with achievement and are more important in modern Western societies. Winning and losing are the most important reversals in most competitive games, and they will remain so in Western society' (ibid.: 55). Beyond this, Sutton-Smith even assumes that in Western societies with an increase in 'phylogenetic complexity' the 'quantity of play' increases and a previously unknown differentiation and intensification of play takes place. Referring to his own intercultural investigations, he asserts 'that societies display a greater variety of games the more complex they are' (Sutton-Smith 1973: 610). At the same time he praises Western society as compared with those cultures 'in which the children are introduced at an early age to the adult world of work, e.g. knotting carpets or looking after animals, which hardly gives them time or encouragement to play. Wherever the roles of the adults are rigidly prescribed for reasons of survival and the contribution of the children to this survival is essential, play is hardly promoted. Frequently it is actively opposed' (ibid.: 610).

One does not have to idealize the relation of 'play' and 'work' in non-modern cultures in the sense of a presumed identity in order to call

Sutton-Smith's assertions into question. 'With at least the same degree of plausibility, one could assume an impoverishment of children's play, left to its own devices in industrial societies, whose goal-orientation tends to simplify social relations (e.g. in the family, by school and the workplace)' (Eichler 1979: 126). As evidence for this one can take the study by the child psychologist Hildegard Hetzer, who notes the following tendencies in the Federal Republic of Germany in the 1950s:

1. A noticeable decline in genuine games involving creativity in favour of games that are in the proper sense mere gratification of physical urges and do not deserve the name of game, because they lack shape and rules. 2. A favouring of the simplest forms of play, the simple activity games (function games) of children of an age where they ought long since to have outgrown preferential treatment. ... 3. The preference for games founded on chance rather than games in which the decision is arrived at through the use of the player's own powers, skill or inventiveness. (Hetzer 1957: 16, cited in Eichler 1979: 126)

It may be left open whether children's play in Western societies is really becoming 'impoverished', or whether instead children are developing new activities with which they react to the restriction of possibilities and areas of action in a perfectly independent and creative way – up to and including the conscious exceeding of the limits that have been set for them by their exclusion from socially relevant processes of 'work'. What is clear is that children in Western societies are referred to a constructed 'play' world with 'toy' reality and that in this way the 'childization' of their lives, which was introduced with the concept of childhood of the European Enlightenment, is carried to extremes.

How work and play may be related to and linked with each other in a different manner presumably more likely to serve mankind will be shown by the example of several non-Western societies. This is done not in order to recommend models for imitation but in order to counter the 'civilizatory' arrogance to be found (also) in Western theories of children's play, and to give food for thought about possible relations between play and work in contemporary Western societies as well.

Work and play in non-Western societies

In the indigenous societies of the South American Andes, people still practise work today 'as a playful competition between groups. Work is accompanied by song and dance, laughing and betting. While working, one will parody another, imitate and dramatize the roles ascribed to him. Work can be an opportunity to have fun, to improvise. In a well-balanced family, the children learn that work is pleasurable, like a game, a useful game. Sharing work means affection' (Ortiz Rescaniere 1994: 34). Play is not regarded as the opposite of or compensation for work, but as part of daily life. In the Andean culture, 'play [*pukllay*] is not only seen as an amusing and relaxing activity that follows the harvest, but as a ritual demonstration of thanks and the precursor of well-being and fertility' (Rengifo Vásquez 2001: 1). Separating play, work and life would appear to the people of the Andes as if nature had been transformed into a resource to be exploited. 'When play is in progress, the whole community plays, not only the children. There are no distinctions according to age groups. Play runs through the lives of adults, children and adolescents' (ibid.: 2). The objects and animals that serve as toys are also of significance for work. Accordingly, the 'toy' is not a means for the development of the child; playing, working and learning form a unity in the lives of the rural population as a whole.

Among the Tonga of the south-western Pacific, too, one can 'observe no precise separation of work and play, or a split between leisure and work' (Meiser 1997: 208). Many kinds of work are 'performed playfully and are connected with social relations, encounters, song and *joie de vivre*' (ibid.: 208). When children, in accordance with their age, perform certain activities that contribute to the family economy, work and play aspects are closely interwoven.[3] In the study by Meiser on cultural anthropology, such an action situation is given an exemplary description: 'Children and adults sit together in groups to make roofing for houses, flower decorations, ropes, etc. They laugh, joke, sing and dance while working; the children interrupt activities to play a game or go off on expeditions. When they are tired, they lie down on a mat and sleep for a while. When a feast is being prepared, they joke while working all night to get the decorations and garlands ready and to prepare the food for the earth oven'[4] (ibid.: 218). Meiser never experienced these processes as 'work' in the sense we understand it. 'What I observed was activities that were performed with pleasure and calm. Even when they had to be finished by a certain point in time, the rhythm was no different from usual. I was repeatedly surprised at the calmness with which the work was done and how punctually the products were finished' (ibid.: 218).

Similar practices are reported from the Rarámuri, an Amerindian people in the Mexican state of Chihuahua. From the age of about six, the children already take on responsible jobs, for example looking after cattle. 'While looking after cattle, the transition between work and play is fluid. Thus on the one hand the children practise throwing stones skilfully to guide the herd; on the other, there are some games played by children and adults in which the point is to throw stones a long way accurately' (Kummels 1993: 256). At the same time, the children's responsibility is great: thus they have to take care of the animals, and prevent them being savaged by coyotes, getting lost or damaging plants. A recent study on childhood among the A'uwê-Xavante in the Brazilian rainforest reports on similar combinations of play and work (see Nunes 1999: 158ff).

In the nomadic society of the Kel Adagh in central Africa, the first job entrusted to children is looking after young animals, 'with which they are often compared, and with which they have in common not only their age, lightness and agility, but also playfulness' (Klute 1996: 216). When the children gambol around with the young goats and camel foals, work and play fuse.[5]

In the rural areas of Ethiopia, when the children are looking after the cattle in the open field, they play the most varied games, put on races and tell each other stories (Melaku 2000: 29). In the towns and cities of Ethiopia, the shoeshine boys play while waiting for customers. In the streets of Addis Ababa, Melaku observed how the working children not only combine work with play, but also help each other. 'When one child has no shoe polish left, the other children will lend him some. When older children attack them, they come to each other's defence' (ibid.: 29f).

As a further 'ethnological' example, the Australian Aborigines may be cited, in whose language there are no words to distinguish work from play. The photographer Donald Thomson and the ethnologist Isobel White had the impression that the children, 'full of enthusiasm', spent much time

> helping the adults or imitating them while they worked. ... Girls go with their mothers, grandmothers and aunts on the daily search for food, roots and tubers, leaves, fruits, small animals, lizards and molluscs, and thus provide the community with its main food products. Boys practise hunting, aiming at birds, lizards and other small animals. Fathers find it fun to make small tools and weapons for their children – little sticks for digging for the girls, spears and spear-slings for the boys. Children are congratulated when they contribute to the food supply. ... The children learn very early to recognize animal tracks and the footprints of each member of the community. When a child begins to walk, everybody is called to see his footprint, so that in future everybody will recognize him from it. A favourite game played together by children and adults is imitating the tracks of various animals by pressing the ball of the thumb, the fist or the finger in the sand; thus the children learn an essential skill. (Thomson and White 1993: 373ff)

It is reported of numerous non-Western societies how children imitate, dramatize and vary the work of adults in their play. We will present a few examples from Africa here. Wherever cattle-raising is practised, the three- to four-year-old boys already begin to play 'looking after animals', using animal bones, fruits, stones, berries, snail shells, corncobs, goats' feet, etc. 'The herd is properly fenced in, taken to pasture, attacked and stolen, given medical treatment, bargained for and praised. Bulls are castrated, cows milked, cattle bled to drink the blood mixed with milk, oxen are fattened to be slaughtered for a particular feast' (Paul 1997: 197). In many places, the small children start making whole herds of cattle out of damp clay with beautifully and originally shaped horns. The clay cattle made by children sometimes play an important part in myths or initiation rites: 'Thus the Bira in Burundi tell how the Hima became their masters because Bira boys had left their clay animals outside one night. The Hima came, stole them and were henceforth the owners of the herds' (ibid.: 197, referring to Geluwe 1957). Among the Zigua in Tanzania, the initiates are shown animals and other clay objects to demonstrate that they have now left their childhood behind them (ibid., with reference to Cory 1956).

The danger posed by beasts of prey demands much attention and courage while looking after the animals; this is dramatized in group games such as 'hyena and sheep' or 'leopard and goats'. In the case of the West African pastoral people of the Fulbe, the strongest children represent the hyenas, the smallest the sheep and the medium-sized ones the guardians (ibid., referring to Traoré 1940). Among the Logo and Mamvu of the eastern Congo, the custom of rewarding with beer the help of neighbours in clearing bush is played by small girls, who make a drink for the guests from fruit. The 'workers' drink this copiously as if it were real beer (ibid., with reference to Costermans 1948). Children who go to market with their parents then play 'market' at home, offering ready-made dishes, grain, spirits, cola nuts, tobacco, oil, etc. with the corresponding cries and prices for bargaining (ibid., with reference to Béart 1955). Girls anticipate in play the housework in which they little by little take part seriously. They pound and grind grain, collect fruit as extras, cook and invite the boys to self-prepared meals. It is reported of the Lovedu in South Africa that the 'beer' brewed by the children themselves is praised with dignity and respect (ibid.: 198, with reference to Krige 1978).

Schildkrout (1981: 94) reports of the Hausa in the Nigerian city Kano that she was often told by children and adults that the activities of three-year-old children – such as 'going to Mecca', 'cooking food for sale', 'shopping', or 'marrying' – which she took for 'imitative play' were in fact their work. In the case of girls aged nine to ten, she noted that they baked little cakes to sell to other children. 'These cakes are made of flour and water and fried in a small quantity of oil. They are about 5 cm in diameter, and they are not food that any adult would consume. However, children buy them for cash and even obtain credit. This activity generates income (one girl obtained enough money to buy a pair of shoes), but it is regarded, nevertheless, as play (*wasa*), for at this age girls are aware that cooking is an activity performed by adult women' (Schildkrout 1981: 94).

In many cultures of Africa, the playful imitation of certain kinds of work merges imperceptibly with the production of useful articles. An example is craft products. 'Clay vessels are shaped and sometimes also fired with the help of adults and the weaving of baskets and mats, and spinning and weaving, are tried out at an early age. Children construct their own musical instruments, make music, sing and dance their own tunes or those of the grown-ups' (Paul 1997: 198). Paul also mentions imitations of European technical apparatus such as telephones, cameras, bicycles, or aeroplanes, and shows herself impressed by the 'technological understanding' that they demonstrate and their 'creativity', for example in making drumming cyclists 'for whom there was no model present' (ibid.: 198).

Evidently the children in their 'play' not only simply simulate adult activities, but also produce products and acquire skills that at least from their perspective have a meaning important for life, a 'utility value'. This character of the actions of the children, which is alien to our thinking about 'childish play', had already been described in clear terms by US anthropologist Margaret Mead in the 1920s and linked with problematizing reflections on the exclusion of children from work processes in US society. In her studies in Samoa in the Pacific, she had observed: 'The distinctions between work as something one has to do but dislikes, and play as something one wants to do; of work as the main business of adults, play as the main concern of children, are conspicuously absent. Children's play is like adults' play in kind, interest, and in its proportion to work. And the Samoan child has no desire to turn adults' activities into play, to translate one sphere into the other' (Mead 1928/1963: 135).

The key to this integration of play and work does not lie, as is frequently asserted by apologists of Western industrial society, in the highly favourable climate, the fertility of the soil and/or the wealth of animal life, or even in the lack of 'functional differentiation' or 'complexity' in these 'primitive' societies. It lies in the fact that the activities of the children, intended seriously by them, are also taken seriously by society (the adults). To label them with the term 'play' common in Western societies already entails a 'devaluation' of the children's activities. To conclude the ethnological considerations, we may quote Margaret Mead with her 'comparative cultural' reflections – published in 1928:

> Samoan children do not learn to work through learning to play. ... Nor are they permitted a period of lack of responsibility such as our children are allowed. From the time they are four or five years old they perform definite tasks, graded to their strength and intelligence, but still tasks which have a meaning in the structure of the whole society. This does not mean that they have less time for play than American children who are shut up in schools from nine to three o'clock everyday. ... American children spend hours in schools learning tasks whose visible relation to the mothers' and fathers' activities is often quite impossible to recognise. Their participation in adults' activities is either in terms of toys, tea-sets and dolls and toy automobiles, or else a meaningless and harmful tampering with the electric light system. ... So our children make a false set of categories, work, play and school; work for adults, play for children's pleasure, and schools as an inexplicable nuisance with some compensations. These false distinctions are likely to produce all sorts of strange attitudes, an apathetic treatment of a school which bears no known relation to life, a false dichotomy between work and play, which may result either in a dread of work as implying irksome responsibility or in a later contempt for play as childish. (ibid.: 133f)

Work and play in Western societies today

To draw attention to the 'intensive dialectic of work and play' in European societies, the German scholar of popular culture Hermann Bausinger calls to mind studies by Édit Fél and Támas Hofer on a Hungarian farming village. One of these contains a long chapter on 'instruments of play', containing the passage:

> The first plaything of the boy was usually a whip, with which he drove his 'foals' or 'team of oxen' made of stripped corn cobs. The foals had their harness, which became more perfect year by year the more the boys became acquainted with the real horses' harness and the craft of harnessing them. The cart that was to be pulled by the team was, to begin with, symbolized by a piece of wood or a broken tin pot; later the boys would make proper carts from pieces of board. These carts were also laden with earth or grass, and so the children drove them. Sometimes they harnessed the foals to an old barbed collar (for dogs)

and harrowed the dust with this. In their play, the children followed the annual rhythm of work; when harvest-time came, they went 'cutting' with reed-cutters or small scythes made of sunflower stalks. (Fél and Hofer 1974: 299, cited in Bausinger 1983: 56f)

According to Bausinger, this makes it clear that the play was oriented to the procedures and tools of farm work. A further observation shows how play and work were directly related to each other, indeed connected seamlessly. While the children of the day labourers continued to play, indeed had to do so, the farmers' sons, who 'were able to play with their own things', gradually began, from the age of seven or eight, 'to stop playing, and help their fathers not only in the animals' sheds but also with other tasks such as pruning trees, preparing the threshing floor, etc. A ten-year-old was already hoeing in his parents' garden, and also tried digging with a spade. The more adroit began carving and drilling, before their feet could reach the treadle of the workbench. Getting to know a tool is a real pleasure for the child, which can hardly wait to get its hands on one thing after another' (Fél and Hofer 1974: 299). Bausinger concludes from this description that 'play was not really abandoned at all, but transferred to work or preserved as work' (Bausinger 1983: 57).

It is frequently assumed that the separation and polarization of work and play in the modern era in Europe was inevitable and is irreversible. If this were the case, reports from 'indigenous' societies of America, Africa, Australia, Oceania or rural areas of Europe would be nothing but a romantic reminiscence. Disregarding the assumed reasons why 'work lost its playful element' (ibid.: 58), the fact that this loss can 'only inadequately be compensated for by autonomous or, to put it more cautiously, unconnected play' (ibid.: 58), and that it 'goes against the grain' of many people, especially the young, should give cause for reflection. Working children who struggle through life today in the mega-cities of the South daily invent, despite extremely unfavourable living conditions, new ways of making life more enjoyable, without giving up work and allowing themselves to be shut up in ghettos of playing or learning (see Invernizzi 2001; Liebel 2001a). In our latitudes, too, the signs are increasing that new combinations and mixtures of work and play are desired and being practised, particularly by the young.

With regard to the 'spectrum of activities' of children and adolescents in contemporary Western societies, Hengst (2000: 73) has collected a large number of examples of how 'fluid transitions between playing, learning and work and between self-reference and community relevance are observable in social and cultural activities'. For instance, he points out that the many children who engage in work today do so not only to earn money but also to 'have fun'. Or that children and adolescents use modern communications technology in a way that combines elements of play and work. 'The computer and Internet kids play, learn and work with the same hardware and software as adults use in the world of work. They simply place the software emphases differently' (Hengst 1998: 246).[6] Lacking in the many kinds of sport favoured by children and adolescents today, too, such as BMX, break dancing or skateboarding, is 'the as-if dimension characteristic of traditional children's activities. They are reality' (ibid.: 246). According to Hengst, these and many other 'leisure activities' practised by children and adolescents today show 'how little the traditional categories for the identification of marginal and central spheres, work or non-work, adult and children's activities, now apply' (ibid.: 246f).

A recent study by the German Youth Institute on the extra-school learning of ten- to fourteen-year-old children comes to the conclusion that having fun and achieving something are not a contradiction to children. In order to pursue their interests, the children were even prepared to undertake considerable effort. 'The children had most fun when the activity was "their thing", i.e. when they identified with it and were also able to carry it out largely on their own. Thus considered, it was of secondary importance whether the activity concerned was "play" or "work"' (Lipski 2001: 103).

As early as the 1970s, the American cultural researcher Mihaly Csikszentmihalyi (1979) pointed out that the usual distinction made between work and play was becoming increasingly invalid. He argued that there is a quality (which he called *flow*) of life that is to be found in any context in life, whether work or play, characterized by a blending of action and consciousness and a concentration of attention; it appears whenever one is completely absorbed in an activity.

The separation and opposition of play and work are not, as most theories of play and work still dominant here would have us believe, a kind of natural law; it is rather to be seen as a special historical case of a society that is able to imagine work only as a burden and a strain and performs it accordingly. We should realize that 'it is social convention that defines what is "play" and what is "work"' (Eichler 1979: 110). Play does not inevitably have to be seen as a 'leftover' of industrial work, particularly in its predominant form under capitalism of wage labour, but rather the latter should be seen as a special case of a more complex form of human behaviour which also contains elements of play.

The mutual exclusion of play and work is an 'idealistic separation' that reflects the alienating character of gainful employment in capitalist society and seeks to legitimize it, but also points to a possible 'reconciliation of work and play under non-alienated conditions of life' (Meyer-Bendrat 1987: 3). The 'strict separation of work and play and the postulated freedom in play and compulsion in work are born from the alienation and lack of freedom in work situations. The idea of freedom in play complementarily corresponds to that of alienation and lack of freedom in work' (ibid.: 22). When it is recognized that the idealization of play as contrary or alternative to work is only the obverse side of the perversion of work into a 'spiritually empty operational function for an alien goal that is neither agreed with nor of interest', it becomes clear that play as a 'superfluous activity' is merely 'an historically conditioned, transitory phenomenon that results partly from the still undeveloped character of work, and partly from its formation-specific origin. Play as a special detached category of life is an ideal product of the history of the development of concrete conditions of human living in which social production and reproduction became more and more separated' (ibid.: 38).

Meanwhile, this had and still has not only ideal but also quite concrete consequences. The idealization and prettification of play as a supposed way of avoiding at least part of the time the stressful and destructive effect of work chain the individual emotionally all the more powerfully to the latter, and cause him to tolerate it as a 'necessary evil', or to reserve it for his later life. The ideological separating off of play as a 'privilege' of children becomes a means of fobbing them off with their role as 'outsiders of society' (Zeiher et al. 1996) and making them long for a life in which they will finally be taken seriously as 'adults' with 'proper work'.[7] However varied the design of the 'toys' created for children and the 'playgrounds' made for their use, the world of the child thus limited to the sphere of play is characterized by social isolation. 'Precisely through their social isolation, *games* have a redundant character, because they convey no gain through information, i.e. experience. The whole tradition of well-meaning (and no doubt in specific functions important) encouragement to pursue games and hobbies has its roots in the ideological separation of "work" and "play/leisure" and points to the generally accepted reduction of play to the redundant level of an object' (Eichler 1979: 129; emphasis in the original).

The German philosopher Ernst Bloch (1967: 1,066) illustrates the extent to which play and work are dialectically interdependent, either negatively or positively:

Handymen, small garden owners and many other people make their hobby an image of the occupation they have failed to pursue, or which in the stern reality of life does not exist at all. Such things are often only atrophied, with a distant sense of work without compulsion, a private semblance of what work done with pleasure and love might mean. In places like America, where people's employment or job is almost incidental and does not fill their lives, the most hobbies are accordingly to be found. And amateur occupations will only die out when they become proper occupations or trades. Up to that point, hobbies can teach us how fulfilled leisure is privately dreamed, as work that appears leisure.

It is surely no accident that it has increasingly been observed recently in social science and educational studies that we are departing 'more and more from the older dichotomies between work and play' (Sutton-Smith 1983: 68). The opposition of work and play is termed 'ideologically suspicious' and 'dangerous as to its consequences for the education of the individual' (Eichler 1973: 177).

> Play as a process of appropriation and shaping of the environment can therefore only take place when all the levels of this environment up to and including the requirements for learning, i.e. working, are open to explorative, inquisitive, testing access. For the child there is no fundamental opposition between play and work, work and leisure. It learns from adults that work is a particular, not very pleasant and rather overpowering game; it learns the distance between work and leisure, the devaluation of work. Culturally, the separation of work from play leads up a cul-de-sac. (Eichler 1983: 234)[8]

Anyone who has observed the spontaneous play of children, where this is possible, 'will notice that children's play really has a great deal to do with what is called work' (Werth 1997: 1). This is the case when we have a view of work that is not restricted to earning money, not to mention controlled wage labour, but see as work all activities that have a deliberate effect on the environment and produce beautiful or useful things. To do this is the desire of children from their first years of life onwards – the desire to test out their powers and skills, and show others that they can produce a useful result.

The way in which children at various age phases deal constructively with materials had already been described in the 1930s by Hildegard Hetzer (1931). If a small child is given unfamiliar materials such as building blocks, paper and crayons or plasticine, an unspecific reaction first occurs (e.g. sticking things in its mouth), followed by using the item in a way specific to the material ('scribbling phase'), and then, already discernible in two-year-olds, an interest in dealing with the product (which has resulted possibly by chance): it is more closely considered and shown to others. The intention of creating something (e.g. painting a picture) is first stated by children of about three, and not until they are four do they utter the intention to make something definite (e.g. to paint a house). When a task is set by an adult, a child is able to pursue this goal rather earlier. Only from about age six do children stick most of the time with the task that they have set themselves or that an adult has set them. Hetzer's observations and age-specific classifications would certainly vary in different cultural and historical contexts and situations in life, but they give an approximate impression of how children at various stages of their lives can and wish to work with objects.

The result intended by a small child may frequently be something other than a generally usable result, and it may rather be guided by an interest in a certain experience or effect. But when already in the first three years of life children are able to see a result as the consequence of an action, it may be imagined what – especially as they grow older – they might be capable of if offered corresponding opportunities or challenges. As we know, this is hardly any longer, or not yet again, the case in the 'developed' Western societies.

To try to remedy this situation, it is no use artificially creating 'tasks' or 'serious situations' in which children are supposed to abreact or learn something.

If a child is given a task, it only has a meaning for the child when it is not an 'educational' task (e.g. watering flowers, so that the child gets used to having duties), but a really necessary essential and generally useful requirement, thus also for the child. The child must already have experienced that it is essential; it must have seen how others did it and that the results were useful. Performing such tasks is made easier for a child when it is included in the action from the beginning, i.e. performs the activity together with adults and is not just left to itself. This cooperation of the child must not be declared to be 'help' for the adults, but must be understood as what it is: cooperation in which those involved make a contribution corresponding to their abilities to a common goal. … After all, a child cannot comprehend the sense of the cooperation quite directly: it is not only necessary to treat each other in a friendly manner, but particularly that the task is performed together more quickly and better (so that the child can get back to painting after the meal, or Mother now has some time to read to it). (Ulmann 1979: 30)

The ideological opposition of play and work, which is repeatedly insisted upon, loses its basis when the subjects are not compelled to abandon themselves to their work and are enabled to decide its goals and processes themselves. The point is not to strive for the identity of work and play – this would be an illusion again – but rather the transformation of work into 'free activity', where, as Marx formulates it (1953: 505), 'external goals drop the appearance of an external natural necessity, and are given as goals that the individual himself set'. For children, this means that they must be given the opportunity to escape from the unreal playing and learning ghettos that have been constructed for them and to perform activities decided by themselves and cooperatively organized, which have – for them too – a recognizable relevance for their own needs and those of others. Thus, children who are told to go and play could become children who 'join in the game' and 'play a part' in society.

Notes

1. 'All modern social scientific theorists of play have seen it as contributing to child development in one way or another' (Sutton-Smith and Kelly-Byrne 1986: 308).

2. The line of thought influenced by Romanticism, in contrast, stresses the subversive power of play directed against 'modern civilization'.

3. The sports scholar Rüdiger Schwartz, too, in his study on children's play in Tonga and Western Samoa (1992: 14), was also moved by 'the question as to whether the evident separation of play and work can be accepted in all cultures'.

4. In Tonga, the earth oven is the traditional device used to prepare food. A pit is dug, and the food wrapped in banana or taro leaves, covered with hot stones and so cooked.

5. See also the autobiographical account of R. Mugo Gatheru (1967: 43ff), a member of the East African Kikuyu people born in 1925, who describes his work as a shepherd and goatherd as 'a real pleasure': 'Usually it was great fun to try to ride the big billygoat as Europeans ride their horses, or to play with the tame black goat Kiumu that followed me everywhere; or to get the sheepdog called Simba ("the lion") to fetch things, or to tussle with the other boys that sometimes looked after their animals near by. ... We sometimes played a game in which we formed two groups and each group gave the other a riddle in song, or challenged them: "Goats belong to us! Sheep belong to us! Heaven belongs to us! The sun belongs to us! Do you dare to fight?" And there was nothing more exciting than a good fight between our dogs. Sometimes we passed the time cutting bows and arrows with tips made from pigs' bristles, and challenged each other to shoot birds. We also put out cunning bird traps.'

6. Tapscott (1998: 28) sums up his experience with children of the Net generation by stating that they are not afraid of hard work 'because working, learning and playing are the same to them anyway'.

7. Eichler (1979: 131) speaks of a '"barrier of play" erected by the "proper world", the "serious games" of adults. The child is not allowed everywhere to "play too"; it must first learn to fulfil central roles, paradoxically in an area, school, which is cut off from society.'

8. Elsewhere Eichler (1979: 129) asserts that clearly 'the traditional conception of play, defined negatively against "work", can no longer be upheld'.

8 | The economic exploitation of children: towards a subject-oriented praxis

§ THE International Convention on the Rights of the Child grants children the right to protection from economic exploitation. But what does economic exploitation of children consist of? Why does it come about? What effects does it have on children? How can it best be combated? For years, controversial debates have been taking place on these questions, without satisfactory answers having been found.

In this chapter the most important typological and theoretical approaches to the description of the economic exploitation of children will first be critically discussed. Next, approaches towards an explanation of the economic exploitation of children will be discussed and examined as to their meaning and possible effects on working children. In conclusion, how the exploitation of children can most effectively be opposed will be considered. The approaches described relate to children's work in both the North and the South.

Typologies of children's work

The exploitation of children is almost always seen in connection with 'child labour'.[1] For decades it was usual to equate children's work with exploitation, and to talk of exploitation it was enough to note that work of some kind was performed by a child. 'Exploitation' was a kind of metaphor intended to mean that the very fact of a child working was reprehensible and to be rejected.

In the meantime the perspective on children's work has become more differentiated. It is understood that children's work covers a wide spectrum ranging from slave-like forms of work (e.g. bondage through debt) via forms of wage labour to work that is self-determined and desired by the children themselves. Within the international experts' debate, several typologies have been developed in order to distinguish various forms of children's work, whether or not the work is harmful or beneficial to the children.

Most widespread is the distinction introduced by the ILO in the 1980s between *child labour* and *child work*. The expression *child labour* stands for the forms of work regarded as exploitative, considered harmful to children and to be abolished. By contrast, the expression *child work* is related to the forms of children's work that are considered not harmful and that should be 'tolerated'.

From the point of view of typology, it has sometimes been pointed out that the distinction between *labour* and *work* is too coarse to define adequately the numerous forms and fields of children's work. Thus the International Working Group on Child Labour notes: 'Most children work in circumstances that fall somewhere between the extremes of intolerable and beneficial' (IWGCL 1997: 5; see also White 1994; Lavalette 1999; Liebel 2001c).

A more differentiated typology of the forms of children's work is contained in the so-called *balance model*. With regard to the various working conditions, the advantages and disadvantages that work brings for children are balanced against each other, bearing in mind the children's living conditions (see Mortimer and Finch 1996; Hobbs and McKechnie 1997; IWGCL 1998; McKechnie and Hobbs 2002). Another typology places the various forms of children's work within a continuum that covers several intermediate forms between 'harmful' and 'helpful' children's work (see White 1994; IWGCL 1998; on the discussion see Liebel 2001c). In this sense, UNICEF states that 'to treat all work done by children as equally unacceptable is to confuse and trivialize the issue', and proposes instead 'to distinguish between beneficial and intolerable work and to recognize that much child labour falls into a grey area between these two extremes' (UNICEF 1997: 24).[2]

Today an attempt is usually made to identify the exploitation of children by means of criteria by which, for instance, excessively long hours of work, excessively hard work, humiliating treatment or the withholding of recreation periods or of working rights are listed.[3] This renders it possible to establish more precisely the extent and degree of exploitation, but implies a fundamental problem that has hitherto hardly been mentioned in positions on and analyses of children's work.

The criteria give the impression that exploitation consists of or results from a mixture of features that are somehow given, or not, as the case may be. There is no visible link between them; the points of reference are extremely disparate. Sometimes the criteria refer to age (' ... at too early an age'), sometimes a certain view of the 'development of the child' or 'human nature' is implicitly contained in them, or certain views of human dignity ('... undermines their self-esteem'); sometimes they refer to working conditions (' ... excessively long working hours', ' ... too little remuneration'), sometimes to work processes (' ... monotonous and repetitive', 'dangerous work'), sometimes to restrictions on the freedom of the child (' ... cannot withdraw from work', ' ... unable to dispose of their wage themselves'), sometimes to the exercise of arbitrariness and violence, to rights missing or ignored, sometimes quite generally to social or political conditions ('inadequate access to health and education institutions', ' ... social insurance benefits'), and more.

The arbitrary mix of criteria and the disparate points of reference obscure, or at least render it hard to recognize, the fact that (economic) exploitation is a specific social relationship in which one person profits from another or gains advantages at his expense, and which clearly presupposes and helps to reproduce certain social structures and power relations.

The ILO definition of the exploitation of children

One of the few attempts to define the exploitation of children systematically was made under the aegis of the ILO. According to this, children's work can always be seen as 'exploited labour' when it takes place outside the family 'for others' and is 'productive' in the sense that it produces calculable 'values' and aims at some kind of income necessary for subsistence. This kind of work is, as already mentioned while describing the typologies, termed *child labour* by the ILO and distinguished from *child work* as a kind of activity that is 'reproductive', is practised at home for the child's own family, and is not rewarded.[4]

Apart from the reproach of insufficient differentiation, objection must be made on the empirical level that by far the most work done by children that falls under the ILO criteria of *child labour* by no means involves disadvantages for the children. Thus many working children are proud just because they are doing something 'necessary' that 'is useful to others', for example contributing to earning their family's living, or with their earnings making possible school attendance, which they would otherwise not have been able to afford.

The distinction between *labour* and *work* in the form observed by the ILO implies a social logic that is blind to the realities of life of most children. According to this logic, work done by children is only permitted when it is unpaid. If it is paid, this may only happen when it is not really essential ('a little pocket money'), but not when the income from the work is required to cover the costs of living. Children are only to be allowed to help their parents to improve their income (and to gain pride and satisfaction from this) when the parents are financially independent, i.e. possess their own means of production. But they are not allowed to when their parents are without possessions and dependent on income from dependent wage labour (see White 1994: 873).

The ILO's distinction between labour and work is accompanied by evaluations that amount to a double discrimination against children. On the one hand, social recognition of their performance and 'work' is refused precisely when they are doing something essential and making an important economic contribution. On the other, merely because they have not yet attained a certain age (decided on by adults), the only activities permitted them are those which by definition are worth nothing. These used to be termed 'help', to underline the fact that they do not consist of 'real' work and therefore do not deserve to be taken particularly seriously. With a view to the (possible) social status of children, this excludes them from playing an essential and active part in economic life, even in the sense of making a serious contribution to supporting their families.

Another aspect is no less serious. Permitting children to perform only unpaid or lowly paid work not only means preventing them from earning money, but may also serve to veil or legitimize less visible forms of the exploitation of children. These consist of refusing them recognition and payment for their work with respect to their age, or, as often happens precisely in the case of work undertaken for their own parents, of preventing them from claiming the monetary equivalent of their work.

Considered from an analytical point of view, the ILO with its distinction between child labour and child work, makes wage labour instituted by capitalism the universal yardstick. By ascribing 'value' only to this, all other forms of work, especially those termed 'reproductive', are devalued. From such a perspective, by far the greater part of the work perfomed by children today can be neither adequately analysed nor evaluated. This applies equally to the South and the North. In the societies of the South, despite the structural and cultural differences, wage labour, particularly in the context of formal employment, is much less widespread among children than work in the context of the family economy or in the so-called urban informal sector. Work within the family economy, which as a rule is unpaid, embraces three categories of work: 'a) activities that extract resources from the physical and social environment; b) activities concerning the "unpaid" allocation, preparation and distribution of these resources; c) activities that concern the care of human beings' (Nieuwenhuys 1994: 17).

Such activities in the family household are falsely classified as 'economically valueless'. This undervaluation itself is an 'important aspect of the exploitation of children in the Third World' (ibid.: 18). Meanwhile work in the context of the family is not something outside capitalist structures, but part of them. It functions precisely because it is undervalued as 'free labour power'. The depreciation and undervaluation of the work of children within the family is a consequence of gender- and age-specific hierarchies which will be examined more closely below. Schildkrout (1980) and Elson (1982: 491) argue that children's work in this context is often minimized because as a rule it takes place under the supervision of women.

Moralization and exploitation

In regard to children's work, it is becoming increasingly common to use 'exploitation as a synonym for abuse, maltreatment, excess, over-burdening' (Cussiánovich 2001a: 129). Whereas in the case of adults 'exploitation' is regarded as an economic category, in that of children it is measured only in terms of whether the work is harmful or beneficial to them. Exploitation is 'in the world of childhood ... first and foremost a moral category' (Nieuwenhuys 2000a: 280). The conceptual and practical equation of exploitation with damage leads to a simultaneous inflation and watering down of the notion of exploitation. This not only makes it harder to see things clearly, but also implies a general identification of children's work with exploitation. Beyond this, Nieuwenhuys supposes that this 'moral' view of exploitation 'betrays a greater concern with the threat posed to society by deviations from what are seen as acceptable forms of socialization than with the welfare of working children' (ibid.: 279).

Thus a demand has rightly been made 'to distinguish between a situation of risk, high risk, harmfulness, dangerousness, exclusion, marginalisation, oppression etc., and exploitation' (Cussiánovich 2001a: 129). Suppression and social exclusion, for example, cannot simply be adduced from the conditions of employment, but are related 'to the status of childhood in society, which is to say the non-recognition of their social role, their economic and political activity' (ibid.: 130). This is also bolstered by programmes and practices aimed at the 'outlawing' and 'abolition of children's work'. Talk of 'harmfulness' also draws attention to working conditions, but also, like talk of poverty, requires a search for the deeper causes, 'which relate to economic, social, political and ideological structures' (ibid.: 130).

That this rarely happens with regard to children's work imparts a high moral tone to the discourse on exploitation which is none the less totally depoliticized. For a long time, critique of exploitation was part of the critique of the lack of equality and justice in the capitalist social system; today, exploitation is seen almost exclusively as a problem of children, regarded only as an indicator of a lack of development in the sensitivity of adults towards an age group presented as helpless and in need of protection. When, for instance, children are said to be more easily exploited than adults, this implies that this is in the nature of 'being a child', and that it can be solved only by more protection and care, or even by excluding children from the 'world of work' altogether. In this sense, the ILO intends 'to protect children from work that interferes with their full development and to pursue economic efficiency through well-functioning adult labour markets' (ILO 2002: 7).

If we really want to trace the social context of the exploitation of children, it is necessary to see it as an unequal social relationship between persons or social groups (classes) in which one side obtains economic advantages at the expense of the other side by means of its greater power, and perhaps also by the use of violence. The essence of this situation is that one side becomes the object of the other side.

Exploitation is not restricted to classic wage labour (although it is a sine qua non of this), but is possible in all conceivable kinds of work situations in which the workers are in a situation where they are more dependent on other persons or groups than vice versa.

Exploitation is also not to be understood only economically, in the sense that workers are deprived of the monetary equivalent of their labour. This aspect – which is by no means unimportant – needs to be complemented by the 'qualitative' aspect, whereby workers are prevented from controlling the conditions of their actions as workers, and shaping them according to their own requirements. In other words, what is involved is external control of a situation, placing the workers in the position of objects. This control from outside is the expression of an imbalance of power, and has the consequence that the workers have conditions and activities dictated to them which tend to be disadvantageous for them.

Obviously exploitation in the sense sketched here is widespread in contemporary capitalist societies. It is true that the forms and courses of exploitation have changed in the course of history, and that to some extent violence and arbitrariness in working conditions have been reduced or 'regulated' with the aid of legal norms; but since economic and political power continue to be unequally distributed, exploitation continues to be current reality. With today's worldwide 'deregulation' of employment and the labour markets, exploitation is in fact again assuming crasser forms and dimensions. And in the globalized and regulated economy children's work plays by no means a marginal part.

Exploitation beyond the sphere of work?

It also needs to be considered that economic exploitation is not limited to employment situations. Today it also takes place increasingly in the consumer market. Young people in particular are made tempting offers to persuade them to boost the design and marketing of products as 'trendsetters'. In a study on the battle of the global players for market power, Naomi Klein presents a large number of examples. With reference to the USA, she reports on market researchers conducting an experiment in which children and adolescents were sent home with disposable cameras to take pictures of their friends and families; in one task set by the sports equipment firm Nike, they were to return with documentary material on 'the place they most liked to be at'. Such exercises are legitimized by the market researchers as 'educative' and 'ability-enhancing', and are even approved by some educationists. Thus the headmistress of a primary school in Massachusetts explained the purpose of a taste test involving a brand of breakfast flakes as follows: 'It's a learning experience. They had to read, they had to look, they had to compare' (Klein 2000: 94).

Other market research enterprises, such as Channel One, go a step farther. They recruit teachers as 'partners' and together with them develop models of teaching situations in which the pupils are to draft a new advertising campaign for Snapple or develop a new design for drink-dispensing machines for Pepsi Cola. In New York and Los Angeles, high school pupils devised thirty-two cartoon commercials for Starburst fruit sweets, and in Colorado Springs pupils designed ads for Burger King which were displayed in their school buses. 'Finished assignments are passed on to the companies and the best entries win prizes and may even be adopted by the companies – all subsidized by the taxpayer-funded school system' (ibid.: 94). Klein also found in a school in Vancouver, Canada, that pupils worked for several months for the restaurant chain White Spot to develop the concept and packaging for an instant pizza, which is now on their kids' menu. The following year, the pupils developed a complete plan for birthday parties in the restaurants of this chain. The pupils' presentation included 'sample commercials, menu items, party games invented by the students and cake ideas' (ibid.: 94f). Aspects such as general safety, possible food allergies and low costs, as well as sufficient flexibility, were taken into account. According to one nine-year-old boy, the project meant 'a lot of work' for him (ibid.: 95).

One more example from Naomi Klein's account, which the author terms 'perhaps the most sinister of these experiments': in the USA, Coca-Cola organized a competition at various schools in the course of which a strategy was to be developed for the distribution of free cola coupons to pupils. The school that developed the best advertising strategy was to win five hundred dollars. One school in Georgia that took the competition particularly seriously proclaimed a Coca-Cola day on which all the pupils came to school in Coca-Cola T-shirts and assembled for a photograph in a formation representing the name 'Coke'. They were instructed by leading employees of the firm and learned everything about the black bubbly fluid. But then something went wrong. One pupil ventured to come to school in a Pepsi T-shirt. For this sin he was promptly excluded from class. The headmistress justified this exclusion with the words: 'It really would have been acceptable … if it had just been in-house, but we had the regional president here and people flew in from Atlanta to do us the honor of being resource speakers. These students knew we had guests' (ibid.: 95).

These examples show that the exploitation of children is not limited to the traditional sphere of work, and that particularly in the case of young people work and non-work can no longer be strictly separated with regard to space or time, or conceptually. The tasks taken on by the pupils or imposed on them have considerable economic significance, although they are considered rather as 'leisure pursuits' in the traditional sense or even legitimized as part of the school's task of education. At any rate, their economic yield for the firm that commissions them is considerably higher than the 'reward' – if any – given to the children and adolescents. From at least two of the examples, however, it also becomes clear that the children are certainly aware that their activities are work, and a type of work from which others profit rather than they themselves, and which is thus not accepted without protest.

The exploitation of children as a structural phenomenon of capitalist societies

It is generally assumed today that the economic exploitation of children is a direct consequence of poverty. This overlooks the fact that children's work does not necessarily assume exploitative forms even in 'poor' societies that are dependent on children's work. On the contrary, it may be part of a socio-cultural system that attaches a high value to children's work for the socialization, education and personal development of children and which, for this reason, respects children precisely as working children. Such an attitude to children is still to be found today – under capitalist conditions – in many families that live in poverty and in which it is natural that all the members of the family support each other and assume economic duties corresponding to their abilities and powers. In such families, as a rule attention is paid to the work expected of or assigned to children, taking account of their age-related physical and psychological constitution, and not exposing them to unnecessary risks.

When it comes to the economic exploitation of children, there are reasons involved that are rooted in the structure and mode of functioning of the economic and social system as a whole. Children's work is to be 'locate[d] ... within wider socio-economic processes' (Lavalette 1999a: 39) and their exploitation cannot be understood when separated from the 'global form of exploitation' of a society, in which class, gender and age are interwoven (see Nieuwenhuys 1994: 205). Whether the economic exploitation of children takes place depends thus above all on the social forms in which work essential to survival is organized and distributed, and the social status assigned to the children within the relationship of the generations, particularly regarding the generational division of labour.

In societies in which work essential for survival is regarded as a common task of all and in which everybody shares in a similar way in the production of essential products, it is less likely for work to assume exploitative forms. Exploitation becomes probable where part of society takes advantage of the work of other parts of society and is able to decide in what forms and under what conditions work is performed. That is, exploitation takes place in all societies in which there are unequal power relations, and the powerful section of society is able to tap the productive potential of those excluded from power.

Capitalist society is a special form of such societies. Its mode of functioning is based on the fact that the overwhelming majority of the population do not work to satisfy their own requirements, and are not able to benefit freely from the 'value added' and the products of their own work together and by their own choice. They are obliged to place their labour potential at the disposal of those who possess the most important means of production, and can only hope (or fight) for an at least approximately just remuneration, or that they can share in the wages of those who receive any. In such a society, any work done in the form of wage or domestic work or in other forms of 'dependence' is always also exploited work in a functional sense. Even 'independent', self-desired or even self-decided work is not exempt from the exploitation context of capitalist society.

In this comprehensive sense, the work of children, in so far as it is subjected to the system imperatives of capitalist society, is also exploited work. And this applies – as Nieuwenhuys (1994 and 2000a) has convincingly shown – not only to wage labour in the narrow sense, but also to the usually unpaid work within the sphere of the family economy.[5] In order to find the reasons for the exploitation of children, it is therefore necessary to consider children's work in its system-conditioned social forms, and to enquire how the conditions come about which degrade children to the status of objects of 'economic advantage', that is, a mere embodiment of labour potential whose 'value' is measured solely by whether they promise economic gain or profit.

However, just as there are differences in the work of adults in the degrees and forms of exploitation, and thus also varying ways to influence the conditions of one's own working activity, not all exploitative employment situations involving children are similar. In order to grasp the effects and meanings of work for children, it is therefore not enough only to speak of 'exploitative' work. It is necessary to consider more exactly the conditions under which it takes place and to characterize them. Here, above all, the important question is how far the children are subjected to the power or even arbitrariness of others, i.e. how limited their scope for action is. In the case of 'exploitative' work, it needs in particular to be asked whether the conditions under which it takes place can be improved or influenced by the children themselves, or whether alternatives must be found or created for and with the children.

One way to understand the special character of the exploitation of children is to enquire why their labour potential is rated lower than that of adults and exploited more. This is expressed, for example, in the fact that their work is generally lower paid than comparable work done by adults, or that no pay at all is given, with the claim that it is not 'proper' work but a form of 'helping' or 'learning'. Or that the remuneration is paid not to the children but to their parents, and the children's work is treated as a natural component of the family labour potential. Or that children are rewarded in kind rather than in cash. Or again that it is not considered necessary to grant working children the same working rights that apply to adults.

Like the economic exploitation of adults, the exploitation of children is a 'structural feature of modern capitalist economies' (Lavalette 2000: 214). It is important to emphasize this in view of the widespread view that the exploitation of children is essentially to be attributed to the 'moral defects' of individuals in dealing with children. If one sees the exploitation of children as a 'structural phenomenon', it helps one to realize that it is not abolished by the introduction of 'modern' methods of production or by economic growth. This is shown by the fact that the exploitation of children is still general in the 'modern' globalized economy, and that it exists both in the dependent societies of the South characterized by poverty and in the 'advanced economies' (Lavalette) of the North.

By reason of the mode of functioning of the capitalist economy, there is a tendency to reduce people to their characteristic of representing (exploitable) labour potential, degrading them to a mere source of profit. This is not essentially changed when – as is increasingly common today – people have to deal with the marketing and application of their labour potential themselves, either in the South as 'mini-entrepreneurs' in the informal economy, or in the 'advanced economies' of the North as apparently autonomous 'labour entrepreneurs'. The worldwide capitalist economy produces a great quantity of goods ('material wealth'), but also a great number of people who are poor and disadvantaged, whether because – as in the South – they live from hand to mouth and must fight for survival, or because – in the affluent societies of the North – they are threatened with missing out, are pushed to the margins of society, or are dependent on 'assistance'. The 'poorer' and the 'more needy' people are, the more they are obliged to bow to the existing conditions, and put up with work and working conditions that have disadvantageous consequences for them. Or they have little alternative to acting in a manner that is criminalized, whether by robbing a supermarket, rebelling in the street or sabotaging the mode of functioning of the 'system'.

More detailed approaches to explaining the exploitation of children

A general reference to the structures and modes of functioning of capitalist economies is not sufficient, however, to explain the particular risks of the exploitation and disadvantaging of children. Nor can it explain the varying degrees of risk and the specific and quite different forms of exploitation to which children in the South and the North respectively are exposed.

For the societies of the South, there is agreement, from children's movements (see Chapter 1) to the World Bank (see Fallon and Tzannatos 1998), that 'poverty' is a constituent factor in the economic exploitation of children. This does not mean that poverty necessarily has to lead to exploitation, or that exploitative children's work can only be explained in terms of poverty. For example, there are numerous poor families whose children are not employed, or which take the trouble to protect their children from exploitation. But the greater the poverty the greater is the pressure to neglect the negative consequences of certain kinds of work for children in relation to the relief given to the family by their children's income or the effect of the children's work. For the children themselves, too, poverty means fewer options to refuse unacceptable work or working conditions. In the 'affluent' societies of the North, the poverty factor is much less important for the exploitation of children, but it is not completely irrelevant here either. This can be seen, for instance, in the fact that children from poor families usually have to make do with worse-paid jobs.

The low social status of children within the age hierarchy can be regarded as a further risk factor in the exploitation of children which cannot be derived *immediately* from the functional laws of capitalist economy. Terming this 'weakness', as is commonly done, is unsatisfactory, inasmuch as it suggests that what is involved is primarily a biological phenomenon. In fact, the 'weakness' of children that makes them susceptible to alien interests and purposes is the result of a 'social construction', i.e. it results from social power relations and is thus also susceptible to change. The 'weakness' of children manifests itself in two ways: as failure to respect their subjectivity, and as exclusion from social responsibility.

Children's subjectivity is disregarded above all in authoritarian and strongly hierarchically structured societies, in which postulates of equality and individual rights are largely ignored. This is often the case in societies of the South in which communal forms of life and work based on reciprocity are being dissolved under the pressure of modernization and individualization, without new rules or institutions of community life or social responsibility having been able to develop. Here, the traditionally important inclusion of children in work processes, which used to be accompanied by respect for their peculiarities and development requirements, is often (especially in the urban context) perverted into the mere exploitation of an economic resource under the pressure of the individualized struggle for survival dictated by the need for money. The lack of protection and children's rights that goes with this may be further strengthened by dictatorial or 'caudillistic' political structures in which human rights and dignity in general count for nothing.

In societies of the North, although the subjectivity and protection of children are accorded a higher value, the children are at the same time excluded from the 'society of adults' and 'infantilized'. Here it is above all the ideology of childhood which places the children in a status of dependence, disadvantages them on the 'labour market' and in employment situations, and makes them more easily available. On the assumption that it is not them but their fathers who provide for the family, and that they are thus cared for, children can only 'gain their work experience through filling in certain economic niches left empty by the adult world' (James 1984: 11). They are channelled into jobs which, as typical jobs for children or school pupils, are rewarded merely with a kind of pocket money, or, where they do find work within the adult sphere, they are fobbed off with lower remuneration, justified with reference to the non-essential nature of their work, and have to accept unregulated working conditions not backed up by contracts (see Lavalette 1999: 221). Their disadvantaging and risk of exploitation may be further strengthened by the fact that they perform or wish to perform a kind of work that is forbidden them by law. In general, children's work activities are marginalized in terms of their economic value and social significance.

Elson (1982) attributes the 'dominant' forms of work that disadvantage children to three 'authority sources' which, according to her, mark the 'seniority system' of contemporary capitalist societies: 1) the authority of the adults in the family; 2) the requirements of the educational system, which is also governed by adults; 3) capitalism's 'need' for the easy and profitable utilization of labour.

> The seniority system obviously encompasses a range of gradations, not simply the division between children and adults, but children are at the bottom of it. And this means it is extremely difficult for them to secure full recognition in monetary terms for the skills they possess and for the contribution they make to family income. Only when they have passed over to adult status can they be recognised as 'skilled' or 'breadwinners' – or rather, only when the boys have passed over to adult status, for the girls the problem remains. (ibid.: 493)

The low status of children has the result that a) the children's abilities are poorly regarded; b) children are primarily given tasks that are considered economically less valuable, especially so-called 'reproductive' jobs; c) despite the large quantity of work they do, children are not recognized as workers with their own rights (see ibid.: 491; Nieuwenhuys 2000a: 287).

Elson brings the educational system into the picture, because the 'pupil role' that it assigns to children makes their out-of-school work appear a marginal activity compared with their school obligations, which deserves no particular recognition and may even be devalued and discriminated against as a possible source of disturbance in terms of really important achievements at school. James (1984) adds that obligatory attendance at education institutions limits children's possibilities of getting paid work and also strengthens the appearance of their 'immaturity' in the age hierarchy. In turn, this assumed 'immaturity' and the view of their paid work as an activity done in their 'spare time', has a negative effect on payment and the general conditions of their employment. 'The major structuring principle governing such work experience is the marginal social position of the school child to the main labour force' (ibid.: 12). Lavalette, too, stresses as one finding of his historical study on the development of children's work in Great Britain that, with the growing dominance of the school system, the work activities of children became 'marginalised' to out-of-school work, and limited to the kinds of jobs that could be combined with attending school, finally to be identified as 'kids' jobs', not to be taken particularly seriously (Lavalette 2000: 225, 227).

In the societies of the South, this problem appears in reverse. Here work is the chief activity of the majority of working children, and they frequently endeavour as best they can to harmonize their work with their educational interests, at times including school attendance. Not a few children would not be able to attend school at all without their earnings from work. From the viewpoint of those who wish to push forward 'development' in the direction of more 'modernity', children's work is, however, regarded as the main barrier to regular and success- ful attendance at school, and enforcing school attendance is accounted the magic means of extirpating children's work (for a critique of this position, see Liebel 2001b). The working children's organizations see in this a perspective that is not necessarily of advantage to them, as they rightly fear being pushed into a marginal social position that reduces rather than expands their chances of achieving an improvement in their conditions of living and working. Basically, they are resisting a develop- ment described by Elson, in terms of 'advanced' capitalist society, as the 'seniority system', with the disadvantageous consequences for children that she points out.

Elson describes the seniority system as a socially constructed age hier- archy 'in which those in junior positions are unable to achieve full social status in their own right. They are not full members of the society ...' (Elson 1982: 491). Their subordination does not mean, she states, that they lack the personal capacity for autonomous behaviour; indeed, many children have more ability than many adults. What it does bring with it is the 'lack of public means for recognition of the right to autonomy; and the lack of public means to sustain and extend autonomy' (ibid.: 492). In the seniority system, the lack of readiness of adults to question their own power over children manifests itself. 'The desire of adults to preserve adult power over children, through constructing certain forms of family, for instance, and certain forms of education, has given children an unenviable choice between exploitation at work and subservience in home and school' (ibid.: 494). Rather, children should be granted an ap- propriate income of their own as their right, as well as a firm connection between education and income-generating activities. The exclusion of children from the sphere of work, even if this is in the capitalist labour market, 'simply changes the way in which children are subordinated, rather than ending that subordination' (ibid.: 495).

Working children's potential for coping and resistance

The fact that children become the object of social structures and the actions of adults raises the question as to what this means to the children subjectively and how they deal with it. Economic exploitation is a particularly serious form of this behaviour, which degrades children to the level of objects. But also the exclusion of children from the sphere of work, on the grounds that this preserves them from exploitation, treats them as objects. This dilemma cannot be eluded by envisaging exploitative work as harmful to children and conjuring up work regarded as harmless and free of risks as an alternative. This is an abstract manoeuvre which at best holds its own on the drawing board.

This is not to deny that there is some point in keeping an eye open for forms of working and living in which children are respected as subjects, and in fighting for these. Logically, children who think about the working and living conditions that are forced upon them live in hope that their position may improve, and work for this in various parts of the world through organizations of their own. What I want to do here is make clear that exploitative work demands a more precise and differentiated analysis because it cannot simply be abolished and will continue to determine the reality of the lives of many children.

It is clear not only that are there many intermediate forms within the range of children's work, and that exploitation itself has many different forms and degrees of intensity, but also that even exploitative work does not simply abolish the working subjects. Certainly there are forms of exploitation that reduce their scope for action almost completely – this is the case above all in conditions of exploitation based on immediate personal dependence and in which the working subjects are socially isolated. But frequently the exploitation also arouses in those affected – whether adults or children – feelings of discontent and dissatisfaction, and may even provoke them to action, in circumstances that they are able to influence.

One essential reason for this is that even exploitative work has productive and communicative elements. It too produces utility values, brings workers together, and may give them feelings of pride and a common interest. This is a state of affairs that has long been self-evident among adults; why should it not apply to children too?

For instance, Antonella Invernizzi, in a study on children earning their living in the streets of Lima as vendors, identified playful, useful, relation- and identity-specific components, and points out that work has a 'double function' for the children: on the one hand, it renders survival possible, and on the other it contributes to their socialization. In the child's experience, the various elements combine to form a whole from the subjective perspective of the working child. The child's work is made concrete through the 'combination of links built by the child and with him through the daily transactions. ... Such an approach can only be actually developed by taking into account the relational and subjective aspects of each specific activity of the child and of the various children' (Invernizzi 2001: 51f). It is to be noted that the 'survival activities' analysed by Invernizzi are forms of work which, according to the view of the ILO, are harmful to children and should thus not be tolerated.

In the context of the movements of working children, such a viewpoint is termed a 'critical appraisal of children's work'. It proceeds from 'a dialectical standpoint. Whilst accepting that there is a problem ... it faces up to the unsolved tension between two poles: the dimension of coercion, violence and exploitation, and the dimension of individual and collective response against poverty and exclusion, that is, the dynamic reactivation of the so-called "silent responses" of the popular sectors, opening up a horizon of experience and socialisation in which identities, demands, hopes and projects grow and take root' (Schibotto 2001: 28). A critical appraisal of children's work thus serves by no means 'to accept exploitation, but to consider working children as potential active subjects in the critique of the mechanisms of injustice, to acknowledge their historical emergence and their right to be recognised as a social group (and not merely an aggregate of individual despair)' (ibid.: 28). It is based on the assumption that not only adults but also children are already in principle able to recognize the problems connected with their work, and to tackle these.

In order to understand the effect of the exploitative experience of work on children and how they can tackle it, it is not enough however only to consider the work and the working conditions, in however precise and differentiated a manner. It is also necessary to investigate the social, economic and cultural conditions that mark the lives and self-image of the children, and their individual motives, capacities and resources. The following aspects appear to me to be particularly important:[6]

- the socio-cultural context, e.g. whether the children's work is embedded in a culture that recognizes, or rejects, the work of children;
- the socio-economic situation of the children, e.g. whether they work from material need or from motives of their own;
- the motivation of the children, e.g. whether they identify with their work (because they find it interesting, or wish to help support their family) or experience it as a burden;

- the mental and psychological resources of the children, e.g. whether they are able to judge their experience of work and process it mentally, and are aware of their rights;
- the social status of the children, e.g. whether they receive support from the neighbourhood or through educational projects, or have organized themselves in order to be able to defend themselves better.

These aspects do not apply equally to all societies or to all working children. The social recognition of children's work is more likely to be encountered in rural regions with indigenous traditions, and in cities where the work of children is connected with income necessary for the survival of the family. It is no guarantee that the individual rights of the children are also respected, but rendering it possible for the children to be committed to their work and to recognize their own 'value' and social significance makes it easier for them to insist on their human dignity and to tackle unacceptable conditions of living and working.

When children and their families are in a situation of material need, as a rule they are obliged to take what they can get, so that the children have fewer opportunities to choose a kind of work that is of interest or advantage to them, or to limit the time taken up by work so that they have sufficient time for other activities, for example for playing or attending school. But even in such situations, the 'necessity' of the children's work is not to be confused with 'compulsion' to perform a particular kind of work. In families with an understanding of the children's own interests and requirements, it is usual for the children to be proud of making an essential contribution to the family's living. In such situations, the children approach their work with greater interest and are more able and willing to insist on tolerable working conditions and being treated with respect.

A self-aware attitude to work situations is also reinforced when the children know their rights and possess the ability and the self-confidence to speak up for these rights in their own words. This does not necessarily require a secondary education, but results from group experience with other children and from the mutual help in difficult situations that is quite normal among working children. Here, it is of prime importance that the children see themselves accepted by people they esteem, and grow up in an environment that shows understanding for their 'peculiarities'. Educational projects that respect children as subjects and appreciate their work may be able to compensate to some extent for the lack of understanding in the children's environment, and to increase the children's capacity not to let themselves be downtrodden by stressful work situations.

What can be done about the exploitation of children?

On the question of how to fight the economic exploitation of children there are two fundamentally different views. One considers work as such as damaging to children and therefore strives to eliminate their exploitation by removing children from the world of work. The other sees in work a potential positive value for children, and therefore tries wherever possible to resist exploitation by improving conditions in the children's favour, or creating work possibilities that benefit children. The first position is as a rule termed *abolitionism*, and the second the *critical appraisal of children's work*. Between these positions there are a number of variants.

The ILO and parts of UNICEF today propagate a kind of graduated abolitionism. They distinguish between harmless, bad and the worst forms of children's work. The first kind, termed *child work*, is not taken particularly seriously, and is accorded little attention. Particular interest is devoted to the 'worst forms' of children's work. ILO Convention no. 182, passed in June 1999, considers as such: child slavery, forced labour, child trade, recruiting of children for action in armed conflicts, the use of children in prostitution, for pornographic purposes and in forbidden activities such as drug production and trade, and finally particularly injurious kinds of work. Under this heading falls any kind of work which, because of its nature and the conditions under which it is performed, is likely to endanger the health, security or morals of children. The abolition of these kinds of *child labour* is seen as the priority goal, and the first step on the way to the abolition of all children's work.

Work on the new ILO convention, which occupied more than two years and in which organizations of working children were at times involved (see Sanz 1997), embraced the hope of a substantial improvement in the lot of millions of children who spend their lives labouring under particularly undignified and inhuman conditions. However, in its finally agreed and passed form, the convention failed to fulfil these expectations. Despite its reference to children's rights, it does not perceive children as thinking and acting individuals but only as victims who are to be 'rehabilitated'; and it considers children's work exclusively from a negative perspective, stressing practices that are predominantly *criminal acts* directed against children but are not their *work* as such. This means in fact discriminating against children's work and threatening it with additional criminalization.

In the context of the abolitionist logic that governs the ILO convention, there is room neither for a differentiated view of children's work nor for the concrete experience and perspective of working children. Those who are interested only in that which is 'bad' or 'worst' about children's work will tend to characterize as many kinds of children's work as possible as 'bad' or 'worst'. During the debate on the draft for the convention, a number of delegations competed in phrasing the criteria for the 'worst' kinds of children's work as broadly as possible, in the erroneous belief that this would help the greatest number of children. The absurd consequences to which the abolitionist logic of the ILO convention can lead are illustrated by the fact that the African organizations of working children characterize the number of 100 million children given by one UN document as working under the 'worst' conditions as exaggerated and counter-productive for their work (see Enda 2001b).

Another criticism of the ILO convention is that it is based on a reduced view of exploitation. With its definition of the 'worst forms of child labour', it covers only the forms of exploitation that stand in the way of the modernization and rationalization of the capitalist economy, those that are as it were outdated, and thus suggests that the exploitation of children is not essential to capitalism and could be eliminated without fundamental changes in the economic system (see Nieuwenhuys 2000b). This, however, leads to no practical measures to tackle the existing forms and causes of the exploitation of children.

The position of a *critical appraisal* of children's work, by contrast, proceeds from the consideration that the exploitation of children can be combated only when the scope for action and the options of the working children are expanded as far as possible and their social status is strengthened. This means, first of all, that their work, without regard to the conditions under which it is performed, must be accorded social recognition as value-creating. And this in turn requires that a culture of work be revived in society which sees work in its various possible meanings for human existence and human dignity, and relates these to children's work. This means that children's work must no longer be devalued and disregarded, simply because it is performed by children.

In the framework of the capitalist mode of production, it will not be possible to abolish either poverty or the exploitation of children in general. But just as adults are not excluded from the 'world of work' for this reason, it is not helpful to children to refuse them work. Instead, what is needed (especially where children's work is necessary to ensure the livelihood of their families) is to grant children, wherever they work and are affected or threatened by economic exploitation, at least the same rights of protection and participation as apply to adults or are considered requisite.

Since poverty and exploitation are essential components of the economy based on capitalist maxims and – considered worldwide – are being reinforced rather than reduced by the globalization of capitalism, anti-capitalist movements such as are developing today in the struggle against the structural adaptation programmes of the International Monetary Fund (IMF) and against the deregulation of the world economy are also in the interests of working children. And it is desirable that these movements also take up the topic of children's work. But it is precisely those who recognize capitalism as the essential reason for the exploitation of children who ought to take the trouble to imagine what a better society would be like and the part that children could play in it. Equating the fight against capitalism with the 'fight against child labour', as occasionally happens in this context (see Lavalette and Cunningham 2004), shows a lack of imagination. Such thinking remains caught up in the context and conditions of the capitalist economic system, and additionally in paternalistic patterns of thought in which children feature only as convenient objects – under capitalism as the objects of exploitation (or compulsory schooling), and in its mirror image anti-capitalism as the objects of the good intentions of well-meaning 'friends of the children'.[7]

The problem lies in the fact that these changes, located on the macro-level of the economic and social system, can only be achieved slowly and with difficulty. The majority of actions and measures related to the exploitation of children are therefore limited to the micro-level, which appears more accessible. At the same time, action on the spot is at least equally important, as long as the wider context is not lost sight of and excluded from action. For action on the micro-level, I believe the following three principles are indispensable.

In the case of all actions or measures, it should be observed whether they do in fact benefit the affected children and their families. This *child-centred approach* is fundamentally different from the hitherto dominant approaches, which only or primarily regard children as 'human capital' for the future of society or economic development (*human-capital approach, labour-market approach*) (see Boyden et al. 1998; Myers 2001). The child-centred approach enquires, for instance, whether an action based on prohibition brings advantages for the children affected. At least for children who work in the so-called informal sector (who are in the majority, unlike in the era of early European capitalism), the prohibition of children's work is directed against them and their families more than against those responsible for their exploitation. The prohibition of children's work also contributes to working children being deprived of rights, and prevented from defending or organizing themselves. Measures forbidding children's work in particular places or enforcing prohibition with the threat of trade boycotts have negative rather than positive consequences for the children, as concrete cases in Bangladesh, India, Morocco and Zimbabwe have shown (see Lolichen and Ratna 1997; Badry Zalami 1998: 29–30; IWGCL 1998: 84–6; Bourdillon 2000: 147–72). In order really to benefit working children, measures must therefore be directed to expanding the working rights of children on the spot, and introducing work and educational alternatives that correspond to the children's conditions and experience of life and which are accessible to them.

In the case of all actions and measures, it must be ensured that the children (and their families) are consulted, and that decisions are not taken over their heads. At their first world meeting in Kundapur (1996),[8] working children therefore particularly opposed the boycotting of products made by children, because their own experience and ideas had not been taken into account. Consulting those immediately affected not only corresponds to democratic principles and the idea of children's rights, but is also a decisive condition for the actions being attended by the hoped-for improvements.

All actions and measures directed against the exploitation of children should improve the ability of the affected children to resist on the spot; that is, they should strengthen working children. This can best be done by promoting the social recognition and self-confidence of the children through dialogue, and making it easier for them to organize themselves so as to help enforce their rights and interests. This could entail, for example, the trade unions admitting children or, where this is not yet possible for legal reasons, helping them to combine in organizations of their own and achieve legal recognition. There are already positive examples of this in India, Bolivia and Senegal.[9] In Germany, at least the IG Metall-Jugend (the youth wing of the metal-workers' union) supports the recognition of working children's organizations.

Notes

1. This is not necessarily the case where 'sexual exploitation' is involved, unless it is related to forms of 'commercial exploitation'.

2. This perspective results from the International Convention on the Rights of the Child which, contrary to widespread opinion, does not oppose children's work in general, but in Art. 32 expressly stresses children's right to be protected from exploitation.

3. The most commonly used criteria are described in detail in Liebel 2001c.

4. Beyond the 'economic' argument there is also the observation that *child labour* is the appropriate term when it takes place on a *large scale* and displaces school attendance, whereas *child work* takes place only on a *small scale* and in tandem with school attendance (see ILO 1993).

5. Particularly since 'employment is not the typical feature of children's exploitation in Third World societies but unremunerated work within the family context' (Nieuwenhuys 1994: 21). According to Nieuwenhuys, the exploitation of children takes place in three ways: a) via goods produced directly by children's work; b) via the savings made on the cost of adult labour; c) via the saving of the social cost of bringing up new generations of workers (see Nieuwenhuys 2000a: 287).

6. These aspects are to some extent discussed in research on dealing with stress, under the heading of 'resilience'.

7. In contrast to this, it should be recalled that Karl Marx not only considered the idea of the abolition of children's work under capitalism an illusion, but also accorded the work of children great importance for the overcoming of capitalism and beyond. In 1875, he noted critically on the 'Gotha Programme' of the SPD of the day, in which a general prohibition of children's work was demanded: 'A general prohibition of children's work is incompatible with the existence of major industry, and is thus an empty pious wish. Its implementation – if it were possible – would be reactionary, as, given the strict regulation of working hours according to the various age groups, together with other measures for the protection of children, the early combination of productive work with instruction is one of the most powerful means of change in today's society' (Marx 1969: 32). In the first volume of *Das Kapital*, Marx states more concretely how children's work must be 'in its unmodified, brutal capitalist form, where the worker exists on behalf of the process of production and not the other way round, the pestilential source of ruin and slavery' (Marx 1979: 515f), but under different social conditions it can become 'on the contrary a source of human development' (ibid.: 516).

8. The text of the declaration is reproduced in Liebel et al. 2001: 351.

9. These are reported on in several contributions contained in ibid.

9 | How working children resist exploitation and strive to share in decisions about their work: experiences and examples from various continents and periods

§ HITHERTO, working children have hardly been perceived as acting individuals. Therefore, little is known about what they have thought in the past about their work, or how they have tackled their conditions of working and living. In the annals of trade unions and labour parties, they almost only figure as beings that do not belong in the world of work and should be removed from it as quickly as possible. Historians and sociologists, too, have so far seen working children almost exclusively as the victims of inhuman work practices, but not as subjects who have their own ideas and are able to defend themselves. Only recently has interest grown in the 'voices of the children' and their active role in the struggle for better working and living conditions.

In this chapter, I shall attempt some reconstruction of the actions of working children. First, I shall refer to the 'history of action' of working children in the capitalist industrial societies of the North, necessarily limiting myself to scattered sketches for lack of more widely available sources. In the following section, I shall try to give an impression of how working children in the present societies of the South tackle their working and living situations. This area is better documented, thanks to the working children's own social movements. Following this, I shall examine to what extent working children in both the South and the North develop interests, ideas and initiatives for forms of work decided by themselves. In this case it is necessary to distinguish between those who attempt to improve their conditions of work and those who aim for completely new forms of work.[1]

Early working children's history of action

The earliest reported example of a common initiative by working children is from Manchester (UK). In 1836 a group of children working in the textile industry sent a petition to the British parliament. As part of the international campaign for the reduction of the extremely long working hours in the growing industry, the children supported their interests with plain words: 'We respect our masters and are willing to work for our support and that of our parents, but we want time for more rest, a little play, and to learn to read and write. We do not think it right that we should know nothing but work and suffering from Monday morning to Saturday night, to make others rich. Do, good gentlemen, inquire carefully into our concern.'[2]

The Belgian historian Bart De Wilde has found early documentation of independent action by working children in his country, too. In 1839, at the peak of an economic recession, there were protests, which were bloodily suppressed, on the part of several hundred textile workers, who were led by a fourteen-year-old boy and of whom 'most were small boys' (Deneckere 1994, cited in De Wilde 2000: 15). At other workers' protests eight years later in Ghent and Brussels, most of the 'agitators' arrested by the police were children between eight and fourteen years old (De Wilde 2000: 15).

De Wilde (ibid.: 18) notes that his search for statements made by working children in the nineteenth century proved extremely difficult because the public debate on children's work and its final prohibition in Belgium were determined exclusively by adults. The same may be assumed with regard to other countries. The German historian Jürgen Kuczynski, who has dealt with the history of the workers' movement more intensively than almost anybody else, states that 'small events' such as those where children and adolescents 'took matters into their own hands' have mostly vanished from literature and history, but were presumably more frequent 'than we know' (Kuczynski 1968: 212). Nevertheless, there are some written records from Germany. In an 'Urban Yearbook' from Berlin dating from 1870, there is a sympathetic report of a children's strike:

> We may here mention a small intermezzo, particularly as it provides a contribution towards the characterization of the young people or children of Berlin. In Decker's factory, about forty boys who were employed there for pointillé and laying work went on strike and, what is more, carried it out victoriously. When on Saturday 1st August at break-time their weekly wage was to be paid out, these boys demanded 5 Sgr. a week extra per head. This was refused, so the forty boys stopped work, and diverted themselves on the Wilhelmsplatz with childish games. But the paper *Fremdenblatt* had to be printed, so that the Oberhof printers saw themselves forced to send a supervisor to the square at 11 o'clock with instructions to fetch the boys back. The boys came, but only recommenced work when the 5 Sgr. extra for the past week had been paid them. ('Berlin und seine Entwicklung' 1870: 286f)

Ruth Hoppe, a colleague of Kuczynski, heard of another children's strike by chance during a conversation with a man born in 1877. Her report runs:

At the age of eleven, he worked five and a half hours a day (and eleven in the holidays) in Köhler's steel wire braiding factory in Harta, where his job was to weave iron wire into rings. Twenty pfennigs were paid for 1,000 pieces. In 1888, there was a children's strike in this factory when two girls and four boys were given work that was so hard that they worked the whole week without earning a cent. In the holidays, when the owner was absent, they went to the foreman and asked for better payment, which he declined. Thereupon the children no longer went to work, but played in the forest. None of them told their families what had happened, except for one boy whose father was a social democrat and distributed progressive literature (e.g. the *Pfaffenspiegel*) in Harta. The next day, the procedure was repeated. Although the foreman threatened 'school punishment' (i.e. a severe beating!) and to fetch the police, the children went to play again. On the third day, the owner returned, and the children went back to their old wage. (cited in Kuczynski 1968: 211)[3]

Another form of resistance to unacceptable working conditions that was presumably widespread at that time, 'in which children could take an active part together with their parents, was "sabotaging working time": the children came late to work and prolonged the breaks as much as possible' (ibid.: 113).[4]

The SPD newspaper *Vorwärts* reported on 13 June 1914 on an action by children working in agriculture in the following words:

The children too are resisting. Like most of their fellow workers, school-children from the surrounding villages had been recruited by the lessee of the estate of Bilderlohe [in the provice of Hanover] to pull turnips and do weeding. For this tiring work, the children had been promised a wage of 60 pfennigs an afternoon. In fact, however, the boys got only 20, 30 or 40 pfennigs. Thereupon they told the carters who were to fetch them later on to tell their master that they would no longer work for such a small wage, and the carts went home empty, to the applause of the children. (cited in Kuczynski 1968: 212)

Two other 'classical young people's strikes' (Kuczynski) are also reported from the first two decades of the twentieth century: the strike of the 'Rollmöpse' boys in Berlin in 1909, and a strike of young people in Brunswick in 1916.

At the time of their action, the 'Rollmöpse' were between fourteen and sixteen years old. They accompanied delivery vehicles and had the job of carrying freight goods to customers or fetching them from them. They also had to guard the cart and protect the freight from thieves. Any tips they received were to be given to the driver. The boys were not in agreement with this, and demanded of the union of transport workers to be included in the delivery workers' tariff, i.e. to get regular pay for their work. When they saw that their older fellow workers would not support their demand, they took matters into their own hands. 'They organized a number of actions which threatened to paralyse the whole of Berlin's road haulage traffic. Unharnessing the horses, cutting the reins, and similar actions to obstruct the proper execution of delivery traffic led to violent public arguments' (Deutschlands Junge Garde 1955: 47f). Through their action, the young people succeeded in getting paid a fixed weekly wage of 12 marks and 'in the older workers at last recognizing their young fellow workers as having equal rights and seeing that they could all only get their demands of the entrepreneurs met by acting together' (ibid.: 48).

The strike of young people in Brunswick, which took place during the First World War, was directed against a decree issued by the military leadership ordering that the wages of adolescents should partly be retained as a measure of 'compulsory saving'. To protest against this decree, many young people failed to return to work following the demonstrations on Labour Day, 1 May. The journal *Jugend-Internationale* (no. 5, 1 September 1969) contained the following report:

On 2 May, the strike that had begun during the May Day demonstrations extended. ... a meeting of 800 took place at which it was announced that the General Command had partly rescinded its order. The rate of pay had been raised from 16 to 24 marks. Unimpressed by this concession, the young people resolved to maintain their struggle, and the strike extended still further, with some firms unable to function. On 3 May a meeting took place in the street at Mastbach attended by almost 1,800, including nearly 300 girls. At the same time, unrest broke out at the potato market in the city centre because of the shortage of potatoes, with the habitual police attacks contributing to the embittered feelings. The authorities appealed to the representatives of the labour organizations to 'ensure peace and quiet'. A delegation of young people set off for Hanover to get in touch with the party leaders and convey the demands of the young people to the General Command. The General Command attempted another compromise, 'excluding the lifting of the savings order', but promising further concessions. A big meeting took place in the Wählhausgarten, where the adults exhorted the young people to resume work. But they stood firm. The strike spread still further. In the evening, there were clashes at some points with the soldiers, who hit out at the young people with the butts of their rifles. In the session of the trade union committee, a sympathy strike of adult workers was considered. The next day, 5 May, the General Command cancelled the savings decree completely. (cited in Hoppe 1969: 206)[5]

Further remarkable reports on the organized activities of working children come from the USA (see IWGCL 1998: 61; Nasaw 1985: 167–86). In 1902, together with their adult fellow workers, children working in a coal mine went on strike against the particularly inhumane treatment of the children and in pursuit of higher wages for all the workers in the mine. Unfortunately, nothing is known about the part played by the children in the strike, or its result. The other example dates from 1899 and relates to newspaper boys (so-called newsies) in New York. They had founded a trade union of their own, to resist the lowering of their sales commission that the press barons had decreed. In this case, it was reported that the children were successful in cutting back the circulation of the two afternoon papers and forcing the two most powerful publishers in the United States to alter their distribution practices. The following years newsies in other cities also formed unions, giving a stimulating example to other working children, such as messengers and shoeshine boys.

> The children's unions owed their existence – and whatever strength they possessed – to the informal networks that preceded them. The boys knew and trusted one another from the neighborhood and the streets. No extensive organizing campaigns were necessary to convince boys to join a union with their friends. … When their earnings were threatened, they did what they had to do in order to protect them. They cemented their informal communities of the street into quasi-formal unions, held mass meetings, elected officers, declared strikes, paraded through the streets shouting their demands, 'soaked scabs', and held together as long as they possibly could. Along the way, they tried to have a good time. The children's strikes were serious matters, but they were also occasions for community celebration, for marching en masse up the avenue, for playing dirty tricks, for making and wearing signs, and for ganging-up against troublesome adults, especially the boss's still loyal employees and the police who tried to protect them. (Nasaw 1985: 177, 168)

A further example comes from Denmark. There was a strike in the tobacco industry there in the 1890s in which children played an active part. In March 1901 the strikes had also reached a tobacco factory in the small town of Holbaek in Seeland. In the newspaper *Holbaek-Posten*, the following report was to be read under the heading 'A lost battle':

'The small tobacco children who were so joyfully striking yesterday are labouring in Herr Andersen's factory today for the same wage as before. The only result of their action is that some of them, it is said, got punished at home for their foolishness. This is sad ... ' (cited in Coninck-Smith 2000: 210–11).

A rare report on an action of working children in the 1950s comes from the Weser-Solling area in Germany. A group of children there stopped work to support their demand for a 'fair' wage:

There were twelve of us boys, most of us about thirteen years of age. We were to pull turnips on a farm in our village. The sun was burning down from the sky – we did not feel like working at all. We were only doing it for the money. In the neighbouring village, on Götzenhof Farm, the children were getting two marks an afternoon. We wanted the same! When we told 'our' farmer we would not work unless he gave us two marks as in Bodenfelde, he did his nut. He raged and shouted, but none of us gave in. Ten minutes later, the strike was over: the farmer agreed. But it took him several days to recover from our action. (Schäfer 1916: 139–40)

Contemporary working children's actions

Reports of actions carried out by working children in recent years have come so far almost exclusively from countries of the South. Two types of action can be distinguished. On the one hand, those with the goal of improving working conditions immediately or in the short term, or to compensate for negative consequences; among these are, for instance, actions of mutual assistance, which are mostly undertaken at a local level or by small groups. On the other there are those that aim to create better framework conditions in the medium or long term. These mostly take the form of demands or suggestions directed at adult organizations or institutions, i.e. state institutions, trade unions or children's rights groups, which are expected to have more power and influence than the children themselves. Both types of action are often combined with an attempt through the media to interest the general public in the children's situation and demands, and thus to 'sensitize' the (adult) population to them.

One example of the first type is that of the 'fish pirates' in the Peruvian coastal town of Chimbote. They have formed small unions (*sindicatos*), partly in order to organize their work better, and partly to resist the owners of the fish factories and the truck drivers, who obstruct their work and frequently even take the law into their own hands. The children earn their living 'illegally' by following the trucks that take the fish from the harbour to the factory with linen bags on their shoulders, jumping on the trucks and filling their bags, which they then throw to other waiting children. In their *sindicato*, the children not only plan their work, but also consider how they can defend themselves better from attack. By means of a common fund (*caja común*) to which all the children make a small contribution, they organize common actions to draw attention to their situation or to help a *compañero* in need (see Dücker 1992: 54ff).

Another example is that of the shoeshine children in La Asunción, the capital of Paraguay. They allocate their workplaces by deciding who is to work where in the morning and who in the afternoon, so that they can attend school during the other half of the day without worrying about finding a site. A similar initiative is reported of the 'parking boys' of Zimbabwe. They agree among themselves who will guard parked cars at which sites, and in this way manage to preserve their workplaces (see IWGCL 1998: 62f).

When the Nicaraguan government decided to drive the children who earned their living at the traffic lights of Managua in various kinds of jobs from their workplaces, the movement of working children (NATRAS) declared its solidarity with the children. They organized meetings at a road junction and demanded that the government should instead make a serious attempt to fight poverty, and see to it that the children no longer had to pay to attend school (see Dulisch et al. 1997: 40ff).

A form of action widespread in the children's movements in several countries is mutual assistance in cases of need. Thus, for instance, children made it possible for a boy whose shoeshine box had been stolen to acquire a new one. Or they persuaded the boss of a girl who had fallen ill to pay for the costs of necessary medical treatment. Some children's groups have instituted a solidarity fund or a common account from which the essential expenses of individual children who would otherwise be unable to deal with their situation are paid. The money is obtained through requests to businesspeople, doctors or other affluent citizens, or the children contribute part of their earnings. In one case (see Swift 2001: 183), with the support of adults, children founded a credit cooperative into which they regularly pay small amounts. This enables especially needy children to gain access to school, training courses or medical care. The granting of credits to children's groups, to make it possible for them to found their own cooperatives, is also planned (see Ennew 2000: 137).

Actions of mutual assistance related to conditions of work are also described in one report on children's unions in India. In one case a boy had been beaten up by a security guard and wrongly accused of having destroyed the windscreen of a car. Some other children had observed the scene, and complained to the police. The car owner had to apologize and pay the costs of the boy's medical treatment. In another case, a boy had been abused by a hotel owner and thrown out of the hotel; the owner also kept back his pay. The children's union group, to which the boy belonged, decided that it was too dangerous for him to return to the hotel to demand payment of his wage. They resolved that they would all make a contribution, so that the boy could instead buy a basket for the sale of vegetables (see Swift 2001: 189).

A direct influence on working conditions has also been exercised by the initiatives of shoeshine boys in various countries to acquire shoe polish in large quantities to reduce costs, and to gain access to rooms in which to keep their working materials secure overnight or during their absence. Children active in street trading often protect themselves from the loss of their takings by asking adult traders whom they trust to keep them for them. It is reported from Colombo, the capital of Sri Lanka, that children sleeping in the street keep their money in their mouths (see Ennew 2000: 136ff). In Johannesburg (South Africa), children working in the street have organized a kind of savings and credit system among themselves, with the aid of which they deposit their takings for later use or for emergencies (see Swart 1990).

The second type of action includes those by means of which employers and others having responsibility for the working conditions of children are put under pressure. Such typical trade union forms of action can be found in many countries of the South. When it became known in the Indian city of Bangalore what terrible working conditions obtained in some hotels, the local children's union organized demonstrations in front of one of these hotels. They had found out that twenty-six children were lodged in one room with no windows, light or fresh air. These children had to work from four in the morning until midnight. To wake them, they regularly had boiling water poured over them. Blows were routine. Frequently, too, both pay and food were withheld. When the children learned that the hotel owner came from a village in which some members of the children's union also lived, they began to demonstrate in front of his house as well. After the hotel was closed down, the children sued for payment of their wages (see Swift 2001: 190).

Other actions carried out by children's organizations are directed at political institutions and civil social organizations, to persuade them to be active in the interests of working children. For instance, children exhort the government to erect small huts at road junctions or other children's public workplaces, in which they can protect themselves from the sun, rest, and keep their working materials. Or they demand that the police protect them at their workplace from aggression and stress. Or again they demand of the health and school authorities that working children should no longer be disadvantaged or suffer indignity in hospitals or schools. In Nicaragua and Senegal, children's organizations succeeded for a time in making contractual agreements with the government. In Peru, after protracted negotiations, working children were finally included in social insurance. In Senegal (West Africa), girls who have migrated to the city and work as domestic servants are pressing for living conditions to be improved in their home villages sufficiently for them to be able to return and fend for themselves there.

In some countries, children's organizations also attempt to influence legislation. For instance, they demand that children be granted the same working rights as adult workers, such as the same wage for the same work, protection against dismissal, or protection against discrimination in the workplace. Or they petition institutions that working children can address without the mediation of adults for the rights formulated in the UN Children's Rights Convention, and to enforce effective protection at work. In India, for example, Bhima Sanga, an organization of children who work in the informal sector in the city of Bangalore, has pressed the local and national governments to recognize them legally as workers with equal rights (see ibid.: 187ff).

When children concern themselves with working conditions, as a rule ideas also arise as to possible alternatives. The still widespread assumption that working children wish nothing more ardently than to stop working does not correspond to the facts, according to my own experience and the studies I know of. On the contrary, the desire to work on condition that their own will, needs and human dignity are respected is much more common. Above all, when the hope of achieving some improvement in working conditions turns out to be difficult or even impossible to realize, children begin to want to undertake work of a quite different kind, over which they can exert an influence.

In terms of the origination of independent forms of work by children, two approaches are to be distinguished. On the one hand, there are those that come about in the course of the children's daily lives and are created by them, partly in conjunction with neighbours, parents, etc. On the other are those that are created as part of policy and educational measures of support by adults for and with children.[6] The two kinds of approach cannot always be strictly distinguished; for example, in the organizations of working children the children's own initiatives are mixed with the supporting activities of concerned adults.

Working children's own initiatives with the aim of practising independent forms of work are to be found above all in the societies of the South,
but in recent years have also been evident in Europe. The conditions of
their origin and their forms of realization vary widely, however.

Self-determined work by children in the South

In the South, initiatives on the part of the children themselves to
originate self-determined forms of work arise mainly from the poverty-
induced necessity to take their survival into their own hands and to
'invent' a kind of work that renders survival possible.

> Someone living on or beside one of the mountains of garbage on the
> fringes of the big city may become a collector of glass or metal, or will
> attempt in some other way to live off the city's garbage. In the bar-
> rios [slums], which are far from access to the public water supply, they
> become water-carriers, and in the sluggish city traffic the red phases of
> the traffic lights are used to clean the cars' windscreens. Where there is
> no chance of any kind of work, it is sometimes created artificially, for
> instance where the children erect obstacles in the roads leading out of
> town and collect payment to remove them. (Schimmel 1993: 79)

A similar example is that of the children who on their own initiative
mend the potholes on cross-country roads, expecting drivers to reward
their services.

In the case of such initiatives, the achievement of self-determination
of the work is not the goal as such; it emerges as it were as a side
effect in a situation in which the children have to rely on themselves.
Also, it is a kind of self-determination that is always threatened, as the
children are never completely autonomous but are frequently dependent
on adults (e.g. middlemen or customers), and because their work often
takes place in an environment that endangers their health or even their
lives. Furthermore, they have very limited possibilities for exerting an
influence on their surroundings and altering them in accordance with
their wishes. It is therefore wrong to pretentiously term children who
take their work in their own hands in this way 'entrepreneurs'.[7]

At the same time, the fact that it is indeed important to the children
to preserve as much independence as possible and to make their own
decisions while working should not be overlooked. In a study on children working in the streets of the Uruguayan capital Montevideo, it is
stressed that, together with the self-earned income, what particularly
satisfies the children is acting themselves and not being dependent on
the benevolence of others.[8] To them, 'the independence of the street is

an important value, even when the child belongs to a group' (Lucchini 1998: 42). This independence is also sought when the child recognizes that there are numerous difficulties in the street. From the perspective of 'independent' children, children working for a third party lack the necessary skills, especially the necessary cunning or slyness.

It is precisely among children working in the streets of cities that informal forms of work organization often come about which serve to secure or expand their scope of action. For instance, they agree on the places and times at which they work, or they combine to defend themselves against adult competitors who compete for their workplaces.[9] Children working as shoe-cleaners are as a rule proud of their activity and show outwardly by their behaviour how important their personal independence and dignity are to them.

Attempts to render self-determined work possible for a number of children at the same time in an organized form go beyond the forms of self-help that are otherwise possible in daily life. They are seen as collective attempts to replace forms of work based on exploitation by forms of work in which the ethical maxims of solidarity, respect and human dignity are guaranteed. In this way, within the framework of the movements of working children, the beginnings of an economy of their own can be seen, enabling the children to work under conditions influenced by them and to earn their own living. These exist in many countries of the South, as will be illustrated below by several examples.

In the Colombian capital Bogotá, a project came into being in the largest market of the city, La Plaza, calling itself La Cosecha (the harvest). Children who had hitherto worked at the market in undignified and health-endangering conditions as carriers, garbage collectors and so on combined in five groups of ten each with a number of adult women. They make agreements with restaurants and private households concerning the delivery of fruit and vegetables. According to demand from their business partners, the Cosecha groups buy the goods at the market in the early morning in large quantities and at the most favourable prices, and deliver them directly to the agreed destinations. In this, they are helped by the experience and knowledge they have acquired as 'insiders' of the market scene. The organization of purchase and sale, and financial affairs, are in the hands of the group as a whole. The space required for storage in the market and a small delivery van used on a rota basis by all the groups are placed at their disposal for a small consideration or on a credit basis by a foundation (El Pequeño Trabajador) that promotes projects involving working children.

A further example from Bogotá is the group Choqui Raps. In this, a number of girls from eleven to thirteen years of age together produce various kinds of sweets and sell them in their quarter of town. As a rule they have acquired the necessary know-how from their mothers. Other children from the same quarter have combined to produce jam and fruit juices. They take care that their products are of better quality than comparable products sold in their quarter. In the production and marketing, they obtain advice from expert adults, but without abandoning their own scope for decision-making.

In a Lima slum, as a 'productive project' of the movement of working children of Peru (MNNATSOP), a workshop has been instituted in which nine boys and girls aged between thirteen and seventeen make simple metal furniture under their own management. They have been active in the children's movement for years and thereby acquired the idea and the necessary technical and organizational knowledge to run the workshop. Instead of working many hours, as in the jobs they performed previously, they now work no more than four hours a day, and attend school in the afternoons. In making the furniture, they take account of the desires and suggestions of neighbours; meanwhile their customers are so numerous that, according to them, they earn an adequate income.

The creation of self-organized places of production has been propagated for years by the Peruvian children's movement MANTHOC. On its initiative, for instance, firms have been founded in which candles, congratulation cards, leather goods, biscuits or bread are made. The age of the children and adolescents varies according to the type of product. Working in a candle workshop are ten girls and two boys between twelve and sixteen, who at times pass on their experience and knowledge to younger children. Boys and girls aged between twelve and fifteen are involved in biscuit-making. The production is done partly to order, and the products are also to some extent sold by the children in the street or the market. A bakery in Lima run by two boys and a girl has its own sales shop at a favourable location. As a rule, the businesses are owned by MANTHOC, which also supports the children and adolescents in obtaining the necessary investment, carrying out training and organizing sales.

A particularly remarkable project is a cooperative for the manufacture of greetings cards, in which eighty-three children from eleven to thirteen years of age are involved, approximately half girls and half boys. The children live and work at different places all over Peru, and use the e-mail connections installed by MANTHOC to coordinate production and sales. The cards are painted and printed by the children themselves. They arrange the work in such a way that they have enough time to play and to attend school. Sales take place largely in the street, but thanks to the international contacts of MANTHOC also extend to European countries. With the income, the children support their families, but also organize common excursions and maintain a fund for special events (e.g. Christmas presents). Part of the income is used to reinvest in production and sales. The children identify themselves so strongly with their cooperative that they have given themselves a special name, calling themselves Tarjeta-NATs (*tarjeta* = postcard, *NATs* = working children and adolescents) (see MANTHOC 2002).

In Nicaragua, the movement of working children (NATRAS) has set up a photo lab and runs photography courses during which the children learn to use a camera, develop films and enlarge and process photographs. The children who take part in the photography courses as a rule already have some journalistic experience as reporters or correspondents for the journal of the children's organization, or for local newspapers or radio stations. They use the photo lab and their newly acquired knowledge of photography to make photographic reports or exhibitions on the lives of working children. On various occasions, the photos are also sold, providing the children with some earnings of their own.

Similar projects involving self-organized work also exist in other countries of the South. In Africa, they are frequently termed *self-sustaining economic projects*, and in Latin America *iniciativas solidarias económicas*, and they are often also seen as part of an 'economy of solidarity' going beyond the sphere of action of the children. Where they are set up and supported by independent organizations of working children, they serve not only to improve the material situation and expand the independence of the children immediately involved, but also to strengthen the independence of the children's organization itself. One example of this is the production and sale of newspapers of their own. Their sales provide the children with an income, but at the same time serve to finance the activities of the organization and to spread its ideas and demands. Sometimes the children's self-determined economic projects are also a component of neighbourhood self-help actions, with the aid of which the inhabitants of slums attempt to improve their living conditions and to contribute to the development of the community.[10]

Self-determined work by European children

In Europe, too, for some years now forms of work by children far removed from the usual notions of children's work have been taking shape. In contrast to what happens in the countries of the South, they do not as a rule grow out of a situation of material need, but result from the children's wish to break out of the ghetto of childhood intended for them, where they are restricted to play and (school) learning. It seems that an increasing number of children at an increasingly early age see 'work of their own' as a way of securing skills and social significance and giving their lives new meaning.

In the few studies on children's work today in the 'affluent' societies of the North, attention is almost exclusively directed to children's wage labour, or doing 'odd jobs' for pay. Here, it becomes evident that many of the jobs done by children have little to do with exploitation, and leave some room for the children's personal initiative and creativity – for instance, in the case of gardening, private lessons or caring for old people. But the fact that apart from such jobs there is a broad spectrum of work in which the children themselves set the scene has been overlooked. One example of this is the rapidly growing number of children who sell their outgrown playthings, books and so on in public places or on market days, or persuade passers-by with performances of music or dancing to pay attention to them and cough up a few coins. Another example is the 'children's flea markets' that are rapidly becoming popular, which often come about only with the support of adults, but would not be thinkable without the children's own initiative.

In a remarkable study on children's work in Russia today, it is pointed out that a growing number of children from the age of seven 'organise their own labour and utilise the resultant income for their own wants and needs' (Mansurov 2001: 153). This work is semi-legal in character, as the children do not possess the permits and patents required for private trade, for instance, and often impinges on the criminal sphere. Because Russian children often take to this kind of work in an emergency situation, it resembles the self-help activities of children in the countries of the South more than those seen in the countries of western Europe. But it also shows similarities to these, inasmuch as the children are guided by their own wishes and needs.

In the recent debate on the sociology of childhood, the view has been put forward that children's work in the post-industrial societies of the North has not only taken on new forms and meanings but is increasingly marked by 'fluid borders between playing, learning and working' and is linked with 'social and cultural activities' (Hengst 2000: 73). The work of children today is no longer restricted to wage labour in the traditional sense. The service sector in particular has become so widely varied that many new jobs and kinds of employment have come into existence that are no longer on the same level as the forms of children's work that were usual here in former times and still are in the societies of the South.

There are now 'possibilities of work that are closer to hobbies and at the same time less age-specific, and thus more adult and stimulating' (ibid.: 88). They are enhanced by the new communication technologies, as can, for example, be seen in the wide-ranging and independent use of the computer by children. Children are also taking on new tasks and intervening in fields and affairs that used to be reserved for adults. Hengst interprets these processes and 'new spectrums of activities' of children 'as early attempts to come to terms with a society ... that will no longer be determined by the model of a standardized employment situation, that is, a society in which mixed forms will become the rule, new relations between work and other activities will come about, which ... in some respects may be reminiscent of pre-industrial kinds of employment, but in which quite evidently future forms of working and living become apparent' (ibid.: 88).

An interim stock-taking

Children who work give their work thought, and in many cases resist the conditions under which they have to work. A history of working children as actors is yet to be written, and would require more precise source studies. In the countries of the South, the struggle for acceptable conditions of work and living is a part of daily life for many working children. It shows that children do not wait for things to be done for them, but themselves take the initiative to obtain forms of work that benefit them, and in doing so show a creativity that is still underestimated. In the countries of the North today, children are equally in search of opportunities and forms of work that are interesting to them and enable them to introduce their own ideas.[11] The activities delivered and chosen by children no longer fit in with a traditional view of (wage) labour, and require new consideration regarding the concept of work in societies that are no longer marked by formally regulated industrial work or the separation that goes with this between work and 'leisure'.

The approaches developed or shared by children to an 'economy of solidarity from below' are confronted by many difficulties and will become involved in contradictions similar to those faced by all attempts to make an (ethical) virtue out of (economic) necessity. In any case, they provide striking evidence of the fact that children's work can take on quite different forms and meanings from those usually associated with 'child labour'. They show that work does not have to be equated with exploitation, that it does not have to run counter to the children's need for play and learning, and that it can even contribute to promoting the development of the children's personalities. Thus it also stimulates the ability to imagine alternatives to a form of economy and society based essentially on the exploitation of human labour potential.

Notes

1. In the next chapter adult ideas and initiatives will be presented which are intended to offer 'positive' experiences of work for children and promote their education. At the end of this chapter I shall trace the pitfalls and development possibilities of the various work projects, also taking account of issues from the debate on the educational theory of work.

2. Submission from Manchester's Factory Children Committee, sent to the House of Commons in 1836. Accessible via <www.spartacus.schoolnet.co.uk/Irmanchester.child.htm>.

3. On this report, Kuczynski (1968: 211) remarks: 'This shows once again how fortuitous it is to get information on the class struggle of our children.'

4. On this, Kuczynski (ibid.: 113) quotes at length from a letter from a factory-owner to the Prussian Crown Prince, in which he protests about the fixing of a maximum of ten working hours for children in Prussia (see also Hoppe 1969: 95ff).

5. There were similar actions in Hanover, Magdeburg and Halle (see Kuczynski 1968: 120).

6. These will be presented and discussed in the next chapter.

7. Such designations can, for instance, be found in Faltin and Zimmer 1996 or Klein and Sell 2000, as well as in the publications of the children's rights group KRAETZAE, which is active in Berlin.

8. This is also a reason why most children are averse to begging and fall back on it only in severe emergencies. Most begging children are forced to do so by their parents or other adults.

9. Reference was made above to the mutual assistance of children in emergencies, in terms of the improvement of working conditions.

10. For the debate on the forms and development opportunities of the 'economy of solidarity' in Latin America, see Razeto 1997; Quijano 1998; Serrano 1999.

11. In both the North and the South today, many new forms of work by children are coming into being in the context of educational initiatives and institutions. These will be referred to in more detail in the next chapter.

10 | Ways to self-determined children's work? The significance and problems of educationally conceived work projects

§ THROUGHOUT the world, the number of working children is on the increase. Especially in the societies of the South, most of these children work under conditions that damage them and threaten their development. But by no means all those who are worried by this situation draw the conclusion that children's work as such is harmful and that child labour must therefore be abolished.

The movements of working children in the societies of the South are to be thanked for the insight that what is a problem for the children is not work as such, but the conditions under which it is carried out. A growing number of children today put forward the view that an improvement in the overall conditions of work – wherever possible – is to be preferred to measures that attempt to remove children from their workplaces at all costs. The sociologist Ben White, who works in the Netherlands, used for this position the memorable formulation 'not to *remove* but to *improve*' (cited in IWGCL 1998: 39).

It was shown in the last chapter how working children have again and again attempted to improve working conditions in their favour, and to create or demand new forms of work that benefit them. Today proposals are being developed also by educationists and sociologists, and educational workers on the staff of children's rights and aid organizations in many parts of the world, on the nature of work that can be supported and which is of benefit to children, and how to achieve this. And in the context of educational and caring institutions for and with children, many projects of 'self-determined' work are being set up.

This is the case in Europe as well. The point of departure here, however, is not so much concern about the exploitation or abuse of children, but rather the insight that the exclusion of children from economic processes has negative rather than positive consequences. Additionally, there is the observation that a rapidly growing number of children are breaking out of the 'unemployed' ghetto of childhood intended for them, and want to earn money, have new experiences or make themselves useful.

To begin with, some initiatives and proposals aimed at an improvement of the working conditions of children will be presented. Then some educationally conceived work projects will be discussed, beginning first with experiences in the South, and going on to experiences in the North. In conclusion – also with recourse to what was presented in the previous chapter – some pitfalls and possible perspectives for self-determined work by children will be discussed.

Initiatives for the improvement of children's working conditions

In countries of the South, initiatives on the part of adults for the improvement of children's working conditions are based mainly on the insight that children's work represents a contribution to their families' living that simply cannot be done without. They are regarded as alternatives to programmes and measures whose primary aim is to remove children from their workplaces, since, despite their good intentions, these measures frequently have the effect of putting the children in still more dangerous or harmful situations, for example exposing girls who had worked in carpet manufacture to prostitution (for specific instances, see Lolichen and Ratna 1997; IWGCL 1998: 84–6; Save the Children 2000: 41–2). Partly for this reason, working children oppose the boycotting of goods made by children (see the Declaration of the 1st World Meeting of Working Children, 1996, in Kundapur, India, in Liebel et al. 2001: 351).

Proceeding from the fact that many children must work or want to work and do so in small businesses, one member of staff of the British children's aid organization Save the Children has made proposals as to how, 'in the best interests of the children', the overall conditions of this work could be improved. She suggests wherever possible adapting the technology to the children's body size, to reduce risks; shortening working hours, to render school attendance possible; paying the children a 'fair wage' corresponding to the wage paid to adults for the same work – this would make it possible for the children to work shorter hours and improve their standard of living; guaranteeing health and safety measures, for example providing protective clothing and making the children familiar with safety regulations; providing social services and infrastructure for both children and adults, such as meals, health services, the care of small siblings, possibly even accommodation and separate recreation rooms for girls and boys; rendering possible accompanying educational courses, for example by financial support for the building and equipment of schools (Marcus 1998: 10f).

One example of this is the programme developed together with farmers by the Farm Orphan Support Trust in Zimbabwe. The farmers place land at the disposal of village communities, to be cultivated by families who are prepared to employ and care for orphans. The trust supports such initiatives by equipping the schools that are set up on the farms with materials and furniture. There are also plans to provide the families and the farm staff with the necessary knowledge to set up play centres for children, to promote the development of existing primary schools, and to offer health services (see Save the Children 2000: 67).

Attention is sometimes drawn to the fact that it is above all the responsibility of the employers to make work safer for children. It is not surprising that they have hitherto fulfilled this responsibility inadequately, not only because they have no economic interest in doing so, but because the prohibition of children's work that applies in nearly all countries makes the improvement of working conditions impossible. Those who support the improvement of children's working conditions are easily suspected of legitimizing the economic exploitation of children by making it less obvious (see Boyden et al. 1998: 225).

It should also be borne in mind that the majority of children do not work in 'formal' employment situations, in which an employer is clearly identifiable and can be called to account, but in 'informal' employment where the work roles and responsibilities are considerably less clearly defined and still less legally regulated. At the same time, it can be discovered even in 'informal' employment situations to what extent and in what ways children work in a self-determined way or otherwise, why they are dependent and on whom, and what opportunities there may be to arrive at more self-determined forms of work (on this see Liebel 2001c).

In this context the Nigerian section of the International Working Group on Child Labour has formulated some criteria by which efforts for the improvement of children's working conditions should be oriented:

• safety from external physical and social environments;
• protection from the inherent negative factors of work;
• hazards that have varying negative impacts on different age and gender groups;
• economic and psychosocial remuneration;
• the amount of training provided;
• the social placement value of the task. (IWGCL 1998: 9)

These criteria are very abstract and demand to be made concrete. But they offer the possibility of developing proposals or demands, according to the economic or cultural context, which offer working children realistic chances of improving their situation.

Another way of improving working conditions is seen in giving children the necessary knowledge and self-confidence the better to influence their work situation themselves. In this context the Canadian children's aid organization Street Kids International (SKI) has developed a curriculum for the further training of street social workers, aimed at providing street vendors and other children working independently in the street with basic knowledge of business procedures. It takes the form of a story about a small group of friends who work together and contribute their own special talents – related to typical business functions such as product development, sales, production, etc. – in a manner that permits them to be successful in their work, education and personal lives. This approach gives a healthy image of working children as clever, responsible, ingenious and able to solve their problems, and aims to strengthen these characteristics in the children (see Boyden et al. 1998: 224).

In addition, SKI has developed business schemes to promote the employment of children under conditions favourable to them. The first project of this nature came about in Khartoum, capital of the Sudan. There, business people and NGOs had experienced great difficulty in communicating with each other, as the postal and telephone services hardly functioned. They trained children in the identification of street names and in riding bicycles and negotiating traffic safely, then gave them each a bicycle and a uniform. The children are paid daily for their errands, with extra for long distances or deductions in case of non-fulfilment of the tasks. If a bicycle is lost, the child has to pay for it. On this project, Judith Ennew (2000: 138ff) notes that, among other things, it requires a relatively high investment, and exposes the children to high economic and traffic risks; it is ultimately less suitable for 'street children' than for adolescents looking for a job.

In several Latin American countries, the practice of street workers helping children who work in the street and who have similar jobs to combine in groups is widespread. In this way, they should be better able to help each other and improve their working conditions. There are two examples from Guatemala. A group of eight boys who wash cars in streets and parking lots is supported in looking for regular customers with whom they conclude contracts. In this way, the boys can calculate their earnings better and work under more tolerable conditions, for example in a courtyard instead of in the middle of traffic, or in the shade of a garage instead of in the burning sun. The other example is of three girls who used to go from house to house, and who were helped to conclude a contract with a restaurant that permits them to sell tortillas, and in addition self-made fruit juice. They too now have a more stable income and do not have to shout themselves hoarse in the street. They also support each other in case of illness.

In Mexico City, the municipal administration is trying to obtain better working conditions at least for the older children, thousands of whom are employed packing goods for shop customers (*empacadores*). Hitherto, the children received no wage for this but were dependent on the customers' tips. They also had to provide their working clothes themselves. The municipal administration finalized a contract with the entrepreneurs' association responsible for regulating working and break times and health protection, which grants the children access to state social insurance. Furthermore, the municipal administration runs seminars that promote the children's self-confidence and are intended to help them to take care of their health and utilize opportunities for education. Social workers employed by the municipal administration see to it on the spot that the regulations are observed, and urge the children to form organizations of their own to achieve further improvements in their working conditions (e.g. regular payment, free working clothes). This initiative does have a downside. Being restricted to children of at least fourteen, it has meant that younger children are practically excluded from this kind of work. The social workers are even instructed to check that the minimum age requirement is observed for employment in the supermarkets.

Initiatives for self-determined children's work in the South

The idea of work as 'self-determined', 'non-alienated' or 'non-exploitative' has characterized the history of capitalism from the beginning. Its early expression was in the proposals and initiatives of the 'Utopian socialists',[1] and later in various variants of the cooperative movement and anarcho-syndicalism, and it is found today in the numerous and varied initiatives and proposals that are discussed and practised partly in the South and partly in the North under labels such as 'economy of solidarity', 'social economy', 'community economy', 'alternative economy' or 'new labour', etc. These ideas, initiatives and movements were and are often linked to the idea of creating new forms of education and learning together with the new forms of work.

On the other hand, the history of educational theory in many parts of the world is rich in conceptions, theories and practical experiments in linking working and educational processes. The approaches of Rabindranath Tagore and Mahatma Gandhi in India may be mentioned as examples (see Talib 1998); also the long and varied history of socialist education and the education theory of liberation (*educación popular*) in Latin America and Africa, in which the idea of the 'production school' is repeatedly articulated and put into practice in various forms; the international movement of community schools; and finally the concepts of a 'work school' or 'polytechnical education' developed in the European school of 'progressive education' and socialist educational theory, of which in particular the ideas of the Russian educationist Andrej Blonski and the French educationist Célestin Freinet should be mentioned.

In the writings known to me on self-determined, non-alienated forms of work, and educational approaches to the linking of work and education, the question of 'child labour' is not touched upon, or only marginally. In the former case, the authors have to all intents and purposes only adults in mind as subjects of the new forms of work and economy. At best, children appear as profiting from the new forms of work and its socializing and emancipatory potential. In the second case, the question of children's work is mainly mentioned only in terms of educational institutions and educative aspects, without explicitly considering daily living circumstances and practices in the lives of the children. Meanwhile – both in the South and the North – a recent tendency in the educational debate attempts to relate the question of learning and the development of the personality directly to the problems and the context of the lives of children, and to develop new forms of working and learning *with* children.

We may quote as an example of this the ideas of an NGO seeking solutions to the problems of working children, their families and neighbours in a slum in Mexico City. To find such solutions, the staff of the NGO think it

> necessary to revise the concept of children's work, not only with a view to the norms that regulate children's work, where it is inevitable, but also with a view to the rights that the child ought to have to work with fair remuneration and under suitable conditions. To be consistent, children should be offered alternatives of their own to be able to liberate themselves from social repression and total economic dependence. Work appears to us in this way not only as an economic necessity but also as an opportunity for the children to develop their natural talents. When children's work is performed under conditions different from those of today it becomes the basis of the development of boys and girls. Legislation in favour of working children cannot relate only to current conditions – this would be tantamount to a justification of the exploitation of the children – but must relate also to a model of work that guarantees their development. (Griesbach Guizar and Sauri Suárez 1993: 87f)

The forms of work presented and discussed in the following section came about in the context of educational projects in and out of school, or are part of educational concepts that set out to link learning and working.

Not included are projects and concepts in which work is merely simulated or played, to learn something without economic significance or a certain degree of seriousness. By contrast, educational concepts such as that of the French educationist Célestin Freinet are of a different quality, since work here is serious in character and is more than a mere dry run.

School work projects in rural areas

With regard to the countries of the South, a recent publication states: 'Much is to be gained by creating appropriate opportunities for children who want and need them. Ideally, these should be systematically incorporated into an educational framework, structuring children's work in such a way that it becomes a vehicle for learning and social advancement as well as income' (Boyden et al. 1998: 340). According to the authors, the literature on non-formal education in particular, especially in Africa, is 'rife with experiences of this type' (ibid.: 225).[2] 'Programmes based on "learning by doing", in which the students earn money in a particular trade while in the process of learning it, have a long history, including through traditional apprenticeship systems. In modern times, many attempts have been made to meld the "hands-on" and income advantages of learning through apprenticeship with the efficiency of school instruction in groups (ibid.: 225; on the apprenticeship systems, see Overwien 1997 and 2001).

Reference is made to the Swareng Hill School run by the Foundation for Education with Production in Botswana: 'Children and young people would receive basic educational instruction in reading, writing, and maths within the context of operating a group development project, commonly in agriculture or construction. Under the guidance of one or more teachers, the group would undertake practical money-making activities which would serve both as a learning vehicle for the children and a source of financial support for both the children and the programme' (Boyden et al. 1998: 225).

In Africa, these approaches were pursued above all during the 1970s and discussed 'as a possible new model of popular education and local economic development' (ibid.: 226), but were not able to prevail owing to the hierarchical structures and rigid procedures of the state authorities. Boyden et al. believe that these approaches are more likely to succeed in the non-state area.

In India and Latin America, such educational approaches, to some extent with recourse to colonial experience, have a still longer tradition. In India, from the early twentieth century on, as a contrast to the elite colonial educational system, Rabindranath Tagore and Mahatma Gandhi developed concepts of education in which craft and agricultural work occupied an important place. They were guided in this by the idea of the traditional Indian *ashram*.[3] To Tagore, learning a craft is a means for the promotion and development of the creativity of the learner. It should help him to express himself, to find his place in the social structure, and thus also to find his own identity. In the school founded by Tagore (*Santiniketan*), which still exists, teaching takes place mainly in the open air; trees are planted, fields are cultivated, craft products and works of art made by the pupils are presented to the public.

Gandhi aimed at the foundation of 'autonomous village republics' in which the educational institutions (*Nai Talim*)[4] were to support themselves financially and materially by means of craft work. The place of learning for teachers and pupils was at the same time to be the place of production. Correlated subjects of study, connected interdisciplinarily, were grouped around the particular craft being practised. Lang-Wojtasik (1999: 9) makes this clear from an example:

> While a child tried processing wood in practice, it was able to learn something about the various kinds of wood and the places the wood comes from (geographical knowledge). In connection with the way a wooden bowl was made, there were many ways to understand the basic laws involved (general science), and for instance to acquire skills in the calculation of length, area and extent (mathematics). By making simple drawings and plans for the construction of the wooden bowl, basic knowledge in drawing (art) could be transmitted. Parallel to this, a song (music) from the Hindu tradition on the situation in life and the liberation of forest workers could be sung (social studies, Hindi). This song could be translated into the maternal language of the pupil (mother tongue) or the children could invent a way of adapting it musically. In addition, relaxation exercises could be tried (physical education) and a sporting game, e.g. a relay race using wooden bowls (sport) could be carried out.

To both Gandhi and Tagore, education always meant a means for liberation, both from alien colonial domination and from the structural violence and oppression inherent in the traditional Indian caste system. The inclusion of productive work was intended to render it possible for children of the oppressed and marginalized classes to exercise their right to education independently of the prescriptions of the ruling social groups and the colonial state, and enable them to liberate themselves from the ascribed status of social subjection. When Gandhi encouraged the children in particular to perform craft work and help their parents in such work, it was expected that they 'develop a sense of belonging not only to parents but also to the village and to the country. Learning through productive work made children self confident as they could pay for their own education through their own produce' (Talib 2000: 58).

In the pre-Columbian societies of America, especially among the Inca and Maya, 'work was one of the most essential forms of educational communication; instruction at school meant, also though not exclusively, being productive, i.e. providing part of the contribution to be made by the collective, sharing in work of the most varied kind – agricultural, craft, military, administrative, religious – and thus at the same time acquiring training in these fields' (Schroeder 1989: 152). The separation introduced with Spanish colonization between school learning as moral-religious instruction and 'training' in practical handicraft was further strengthened in the 'bourgeois' schools of the formally independent countries according to the European pattern: work, particularly in a productive form, had no place in this school, which served for the memorizing of pre-digested knowledge. In the course of the movements for independence in the early nineteenth century, however, there were attempts to make productive work (once again) an educational principle. In school models that resulted from this, not only was the subject of 'work education' introduced, but directly productive work was also performed in the workshops and fields belonging to the school.

The inclusion of productive work in the school curriculum was justified educationally with the argument that only thus was 'versatile' education possible, to overcome one-sided intellectual learning and enable the children to make their way in practical life. The concept of work from this educational point of view has two dimensions. On the one hand, the linking of work and learning is seen as something like learning by doing, in which the absorption of the subject matter to be learned takes place by practical application; on the other, it is understood as work 'producing utility value', making a direct economic contribution to society, the school or the individual pupil. In this way, educational considerations are merged with economic and social ones. The work integrated into the school curriculum was also to contribute to covering the costs of upkeep, keeping the schools independent of the public exchequer, and also rendering it possible for poor children to claim their right to education. Finally, in this way the school was also to exert a direct influence on the economic development of the environment.

To illustrate this concept of school, the Escuela Productiva (productive school), which has existed in practice since the 1970s in several regions of Peru, can be cited as an example. It sees itself as a possible answer to the growing problems of survival in rural areas and the urban slums, and is intended to contribute to reviving an economy of self-supply and rendering an autonomous and satisfying life possible for the people and their communities. The initiative proceeds mainly from social movements among the poor population and NGOs oriented to the basic ideas of *educación popular*; sometimes it is also the consequence of 'educational movements' supported by teachers and their trade unions. To some extent, an attempt is made to transform the state school into a 'productive school', and to some extent non-state schools are specially founded as communal institutions.

It is very common in rural areas to establish school gardens or keep commercially used animals (e.g. rabbits). They are looked after by the children, with support from the teachers and competent villagers. They serve both for the better nourishment of the children, and sometimes also of parents and teachers, and for the acquisition of knowledge that is fundamental for living and working in the country.

Some reports originate in the region of Grau in Peru. From two primary schools in Huancabamba, several teachers report:

> In all phases, we and the children have cultivated the school garden together, from the preparation of the soil to the harvest, and after that prepared the salad and vegetables for consumption. We can say with certainty that this activity has motivated our children greatly, and we have found them very contented and cooperative. On the other hand, we have also made a contribution to attacking the very serious problem of undernourishment, by supplementing the usual menu with the vitamins and minerals contained in the vegetables. In this way the children were able to strengthen their organisms, and avoid becoming an easy prey to illness. (cited in Mendoza Gálvez 1991: 15f)

From a primary and secondary school in Piscán (Yamango Morropón), a teacher reports experiences with a school garden and rabbit breeding:

> The pupils participated in the context of work study [*formación laboral*], natural science and social science. The parents shared the experience, and the qualified farmers passed on their knowledge on the preparation of the soil, sowing, pest control, etc. The parents also initiated and supported the committees for school breakfasts, to whom some of the foodstuffs made were handed over to improve the nourishment of the pupils. We purchased the rest in the village at a low price, with the aim of promoting both knowledge about suitable food and receiving a financial contribution for the requirements of the school. (ibid.: 16)

From a primary and secondary school in Lajos (Yamango Morropón), a teacher reports that the idea of a school garden came about above all

in order to promote among the pupils an awareness of the problems of the village community, such as the backwardness of the *campesinos*, the exploitation by the wholesalers to which they are exposed, undernourishment, and the need to organize themselves to solve these problems. At the same time, the school garden is to serve to improve the nutrition of the children and the community as a whole. Instruction in work study and natural science is largely built on the experiences with the school garden, which helped us to overcome the hitherto usual boring and unproductive forms of learning. It is also important to mention that work in the garden takes place not only in lesson-time but also afterwards. (ibid.: 17)

Another teacher reports: 'When the children choose the plants or seeds, and distinguish the various kinds of soil or climatic conditions, we are doing natural science. We are using mathematics when we measure the ground and the area to be cultivated or divide up the plots. In the language workshop, the children write poems, tell of their experiences in the garden, or re-enact them in play. In the drawing workshop, the children make comics [*historietas*] about the whole production process' (Sifuentes et al. 1991: 18). The same teacher describes the goals of the production school as follows:

First and foremost, we want to achieve an attitude that defends life, by making a contribution to survival with the children. This allows the child to introduce himself as a subject that participates, produces and collaborates with his community. In second place, we want to overcome the traditional conception of school according to which the child can only learn in the classroom. What we want to achieve is the opening of the school to the outside world, to place it in direct contact with reality, with the community, with the physical and natural surroundings, with living things, where the child is able to observe, study, work and create new things. Thirdly, we want to awake in the child the love for work and in this way give him the feeling that his own work is useful for life and makes it possible for him to enter into relations with others and to act with solidarity. We attempt to contribute to the child being self-sufficient, critical and creative, and acquiring an adequate capacity for tackling his own problems and solving them. (ibid.: 18f)

From a primary school in San Julia (Piura), a teacher reports how the pupils 'felt very contented' through their work in the school garden.

Above all, 'the community and solidarity' of the work had pleased them, and the fact that they 'could take home the products of their own work' (Mendoza Gálvez 1991: 19). As a rule, the children organize themselves in working groups, and each group elects a coordinator who cooperates closely with the teacher (see Sifuentes et al. 1991: 18f).

A further example is the programme Educación Rural Andina, which is practised in sixty communities in the Cusco area with primary school children. According to one report (Masson 1992), in the early 1990s it covered 114 tracts of land, which were mostly cultivated on an organic basis, and seven animal farms. Each child is given a plot or two animals for which it is responsible. In the course of the work, the children learn to calculate and measure the growth of the plants, and acquire knowledge on, for instance, natural insecticides, the use of urine, etc. This is intended to make the children aware of their own resources and enable them later as *campesinos* to free themselves from dependence on the pharmaceutical multinationals (e.g. BAYER).

These examples show that children's work has real significance in terms of the solution of daily problems, and for this reason can be interesting and satisfying to the children. The intention of promoting the learning process by means of work experience is not unconnected to the material aspect of work. 'As a place of education, the school needs a production centre, but this centre must be part of the local production system' (Gallardo et al. 1992: 191). We may assume that, in this way, for the children school acquires more relevance to their daily lives, in which they are also involved in work processes in the context of the family. The forms of work created in the school are not explicitly seen as an alternative to forms of work that are exploitative or otherwise excessively stressful for the children, but presumably contribute to strengthening their self-esteem and give them criteria by which they are better able to assess their daily conditions of living and working.

From a more recent study (Ames Ramello 1999) it emerges that the production schools set up in rural areas of Peru continue to exist despite many difficulties, and are even spreading.

In Nicaragua during the 1980s, the school model of the Escuela Rural Educación-Trabajo (ERET), which was founded during the Sandinista revolution, played an important part. Agricultural work was thus integrated into the curriculum of the rural primary school in such a way that the pupils' own actions acquired great importance for the learning process. A dynamic connection was established between school and community, and the pupils were included in socially useful tasks that contributed to the development of the community. The pupils were allowed to take home the products harvested, which were also sold in the community at cost price and consumed by pupils, parents and teachers on the occasion of functions at school. In this way, the supply situation in the community, which was as a rule difficult, and the learning conditions of the children were substantially improved (see Arrien and Matus Lazo 1989: 219ff).

In the school in Brazil that came into being during the land occupations undertaken by the landless movement from the early 1990s onwards, the children also perform productive tasks. 'Helping in the fields and the view of work as a human right are a natural part of the educational and socialization process of the children of the landless' (Recknagel 2001a: 244). The problems dealt with in school have a direct and concrete relation to the reality of the children's lives. Daily life in and out of school go hand in hand; the problems familiar to each child, such as racism, repression and violence, are addressed and tackled through values such as respect for others, their colour, culture, faith or gender. The imparting of knowledge is related to experience and action. As well as working together, song and dance are important media for understanding the children's own history, and for the search for solutions (see Leite García 1997).

School work projects in the urban context

In the urban context, too, there are numerous attempts to realize self-determined work by children in the context of educational institutions, but with differences. Here what is involved is mainly projects in 'social education' that are set up for the direct support of the working children. They are conceived as places where the children obtain respite from their usually precarious situation, and which strengthen their self-esteem and encourage them to push for their interests and rights. A growing number of these projects are linked to 'school' and 'occupational' educational measures that are useful for the children either in terms of improving their work situation or of opening up safer forms of gainful employment. To begin with, I will give an outline and some examples of 'schools' that have come about in the context of such projects and whose approach to learning and action is centred on work and production.

They are explicitly addressed to working children who are disadvantaged in regular state schools and have frequently been obliged to stop attending them. As a rule, they come about on the initiative of parent or youth groups, communal action or Christian communities, or in the context of social work projects in the community or the street. Sometimes the children too play an active part in the foundation of such a school. They rarely operate in buildings intended for school use. Much more frequently, they begin at a street corner, under a tree, in a family courtyard, in a church community centre, or a former vegetable shed or storeroom.

In many cases, they resemble informal study circles, without a curriculum, formal procedures, compulsory attendance or grades. In other cases, the learning process is more strongly systematized; working groups or classes are formed and an attempt is made to ensure fairly regular attendance.

As a rule, the schools are closely connected with their environment. They are situated in the middle of the area of town or near the houses or huts in which the children live, or where the children work, for example on the site of a market or on the fringe of a garbage heap. Even when the school does have a building of its own, teaching does not all take place within its walls. Any place at which the children live or work becomes a place of learning. The work experience of the children is taken up and used for the learning process. In the context of the school, the children are given new work experience, to enable them to learn in a way familiar to them and to understand better how they can use that which they have learned at school.

The initiators of the schools discussed here are not content with just any kind of formal 'school education'. They are concerned that the children should acquire knowledge and skills of practical significance for their survival and changing their living conditions. They learn how to make practical use of their knowledge of reading and arithmetic, and come to realize at school what use this knowledge has for them. In a number of these schools, the acquisition of such knowledge is not even paramount. In one school in Peru, for instance, 'the most important thing for the children is to learn to talk, for they live by being able to sell their goods. Therefore they want above all to learn how they can best attract the customers' attention. We have found that progress in this form of communication makes the transition to writing much easier' (Cussiánovich 1988: 92). Teaching is often embedded in a number of activities into which the children can introduce their own experience of life and work.

In the evaluation report of a school in Neiva, a town in Colombia, an account is given of the expectations with which the children come to school, and how an attempt is made to satisfy them.

It is the working child, occupied with productive activities essential for survival, that comes to the school, in order to make the utmost use of his or her time, above all for the acquisition of skills that will help to perform work outside the school better. It is impressive to observe the interest shown in mathematics and for tasks that require physical effort and mobility. The child comes to school as a place that offers it the chance to realize itself as a child, stimulates its imagination and creativity, and offers relatively favourable conditions for it to figure as an individual. In an environment that accepts and values positively its own cultural forms, the child shows great spontaneity and communicates easily where it can express itself verbally, physically, artistically and critically in a non-regimented manner. (Colectivo de la Escuela Popular Claretiana 1987: 45)

Wherever possible, in these schools practical tasks are carried out with the children which have a recognizable utility. Since as a rule little space is available in urban areas, agricultural activities or even a school garden are rarely possible. Recourse is had to learning crafts, or outside the school premises tasks are performed that are relevant to home life or are met in the course of the children's work. The school at Neiva, for instance, has a small printing shop in which, influenced by the educational principles of Freinet,[5] texts selected by the children are produced, printed and published. An important element of the school is also the 'research excursions', on which the children study, for instance, how the stream flowing through their district is poisoned, what poisons it contains and the effect on the lives of the inhabitants. Or they examine the features of the mosquito, the conditions of its growth and its function as a bearer of malaria or other diseases. Or they investigate the living and nutrition habits of the inhabitants of their district and revive forgotten traditions of healthy nourishment, such as the production and consumption of a certain drink based on maize.

In one slum in the Peruvian capital Lima, on the initiative of some teachers and pupils, a workshop was instituted in which paper bags are produced. The central motive was to pay for school fees, uniforms and materials out of the income. In order to realize the project, the pupils collected used paper and tools (scissors, rulers, etc.), furnished the workshop, arranged working hours, acquired the knowledge required for making the paper bags, and formed a committee responsible for quality control. With some support from parents, they made contact with traders. The main problem turned out to be that there was hardly any demand in the quarter for paper bags, which were used only for packing eggs. Then the pupils found out that chemists, for instance, were interested in bags made of white paper, made the corresponding change in production, and met with more success. They also succeeded in obtaining a contract for sticking transparent paper in envelopes and making a profit on this. The evaluation states that with this work the pupils attained their aim of financing the costs of their schooling, at least in part. Their experience of the production project was rated by the pupils on a scale between positive and enthusiastic. They learned through their own actions and experience how articles can be produced and marketed. They learned the value of shared organization and democratically made decisions, treating one another with solidarity, and how to appreciate the exchange of ideas (see 'Una experiencia de educación y producción en el C.E. "Madre Admirable" de El Agustino' in TAREA-TINKUY 1989: 32–4).

At another school in Lima founded on the initiative of the children's organization MANTHOC, educational-productive workshops are of central importance. In the school, work forms 'the coordinate axis of the education. This is not primarily education for work; work itself is the source of the learning process' (MANTHOC 1995: 42). In the workshops, the starting point is always concrete problems, the solution to which is sought with the children and recognizing their specific experience and skills. The traditional canon of school subjects has been replaced by concrete production processes or other practical tasks of vital importance, and the knowledge to be acquired is related to these. With, for instance, the manufacture of leather goods (pen cases or other such items, bags, shoes), instruction deals with the topic of leather, proceeding from biology (which animals provide us with leather?), history (why and since when have people processed leather; how did cattle and sheep come to Peru?) and marketing (what leather products are in demand; at what price can we produce them?). The production of the products is an occasion to enquire into whether the knowledge acquired is adequate, whether the quality necessary for sale has been achieved, and what could be done better in what ways.

The production projects carried out at the MANTHOC school are not only selected and considered from the point of view of marketing, but also judged according to the extent to which they correspond to the children's requirements and contribute to the solution of their problems. Thus, for example, at the suggestion of the children a canteen was installed in the school to compensate for their growing poverty and the increasing cost of food. As a field of learning, the canteen contributes to developing a number of vital skills and furthering the children's self-organization. The children form a team that tackles the jobs to be done daily: checking income and expenditure, hygiene in the kitchen, dining room and toilets, the buying of foodstuffs, the drafting of a balanced and economical menu, and the inclusion of new children with as yet little experience. Together with the acquisition of practical knowledge and the production of marketable products, attention is also paid to furthering the imagination and artistic creativity of the children. Thus in the leather workshop it can certainly happen 'that particularly beautiful leather pendants or other decorative articles are made from leather for which there is no market, but which gave the children special pleasure to make' (Recknagel 2001a: 242).

In the Colombian capital Bogotá, a 'workshop school' was set up in which working children and adolescents who have difficulties at the regular school not only have extra coaching and 'problem supervision', but are also offered apprenticeships as furniture-makers, tailors or bakers, computer courses lasting several months, or quickly acquired qualifications as broom-makers or makers of cleaning cloths.

> By means of work and discussion circles, the attempt is made to promote the social values and visions that render possible both the stability of the individual and solidarity in and with the group. This combination of practice-oriented learning, technical training and social sensitivization repeatedly causes some of the young people, on concluding their training, to seek mutually organized alternatives for working and living. For some years, there have been various cooperative ventures that endeavour to create stable jobs for them and their families, with the support of the workshop school, but also independently. (ibid.: 243)

At the school, meetings are held and shared actions planned, from neighbourhood campaigns to the removal of garbage from the local streets, through sporting events to political protest actions and peace marches.

Social educational work projects

Projects such as the workshop school in Bogotá or the MANTHOC school in Lima have little more than the name in common with the usual type of school, and regard themselves as an alternative to these. Learning and working projects with children explicitly conceived as 'non-school' or 'out-of-school' were launched during the 1990s in several countries of the South. They are mostly supported by NGOs or are due to initiatives by Church institutions or neighbourhood groups. They are principally aimed at children who work and sometimes also live in the street. As a rule, they are concerned with giving the children basic occupational qualifications, and expanding their options for less demanding or risky ways of earning. In addition, they are intended to promote working children's self-confidence and make it easier for them to push for their interests and rights. A few examples from Central America and Mexico, then some from Africa and India, will be presented in the following.

Since the early 1990s, in several cities in Guatemala, initially by the NGO SODIFAG and then – after its dissolution – by other NGOs, the goal has been pursued of forming production and service cooperatives with working children between the ages of ten and fifteen, which would contribute to their living and be administered by the children themselves. They develop from the shared learning of a trade in a kind of teaching workshop which the NGO equips. This may be a carpenter's shop in which, for instance, toys are produced, an offset printing shop for making visiting cards, book covers, etc., a workshop for making marimbas (a traditional musical instrument resembling the xylophone), a painting workshop or a flower-binding shop. The products are sold through middlemen or by the children themselves at markets. A stationery shop was also set up for the children in which they are able not only to acquire and test business and administrative knowledge but also to earn income with various services (photocopies, sealing identity papers in plastic, etc.) with small means. The children work in the workshop four hours a day, and receive a fixed monthly wage, plus a daily subsidy for two bus journeys, and a free lunch.

As a rule, the workshops are housed in buildings that also offer space for study circles and leisure activities. Here, the children of the cooperatives, in addition to their work, take part for four hours a day in an educational programme covering both vocational and general knowledge, including 'cooperativism'. Once a week, they meet to discuss everyday problems (e.g. cleanliness and hygiene, group conflicts, the financial situation), to find solutions and make decisions that are binding on all (including the adult staff, trainers, etc.). Now and again, they undertake an excursion together, and take part in sports competitions or similar activities. The buildings, with their educational and leisure programme, are also open to children who are not (yet) integrated into the cooperative. They are intended as a kind of base at which the awareness of common interests and a collective identity as working children can be developed.

In another project supported by the Centro Popular de Educación VECINOS in San José, the capital of Costa Rica, provision of work, simple contract work (packing, production of boxes, errands, etc.), training and the establishing of firms are linked. In the workshops wooden toys, needlework, screen printing and other simple art and craft products are manufactured. The training covers not only technical aspects, but is also intended to stimulate and enable the children and adolescents to look after their own interests as workers and local residents, and to run a small firm themselves. The workshops are to be gradually transformed into small firms, and fulfil a double function – that of being a source of income for the young people and of motivating and qualifying them to function as multipliers.

Since the early 1990s in Nicaragua, two forms of work project have developed. In one case, young people from the age of fourteen, who previously performed various activities in the street, are found places as 'apprentices' in existing workshops and supervised by the educational staff of an NGO. The young people receive a grant and are able to use the NGO's facilities for leisure, education and advice. An attempt is made to promote a feeling of cohesion in the group and a consciousness of common interests. Some of the young people who conclude their apprenticeship successfully and have been particularly active and taken on responsibility in the institutions of the NGO are supported with small credits, to enable them to market the knowledge they have acquired independently.

In the other case, workshops for the children and adolescents are set up by the NGO, similarly to the projects described in Guatemala and Costa Rica. In the Centro Juvenil de Capacitación y Convivencia (CJCC), which was established in the capital Managua on the initiative of inhabitants of a slum, the workshops are part of an open youth centre with various leisure, advisory and educational provisions, including a school for working children. In the workshops, training is linked from the beginnning with productive activities. These include a furniture workshop, a men's and women's hairdresser, a screen printing and leather workshop, a beauty salon, a typewriter and computer workshop, and a teaching kitchen. The 'apprentices' are between twelve and eighteen years of age, mostly come from the same part of town, and as well as their four hours of work in the workshop also work in the street or with the family.

In the workshops, the children and adolescents have far-reaching participation rights, and elect delegates to represent their interests with the institution. It is expected of them that they also take an active part in activities in the district (e.g. vaccination campaigns, a population census). Profits from the sale of products or services are, according to an arranged scale, partly paid to the apprentices, and partly used for the purchase of more raw materials and tools, the development of the workshops, and other project activities. On conclusion of their apprenticeship, the young people are able to continue to use the workshops on payment of the net cost. They are also helped to form small cooperatives under the institutional umbrella and with the advice of the staff of the youth centre, and with the aid of credits. In the case of the screen printing workshop, three young people, on conclusion of their own training, took over the workshop to train new apprentices.

The NGO EDNICA, which runs projects in a part of the Mexican capital involving children who work in the street, aims to develop with the children work alternatives with an exclusively positive meaning for the children. For this purpose, it has developed a model that provides for gradual improvements up to self-determined forms of work. The process is regarded as closely linked to improvements in the children's living conditions and the development of a 'community identity', meaning the identification of the children with the community and their inclusion in it. The model is intended to enable the children and adolescents to develop, in the long term and independently of institutional support, skills, knowledge and habits that they need to perform productive activities in accord with their specific interests and abilities. Furthermore, it is meant to promote the development of the community, in order to render possible the common mobilization of economic resources that the child needs to be economically independently active. This involves not only securing the independence of the firms to be created, but also enabling children and adolescents to be creative, to pursue their own need for play, to develop their abilities and self-esteem, to achieve an attitude of solidarity towards each other, and to strengthen their sense of justice (see Griesbach Guizar and Sauri Suárez 1997: 263ff).

A common feature of the projects mentioned is that, when organized in a democratic way and in the context of the community, work per se has an educative value, and therefore training and productive activity can and must interact. The children and adolescents are regarded as members of a community with equal rights, who have a claim to participation in the planning of training and work processes. Their previous work, which usually took place in the street, is not denied or devalued, but recognized as an activity essential for survival, and the experience and identities connected with it are built upon.[6]

In other countries of the South, too, comparable approaches are to be found attempting to promote and create self-determined forms of work by children. We will now describe two examples from Ethiopia and India.

In 1991, in the Ethiopian capital Addis Ababa, a circus was founded, the members of which were exclusively children who had previously earned their living with odd jobs, theft or prostitution in the street. The initiative originated from a Canadian teacher who worked at the international school in Addis Ababa, and who did not agree with the purely charitable nature of the projects for street children. Instead of reducing the children to mere objects of aid, he wanted to take up their creative potential and give them the opportunity once again to become active in earning their living. Following the circus in the capital, similar projects soon came about in other Ethiopian towns.

In the circus, the children receive training as acrobats, and are rapidly integrated into the groups that already put on performances. Each child can introduce its own ideas and help to decide on the programme, and which of its talents is to be brought out. They invent brief plays and scenes, find suitable music, design the scenery and costumes, and acquire or make the equipment and utensils needed for a performance. They also advertise the performances, evaluate the reactions of the audiences and the media, organize tours to other regions of the country and to other countries, advise other groups on the founding of their own circus, and other things. The performances include various kinds of acts such as acrobatics, comedy, plays or music, and take up cultural traditions from various regions of the country. They are mostly devoted to topics experienced and selected by the children themselves, such as the AIDS problem, living in the street, rape, hunger, pickpocketing, the problem of landmines, the gulf between rich and poor, or the disregarding of children and their rights.

The performances of the circus in Addis Ababa and other places in Ethiopia have been very popular since their inception. Even tours abroad have been organized for some years. The circus meanwhile supports itself, and gives the children their living. A strong feeling of cohesion has come about among the children, and they are convinced that they can solve their problems through solidarity. 'Through the circus, they have acquired quite a new place in society; they are respected, even admired. They have noticed that with their own initiative, creativity and persistence they can achieve and change things' (Melaku 2000: 84). One boy states: 'Life has been much more fun since I have been in the Ethiopia Circus. I will not wait for problems to arise. At the moment I am trying to put on a show with my friends and earn some money that way. It has worked well. We have taken our fate into our own hands' (Oxfam 1999, cited in Melaku 2000: 84).

In New Delhi, capital of India, the outpatient health services for children living and working in the street offered by an NGO (Butterflies) gave rise to a health cooperative that is in the hands of a group of children and adolescents. They had previously worked in the health teams going round the slums and the city centre to give first aid mainly to children, but also to adults in need, to get medical treatment for the sick or injured, to carry out vaccination programmes, to give sex advice, especially relating to AIDS, and so on. The young people and the older children resolved to make a project of their own out of this, with which they earn their living, and which also ensures their own medical treatment. They laid down the criteria for membership, allotted the tasks, and drew up regulations and work plans. In a similar manner, a restaurant was also founded, which is now run by twelve young people (see Swift 2001: 183).

Initiatives for self-determined children's work in Europe

In the 'affluent' societies of the North, approaches to self-determined work in the context of educational projects are as a rule not developed in order to counteract exploitative children's work, but to give children alternatives to a life that they find unsatisfying and 'empty'. This includes the consideration that, by means of their own work experience, which is felt to be positive, skills can be promoted that make it easier for the children to make their way later on in their working lives, and perhaps even to set up their own firms.

An early initiative in Sweden

In the early 1980s, an initiative was founded in Sweden to enable children to take on productive jobs in the neighbourhood in the field of the social services. They were to take part in the 'local cooperative production of goods and services for which there is a need in the neighbourhood, schools, etc.', and should be able to assume 'cooperative responsibility for restaurants, cafés, cultural and recreation facilities' (Henriksson 1985: 155). In this way, the children were 'to learn the value of work' and 'experience participation and solidarity in practice' at an earlier age than usual in Swedish society.

The main starting point for participation in these activities was to be school, where pupils at all stages would perform certain useful tasks once a week. 'For instance, they could assist a domestic help during a school year and get to know their job. The following school year, they could work in the production cooperative, and in the one after that prepare the food for school meals, clean school rooms, carry out minor repairs, etc.' (ibid.: 155). It is expressly stressed that the aim of this was not to undermine the public institutions and their work, but to give new tasks to the educational staff. Instead of relieving the children of all such tasks and imparting to them only information and supervision, they should now be more active as 'animators' and help the children 'themselves to achieve a higher degree of obligation and responsibility' (ibid.: 156).

The initiative is supported with the argument that children in Sweden are 'materially saturated but socially starved' (ibid.: 146). In the welfare society, childhood and adolescence have become, it is stated, a time of waiting. In view of growing unemployment, even twelve- and thirteen-year-olds lose faith in the future, and leisure increasingly means to them having to kill time. 'We can speak of a life in the vacuum of leisure – or a life in no man's land – a fact that affects most children and adolescents in our society' (ibid.: 142f). The vacuum is reinforced by the separation between children and adults; they no longer work together, and produce nothing in common. 'Never before in our history – but also in other cultures[7] – could people reach the age of twenty-five without having learnt to do a job which others profit from or have use of, without having learnt to help someone who is old, sick or helpless. It is a drastic change in culture, which has pushed most children and adolescents into the perspective of onlookers of society instead of having a perspective of participation' (ibid.: 143).

The Swedish initiative results not only from a critique of culture, but is also based on the observation that many children and adolescents are themselves dissatisfied with their situation[8] and frequently take on a job at the age of eleven. 'In our researches, we found that a new form of children's work has established itself in Sweden. Children do small favours at home in return for amounts fixed in advance; they make their beds, clear up their rooms, go shopping, mow the lawn, do babysitting for neighbours etc.' (ibid.: 145) As 'children are clever negotiators' and as a rule arrange to be paid for their work, within the period under study the 'income' of children rose by about 20 per cent a year. The initiative addressed this tendency and attempted to complement or replace the predominantly material motive with a social motive.[9]

In other European countries, too, attempts have been made since the 1980s in the context of educational institutions and projects to realize forms of self-determined children's work. These range from sporadic attempts to earn money, through more lasting forms of 'supervised wage-earning' to the foundation of 'school-pupils' firms' or 'youth firms'. In the case of most of the projects, earning money is less important than the aim of conveying to the children at an early age certain attitudes and skills that are important in working life. In the case of the foundation of firms or businesses, ideological goals also play a part, in the sense that children are already being taught to see themselves as 'entrepreneurs'.

Supervised wage-earning

In cases of 'supervised wage-earning', the children's wish to find an opportunity to earn money without involving work that exposes them to unacceptable strains is addressed. For instance, in Berlin it was observed of children who regularly met on a building playground that their pocket money was not sufficient and that they wanted to work regularly to earn money. The children declared that they 'would prefer a job that was fun, even if it brought in less money. They would prefer to earn less money legally than a lot illegally' (Wetzel and Sorge 1999: 110). The carers working on the playground had long been worried about the 'illegal earnings' of a large number of their protégés, and resolved to get together with them to develop ideas for work involving fewer risks which could perhaps also give the children more fun and social recognition.[10]

One of the projects enabled interested children to organize the distribution of the weekly advertiser in the Kiez area. The children agreed on who would deliver the papers when, and divided their earnings among themselves. One problem was that the money was not given to the children at once but only the following week. Another was that not all the children were able to read and write. This was solved by seeing that at least one of the three children who delivered the newspapers as a team could read, and was able to prove it. When the project was suspended, this was not the fault of the children, but was due to an irregular charge made by a police patrol which saw in the involvement of children under fifteen an offence against the law regulating youth work protection. Thereupon the newspaper firm felt itself obliged to terminate the agreement with those responsible for the building playground.

Another project that has meanwhile been imitated in other districts of Berlin was the institution of a children's flea market. It takes place during the warmer part of the year once a month in a busy square in the district. For a token charge, each child can occupy a stall, and sell or display whatever he or she likes. In addition to stalls offering disused toys, books and assorted bric-à-brac, children opened a grilled sausage stall or made music with a barrel-organ. Sometimes the children do not wait for the market dates, but open small flea markets of their own on the fringe of adults' weekly markets, in playgrounds, or in pedestrian zones. In the days preceding Christmas, a Christmas market also takes place on the pavement in front of the building playground, at which the children sell home-made items such as metal bracelets, wooden toys, felt balls, Christmas decorations, tree decorations, hot cocoa, coffee or home-made waffles. The profit from this market is used for a Christmas celebration. Since functions frequently take place at the playground, often attended by as many as 700 people, the children also have the opportunity to run food stalls there and share in the takings.

For a time, the children at the playground also tried to sell firewood that they had chopped and bundled or packaged in sacks. Although they went about this with plenty of enthusiasm, the project finally failed because of the difficulty of finding buyers for the wood, the old wood stoves having been replaced in many houses in the district by central heating.

A further idea was to take broken bicycles and parts of bicycles that were to be found on a dump and use them to construct functioning bicycles and sell them. However, this project could not be put into practice as it was difficult to allay the suspicion that the parts had been stolen. The project also ran up against the opposition of local tradesmen and their guild, as commerce in such recognized areas of trade is not allowed without officially recognized occupational qualifications.

In contrast to the projects of 'supervised wage-earning', in the case of establishing firms the stress is more on the learning processes that are expected to result. At the same time, in most cases these are not mere simulations of work processes, but 'serious situations' in which something is really produced and may also be sold. The firms are founded both within the institutional framework of schools or vocational training and in the context of social educational institutions of youth work such as youth centres, adventure playgrounds, etc., and occasionally even in kindergartens. The school projects established in Germany are partly modelled on developments in Great Britain and Ireland,[11] and to some extent in Denmark.[12] It is striking that little recourse is had to basic concepts from the field of progressive or socialist education, or experience from Freinet education, in which work plays an important part. Nor is reference made to the experiences of school cooperatives, which are quite widespread in Italy (see Blandano et al. 1997).

School pupils' firms

In Germany, the foundation of pupils' firms has been going on since 1993, above all by the Institut der Deutschen Wirtschaft[13] and the Federal/State Committee for Educational Planning and Research Promotion (BLK).[14] These two institutions are concerned primarily with 'the promotion of a culture for more independence, an atmosphere of entrepreneurial action' (position statement of the BLK, 1997, cited in Klein and Sell 2000: 89). Whereas in progressive or socialist approaches to work education the focus is on concrete experience in dealing with materials and technologies, in most pupils' firms 'business ideas' and experience with management and marketing have priority. In contrast to the Swedish initiative described above, the Danish production schools, and the Italian school cooperatives, considerations as to how far the products and services originating in the pupils' firms might serve certain needs in the local environment are hardly involved. This is the case, however, in a number of other school and out-of-school work projects originating in Germany from the 1990s onwards. They will be described, with some examples, hereafter.

Since 1996, in cooperation with the Berlin schools administration, the Institute for Productive Learning in Europe (PLE) has, at several Berlin junior high schools, institutions for special education and two out-of-school educational institutions, set up a pilot project called 'Productive Learning at Berlin Schools' (PLEBS). The project's aim is not founding firms, but involving disadvantaged young people in productive work ('social relevance'), addressing their personal educational requirements, strengths and motivations ('personal relevance'), and teaching cultural, social and technical skills through experience in social and occupational practice ('activity relevance') (see Böhm and Schneider 1996: 31).

The point of departure is the critical consideration that young people in urban situations are offered no opportunities to take on social and productive tasks in society, but are kept in a state of infantile uselessness. They should therefore be given the chance to learn on the basis of productive activity in social 'real-life' situations. They should be able to experience doing something of importance for themselves and their environment, and become full members of society. Scenarios are not artificially created; the learners are placed in regular, or innovative, work situations. This may be in a firm, a workshop or a shop, but productive projects are also developed in schools or in the street. These include, for instance, a washing and ironing service, a breakfast and party service, painting and gardening work in the local area, or the construction of equipment for playgrounds. Where profits are made, they are reinvested in the project, or used for final celebrations, excursions or similar communal events. No wages as such are paid.[15]

Meanwhile, initiatives for work projects are regularly established in schools as well as in pre-school and out-of-school educational institutions. They are mostly initiated by teachers or social educational workers, but sometimes also by children and adolescents. Their approaches and motives frequently but not always differ from those of the centrally controlled firm foundations such as those of the 'Junior' project of the German Business Institute or the experimental models of the Federal/State Committee. The focus of interest is no longer the founding of firms as such, but one or more concrete activities that are fun and render possible new experiences. Several examples will be presented below.

At the Richard Keller School in Hermsdorf (Berlin), a special school for pupils with learning handicaps, the children wanted to get out of the 'play situation' and deal with 'proper money' instead of 'play money'. One teacher describes how this resulted in a work project:

> This is how it began. Food was being prepared in a cookery project. Then we thought about selling the surplus among the staff. This went down well, and we had our first earnings. The next step was to make potato soup with sausage for the staff. So we made a pot of potato soup. The profit from this was somewhat greater. Then we tried hamburgers, and earned even more. By now the pupils had acquired the taste. So we decided since it was running so well we would expand it to the other class. So it came about that first a food service was set up, then came provision for teachers' birthdays, then we made whole menus, and the culmination was a buffet for a congress with 100 people and the forum. In the course of time the other teachers saw the potential and we got so many more jobs that we could hardly cope. (cited in Klein and Sell 2000: 111)

Another work project was developed in 1997 by fifteen pupils at the Erasmus School in Hellersdorf (Berlin), also in the context of an optional subject. They grow flowers and plants and sell them on various occasions, for example at the school's open day or Christmas bazaar. They also undertake gardening work for allotment holders, for instance mowing grass, planting trees or collecting apples. Remuneration and proceeds from sales go into the group fund. As a rule, four to five pupils work for one to two hours at a time. From time to time, the pupils participating in the project consult as to what is to be done with the money. The group received a starting subsidy from a foundation. Whereas up to now only the school's botany room could be used for production, a greenhouse or a plot on the school premises or in the allotment area is now being envisaged (see Wetzel and Sorge 1999: 62ff).[16]

At Friedrichstadt secondary schoool in Wittenberge (Brandenburg), on the initiative of two teachers, the pupils' firm 'Culinary Theatre Kids' was set up, in which twenty-two pupils of the seventh grade take part. They put on theatrical performances at festivals in the school and the local area, at which they sell self-produced soup, pizza, cake and drinks. Work done for the firm is measured in points, the units being of time. Attendance at rehearsals, cooking, voluntary cleaning work – all this brings points, and the profits are then distributed according to the points collected. Last school year, DM1,050 marks (= €36.81) were paid out. Some pupils received only three to four, one almost DM100. They made the rules themselves, and the tasks and responsibilities were agreed together. In one newspaper report, the commitment of the pupils was put into the context of the depressed economic situation in East Germany:

Hardly one of the fathers or mothers of the 'Culinary Theatre Kids' is in work. But the kids have work. They reject the stigma of being super-fluous by their own activities. With their firm they defend their human dignity. In an environment that is decaying, their common work makes them young people with self-respect, sympathy and solidarity. Their sense of responsibility and initiative is not geared to the entrepreneurial individual who makes his way and gets on at the expense of others. What counts is concrete usefulness, not abstract profit. Their activity serves to compensate for a lack, the lack of *joie de vivre* and confidence in the future. (Reymann 2001: 19)

Work projects in leisure centres

Out of school, since the 1990s work projects have been established principally in open institutions for children and adolescents and, as the example of 'supervised wage-earning' shows, in the context of adventure playgrounds. In youth centres, the work projects sometimes proceed from the bar, where young people also like to work because they are in the limelight and get free drinks. This is the case in 'Maxim's', a community youth leisure centre in Weissensee, a district of Berlin. In March 1999, eight young people aged between fifteen and eighteen came together to organize film shows, disco meetings and open evenings on their own initiative.

Such activities are not in fact as new as they may seem at first sight. Many 'self-administered' youth centres were set up in the 1970s on the initiative of young people, and thus became their self-determined work-places. Their primary aim was not to put a 'business idea' into practice, found a 'firm' or 'find work', however, but to claim a social sphere for themselves which could be the point of departure for political initiatives and actions. Such projects were and still are largely restricted to adolescents. Younger children were hardly ever included and would have no chance to play a central part in them.

More remarkable are the work projects with relatively young children that have been founded in the last few years. On the relatively spacious site of the Munich farm for children and adolescents,[17] for instance, plots and beds are leased to children to enable them to cultivate vegetables and strawberries according to biological principles on their own initiative. The products are sold to visitors by the children. They also make jam from the strawberries under expert supervision.

Two further examples are to be found in a pre-school institution ('Villa Kunterbunt') at Crussow, a small village in the state of Brandenburg. Here a bicycle workshop run by the children and a worm-breeding unit have been set up. Christoph Klein and Meta Sell (2000) take up the report of a teacher there in their vivid account.

In Crussow, bicycles are

the sole means of transport for children. They are much used and often break down. The older children had the idea of running their own bicycle workshop, to be able to save themselves the irksome journey to the nearest town and expensive repairs. First, the children took the initiative against the teacher's will and enquired as to a suitable location. Finally the teacher agreed and joined in. The bicycle workshop was set up in the cellar. Some of the children are really too old for the Villa but still too young for the youth club. They want to take part, and are allowed to, because leisure provision in the area is very limited. They all assume that, for instance, they will not get the necessary tools for nothing. Then the idea comes up of repairing other people's bicycles too, so as to be able to earn something for themselves. They could thus perform a useful service particularly for the older people in the village. It is faster, costs less and is not so awkward. The children organized a repair service. They used the profit, for instance, to set up their workshop, for the purchase of new play equipment, or for projects or journeys together. They also have the profits that they made from the worm-breeding unit they established in 1996. (Klein and Sell 2000: 110)

The worm-breeding began when the teacher told the children that it was possible to breed worms and sell them to local fishermen.

At first four children wanted to take part. Many questions were raised: 'What does a worm eat? Where does it get air from? What kinds of worms are there?' Earthworms were collected and observed for quite some time in the terrarium. 'How do they move? How do the layers of earth get mixed? What happens to the earth?' From a letter, they learned of Mr Stark, who had been breeding worms for twenty years. Meanwhile a few more children had joined in. 'What conditions does a worm need to live?' The temperature must be right, the density of the soil must be right. If this is not adhered to, then of course the maximum increase of 600 offspring is not achieved. First of all, a worm-box had to be constructed. When the wooden box was finally finished, the materials partly sponsored by the DIY market, and the parts finally properly sawn, they discovered a sobering fact: because the worms must always be kept damp, the wood of the box would rot in time. But they did not give up, and got themselves a plastic box. After it turned out that the mayor would not contribute 50 marks (= €25.56) for the first 500 worms, they went in search of initial capital themselves. The Villa's newspaper was sold in the village for one mark a copy. The rest was made up by cake bazaars. Then came the problem with the flies. At the end of their tails, the worms have a poisonous fluid with which they can defend themselves. But the eggs must also be defended. The solution to the problem was simple. The children put used oil on the sides to keep the flies off. Finally, leaflets were made, and they went on an advertising trip and organized a press conference. Jana took along a pack containing the finest specimens. 'Only Villa Kunterbunt breeds fish magnets like this!' the advertisement proclaimed. The big sales are made twice a year, according to the season, but there are many interested customers in between times. (ibid.: 110f)

Pitfalls of self-determined work by children

The examples described show that self-determined children's work is possible and is desired, sought and, to some extent, created by them. Despite widely differing points of departure, this applies to societies in both the South and the North.

Experience with work projects and enterprises by and with children, however, also raises a number of problems. In the South, they do not solve the problem of continued and growing poverty, which is an essential reason why many children have to work under conditions that are exploitative and detrimental to them. They are growing up in an environment and under conditions that constantly threaten their survival. They are also in danger of being exploited as a cheap and easy resource, in a situation in which the state and society ought to assume responsibility.

In the North, there is the rapidly growing interest among children in becoming independent earlier, in having 'money of their own', taking on responsibility and having experience of 'real-life situations' that school does not as a rule offer them. Today, the problem lies not so much in the children being exploited as 'cheap labour power' but rather in the fact that they are elevated by some into mini-entrepreneurs with the suggestion that they are captains of their fate. This applies above all to those work projects and 'enterprise foundations' in which the emphasis is not on the content and structures of the work but on aspects of management and commerce.

It is true of both North and South that 'independence' and 'independent work' can take on various forms and meanings. It is euphemistic, for instance, to call children who have recourse to their own initiative and creativity to make the best of their precarious and threatening situation 'small independent entrepreneurs'. Their independence stresses their determination not to be kept down and the fact that they have a number of skills that children are as a rule not expected or permitted to have. But it remains an independence that has very little latitude, and has to assert itself under conditions that could at any moment extinguish it.[18]

In a different sense, this also applies to the 'pupils' firms' that have been spreading in Europe since the 1980s. Here, no doubt, an attempt is made to render possible for children and adolescents while still at school or in other educational establishments experience of real-life economic situations in which they can gain exposure to work and make decisions of their own. But this independent action is, even where it is not expressly limited in time,[19] an independence under constant threat; the adults who as a rule are involved are able to put an end to it at any time, and it is usually measured out from the planning stage in such a way that no unforeseen consequences for the pupils involved can result.

The work projects that regard themselves as 'training for entrepreneurship' proceed from 'the independence and entrepreneurship of the child' (Faltin and Zimmer 2000), but independent work action is conceived only with regard to whether it is suitable for the market and likely to survive on it. No inherent significance is accorded either to the practical use of materials and techniques or the question of what concrete use the resulting products are. The children working in the pupils' firms projects may be regarded as subjects with inventiveness and skills, but in practice they are reduced to the role of mini-managers, for whom the 'utility value' of the products and services they produce is ultimately of no consequence, or only of interest to the extent to which profit can be made from it.[20]

A comparable problem also faces the workshops, cooperatives and small firms that come into being outside educational institutions and not infrequently even on the initiative of children and adolescents themselves. They are obliged to find purchasers for their products or services if they are to survive under their own steam. The children and adolescents involved cannot be content with merely observing the work process and carrying it out as satisfactorily as possible; they must also acquire knowledge and experience related to the management of their enterprise. Under the pressure of the market, this not infrequently leads to the original 'social' or 'political' motives that were in the forefront at the foundation of the enterprise being pushed into the background, with the business being regarded as a mini- or small firm 'like any other'.

This does not have to be the case, however. When children seek (to create) independent work, whether in the South or in the North, they are usually concerned with earning their living or extra money, but as a rule they are also pursuing other interests. One strong motive is the wish not to be dictated to by others, and to do work that is useful, interesting, varied and perhaps even exciting. They also hope that it will offer them the time and opportunity to have fun with each other and to communicate in an informal way. These motives are not fulfilled by the kind of firm aiming primarily at 'economic success'; under its conditions, the children and adolescents involved no longer have much time or opportunity to devote themselves to what is fun (unless they already see themselves only as 'managers').

To try to render independent work possible for children makes sense only when it gives the children themselves something, or, in the words of the International Convention on Children's Rights, when it is 'in the children's best interests'. This requires considering and linking three aspects of children's work: the content and purpose of the work, the relations involved in the work, and finally the environment with which the children's work is connected and on which it has an effect.

On the question of the work content, it is worth recalling the considerations that have for decades been formulated and practised by people who have recognized the educative value of work for children. Here, I am thinking above all of the French educationist Célestin Freinet and the US educationist John Holt.[21] Whereas the traditional educational theory of the work school regards work above all from a functional point of view, and thereby promises observance of rules and norms laid down in advance, Freinet and Holt argue for children's work in terms that are critical of the state and society, seeing it as the basis of a liberating popular education and the point of departure for a democratic culture, not least in terms of the relations between children and adults.

Freinet sees work as the mirror image of human development. According to him, work is meaningful for children when it is goal-oriented, socially relevant, combines manual and intellectual components, and can be planned by the children themselves. Under these conditions, 'work can guarantee the harmonious development of all the powers of the child and help to satisfy people's basic needs for survival and for social preservation and reproduction' (Kock 1996: 17). This is based on a view of the child as a 'free and open socially formed being that develops in dealing with its environment and with other people, needs to be challenged by concrete tasks and techniques, and integrated into the social whole in a manner appropriate to its potential' (ibid.: 18). Freinet sees in children's work the kernel of the learning process and the 'highest form of social expression' (Freinet 1950: 103).

In the École Freinet, each child, like each adult, regularly pursues from its first years onwards a kind of work corresponding to its development, its potential and talents, either with a weaver, a carpenter, a smith or a shoemaker, or in some agricultural activity. 'In this way, the children are integrated into social life and responsible and productive work' (Kock 1996: 21). As the child grows older, it is seen as important that the children reflect on their work experience and evaluate it within the social context. Freinet recognizes that the link demanded by him between the material and intellectual dimensions of work is not possible in individualistic societies organized according to the wage and competition principle, but requires its own sphere of experience.

The Freinet school is designed in the form of work studios, partly open and partly with the potential to be closed off, grouped around a class or communal room. The studios include areas for elementary manual work and others for intellectual work projects, frequently also a vegetable and fruit garden and an animal care room. In each classroom there is a lot of material for independent working: tools such as hammers, pliers, saws, nails; materials such as wood or clay; experimental kits; batteries, wires, bulbs; scales, weights, rules, thermometers; bottles and measuring vessels; magnifying glasses; cooking implements; sewing materials. In a number of classrooms there are flower-boxes, others have an animal (bird, fish, hamster), others again are equipped with record player, tape recorder and materials for making technical apparatus (old radios, old motors). With the materials and apparatus the children carry out various kinds of experiment, observe small animals and plants with the magnifying glass, weigh and measure, produce useful objects, toys, technical models, etc. An important element is the design and printing of 'free texts' in which the children express their experiences, thoughts and fantasies and communicate with others. Freinet expressly opposes setting up workrooms separate from the classrooms, because this would create a divide between intellectual activities and manual work.

John Holt, in his ideas for work that is meaningful and advantageous for children, proceeds from everyday observations, and enquires what kinds of work children find fun from an early age. Among these he includes kinds of work in which their fingers penetrate the material ('mud pies', 'to control and use water', 'digging ponds and ditches', 'diverting and damming up water'); work with material that smells good and can easily be modified, and which makes possible a new product through changing its shape. As an example, he takes work with baking dough. 'There is quite a bit of change and magic in it; things start out looking one way and soon look like something else. There is suspense; will the cookies, cake, or whatever come out right?' (Holt 1974: 182). He considers as further important features of work attractive to children that they do not have to wait (too) long before a concrete result emerges; that the products made have a potential use; that tools appealing to the hand and the senses can be used, for example painting with a brush ('the motion of the bristles of a paint brush against the wall'); that the children can easily judge whether they have done the work well or badly. Finally, Holt also includes kinds of work for which the tools are unfamiliar, exotic and even up to a point dangerous, especially when they have to do with heat or fire (for instance, children are fascinated by welding). Holt draws the conclusion that 'any work is good for children in which they can see what they are doing, how much they are doing and how well they are doing it' (ibid.: 183). If the work has a purpose, a child 'can understand, if it takes his strength and skill, and if he can see the results of his work as he works, a child will undertake and stick at very hard tasks' (ibid.: 184).

Apart from the features mentioned by John Holt, which are above all related to the extent to which the work appeals to children as it were anthropologically and culturally, I think it essential that the work not take place on an 'artificial island' or solely for learning purposes, but is of actual meaning for the reproduction of labour and society, and enables the children to feel useful. Holt also considers being 'helpful and useful' as a fundamental motive for children's interest in work (ibid.: 185). Finally, it is important that the work is varied and complex enough for the children to feel challenged and able to use and further develop their skills.

This points to the second aspect of work that has meaning for children and brings advantages for them: relationships during work. This has to do with the question of how the work is organized and distributed among the children, how they cooperate with one another, and their relationship with any adults who may be involved. Whereas Holt above all has the individual child in mind, Freinet stresses the necessity not only to see and organize work on an individual basis, but at least to complement this by cooperative work. It is important for the children that they have the experience of being dependent on each other, and at the same time are able to distribute the various tasks according to their own judgement. This is only possible when the relationships are 'democratically' structured and the adults, if any, are also included in this structure.

From the point of view of work relationships, the question also arises as to the relation between the productive activities, i.e. those related to the making of a product, and other activities, for example communicating freely with each other, play, etc. The competition-oriented organization in capitalist firms excludes such activities to a great extent, or functional-izes them to keep the workers in check and to increase the motivation to work. In the self-determined work of children, by contrast, neither should work and 'leisure' be strictly separated, nor should play and having fun with each other become an 'extra activity' alien to work. In work projects in which children cooperate with each other in a self-determined manner, it can frequently be observed that the organization of work in a manner determined by competition and oriented to speed tends rather to create resistance and is disrupted by the children.[22] At the same time, the realization of relation structures in a work project which are democratic, communicative and characterized by solidarity depends not least on whether the children have the opportunity to keep their work free from the rigid time pressure of production oriented to competition and profit, and also make products that are useful and of interest to them and others, without having to make money from them.

This already brings in the question of the environment and the goals of self-determined work as the third aspect. There is a fundamental difference between work projects that are linked to the labour and goods market that functions according to capitalist principles and seek above all to assert themselves here, and work projects that are linked to a needs-oriented context, and relate their products or services to corresponding, mostly local and specific, needs and demand. In this sense, a 'private economy' pursuing chiefly individual goals could be distinguished from a 'social economy' pursuing predominantly social goals, without for this reason abandoning 'economic' considerations. The 'social economy', which is also termed 'economy of solidarity', 'community economy' or 'communal self-determined work', covers 'all kinds of work necessary for mutually organized self-provision, all kinds of work for the sustenance and organization of life' (Möller et al. 1997: 29). These are based on the 'idea of self-provision and self-help', and have as their goal primarily the 'satisfaction of the needs of the individual working in the community' (ibid.: 18) and the neighbourhood or regional environment.

Work projects by children that develop within this context and with these goals can not only contribute decisively to the improvement of the living conditions of the children, but can also strengthen their position in the community and promote their social recognition. They also enable children to experience themselves as independent and competent subjects with significance for other people, and to acquire social skills and qualities that are indispensable in a community.

Work projects of this kind cannot be realized easily or without contradictions. They must always deal with a social and economic context in which work is regarded above all as an exploitable resource or a source of profit, and in which children in particular are seen only as easy prey or an unimportant incidental. The chances of realization for self-determined work by children in the context of a social economy are the greater the more clearly working children also become an organized influence in social life, insist on their interests and rights as a social group, and initiate social movements.

Notes

1. The term 'Utopian socialism' was coined by Friedrich Engels, and was directed critically against pioneers and theoreticians such as Robert Owen, Jacques Fourier, etc., who did not want to delay alternatives to the capitalist system of production and work until capitalism had reached its 'highest stage of development'. Engels characterized their views as 'Utopian' because he thought them illusory and 'unscientific'.

2. For examples, they refer to Sheffield and Diejomaeh 1972.

3. A precise description of the *ashram* is to be found in Reagan 1996.

4. Hindi for New Education.

5. On Freinet's approach to education and the significance of work experience, see the following section.

6. Comparable projects combining training and self-determined work for a living can also be found in various countries in Africa. There they are known as *self-sustaining economic projects* (see Tolfree 1998; Enda 1999).

7. In a digression, Henriksson refers expressly to African cultures and current threats to them (Henriksson 1985: 149ff).

8. Children and adolescents are quoted as making the following critical comments: 'We have to be grateful to others, while we ourselves are excluded ...' '... others work so that we can attend school ...' 'Nobody wants to take advantage of our help ...' 'I never get the chance to show what I can do ...' (ibid.: 143).

9. Similar considerations are to be found in a German publication: 'Many [children] *wish* to do odd jobs, to escape from their cushioned everyday existence and get out into real life. In contradiction of a general rejection of children's work, where work, in most cases, is not hard physical labour, this can be very meaningful as social experience, after ten years living in a cage' (Grefe: 1997: 95).

10. The following examples are based on the author's own observations, or were taken from the degree thesis of Susanne Wetzel and Martin Sorge (1999).

11. The projects here are 'mini-companies', small working pupils' businesses operating for a limited time only, which were set up in Great Britain and Ireland from the late 1970s onwards, to build a bridge between school and occupational life, and to prepare the pupils for the independent foundation of their own firms. Such pupils' businesses have also existed in Belgium since 1976.

12. This involves above all production schools, an independent school form in Denmark, which was established by the Danish Ministry of Education in 1980 to offer unemployed young people betwen the ages of sixteen and twenty-three an alternative, linking education with production work for the local market.

13. German Business Institute. This is an institution of the Federal Association

of German Employers' Associations and the Federal Association of German Industry. The pupils' firms supported, coordinated and supervised by the Institute are based on the 'junior' concept: 'Young entrepreneurs initiate – organize – realize.'

14. Since 1993, the BLK has supported model projects in schools 'for the promotion of entrepreneurial independence'.

15. Similar projects have also been established in Spain, Portugal, Hungary and Russia (see Böhm and Schneider 1996: 53ff; Institut für Produktives Lernen in Europa 1999). A comparable approach, 'action-oriented discovery learning' in 'real-life situations', is practised in Germany at a Rudolf Steiner school in the form of the 'Gröbenzell Craft Centre' (see Brater and Munz 1996).

16. These pupils' firms and others are widely reported in the media, eliciting either surprise or enthusiastic praise. We cite three newspaper headlines as examples: 'Early practice makes the perfect businessman. Four schools found firms to do international trade' (die tageszeitung, Berlin, 6 October 1998); 'Pupils as entrepreneurs. In Hoyerswerda [Saxony], pupils are successfully running a travel agency – profit-oriented but not greedy for profit' (Die Zeit, 11, 11 March 1999); 'Entrepreneurship in the classroom. About fifty pupils' firms in East Germany make the school year into a business year' (Der Tagesspiegel, Berlin, 28 December 1999).

17. Farms for children and adolescents, which exist in several German cities, see themselves as a form of active playground in which environmental education has a particular priority. The model comes from institutions in the Netherlands at which agricultural work such as cheese-making forms an integral part of the activities.

18. In my attempt to establish a typology of the various types of employment of children in the societies of the South, I speak in this context of 'dependent self-sufficiency' (see Liebel 2001c: 151ff).

19. This is, for instance, the case with the 'junior enterprises' conducted under the aegis of the German Business Institute.

20. This is precisely the trend that can be observed in the deregulated capitalist economy, in which the flexibility and permanent availability increasingly demanded from those working or seeking work are covered by the both ideological and euphemistic formulation 'labour power entrepreneur' (Arbeitskraftunternehmer) (see Voss 1998; Sennett 1998).

21. As examples of educational concepts and projects from the South in which work is accorded great significance in the sense of 'creative-practical activities', we would refer to Rabindranath Tagore and Mahatma Gandhi in India, and Julius Nyerere in Tanzania.

22. This may also be a reason why these projects like to call themselves 'cooperatives'; by contrast, the terms 'enterprise' and 'entrepreneur' are based on an individualistic view of action.

11 | Thoughts on a subject-oriented theory of working children

§ IN the societies of today, new modes and forms of the resubjectification of childhood are emerging. In the societies of the South, they are developing in a different way from those of the North, but share some causes and are coming closer. In both South and North, it is apparent that work is becoming a focal point in the development of a new, enhanced status of children as subjects. The bourgeois draft of childhood that originated in Europe, which is essentially based on the separation of children from socially relevant work and its privatization, has reached its limits and is in the process of becoming completely obsolete. What may succeed it is as yet observable only in outline, but it appears to involve forms of childhood marked by an active relation to society, a kind of participative childhood. With this, a new type of working child is emerging which is compatible neither with the outworn ideas and practices of 'child labour' nor with the 'niche existence' of children hitherto.

In this final chapter, I will sum up the book's main points and connect them with some conclusions which, I hope, point a way forward. For this, I shall examine the various ways in which children in the South and the North have been reduced to the status of objects, and finally enquire how and for what reasons children are acquiring a new status as subjects, or are on the way to doing so. Since the concept of 'subject' occupies a central position in my ideas, I will begin with a critical reconstruction of it.

Reconstruction of the concept of the 'subject'

The concept of the 'subject' is a controversial child of the philosophy of the European Enlightenment, and is connected above all with the names of René Descartes and Immanuel Kant. According to Descartes, man is, on account of his reason, the subject of possible objects with which he is confronted and to which, in the autonomy of his thinking, he is superior. Kant goes beyond mere thought, and 'contrasts his concept of the subject as an idealistic utopia with the class society he experienced, thoroughly regimented, censored and bureaucratized as it was' (Meueler 1993: 21). Kant's utopia centres on the 'categorical imperative', the individual guided by reason, self-aware and autonomous, who in conjunction with other 'free individuals' brings about a 'bourgeois society' that renders possible the full – which he calls 'moral' – development of the subjectivity of all men. Here, Kant has in mind the bourgeoisie of his time, which was gaining in numbers and influence.

Under the influence of the class conflicts that arose with bourgeois society, Karl Marx and Friedrich Engels opposed the idealist subject conception of bourgeois Enlightenment philosophy with a materialist concept of the subject, centring on work and the dispossessed proletariat obliged to sell its labour power. They state 'how those who think themselves autonomous actors are in reality marionettes of a system whose compulsions to act hardly differ from the traditional dependences' (ibid.: 25). Rather than the idealist picture of man, which centres on the concepts of reason and liberty, they stress the historical and social character of human beings and the influence of work. In their work *Die deutsche Ideologie* (written in 1845–56 but published only posthumously) they formulate the basics of their materialist concept of the subject:

> The production of ideas, imagination and consciousness is to begin with immediately interwoven with the material activities and the material intercourse of men, the language of real life … Quite in contrast to German philosophy, which descends from heaven to earth, here the ascent from earth to heaven is undertaken. That is, it does not proceed from that which men say, think or imagine, nor even from man as something said, thought or imagined in order to arrive at the real man; it proceeds from really acting men, and from their real process of life the development of the ideological reflexes and echoes of this process of life is represented. … It is not awareness which determines life; life determines awareness. The first view proceeds from awareness as from the living individual, the second, which corresponds to real life, proceeds from the really living individuals themselves, and considers awareness solely as *their* awareness. (Marx and Engels 1962: 26f)

Marx and Engels see human life and its history as the conscious activity of subjects, but stress that men can in turn shape their lives and history only under pre-existing conditions. In order to survive, they must establish relations with nature and with other people. These two kinds of relation are always pre-existent as objective states of affairs, as the result of the actions of earlier generations. The subject, with his productive, intellectual and other powers and abilities, develops under the pre-condition of these relations and by modifying with them. He develops within practical social activity, by making ever new fields of life the object of his activity and understanding.

These two conceptions of the subject, the idealist and the materialistic, still form two essential fixed and central controversial points of the debate on the 'chances of the subject'. Under the impact of the catastrophes of the twentieth century stemming from human action (the world wars, fascism, Stalinism, the ravaging of the environment), not only did the autonomous and free-reasoning subject of Enlightenment philosophy fall into disrepute, but the optimism of progress embedded in the materialist concept of the subject was also called into question.

Sigmund Freud expanded the spectrum of the concept of the subject by adding the dimension of subconscious mental processes, judging the subject as being only apparently autonomous and free within (see Freud 1969). Max Horkheimer and Theodor W. Adorno saw in a disastrous 'dialectic of enlightenment' the self-destruction of reason as an unstoppable process,[1] and in the end Adorno saw himself confronted with a 'subjectless subject' (Adorno 1970: 35), whose apparent individuality was nothing but an empty show. Michel Foucault proclaimed the 'end of man' with the death of the subject: 'How can man be this life, whose network, whose pulsating, whose hidden power infinitely exceeds the experience of it that is immediately given to him? How can he be that work whose requirements and laws impose themselves on him as an alien compulsion?' (Foucault 1966: 334).

Whereas this criticism principally relates to the idealist concept of the subject, and is a version of points of criticism that are already to be found in the materialist view of the subject, there is a further kind of criticism of the subject that relates equally to both of these positions. A critique that arose with feminism and the social movements directed against capitalist globalization opposes the separation of the human subject from nature and making the latter its object. A text from Peru dedicated to the renaissance of Andean culture takes up a position against the European idea of the subject in the following terms: 'This new, enlightened man that degrades nature to the status of object is the individual, a creature hitherto non-existent in history, which finds its confirmation in contrasting itself with that which it considers as objects. The individual is a lonely being which also opposes itself to other individuals that it experiences as competing for its self-realization. It opposes nature, which it regards as a storehouse of raw materials to be exploited. It opposes God, of whom it assumes that He can disturb the individual's rational explanation of the world' (Rengifo Vásquez 2001b: 46).

In contrast, it is stressed that for the Andean culture, as for other 'indigenous' cultures, there is 'no difference between living and dead objects' (ibid.: 55). 'There is a feeling of equality between men, nature and the protective gods; they are all regarded as persons. ... In this personified world, nothing exists outside of nature. There is nothing supernatural. The protective gods are palpable, evident; intercourse with them is based on community work and not on adoration, for all consider themselves incomplete and each one needs the others for the healthy recreation of life. In the context of this incompleteness, mutuality manifests itself; someone who thinks himself perfect does not need to communicate with others' (ibid.: 55). Knowledge and education are not accounted a privilege of man that places him in a position to appropriate or to dominate non-human nature. Non-human nature too is accounted knowledgeable and educated, and enables man to learn from it, provided he respects it and engages in a dialogue with it in a relationship as between equals.

The question arises as to whether the idea of the subject is a necessary concomitant of the separation and subjection of other human beings and of nature. In my view, it can also be understood in the sense of mutual respect and social recognition, by recognizing dependence on each other as an essential basis of human life.[2] The idea of the subject is then opposed to all forms of oppression and exclusion, without aiming at new oppression and exclusion. This 'social' idea is contained in both the idealistic and the materialist concept of the subject. In the former, however, it is lost in the celebration of the individual, egoistic and seeking his own advantage, and in the second it is lost in the mist of the abstract construction of a collective of the deprived.

The idealist concept of the subject, connected with the rise and triumph of the bourgeoisie, arose out of a situation of repression, but is attached to the individual, thought of as bourgeois or educated, and aims at his dominance over other, less privileged people and over non-human nature. Its modern ideal type is the technically skilled manager-entrepreneur, who will risk anything to make a profit.

The materialist view of the subject also contains elements aiming for dominance and rule, but it sees man in his neediness and his social relations. According to this view, the subject develops by acting for self-preservation, and creates the material basis that makes the lives of all easier. And it develops by entering into relations with other people, in the increasingly complex division of labour and cooperation, and in solidarity in the struggle for survival and a better life. One could speak here of a *social subject*, in contrast to the self-loving and dominating bourgeois subject.

The subject of survival and neediness finds himself in an ambivalent situation. He cannot give up, as he would otherwise succumb. He combines features that – in the words of Leo Löwenthal (1989) – can be termed the 'little ego' and the 'big ego'. By the 'little ego', Löwenthal means the desire directed towards his environment with which the individual seeks to assert and prove himself with reference to himself within a society not conceived as having solidarity. By contrast, the 'big ego' recognizes that individuals in their isolation deny the reality shared with others, by which Löwenthal understands the 'turning away from the reality of the suffering of human and non-human beings'. On this, Meueler remarks that both egos only apparently exclude each other; in fact the 'little ego' can gradually undergo a transition into the 'big ego'. 'The little ego employs all its available strength for its own self-preservation, cost it what it may. If I have eyes only for myself, I will only see, other than myself, that which is of importance for my own survival and welfare. Nothing but this has meaning for me. Pure self-preservation realizes itself via indifference to aggression towards the sufferings and fate of others ... The autonomy striven for only becomes a human value when the counter-concept, dependence on others and that of others on me, is also considered' (Meueler 1993: 90f).

With regard to the 'little ego', Meueler also speaks of a 'more functional subjectivity ... that is in the service of self-preservation' (ibid.: 92) and makes it possible to master everyday life. As men should constantly be looking for hitherto unknown answers and paths, subjects go beyond merely functional self-preservation. Again and again 'one can observe a superfluity of spontaneousness, contradiction, recalcitrance, obstinacy and readiness for conflict, productive material for disturbance in the functionality concept. These superfluities are not only to be found in those who work in far from alienated occupations under good material conditions and can look back on satisfying and stimulating educational experiences. They can also, in different forms, be found in those who are forced to live below subsistence level under humiliating circumstances, quite without security' (ibid.: 93).

It is precisely consideration of the daily lives of people in dire straits which makes one doubt whether the subject is really dead. It appears only to move out of sight when measured with the rhetorical yardstick of philosophical systems. One may also note that the demand for the subject again becomes more lively the more human societies threaten to subside into catastrophe, or when talk is even heard of the end of history. Perhaps there is something in Meueler's supposition that subjectivity 'becomes visible only when it is being lost' (ibid.: 95).

Working children in the contradiction between subject and object

It has become customary today to see children as 'legal subjects' in the sense that they possess and can claim rights of their own ('children's rights'). However, whether they are also 'social subjects' in the sense that they possess the same ability to act as adults remains controversial. The bourgeois view of childhood allows for a certain autonomy and a special value for children, but in relation to 'adult society' the status of subject is denied them. 'Children are ... structurally excluded from all the decisive spheres of life in the modern world, with the exception of those institutions specially created for them' (Kaufmann 1980: 767).

To regard children as subjects is to stress the protest directed against various ideological and practical forms of their degradation to object status. One of these forms consists in denying children participation in socially relevant work, and another in the position that they can work, but have to do this under humiliating conditions and be economically exploited. The first form, which corresponds with the bourgeois concept of childhood that came about in modern Europe, is to be found above all (though not exclusively) in the 'affluent' societies of the North. The second, which at first glance appears to contradict the bourgeois image of the child, is above all (but also not exclusively) widespread in the poor societies of the South. Both forms agree in not allowing children to play an active, influential part in their societies – in other words, to enjoy political participation and to be a socially recognized part of society with equal rights.

In the bourgeois view of childhood, the child is stylized as an object of development. Little people, who are obviously dependent on affection, care and support, become 'immature' creatures who are not accepted as valid until they have 'been developed'. The criteria for maturity and development are arbitrarily laid down by adults, who think themselves developed, in order to legitimize and cement the dependence of the child. Subjective qualities found in the small child are generally devalued as an expression of immaturity that can be overcome by education. The child finds itself exposed to a process of continual and escalating denial of its subjectivity, and its creativity is extinguished. Not until it has unconditionally surrendered to the adults' claim to power is it permitted to become a 'person'.[3] The opportunity to see itself as a subject with self-confidence and initiative of its own is thus considerably restricted.

A variant of the development-object situation consists in degrading the child to the status of the object of care. This takes place when children are no longer treated as objects to be dealt with arbitrarily ('without rights'), but as creatures weak by nature who are above all to be protected from dangers and risks. Supported by the best of intentions towards children, in this sense reservations are defined and established in which the children are to be preserved from the 'evil' influences and the 'rough reality' of (adult) society. This is usually accompanied by ascribing a symbolic role (innocence, fortune, future) to the children. While the child in the one case is the object of paternalistic care, in the second it serves as the object of projections of the adults. In both cases, these are socially conditioned fantasy constructs, which deny children the ability to tackle their own reality and to play an active, formative role in society.

With the separation of children from the sphere of socially relevant work, children that were prized for their 'economic value' become children whose significance lies primarily in the 'emotional enrichment' of adults. The US sociologist Viviana Zelizer has expressed this process in the image of the 'priceless child' that has apparently become valueless. At the same time, she makes it clear – from the example of the insurance business and the adoption trade – that even the non-working child is given a monetary value, although without a contribution from the child itself being seen in this. 'New sentimental criteria were established to determine the monetary worth of child life' (Zelizer 1994: 210). The economic role of the child does not disappear, but undergoes a fundamental transformation. To the extent that work and money still play a part in children's lives, they are no longer defined in economic-productive categories but in educational ones. Zelizer demonstrates this above all by the change in the function of work in the home, which in the case of children no longer expects them to make an essential contribution but rather to practise certain virtues and skills.[4]

The child as object of exploitation appears incompatible with the Western bourgeois pattern of childhood. It is almost exclusively associated with 'pre-modern child labour'. Yet if we consider the exploitative forms of children's work today more closely, it becomes clear that they are rooted not only in the capitalist mode of production – whether 'pre-modern' or 'modern' – but also in the 'modern' ideology of childhood. The latter has been described by the British sociologist Diane Elson (1982) as a 'seniority system'. This means that any economic activity carried out by children is devalued and depreciated just because it is performed by children. This in turn is based on the idea that children by definition are thought of as not developed and thus not particularly productive. On the other hand, children are degraded as objects of exploitation in apparently non-economic contexts, for instance when their creativity and 'liveliness' are used to suck emotional honey from them and make adults feel good. None of these forms of the reduction of children to the status of objects is, however, able to extinguish completely the subjectivity of children. Indeed, they may even help to act as a challenge. The subjectiveness of children has its point of departure in the situation of being subjected to and dependent on those who possess the power of definition and decision in society. The subjective qualities come out in protest, and are the result of a process of adaptation in which biological, economic, social and cultural influences mingle.

Like all human beings, the child has biological-natural resources that render possible its utter degradation to the status of object only at the cost of social or physical death. As long as this extreme form of attack on human subjectivity is avoided,[5] any attempt to make mere objects out of children is doomed to failure, and the child will always show itself to 'have a mind of its own'. 'Elements of independence and obstinacy are … already to be found in the baby precisely through its dependence' (Scherr 1997: 49). In the further course of life, children's independence can be strengthened by cooping them up in reservations of peers, and here as a rule leads to the formation of cliques and other forms of independent behaviour.[6]

In whatever forms children may be reduced to objects – either as non-working children who are apparently valueless, or as working children whose economic contribution is denied – it cannot remain concealed from them for ever that the adults are dependent on them and that they therefore possess value for *them*.

Non-working children are 'priceless' to adults in the economic sense, but their value is at the same time inestimably great. They are ascribed an 'occult value' in the sense that they 'enrich' the lives of adults and stand for a better future. Their (school) education is seen primarily as an investment in the future 'economic development' and productivity of society, and only as such is it also 'valuable' for the child to be 'developed'.[7] This purpose of school, which can hardly be hidden from children, suggests to them the question as to what they themselves get out of it. Simply referring to their future 'profit', as is usual, is a promise recognized today as 'brittle' by many schoolchildren. This may be the most important reason why, for a growing number of children in the North, school is becoming a 'job on the side',[8] whereas they devote most of their attention to activities that 'give them' something, whether it be income they can dispose of, or the feeling of being able to achieve something and play a (recognized and self-determined) part in 'real life'.

We may assume that the exclusion from socially relevant work appears questionable to children above all when and inasmuch as they see in it an unnecessary, 'artificial' prolongation of dependence. At any rate, the fact that a rapidly growing number of children are adopting a new form of existence not provided for in the bourgeois view of childhood cannot be overlooked. This is characterized by the fact that it is no longer supplied and controlled by educational institutions but in immediate interchange with the social life of adults. This new form of existence does not necessarily mean that children now see themselves as 'working children', but its essence is that children are abandoning the passive state of being the objects of development and realizing themselves as socially significant, with a right to a satisfying present.

In the societies of the South, in which for most children work has long been a self-evident part of life, the question of the chances of the subject poses itself the other way round. Here, the children are degraded to the status of objects in that they *have to* work and often do so under conditions that injure their human dignity and rob them of the fruits of their labour. This does not apply to all working children in the same way, and the differences are of an importance not to be underestimated in terms of the chance of recognizing this state as being alterable and practically calling it into question. But the basis for claiming the status of subject is the children's experience that they take responsibility for themselves and others (as a rule their family) and carry out tasks essential for survival. Working children who are economically exploited will call their exploitation into question when and in so far as they become aware of the social legitimacy and significance of their work and their factually achieved independence.

Cultural factors play a mediating and possibly stimulating part in this process. Whereas the bourgeois view of childhood shows itself to be counter-productive, as it transfers to working children a dependence that they have already left behind them, the idea of the individual and social rights of children that is spreading throughout the world contributes essentially to supporting their claim to the status of subjects in society. This is especially true of the rights that are directed at a participative role for children in society. No less important are certain cultural influences that go together with globalization, which make it appear self-evident to many working children in the South today that they can claim the fruits of their work personally and enjoy them.

The implications of globalization

In order to understand the implications of globalization for working children, it would seem useful to distinguish between the structural aspects and changes in the social significance or representations of children's work, while always taking into account the fact that it deals with contradictory processes present in economic, social and cultural dimensions.

Nowadays, children's work is understood as a range of labour forms that vary from self-determined jobs, carried out voluntarily by children in decent conditions, to extremely exploitative types of job that violate the dignity of the children and put their lives and personal development at risk.

With globalization, the number of children who assume social and economic responsibility for their family and/or for themselves – compared with the previous stage of capitalism – rises. That is to say that there are increasingly fewer children who don't have work experience and that there are continually more children who play an important role in the processes of production/reproduction in society. For children, the significances can be very different. They depend on the conditions in which they work and their individual and collective resources in order to interpret and overcome their experiences. These resources depend, to a certain degree, on the social and cultural environments in which the children live and develop. In this context, work cultures and the existence of social movements of children and of adults who support them and their rights are of great importance.

The fact that there are more and more children involved in labour processes calls into question the European and bourgeois model that is based on the exclusion of children from working life, on their isolation and on their preparation in 'protected pedagogical areas'. Now, if a new patron of infancy that directly includes children in society is to benefit them, it depends less on a wide system of protection of infancy. Rather, it depends on whether or not society is capable of recognizing children as subjects that share the same rights and hold the same value as adults do, and which allows them self-determination in life.

Most of the children's work that is promoted by globalization takes place in informal conditions, which is to say conditions that are rarely regulated, be it in the rural or the so-called informal urban sector. Whether or not they are paid, the children are perceived mainly as a source of labour, or they have to perceive themselves as such to be able to compete in the labour market. With the 'informalization' of work, the insecurity and risks in the lives of the children and their parents increase. In this sense, the main and growing part of children's work is distinguished by the 'informality' of work in a subsistence economy, as we know it to be in certain traditional Native American cultures. Nevertheless, modern 'informalization' promoted by globalization has two faces: within it methods of extreme exploitation mingle with methods of economic solidarity. The informalization of work doesn't necessarily equate to reducing children to pure objects but can also open new social spaces in their lives. That depends, once again, on the labour conditions and the socio-cultural environment in which children find themselves and – not least – on the possibilities for them to organize and their capacity to do so.

In the first place, globalization, with its neo-liberal character, is a violent process that may take a material or ideological form. It casts many people out into the abyss of horrendous poverty and puts their physical existence and human dignity in danger. Its forces them to abandon their places of origin, and they are exposed to an insecure lifestyle and to a humiliating treatment that has never been seen before. Regardless, new possibilities are arising for people to guarantee their right to a decent life without poverty and to express these demands publicly. Suffering is becoming less recognized as an act of God or as a fatalistic destiny, but rather as the consequence of a certain policy (in this case a neo-liberal one) that can be converted into an initiative of change.

When children become subordinate in new labour relations (largely of exploitation), today more than ever they are able to recognize this situation as being an abuse of their (children's) rights, and are better able to report it and insist on decent working conditions and a decent life. If a family resorts to using the labour of a child, this situation should no longer be considered the quasi-natural destiny of the child but rather as illustrative of the fact that the family can claim the earnings of the child as its own. If children carry out any labour activity, they are often no longer doing it exclusively to deal with an emergency situation but also to be able to satisfy certain personal needs and to acquire more autonomy.

It is certain that globalization puts at risk the existence of indigenous ways of life and cultures, and threatens the diversity of cultures. Nevertheless, it also creates new possibilities of knowing other cultures and ways of life; engaging in communication with people from other parts of the world broadens one's horizon. The movements of working children have developed international networks and are in the process of converting themselves into competent and able actors at a global level, making use of the possibilities of information-garnering and communication generated by globalization with great self-confidence.

Globalization and the implementation of new technologies are eroding the boundaries of labour organization in such a way that new balances are arising between work and life, and between work time and 'free time'. These are related to the 'resubjectification' of society, whereby each individual must bear more responsibility for the reproduction and planning of life. Both processes can increase the pressure on people to be readily available as labourers ('entrepreneurs of labour'), but – under certain circumstances – they can also broaden their scope to mould their lives according to their own ideas and visions.

New forms and areas of 'action' for children are arising which require them to be active subjects, and where the boundaries between work, leisure or education activities and social activities are no longer well defined. If it is true that this fact increases the risk of children being 'instrumentalized' and exploited, it is no less true that they also have more possibilities for assuming responsibility in creating and projecting their lives.

The requirements of a subject-oriented theory of the working child

In the development of the theory of childhood formulated since the 1980s in the North, the idea is widespread that childhood is currently in a state of fundamental change. This change is seen in the societies termed 'post-industrial' or 'postmodern' in the fact that children are rejecting the role of 'objects of education' and 'recipients of care' imposed by the bourgeois view of childhood, and making themselves felt as 'active individuals' no longer under the control of adult society. Some link the change with a change in the significance of the educational institutions created for children, which are out of touch with real life,[9] as well as the growing influence of children as 'media users' and 'consumers'. 'When the market addresses children as consumers, it treats them like adults, opens up access and possibilities of choice to them, and relieves them from the unacceptable sides of education provided for them by adults. As participants in the market, children acquire a status as subjects not provided for in the utopias of educational theory. It offers children a relative autonomy that coincides with parental expectations of early independence' (Honig 1999: 159). Sometimes, this change is clothed in the image of an 'accelerated childhood' (Zinnecker 1997), or the 'end of Fordistic childhood' is spoken of (Honig and Ostner 2001).[10] This expresses the idea that children today make themselves 'independent' considerably earlier than was provided for by the bourgeois view of childhood – or that adults are making more effort to take account of children's perspectives and claims.

In almost all the writings on the theory of childhood published in German-speaking countries, however, what significance work has or could acquire for the processes of change in children we have noted remains unconsidered. Neither is cognizance taken of the working children of the South, their perspectives and manifestations, nor to any extent worth mentioning of the fact that in the North too a considerable and obviously growing number of children are working or want to work.[11] The still largely unbroken dominance of the bourgeois view of childhood has resulted in the fact that children's work is still perceived either not at all or only in its negative manifestations and aspects. Children's work is accounted a phenomenon of the past, which appeared to have vanished from the scene at the latest with the introduction of compulsory school attendance and the general prohibition of child employment in the North, and which will be abolished in the South too. Where the existence of children's work cannot be ignored, it is nearly always considered as a danger for and threat to children. In a work context, children are seen as vulnerable, passive victims in need of protection. Since only gainful employment is concentrated on, it appears above all necessary to preserve children from 'exploitation' and 'abuse', as well as from the irresponsible use of their money. It is not considered that children might consciously claim work for themselves and use it to escape from the marginalized and privatized reservations of bourgeois childhood.

If we wish to understand children as social subjects, we cannot avoid the question of children's work and its significance. James et al. (1998) emphasize that it is a notable deficiency of childhood research and theory hitherto that such questions have hardly been posed up to the present. They see this as 'part of the invisibilizing of children's work – or the making visible of it only as a problem' (ibid.: 119).

According to them, there is hardly any research that enquires into how children act during their work and what significance it has for them. 'We have remarkably little research evidence on how children themselves understand the different activities in which they are involved: how they handle and use categories of work; which of their activities they understand as work and how this might shift between contexts; what their motivation for engaging in different types of work is; how involvement in work affects and is affected by their kin and other social relationships, and so on' (ibid.: 120). They demand the development of a better understanding of the various motives that cause children to work, and 'detailed work on how children in their relations with their peers and with adult society constitute a sense of their own needs and wants' (ibid.: 120). The few studies that deal with such questions in the North or the South are discussed in this book.

By contrast, Honig (1999) limits himself to noting that in view of the current restrictions in access to employment 'career decisions acquire strategic importance at an early stage', and that 'the legal and economic possibilities for children to earn their own living are extremely restricted' (ibid.: 160). Correct as this observation is, it is important to pursue the question of why these opportunities continue to be restricted and how they could be expanded. And above all it is necessary to take more seriously the activities that are frequently carried out or desired by children today, and to see them in their significance for children's social status and their formation as subjects.

This significance depends decisively, for one thing, on how far the child's work contributes to sustaining life and social reproduction, and for another on to what extent it is based on the child's freely made decision. These two aspects *may* be, but do not *have to* be, opposing alternatives. In the countries of the South, in most cases it is clear that the child's work is essential for survival. In the countries of the North, the child's work contributes to the satisfaction of its own needs or those of others, regardless of whether it is 'paid' or not.

The extent to which working comes about through exercise of the child's free will depends largely on its social situation in life. A child who lives in great poverty and is dependent for survival on the decisions of others has little or no chance to work in a way corresponding to his desires and ideas. These desires and ideas will have to adapt to his situation. The possibility of acting according to his own will also depends on the extent to which opportunities for work that it considers suitable are available to the child. According to how the child is able to develop its own wishes and work in a manner that corresponds to these, he will experience work as meaningful and 'valuable'.

Work essential for survival is of certain specific kinds and thus not a factor of free will. This situation is, however, only insoluble when the child is denied the possibility to decide for itself whether and to what extent it will take on such essential work, and when such essential work has to be performed under conditions that harm the child's human dignity. Working children in the South sometimes put their finger on this point by distinguishing between the 'necessity' and the 'compulsion' to perform a given kind of work (see Liebel 2001a). Only if we see children as 'irresponsible' beings in principle do we have difficulty in seeing that they develop the interest and desire to make decisions about 'essential' work.

What applies equally to working children in both the South and the North is that, in order to assure themselves of their own value and to see themselves as subjects, they require a social environment in which a minimum of social recognition is ensured. 'Becoming a subject means ... not replacing complete dependence by complete autonomy, but expanding the scope for self-aware and self-determined action in social relations. ... Subjectivity is, viewed thus, by constitution "social subjectivity"' (Scherr 1997: 49). The social relations through which social recognition and self-awareness are acquired may to a certain degree arise in the groups and movements of the children themselves, especially when the actors explicitly understand themselves as working children. But beyond this children must find opportunities to intervene in the 'adult world', and their activity – in whatever contexts and forms – must achieve recognition as socially relevant work.

Notes

1. They began their book *Dialectic of the Enlightenment*, which was written during the Second World War in exile in America and first appeared in Amsterdam in 1947, with the sentences: 'Enlightenment, in the comprehensive sense of progressive thought, has always pursued the goal of removing men's fears and making them masters. But the completely enlightened earth now shines in the sign of evil triumphant' (Horkheimer and Adorno 1944/1987: 9).

2. This view of the subject, not related to objects and termed 'intersubjective', is, for example, developed in a study on the language and the view of nature and society among the Maya people of the Tojalabales in Mexico (see Lenkendorf 2000). Here what is stressed is 'mutual understanding and respect as integral parts of intersubjective communication' (p. 36).

3. The reinterpretation and transformation of the biological and social dependence of childhood into a 'socially constructed' dependence on adults that can be prolonged at will is the primary topic of the 'constructivist' sociology of childhood which, proceeding from the debate in Anglo-Saxon countries (see James and Prout 1990), has also brought new emphases into the German discussion of the social status of children (see Zeiher et al. 1996; Honig 1999).

4. On the changes in the function of work in the home by children in Germany, see Zeiher 2000, who connects her study with Zelizer's findings. Zeiher points out that domestic work done by children is today not expected only for 'educational' reasons but rather because mothers are frequently in employment and no longer want to be tied to housework as a supposed duty of women. Children, meanwhile, prefer to engage in housework when it really seems useful, is not demanded of them and does not take place under the direct supervision of a parent.

5. In the countries of the South, this is by no means always the case, as can be seen above all in the extreme form of slavery-type child labour, and in the instrumentalizing of children for war purposes.

6. The German sociologist Oskar Negt (1997: 91ff) has coined the term *Kinderöffentlichkeit* (literally 'children's publicness') for the collective forms of children's expression of their *Eigensinn* (own will), seeing these as a form of protest that it is difficult to pin down.

7. Presumably this is a reason why children in the North often give 'school' as the answer to the question as to what they understand by 'work'. That is, by work they understand above all a disagreeable and perhaps even superfluous burden.

8. As a recent piece of evidence reference may be made to an article by Ulla Hanselmann in the German weekly *Die Zeit* (24, 7 June 2001), which carried the heading 'School as a job on the side. Teachers lament the rising number of working pupils. School performance is suffering, especially among the weaker pupils.'

9. This means, for instance, that school as a hierarchically structured place for the mere transmission of knowledge and inculcation of norms of behaviour is called into question, and confronted with the growing demands of children and adolescents for it to be made an attractive and satisfying sphere for living and acting.

10. 'The educational childhood enforced by the social state of the twentieth century turns out to be a Fordistic childhood which, with the service household, its strong breadwinner norm and the housewife marriage, acquired its shape as an average educational moratorium and will lose it with its disappearance' (Honig and Ostner 2001: 308).

11. An exception to this is Hengst and Zeiher (2000). Worthy of note is the contribution by Wintersberger (2000), who sees the children in the North (again) becoming 'producers', and sees the 'new perception of children's work in the Third World' as relevant to the North as well. Hengst (2000) also takes up in his article the experience and ideas of working children in the South, and enquires into their relevance for the North.

Bibliography

Adorno, Theodor W. (1970) *Aufsätze zur Gesellschaftstheorie und Methodologie*, Frankfurt: Suhrkamp.

Alarcón Glasínovich, Walter (1991) *Entre calles y plazas. El trabajo de los niños en Lima*, Lima: Instituto de Estudios Peruanos and UNICEF.

— (1998) *El trabajo de niños y adolescentes en América Latina*, Bogotá: UNICEF, Documento de Trabajo no. 3.

Ames Ramello, Patricia (1999) *Mejorando la escuela rural: tres décadas de experiencias educativas en el Perú*, Lima: Instituto de Estudios Peruanos, Documento de Trabajo no. 96.

Aragão-Lagergren, Aida (1997) *Working Children in the Informal Sector in Managua*, Uppsala: Department of Social and Economic Geography, Uppsala University.

Ariès, Philippe (1962) *Centuries of Childhood. A Social History of Family Life*, New York: Vintage.

Arrien, Juan B. and Róger Matus Lazo (1989) *Nicaragua: diez años de educación en la revolución*, Managua: Ministerio de Educación.

Aziz, K. M. Ashraful and Clarence Maloney (1985) *Life Stages. Gender and Fertility in Bangladesh*, Dhaka: International Centre for Diarrhoeal Disease Research.

Bachman, Jerald B. and John Schulenberg (1991) *Part-time Work by High School Seniors: Sorting Out Correlates and Possible Consequences*, Ann Arbor, MI: Institute for Social Research.

— (1993) 'How Part-time Work Intensity Relates to Drug Use, Problem Behavior, Time Use, and Satisfaction among High School Seniors: Are These Consequences or Merely Correlates?', *Developmental Psychology*, 29(2): 220–35.

Badry Zalami, Fatima (1998) *Forgotten at the Pyjama Trail: A Case Study of Garment Workers in Méknès (Morocco) Dismissed from Their Jobs Following Foreign Attention*, Amsterdam: IWGCL.

Balagopalan, Sarada (2002) 'Constructing Indigenous Childhoods: Colonialism, Vocational Education and the Working Child', *Childhood*, 9(1): 19–34.

Balding, John (1997) *Young People in 1996*, Exeter: Schools Health Education Unit, University of Exeter.

Barling, Julian and D. G. Gallagher (1996) 'Part-time Employment', in C. L. Cooper and I. T. Robertson (eds), *International Review of Industrial and Organizational Psychology*, 11, New York: Wiley, pp. 243–78.

Barling, Julian and E. Kevin Kelloway (eds) (1999) *Young Workers. Varieties of Experience*, Washington, DC: American Psychological Association.

Barling, Julian, Kimberley-Ann Rogers and E. Kevin Kelloway (1995) 'Some Effects of Teenagers' Part-time Employment: The Quantity and Quality of Work Make the Difference', *Journal of Organizational Behavior*, 16: 143–54.

Bateson, Gregory (1932) 'Social Structure of the Iatmul People of the Sepik River', *Oceania*, 2(3): 245—91 and (4): 401—53.

— (1965) *Naven. A Survey of the Problems Suggested by a Composite Picture of the Culture of a New Guinea Tribe Drawn from Three Points of View*, Stanford, CT (1st edn 1936).

Bausinger, Hermann (1983) 'Spiel unter Dummen. Anmerkungen zur Kulturgeschichte von Spiel·und Sport', in Grupe et al. (1983), pp. 43—59.

Béart, Charles (1955) 'Jeux et jouets de l'Ouest africain', *Mémoires de l'Institut français d'Afrique*, 42, Dakar: IFAN.

Beck, Kurt and Gerd Spittler (eds) (1996) 'Arbeit in Afrika', *Beiträge zur Afrika-Forschung*, 12, Hamburg: LIT.

Becker, Saul, Chris Dearden and Jo Aldridge (2001) 'Children's Labour of Love? Young Carers and Care Work', in Mizen et al. (2001b), pp. 70—87.

Bekombo, Manga (1981) 'The Child in Africa: Socialisation, Education and Work', in Rodgers and Standing (1981b), pp. 113—29.

Bellin, P. (1963) 'L'enfant Saharien à travers ses jeux', *Journal de la Societé des Africanistes*, 33, Paris.

Benes, Roberto (2000) 'Von der Flucht aus der Armut zur Emanzipationsstrategie? Zum Wandel der Kinderarbeit in Italien', in Hengst and Zeiher (2000), pp. 119—32.

Bequele, Assefa and Jo Boyden (eds) (1988) *Combating Child Labour*, Geneva: ILO.

Bequele, Assefa and William E. Myers (1995) *First Things First in Child Labour. Eliminating Work Detrimental to Children*, Geneva: UNICEF and ILO.

'Berlin und seine Entwicklung' (1870) *Städtisches Jahrbuch für Volkswirtschaft und Statistik*, 4, Berlin.

Bidwell, Charles, Barbara Schneider and Kathryn Borman (1998) 'Working: Perceptions and Experiences of American Teenagers', in Borman and Schneider (1998), pp. 160—82.

Blair, Sampson Lee (1992a) 'Children's Participation in Household Labor: Child Socialization versus the Need for Household Labor', *Journal of Youth and Adolescent Development*, 21(2): 241—58.

— (1992b) 'The Sex-Typing of Children's Household Labor. Parental Influence on Daughters' and Sons' Housework', *Youth & Society*, 24(2): 178—203.

Blanchet, Thérèse (1996) *Lost Innocence. Stolen Childhoods*, Dhaka: University Press Limited.

Blandano, Pia, Loredana Iapichino and Mariella Velardi (1997) 'L'autogestione cooperativa: l'esperienza della Scuola M.S., A. Ugo' di Palermo', *NATs – Nuovi Spazi de Crescita. Rivista Internazionale – Ediziono Italiana*, 2: 39—44.

Bloch, Ernst (1967) *Das Prinzip Hoffnung*, vol. 2, Frankfurt: Suhrkamp.

Boesen, Elisabeth (1996) 'Fulbe und Arbeit', in Beck and Spittler (1996), pp. 193—207.

Böhm, Ingrid and Jens Schneider (1996) *Produktives Lernen – eine Bildungschance für Jugendliche in Europa*, Berlin, Milow: Schibri Verlag.

Böhnisch, Lothar and Wolfgang Schröer (2001) *Pädagogik und Arbeitsgesellschaft*.

Historische Grundlagen und theoretische Ansätze für eine sozialpolitisch reflexive Pädagogik, Weinheim and Munich: Juventa.

Bonnet, Michel (1999) *Le travail des enfants: terrain de luttes*, Lausanne: Editions Page deux.

Borman, Kathryn M. (1991) *The First 'Real' Job: A Study of Young Workers*, Albany: New York University Press.

Borman, Kathryn M. and Barbara Schneider (eds) (1998) *The Adolescent Years: Social Influences and Educational Challenges*, Chicago, IL: University of Chicago Press.

Bott, Elisabeth (1958) *Report on a Brief Study of Mother–Child Relationship in Tonga*, Nuku'alofa, Tonga: Central Planning Department (mimeo).

Bourdillon, Michael (ed.) (2000) *Earning a Life. Working Children in Zimbabwe*, Harare: Wever Press.

Boyden, Jo, Birgitta Ling and William Myers (1998) *What Works for Working Children*, Stockholm: Rädda Barnen.

Brannen, Julia (1995) 'Young People and Their Contribution to Household Work', *Sociology*, 29(2): 317–38.

Brannen, Julia and Margaret O'Brien (eds) (1996) *Children in Families. Research and Policy*, London and Washington, DC: Falmer Press.

Brater, Michael and Claudia Munz (1996) *Zusammenarbeit von Schule und Handwerk. Chancen und Wirkungen einer Öffnung von Schule für die Arbeitswelt*, Weinheim: Deutscher Studien Verlag.

Buirski, Nancy (1994) *Earth Angels: Migrant Children in America*, San Francisco, CA: Pomegranate Artbooks.

Burgos, Elizabeth (1985) *Me llamo Rigoberta Menchú y así me nació la conciencia*, México and Madrid: siglo veintiuno editores.

Busia, Kofi A. (1950) *Report on a Social Survey of Sekondi-Takoradi*, London.

Butterwegge, Christoph (2000) *Kinderarmut in Deutschland. Ursachen, Erscheinungsformen und Gegenmaßnahmen*, Frankfurt and New York: Campus.

Cain, Michael (1980) 'The Economic Activities of Children in a Village in Bangladesh', Rural Household Studies in Asia, Singapore: Singapore University Press.

Call, Kathleen Thiede (1996) 'The Implications of Helpfulness for Possible Selves', in Mortimer and Finch (1996), pp. 63–96.

Call, Kathleen Thiede, Jeylan T. Mortimer and Michael J. Shanahan (1995) 'Helpfulness and the Development of Competence in Adolescence', *Child Development*, 66: 129–38.

Camacho, Agnes Zenaida V. (1999a) 'Family, Child Labour and Migration: Child Domestic Workers in Metro Manila', *Childhood*, 6(1): 57–64.

— (1999b) 'The State Generated Child Labour. Rethinking Child Work in the Philippines', *Children, Work and Education*, IREWOC Workshop, Amsterdam, 15–17 November (mimeo).

Campbell, K., P. Marsden and J. Hurlbert (1986) 'Socioeconomic Status and Network Range', *Social Networks*, 8: 97–117.

Carr, Rhoda V., James D. Wright and Charles J. Brody (1996) 'Effects of High

School Work Experience a Decade Later: Evidence from the National Longitudinal Survey', *Sociology of Education*, 69 (January): 66–81.

Castellanos, Julieta and Mirna Flores (2001) *Familia, niñez trabajadora y escuela*, Tegucigalpa, Honduras: Save the Children Fund.

Cecchetti, Roberta (1998) *Children Who Work in Europe. From Exploitation to Participation*, Brussels: European Forum for Child Welfare.

Clayton, Anthony and Donald C. Savage (1974) *Government and Labour in Kenya 1895–1963*, London: Frank Cass.

Codere, Helen (1973) *The Biography of an African Society, Rwanda 1900–1960*, Tervuren.

Cogle, Frances L. and Grace E. Tasker (1982) 'Children and Housework', *Family Relations*, 31: 451–5.

Cohen, Philip (1994) *Verbotene Spiele. Theorie und Praxis antirassistischer Erziehung*, Hamburg: Argument.

Colectivo de la Escuela Popular Claretiana (1987) *Filodehambre. Una experiencia popular de innovación educativa*, Santa Fé de Bogotá: Dimensión Educativa.

Coly, Hamidou (2001) 'An Animator's Personal Experience', in Enda (2001a), pp. 128–47.

Comité Español del UNICEF & IUNDIA – Instituto de 'Necesidades y Derechos de la Infancia y la Adolescencia' (2000) *El trabajo infantil en España*, Madrid: Ministerio de Trabajo y Asuntos Sociales, Materiales de Trabajo no. 68.

Coninck-Smith, Ning de (2000) 'Der Kampf um die Zeit der Kinder. Zur Revision der Geschichte der Kinderarbeit in den nordischen Ländern', in Hengst and Zeiher (2000), pp. 209–18.

Coninck-Smith, Ning de, Bengt Sandin and Ellen Schrumpf (eds) (1997) *Industrious Children. Work and Childhood in the Nordic Countries 1850–1990*, Odense: Odense University Press.

Cooper, Frederick (1998) 'Afrika am Ende dieses Jahrhunderts. Vorstellungen und Erklärungen', *SOWI – Sozialwissenschaftliche Informationen*, 27(3): 220–7.

Cory, Hans (1956) *African Figurines, Their Ceremonial Use in Puberty Rites in Tanganyika*, New York: Grove Press.

Costermans, B. J. (1948) *Spelen bij de Mamvu en Logo in de gewesten Watsa-Faradje*, Belgian Congo.

Council of Europe (1996) *Children and Work in Europe. Report Prepared by a Study Group, 1994–95 Programme of Co-ordinated Research in the Employment Field*, Strasburg.

— (1997) *Combating Child Labour Exploitation as a Matter of Priority*, Strasburg Parliamentary Assembly, Social, Health and Family Affairs Committee, Doc. 7840.

Csikszentmihalyi, Mihaly (1979) 'The Concept of Flow', in Sutton-Smith (1979), pp. 257–74.

Cussiánovich, Alejandro (1988) '"Sie wissen genau, was sie wollen." Selbstorganisation von Kindern in Peru', *Lateinamerika – Analysen und Berichte*, 12: 82–97.

— (2001a) 'Some Premises for Reflection and Social Practices with Working Children and Adolescents', in Liebel et al. (2001), pp. 103–32.

— (2001b) 'The Paradigm of Integral Protagonism Promotion', in Liebel et al. (2001), pp. 309—19.

D'Amico, Ronald (1984) 'Does Employment during High School Impair Academic Progress?', *Sociology of Education*, 57 (July): 152—64.

Da Silva Telles, Vera and Helena W. Abramo (1987) 'Experiencia urbana, trabajo e identidad. Apuntes a una investigación sobre menores proletarios en Sao Paulo', in Diego Carrión and Ana Vainstoc (eds), *La ciudad y los niños*, Quito: CIUDAD – Centro de Investigaciones, pp. 197—214.

Deneckere, Gita (1994) *Sire, het volk mort. Collectieve actie in de sociale geschiedenis van de Belgische staat, 1831–1940*, PhD thesis, University of Ghent, Belgium.

Deutschlands Junge Garde (1955) *50 Jahre Arbeiterjugendbewegung*, Berlin: Dietz.

Dewey, John (1916/1936) *Democracy and Education*, New York: Macmillan.

De Wilde, Bart (2000) 'The Voice of Working Children in Belgium (1800–1914)', *Rethinking Childhood – Working Children's Challenge to the Social Sciences*, international conference, Institut de Recherche pour le Développement (IRD), Bondy, Paris, 15—17 November, Information Bulletin no. 4, pp. 12—19.

Dolorier, Marta et al. (1989) *Educación y sobrevivencia popular*, Lima: Instituto de Pedagogía Popular.

Domic Ruiz, Jorge (1999) *Niños trabajadores: la emergencia de nuevos actores sociales*, La Paz: Programa de Investigaciones Estratégicas en Bolivia.

Dube, Leela (1981) 'The Economic Roles of Children in India: Methodological Issues', in Rodgers and Standing (1981), pp. 179—213.

Dücker, Uwe von (1992) *Kinder der Straße. Überleben in Südamerika*, Frankfurt: Fischer.

Dulisch, Barbara, Manfred Liebel and Elisabeth Marie Mars (1997) *'Bis vor kurzem wusste ich nicht, dass ein O rund ist.' Nicaraguanische Kindheiten*, Münster: LIT.

Eaton, Martin and Carlos Pereira da Silva (1998) 'Portuguese Child Labour. Manufacturing for Change or Continuing Exploitation in the Textiles Industry?', *Childhood*, 5(3): 327—43.

Eberly, Mary B., Raymond Montemayor and Daniel J. Flannery (1993) 'Variation in Adolescent Helpfulness toward Parents in a Family Context', *Journal of Early Adolescence*, 13(3): 228—44.

Eckert, Andreas (1998) 'Slavery in Colonial Cameroon, 1880s to 1930s', in Susanne Miers and Martin Klein (eds), *Slavery and Colonial Rule in Africa*, London: Frank Cass, pp. 133—48.

— (1999) 'Familie, Sklaverei, Lohnarbeit. Kinder und Arbeit in Afrika im 19. und 20. Jahrhundert', *SOWI – Sozialwissenschaftliche Informationen*, 28(2): 131—6.

Eder, Ferdinand and Renate Kränzl-Nagl (1998) 'Schule: Arbeits- und Lebenswelt von Kindern', in Kränzl-Nagl et al. (1998), pp. 209—48.

Eichler, Gert (1973) 'Spiel und Sport in der Freizeiterziehung', in Heinz Walter (ed.), *Sozialisationsforschung*, Stuttgart: Klett, pp. 161—86.

— (1979) *Spiel und Arbeit. Zur Theorie der Freizeit*, Stuttgart-Bad Canstatt: Fromann-Holzboog.

— (1983) 'Spiel und Freizeit', in Grupe et al. (1983), pp. 232—42.

Eisenberg, N., P. A. Miller, R. Shell, S. McNally and C. Shea (1991) 'Prosocial Development in Adolescence: A Longitudinal Study', *Development Psychology*, 27: 849–57.

Elson, Diane (1982) 'The Differentiation of Children's Labour in the Capitalist Labour Market', *Development and Change*, 13: 479–97.

Elwert, Georg (1998) 'Kein Platz für junge Wilde. Unsere Gesellschaft missachtet die kreativen Fähigkeiten der Jugend. Sie hat kaum Freiräume. Alles regeln die Alten. Andere Kulturen geben ihrem Nachwuchs bessere Chancen, Neues und Riskantes auszuprobieren', *Die Zeit*, 14: 51.

— (2000) 'Jede Arbeit hat ihr Alter. Arbeit in einer afrikanischen Gesellschaft', in Kocka and Offe (2000), pp. 175–93.

Enda (1997) *Working Children and Youth of West Africa Get Organised*, Dakar: Environmental Developemnt Action TM Jeunesse Action (mimeo).

— (1999) *Les 12 droits du Mouvement Africain des Enfants et Jeunes Travailleurs (MAEJT). Fondement juridique, plate-forme revendicative ou instrument de développement?*, Dakar: Enda TM Jeunesse Action, JEUDA 104.

— (2000a) *Bénin, Côte d'Ivoire, Sénégal – Ecoute et soutien entre enfants travailleurs*, Dakar: Enda TM Jeunesse Action, JEUDA 105.

— (2000b) *Bénin, Côte d'Ivoire, Mali, Sénégal, Togo – Migrations, confiage et trafic d'enfants en Afrique de l'Ouest*, Dakar: Enda TM Jeunesse Action, JEUDA 106.

— (2001a) *Voice of African Children. Work, Strengh and Organisation of Working Children and Youth*, Dakar: Enda-Editions, Occasional Papers, no. 217.

— (2001b) *Les enfants et jeunes travailleurs décident. 5ème rencontre du Mouvement Africain des Enfant et Jeunes Travailleurs (MAEJT), Bamako – Mali: du 31 octobre au 14 novembre 2000*, Dakar: Enda TM Jeunesse Action, JEUDA 107.

Ennew, Judith (2000) *Street and Working Children. A Guide to Planning*, 2nd edn, revised and updated, London: Save the Children Fund.

Entwisle, Doris R., Karl L. Alexander and Linda Steffel Olson (2000) 'Early Work Histories of Urban Youth', *American Sociological Review*, 65 (April): 279–97.

Entwisle, Doris R., Karl L. Alexander, Linda Steffel Olson and Karen Ross (1999) 'Paid Work in Early Adolescence: Developmental Patterns', *Journal of Early Adolescence*, 19: 363–88.

Erikson, Erik (1978) *Kinderspiele und politische Phantasie*, Frankfurt: Suhrkamp.

Espinoza, Basilico, Benno Glauser et al. (1987) *In the Streets: Working Street Children in Asunción: A Book for Action*, Santa Fé de Bogotá: UNICEF.

Fajans, Jane (1997) *They Make Themselves. Work and Play among the Baining of Papua New Guinea*, Chicago, IL, and London: University of Chicago Press.

Fallon, Peter and Zafiris Tzannatos (1998) *Child Labor. Issues and Directions for the World Bank*, Washington, DC: World Bank, Human Development Network.

Falola, Toyin and Paul E. Lovejoy (eds) (1994) *Pawnship in Africa. Debt Bondage in Historical Perspective*, Boulder, CO: Westview Press.

Faltin, Günter and Jürgen Zimmer (1996) *Reichtum von unten. Die neuen Chancen der Kleinen*, Berlin: Aufbau.

— (2000) 'Erziehung zum Entrepreneurship', in Bernd Overwien (ed.), *Lernen und Handeln im globalen Kontext*, Frankfurt: IKO, pp. 142—51.

Farson, Richard (1974) *Birthrights*, New York and London: Macmillan and Collier Macmillan.

Fél, Édit and Támas Hofer (1974) *Geräte der Atányer Bauern*, Copenhagen: Kommission der Königlich-Dänischen Akademie der Wissenschaften zur Erforschung der Geschichte der Ackerbaugeräte und Feldstrukturen.

Finch, Michael D. and Jeylan T. Mortimer (1996) 'Future Directions for Research on Adolescents, Work and Family', in Mortimer and Finch (1996), pp. 221—35.

Firestone, Shulamith (1970) *The Dialectic of Sex. The Case for Feminist Revolution*, New York: William Morrow & Co.

Fishman, Stephen and Lucille McCarthy (1998) *John Dewey and the Challenge of Classroom*, New York: Teachers College Press.

Foucault, Michel (1966) *Les mots et les choses: une archéologie des sciences humaines*, Paris: Gallimard.

— (1976) *Histoire de la sexualité, I: la volonté de savoir*, Paris: Gallimard.

Frederiksen, Lisa (1999) 'Child and Youth Employment in Denmark: Comments on Children's Work from Their Own Perspective', *Childhood*, 6(1): 101—12.

Freeman, James M. (1979) *Untouchable. An Indian Life History*, London: Allen & Unwin.

Freinet, Célestin (1950) *Essai de psychologie sensible appliquée a l'éducation*, Gap: Editions Ophrys.

Freinet, Célestin and Elise Freinet (1976) *Befreiende Volksbildung. Frühe Texte* (ed. Renate Kock), Bad Heilbrunn: Klinkhardt.

Freud, Sigmund (1912—13/1991) *Totem und Tabu*, Frankfurt: S. Fischer.

— (1938/1993) *Abriss der Psychoanalyse. Das Unbehagen in der Kultur*, Frankfurt: S. Fischer.

— (1969) 'Vorlesung zur Einführung in die Psychoanalyse und Neue Folge', *Studienausgabe*, vol. 1, Frankfurt: S. Fischer.

Frone, Michael R. (1999) 'Developmental Consequences of Youth Employment', in Barling and Kelloway (1999), pp. 89—128.

Fyfe, Alec (1993) *Child Labour. A Guide to Project Design*, Geneva: ILO.

Gallardo, Carlos et al. (1992) *Retos y respuestas a los problemas educativos de la década*, Lima: Tarea.

Gatheru, R. Mugo (1967) *Kind zweier Welten*, Munich: Claudius.

Geluwe, H. van (1957) 'Les Bira et les peuplades limitrophes', *Ethnographic Survey of Africa*, vol. II, London: International African Institute.

Germann, P. (1933) 'Die Völkerstämme im Norden von Liberia', *Veröffentlichungen des Staatlichen Forschungsinstituts für Völkerkunde*, vol. 11, Leipzig.

Goodman, Mary Ellen (1970) *The Culture of Childhood. Child's-eye Views of Society and Culture*, New York: Columbia University – Teachers College Press.

Goodnow, Jacqueline J. (1988) 'Children's Household Work: 1st Nature and Functions', *Psychological Bulletin*, 103(1): 5—26.

Goody, E. (1970) 'Kinship Fostering in Gonja', in P. Mayer (ed.), *Socialization, the Approach from Social Anthropology*, London: Tavistock Publications.

Green, David Lee (1986) *Reading, Writing, and Working: A Study of High School Students in the Part-time Workplace*, PhD thesis, University of North Carolina at Chapel Hill.

— (1990) 'High School Student Employment in Social Context: Adolescents' Perceptions of the Role of Part-time Work', *Adolescence*, 15: 425–34.

Greenberger, Ellen and Laurence D. Steinberg (1980) 'Adolescents Who Work: Effects of Part-time Employment on Family Relations', *Journal of Youth and Adolescence*, 9(3): 189–202.

— (1986) *When Teenagers Work: The Psychological and Social Costs of Adolescent Employment*, New York: Basic Books.

Greenstein, Theodor N. (2000) 'Economic Dependence, Gender, and the Division of Labor at Home: A Replication and Extension', *Journal of Marriage and the Family*, 62: 322–35.

Grefe, Christiane (1997) *Ende der Spielzeit. Wie wir unsere Kinder verplanen*, Reinbek-Hamburg: Rowohlt.

Griesbach Guizar, Margarita and Gerardo Sauri Suárez (1993) *Vivir en la calle. La situación de los niños y niñas callejeros en el Distrito Federal*, Mexico: ednica.

— (1997) *Con la calle en las venas. La comunidad como alternativa para los niños callejeros y en riesgo de serlo*, Mexico: ednica and Foro de Apoyo Mutuo.

Grillo, Gemma and Giangi Schibotto (1992) '... y trabajan en todas las edades ...' *Testimonios de niños trabajadores de América Latina*, Lima: MANTHOC.

Grima, José Manuel and Alicia Le Fur (1999) *¿Chicos de la calle o trabajo chico? Ensayo sobre la función paterna*, Buenos Aires: Lumen/Humanitas.

Gröbli, Roland (2001) *Überleben im Großstadtdschungel. Annäherungen an die urbane Überlebenskultur*, Frankfurt: IKO.

Grohs, Elisabeth (1992) 'Frühkindliche Sozialisation in traditionellen Gesellschaften', in K. Müller and A. K. Treml (eds), *Ethnopädagogik. Sozialisation und Erziehung in traditionellen Gesellschaften*, Berlin: Reimer, pp. 31–60.

Grootaert, Christian and Harry Anthony Patrinos (eds) (1999) *The Policy Analysis of Child Labour: A Comparative Study*, Basingstoke and London: Macmillan Press.

Grupe, Ommo, Hartmut Gabler and Ulrich Göhner (eds) (1983) *Spiel – Spiele – Spielen*, Schorndorf: Hofmann.

Grupo de trabajo infantil (1996) 'El trabajo infantil en España', *Movimiento Junior en marcha*, no. 116 (May/June), Separata no. 38: i–viii.

Gupta, Manju and Klaus Voll (1999) 'Child Labour in India. An Examplary Case Study', in K. Voll (ed.), *Against Child Labour. Indian and International Dimensions and Strategies*, New Delhi: Mosaic Books, Third Millennium Transparency, pp. 85–144.

Hadar, Ivan A. (1998) *Bildung in Indonesien: Krise und Kontinuität. Das Beispiel Pesantren*, Frankfurt: IKO.

Hall, G. Stanley (1905/1969) *Adolescence*, vol. I, New York: Arno Press and The New York Times.

Hansen, David M., Jeylan T. Mortimer and Helga Krüger (2001) 'Adolescent Part-time Employment in the United States and Germany: Diverse Outcomes, Contexts and Pathways', in Mizen et al. (2001b), pp. 121–38.

Hardman, Charlotte (1973) 'Can There be an Anthropology of Children?', *Journal of the Anthropological Society of Oxford*, 4(2): 85–99.

Harms, Robert (1981) *River of Wealth, River of Sorrow: The Central Zaire Basin in the Era of the Slave and Ivory Trade, 1500–1891*, New Haven, CT: Yale University Press.

Haunert, Friedrich and Reinhard Lang (1994) *Arbeit und Integration. Zur Bedeutung von Arbeit in der Jugendsozialarbeit am Beispiel von Projekten freier Träger*, Frankfurt: Peter Lang.

Hedges, J. N. and J. K. Barnett (1972) 'Working Women and the Division of Household Tasks', *Monthly Labor Review*, 95: 9–14.

Hemmer, Hans-Rimbert et al. (1997) 'Child Labour and International Trade: An Economic Perspective', *Entwicklungsökonomische Diskussionsbeiträge*, 22, Giessen: Justus-Liebig-Universität.

Hengst, Heinz (1981) 'Tendenzen zur Liquidierung von Kindheit', in H. Hengst et al., *Kindheit als Fiktion*, Frankfurt: Suhrkamp, pp. 11–72.

— (1996) 'Kinder an die Macht. Der Rückzug des Marktes aus dem Kindheitsprojekt der Moderne', in Zeiher et al. (1996), pp. 117–34.

— (1998) 'Kinderarbeit revisited', in Liebel et al. (1998), pp. 233–49.

— (2000) 'Die Arbeit der Kinder und der Umbau der Arbeitsgesellschaft', in Hengst and Zeiher (2000), pp. 71–97.

Hengst, Heinz and Helga Zeiher (eds) (2000) *Die Arbeit der Kinder. Kindheitskonzept und Arbeitsteilung zwischen den Generationen*, Weinheim and Munich: Juventa.

Henriksson, Benny (1985) 'Materiell übersättigt – sozial ausgehungert', in H. Hengst (ed.), *Kindheit in Europa. Zwischen Spielplatz und Computer*, Frankfurt: Suhrkamp, pp. 138–58.

Hentig, Hartmut von (1993) *Die Schule neu denken*, Munich and Vienna: Hanser.

Hetzer, Hildegard (1931) 'Kind und Schaffen', *Quellen und Studien zur Jugendkunde*, 7, Jena: Fischer.

— (1957) *Das Spiel in der Schule*, Frankfurt, Berlin, Hamburg and Munich: Schöningh.

Hibbett, A. and M. Bateson (1995) 'Young People at Work', *Employment Gazette*, April: 169–77.

Hobbs, Sandy and Jim McKechnie (1997) *Child Employment in Britain. A Social and Psychological Analysis*, Edinburgh: Stationery Office Ltd.

Hobbs, Sandy, Sandra Lindsay and Jim McKechnie (1996) 'The Extent of Child Employment in Britain', *British Journal of Education and Work*, 9(1): 5–18.

Holt, John (1974) *Escape from Childhood*, New York: Dutton.

Honig, Michael-Sebastian (1999) *Entwurf einer Theorie der Kindheit*, Frankfurt: Suhrkamp.

Honig, Michael-Sebastian and Ilona Ostner (2001) 'Das Ende der fordistischen Kindheit', in Klocke and Hurrelmann (2001), pp. 293–310.

Honig, Michael-Sebastian, Andreas Lange and Hans Rudolf Leu (1999) (eds) *Aus der Perspektive von Kindern? Zur Methodologie der Kindheitsforschung*, Weinheim and Munich: Juventa.

Hoppe, Ruth (1969) 'Dokumente zur Geschichte der Lage des arbeitenden Kindes in Deutschland von 1700 bis zur Gegenwart', in Jürgen Kuczysnki, *Die Geschichte der Lage der Arbeiter unter dem Kapitalismus*, vol. 20, Berlin: Akademie-Verlag.

Horkheimer, Max and Theodor W. Adorno (1944/1987): *Dialektik der Aufklärung. Philosophische Fragmente*, Frankfurt: S. Fischer.

Hotz, V. Joseph, Lixin Xu, Marta Tienda and Avner Ahituv (1999) *Are There Returns to the Wages of Young Men from Working While at School?*, Cambridge, MA: National Bureau of Economic Research, Working Paper no. 7289.

Huizinga, Johan (1938/1949) *Homo Ludens: A Study of the Play Element in Culture*, London: Routledge and Kegan Paul.

Ifejant (ed.) (1996) *Niños trabajadores. Protagonismo y actoría social*, Lima: Instituto de Formación para Educadores de Jóvenes, Adolescentes y Niños Trabajadores de América Latina y El Caribe 'Mons. German Schmitz'.

— (ed.) (1997) *Jóvenes y niños trabajadores: sujetos sociales. Ser protagonistas*, Lima: Instituto de Formación para Educadores de Jóvenes, Adolescentes y Niños Trabajadores de América Latina y El Caribe 'Mons. German Schmitz'.

— (ed.) (1998) *Niños trabajadores. Protagonismo y actoría social*, Lima: Instituto de Formación para Educadores de Jóvenes, Adolescentes y Niños Trabajadores de América Latina y El Caribe 'Mons. German Schmitz'.

Iliffe, John (1987) *The African Poor. A History*, Cambridge: Cambridge University Press.

ILO (1993) *World of Work*, Geneva: International Labour Office.

— (1996) *Child Labour. Targeting the Intolerable*, Geneva: International Labour Office.

— (2000) *Action against Child Labour*, ed. Nelien Haspels and Michele Jankanish, Geneva: International Labour Office.

— (2002) *A Future without Child Labour. Global Report under the Follow-up to the ILO Declaration on Fundamental Principles and Rights at Work*, Geneva: International Labour Office.

Ingenhorst, Heinz (1998) 'Kinderarbeit in Deutschland. Motive, Arbeitsbedingungen und Folgen', *DISKURS*, ed. Deutsches Jugendinstitut, February: 56–63.

— (2001) 'Child Labour in the Federal Republic of Germany', in Mizen et al. (2001b), pp. 139–48.

Ingenhorst, Heinz and Hans Wienhold (1992) 'Wie und wofür arbeiten Kinder? Kinder und Jugendliche als Lohnarbeiter', in Christian Büttner, Donata Elschenbroisch and Aurel Ende (eds), *Kinderkulturen. Neue Freizeit und alte Muster*, Weinheim and Basle: Beltz, pp. 80–104.

Institut für Produktives Lernen in Europa (ed.) (1999) *Produktives Lernen in der Lernwerkstatt. Pilotprojekte aus Pécs, St Petersburg und Berlin stellen ihre Arbeitvor*, Berlin, Mirow: Schibri Verlag.

Invernizzi, Antonella (2001) 'The Work of Children is not Only Work', in Liebel et al. (2001), pp. 31–52.

IWGCL (1997) *Have We Asked the Children?*, discussion paper, Amsterdam: International Working Group on Child Labour.

— (1998) *Working Children: Reconsidering the Debates. Report of the International Working Group on Child Labour*, Amsterdam: Defence for Children International.

James, Allison (1984) 'Children's Experience of Work', *ESRC Newsletter*, 51.

James, Allison and Alan Prout (eds) (1990) *Constructing and Reconstructing Childhood. Contemporary Issues in the Sociological Study of Childhood*, London and Bristol: Falmer Press (2nd edn with postscripts: 1997).

James, Allison, Chris Jenks and Alan Prout (1998) *Theorizing Childhood*, New York: Teachers College Press, Columbia University.

Janira, S. (1956) *Kleiner großer schwarzer Mann. Lebenserinnerungen eines Buschnegers, aufgenommen von L. Kohl-Larsen*, Kassel.

Jessor, Richard (ed.) (1998) *New Perspectives on Adolescent Risk Behavior*, Cambridge and New York: Cambridge University Press.

Jodelet, Denise (1989) *Les réprésentations sociales*, Paris: Presse Université de France.

Jostock, Simone (1999) *Kindheit in der Moderne und Postmoderne*, Opladen: Leske and Budrich.

Jugendwerk der Deutschen Shell (ed.) (1997) *Jugend '97. Zukunftsperspektiven, gesellschaftliches Engagement, politische Orientierungen*, Opladen: Leske and Budrich.

Kabeer, Naila, Geetha B. Nambissan and Ranya Subrahmanian (eds) (2002) *Child Labour and the Right to Education in South Asia*, New Delhi: Thousand Oaks; London: Sage.

Kapuscinski, Ryszard (2001) *Afrikanisches Fieber. Erfahrungen aus vierzig Jahren*, Munich: Piper.

Karcher, Wolfgang, Bernd Overwien, Jürgen Krause and Madhu Singh (eds) (1993) *Zwischen Ökonomie und sozialer Arbeit. Lernen im informellen Sektor in der 'Dritten Welt'*, Frankfurt: IKO.

Kaufmann, Franz Xaver (1980) 'Kinder als Außenseiter der Gesellschaft', *Merkur*, 34(387): 761–71.

Kavapalu, H. (1991) *Becoming Tongan. An Ethnography of Childhood in the Kingdom of Tonga*, doctoral thesis, ANU Canberra, Australia.

Keithly, Diane C. and Forrest A. Deseran (1995) 'Households, Local Labor Markets, and Youth Labor Force Participation', *Youth & Society*, 26(4): 463–92.

Kelloway, E. Kevien and Steve Harvey (1999) 'Learning to Work: The Development of Work Beliefs', in Barling and Kelloway (1999), pp. 37–57.

Kett, Joseph E. (1977) *Rites of Passage*, New York: Basic Books.

Kinderarbeit in Deutschland (2000) 'Bericht der Bundesregierung', in Presse- und Informationsamt der Bundesregierung (ed.), *Sozialpolitische Umschau*, no. 186, Berlin, pp. 3–24.

Kirchhöfer, Dieter (1998) 'Kinderarbeit – ein notwendiger Entwicklungsraum der Heranwachsenden. Ein Plädoyer für den Anspruch und das Recht der Kinder auf Arbeit', *DISKURS*, ed. Deutsches Jugendinstitut (February): 64–71.

— (1999) 'Kinder im Leistungssport – eine neue Form der Kinderarbeit?', in: W. Kleine and N. Schulz (eds), *Modernisierte Kindheit – sportliche Kindheit?*, St Augustin: Academia Verlag, pp. 134–47.

— (2000) 'Die Kinder stehen vor der Tür der geschlossenen Arbeitsgesellschaft der Erwachsenen', in M. Dust, C. Sturm and E. Weiss (eds), *Pädagogik wider das Vergessen. Festschrift für Wolfgang Keim*, Kiel and Cologne: Peter Götzelmann, pp. 209–24.

Klein, Christoph and Ursula Meta Sell (2000) *Unternehmen lernen. Entrepreneurship mit Kindern und Jugendlichen*, Science of Education thesis, Technical University of Berlin (mimeo).

Klein, Naomi (2000) *No Logo*, London: Flamingo.

Klocke, Andreas and Klaus Hurrelmann (eds) (2001) *Kinder und Jugendliche in Armut. Umfang, Auswirkungen und Konsequenzen*, Wiesbaden: Westdeutscher Verlag.

Klute, Georg (1996) 'Kinderarbeit bei Nomaden', in Beck and Spittler (1996), pp. 209–23.

Kock, Renate (1976) 'Befreiende Volksbildung: Célestin Freinet. Eine Einführung', in Freinet and Freinet (1976), pp. 9–27.

Kocka, Jürgen and Claus Offe (eds) (2000) *Geschichte und Zukunft der Arbeit*, Frankfurt and New York: Campus.

Köpping, Elisabeth (1993) 'Vom Blasrohr zum Aktenkoffer. Sozialgeschichte der Kindheit in einem Dorf auf Borneo', in Loo and Reinhart (1993), pp. 262–88.

Kränzl-Nagl, Renate, Ursula Riepl and Helmut Wintersberger (eds) (1998) *Kindheit in Gesellschaft und Politik. Eine multidisziplinäre Analyse am Beispiel Österreichs*, Frankfurt and New York: Campus.

Krige, Eileen Jensen (1978, 1st ed. 1943) *The Realm of a Rain-queen: A Study of the Pattern of Lovedu Society*, New York: AMS Press.

Krishna, Sumi (1996) *Restoring Childhood. Learning, Labour and Gender in South Asia*, Delhi: Konark Publishers.

Kruse, Douglas L. and Douglas Mahony (2000) 'Illegal Child Labor in the United States: Prevalence and Characteristics', *Industrial and Labor Relations Review*, 54(1): 17–40.

Kubik, Gerhard (1995) 'Kindheit in außereuropäischen Kulturen: Forschungsprobleme, -ergebnisse und -methoden', in Renner (1995), pp. 148–66.

Kuczynski, Jürgen (1968) 'Studien zur Geschichte der Lage des arbeitenden Kindes in Deutschland von 1700 bis zur Gegenwart', in Jürgen Kuczynski, *Die Geschichte der Lage der Arbeiter unter dem Kapitalismus*, vol. 19, Berlin: Akademie-Verlag.

Kummels, Ingrid (1993) 'Autonomie im kleinen. Einblicke in den Alltag von Rarámumi-Kindern', in Loo and Reinhart (1993), pp. 238–61.

Laines, Lorenza and Fundación Rigoberta Menchú (1999) 'El trabajo infantil desde la mirada indígena', *Grupo de Seguimiento al Tema del Trabajo Infantil*, bulletin no. 4, Guatemala.

Lame Deer, Archie Fire and Richard Erdoes (1992) *Medizinmann der Sioux. Tahca Ushtes Sohn erzählt von seinem Leben und seinem Volk*, Munich: List.

Landrigan, Philip J. (1993) 'Child Labor: A Re-emergent Threat', *American Journal of Industrial Medicine*, 24: 267–8.

Landrigan, Philip J., Susan H. Pollack, Renate Belville and James G. Godbold (1992) 'Child Labor in the United States: Historical Background and Current Crisis', *Mount Sinai Journal of Medicine*, 59(6): 498–503.

— (1995) 'Child Labor', *Pedriatic Annals*, 24(12): 657–62.

Lang-Wojtasik, Gregor (1999) 'Life-long Learning for All – Gandhis Nai Talim', *ZEP – Zeitschrift für internationale Bildungsforschung und Entwicklungspädagogik*, 22(1): 7–11.

Lantos, Tom (1992) 'The Silence of the Kids: Children at Risk in the Workplace', *Labor Law Journal*, 43(2): 67–70.

Lavalette, Michael (1994) *Child Employment in the Capitalist Labour Market*, Aldershot: Avebury.

— (1999a) 'The "New Sociology of Childhood" and Child Labour: Childhood, Children's Rights and "Children's Voice"', in Lavalette (1999b), pp. 15–43.

— (ed.) (1999b) *A Thing of the Past? Child Labour in Britain in the Nineteenth and Twentieth Centuries*, Liverpool: Liverpool University Press.

— (2000) 'Child Employment in a Capitalist Labour Market: The British Case', in Schlemmer (2000), pp. 214–30.

Lavalette, Michael and Steve Cunningham (2004) 'Globalisation and Child Labour: Protection, Liberation or Anti-capitalism?', in Ronaldo Munck (ed.), *Labour and Globalisation: Results and Prospects*, Liverpool: Liverpool University Press, pp 181–205.

Lavalette, Michael, Sandy Hobbs, Sandra Lindsay and Jim McKechnie (1995) 'Child Employment in Britain', *British Journal of Education and Work*, 8(3): 1–15.

Lawrence, Frances C. and Patricia H. Wozniak (1987) 'Rural Children's Time in Household Activities', *Psychological Reports*, 61: 927–37.

Lee, Yun-Suk, Barbara Schneider and Linda J. Wait (2000) 'Determinants and Social and Educational Consequences of Children's Housework', Working Paper no. 19, Alfred P. Sloan Center on Parents, Children, and Work, Chicago: University of Chicago Press.

Leite García, Regina (1997) 'Una escuela donde aprenden a aprender', *envío*, 190, Managua: Universidad Centroamericana (UCA).

Lenkendorf, Carlos (2000) *Leben ohne Objekte. Sprache und Weltbild der Tojolabales, ein Mayavolk in Chiapas*, Frankfurt: IKO.

Lenzen, Dieter (1985) *Mythologie der Kindheit. Die Verewigung des Kindlichen in der Erwachsenenkultur. Versteckte Bilder und vergessene Geschichten*, Reinbek-Hamburg: Rowohlt.

Leonard, Madeleine (1997) 'School Pupils and Employment in West Belfast', in McCloskey (1997), pp. 64–83.

— (1998) 'Children's Contribution to Household Income: A Case Study from Northern Ireland', in Pettitt (1998), pp. 80–106.

— (1999) *Play Fair with Working Children. A Report on Working Children in Belfast*, Belfast: Save the Children Fund.

— (2002) 'Working on Your Doorstep. Child Newspaper Deliverers in Belfast', *Childhood*, 9(2): 190−204.

Levison, Deborah (2000) 'Children as Economic Agents', *Feminist Studies*, 6(1): 125−34.

Lewis, Oscar (1963) *Pedro Martinez. Selbstporträt eines Mexikaners*, Düsseldorf and Vienna: Econ.

Liebel, Manfred (1994) *Protagonismo infantil. Movimientos de niños trabajadores en América Latina*, Managua: editorial nueva nicaragua.

— (1996) *Somos NATRAS. Testimonios de niños trabajadores de Nicaragua*, Managua: editorial nueva nicaragua.

— (1998) 'Arbeitende Kinder in Deutschland', in Liebel et al. (1998), pp. 147−54.

— (2000) *La otra infancia. Niñez trabajadora y acción social*, Lima: Editorial Ifejant.

— (2001a) 'The Dignity of the Working Child. What Children in Nicaragua, El Salvador and Guatemala Think about Their Work', in Liebel et al. (2001), pp. 53−66.

— (2001b) 'Child Labour, Child Work and the International Labour Organisation (ILO). What is Good for Working Children?', in Liebel et al. (2001), pp. 87−101.

— (2001c) 'Yes to Work – No to Exploitation! A Plea for a Subject-orientated Approach to Children's Work', in Liebel et al. (2001), pp. 133−54.

— (2001d) 'Strengthen Children's Rights! Approaches to Participation by Working Children', in Liebel et al. (2001), pp. 171−9.

— (2001e) '12 Rights, and Making Their Own Way. The Working Youth of Africa Organise Themselves', in Liebel et al. (2001), pp. 197−217.

— (2001f) 'A Right to Work for Children? Experiences from the "Third World" for the "First World"', in Liebel et al. (2001), pp. 221−31.

— (2001g) 'Working Children's Protagonism, Children's Rights and the Outline of a Different Childhood. A Comparative Reflection on the Discourses in Latin America and the "First World"', in Liebel et al. (2001), pp. 321−48.

Liebel, Manfred, Bernd Overwien and Albert Recknagel (eds) (1998) *Arbeitende Kinder stärken. Plädoyers für einen subjektorientierten Umgang mit Kinderarbeit*, Frankfurt: IKO.

— (eds) (1999) *Was Kinder könn(t)en. Handlungsperspektiven von und mit arbeitenden Kindern*, Frankfurt: IKO.

— (eds) (2001) *Working Children's Protagonism. Social Movements and Empowerment in Latin America, Africa and India*, Frankfurt and London: IKO.

Lieten, Kristoffel and Ben White (eds) (2001) *Child Labour. Policy Options*, Amsterdam: aksant.

Lipski, Jens (2001) 'Lernen außerhalb der Schule – Modell für eine künftige Lernkultur?', in Deutsches Jugendinstitut (ed.), *Das Forschungsjahr 2000*, Munich: Deutsches Jugendinstitut, pp. 99−106.

Lolichen, P. J. and Kavita Ratna (1997) *Harming Children by Ignoring Their Voices: Experiences from Bangladesh, India and Morocco. Draft Dossier*, Bangalore: The Concerned for Working Children.

Loo, Marie-José van de and Margarete Reinhart (eds) (1993) *Kinder. Ethnologische Forschungen in fünf Kontinenten*, Munich: Trickster.

Loughlin, Catherine (1999) 'The Nature of Youth Employment', in Barling and Kelloway (1999), pp. 17–36.

Lovejoy, Paul E. and Jan S. Hogendorn (1993) *Slow Death for Slavery. The Course of Abolition in Northern Nigeria, 1897–1936*, Cambridge: Cambridge University Press.

Löwenthal, Leo (1989) 'Das kleine Ich und das große Ich. Einspruch gegen die Postmoderne. Rede zur Verleihung des Theodor W. Adorno-Preises 1989 in Frankfurt', *Frankfurter Rundschau*, 2 October: 17.

Lucchini, Riccardo (1998) *Sociología de la supervivencia. El niño y la calle*, Mexico: Université de Fribourg, Suiza and Universidad Nacional Autónoma de México.

Lückert, Heinz-Rolf (1980) 'Kinder in veränderter Welt. Eine Revision unserer Auffassung vom Kind', in *Meyers Enzyklopädisches Lexikon*, vol. 13, Mannheim, Vienna, Zurich: Bibliographisches Institut, pp. 677–81.

Lüdtke, Alf (1999) 'Kinderarbeit – Arbeit und Spiel?', *SOWI – Sozialwissenschaftliche Informationen*, 28(2): 99–104.

McCloskey, Stephen (ed.) (1997) *No Time to Play. Local and Global Perspectives on Child Employment*, Belfast: One World Centre.

McHale, Susan M., W. Todd Bartko, Ann C. Crouter and Maureen Perry-Jenkins (1990) 'Children's Housework and Psychosocial Functioning: The Mediating Effects of Parents' Sex-Role Behaviors and Attitudes', *Child Development*, 61: 1,413–26.

McKechnie, Jim (1999) 'A Peculiarly British Phenomenon? Child Labour in the USA', in Lavalette (1999b), pp. 193–215.

McKechnie, Jim and Sandy Hobbs (1999) 'Child Labour: The View from the North', *Childhood*, 6(1): 89–100.

— (2001) 'Work and Education: Are They Compatible for Children and Adolescents?', in Mizen et al. (2001b), pp. 9–23.

— (2002) 'Work by the Young. The Economic Activity of School-aged Children', in Marta Tienda and William Julius Wilson (eds), *Youth in Cities. A Crossnational Perspective*, Cambridge: Cambridge University Press, pp. 217–45.

McKechnie, Jim, Sandy Hobbs and Sandra Lindsay (1997) 'Bringing Child Labour Centre Stage', in McCloskey (1997), pp. 47–63.

McKechnie, Jim, Sandra Lindsay, Sandy Hobbs and Michael Lavalette (1996) 'Adolescents' Perceptions of the Role of Part-time Work', *Adolescence*, 31(121): 193–204.

MacLennan, E., J. Fitz and J. Sullivan (1985) *Working Children*, Low Pay Unit, Report no. 2, London.

McNeal, James U. (1999) *The Kids Market*, Ithaca, NY: Paramount.

Machaca Mendieta, Magdalena (2000) 'Anderes Konzept von Kindheit. Erziehung, Schule und die Vielfalt in Quispillaccta/Ayacucho', *ila – Zeitschrift der Informationsstelle Lateinamerika*, 235: 11–13.

Madörin, Kurt (1999) 'Positionspapier: Warum eine Waisenorganisation?', Basle: terre des hommes (not published).

Manning, Wendy D. (1990) 'Parenting Employed Teenagers', *Youth & Society*, 22(2): 184–200.

Mansurov, Valery (2001) 'Child Labour in Russia', in Mizen et al. (2001b), pp. 149–66.

MANTHOC (1995) *Propuesta curricular diversificable desde los NATs*, Lima: Movimiento de Adolescentes y Niños Trabajadores Hijos de Obreros Cristianos (mimeo).

— (ed.) (2000a) *Niños, niñas y adolescentes trabajadores: derechos, ciudadanía y protagonismo*, Lima: Movimiento de Adolescentes y Niños Trabajadores Hijos de Obreros Cristianos.

— (2000b) '24 años en la promoción de los niños y adolescentes trabajadores NATs', *Niños Niñas, Autoeducación*, 6, Lima (supplement): 6.

— (2002) *Propuesta pedagógica desde los niños, niñas y adolescentes trabajadores. Educación, trabajo y escuela productiva*, Lima: MANTHOC (mimeo).

Marcus, Rachel (1998) 'Child Labour and Socially Responsible Business', *Small Enterprise Development*, 9(3): 4–13.

Markel, Karen S. and Michael R. Frone (1998) 'Job Characteristics, Work–School Conflict, and School Outcomes among Adolescents: Testing a Structural Model', *Journal of Applied Psychology*, 83(2): 277–87.

Marsh, Herbert W. (1991) 'Employment during High School: Character Building or Subversion of Academic Goals?', *Sociology of Education*, 64: 172–89.

Marx, Karl (1953) *Grundrisse der Kritik der politischen Ökonomie*, Berlin: Dietz.

— (1968) *Ökonomisch-philosophische Manuskripte* (orig. pub. 1844), in Marx and Engels, *Werke, Ergänzungsband. Erster Teil*, Berlin: Dietz, pp. 465–588.

— (1969) 'Kritik des Gothaer Programms' (orig. pub. 1875), in Marx and Engels, *Werke*, vol. 19, Berlin: Dietz, pp. 11–32.

— (1979) *Das Kapital 1*, in Marx and Engels, *Werke*, vol. 23, Berlin: Dietz.

Marx, Karl and Friedrich Engels (1962) 'Die deutsche Ideologie', in Marx and Engels, *Werke*, vol. 3, Berlin: Dietz.

Masson, Rudolfo (1992) 'El programa de educación rural andina', in Gallardo et al. (1992), pp. 164–8.

Mayall, Berry (2002) *Towards a Sociology for Childhood. Thinking from Children's Life*, Buckingham: Open University Press.

Mead, Margaret (1928/1963) *Coming of Age in Samoa*, New York: Mentor Books.

— (1950) *Male and Female: A Study of the Sexes in a Changing World*, London: Gollancz.

Meiser, Ute (1995) *Sie leben mit den Ahnen. Krankheit, Adoption und Tabukonflikt in der polynesisch-tonganischen Kultur*, Frankfurt and Vienna: Brandes & Apsel.

— (1997) 'Spiel, Kreativität und Gruppe: Die Institution der "horizontalen" Gruppen in der sozialen und emotionalen Entwicklung tonganischer Kinder', in Renner et al. (1997), pp. 207–24.

Melaku, Daniel (2000) *Die Situation der arbeitenden Kinder in Äthiopien. Ihre Aktivitäten und Probleme unter besonderer Berücksichtigung der Partizipation in der Gesellschaft*, Science of Education thesis, Technical University of Berlin (mimeo).

Mellaissoux, Claude (2000) 'Looking Ahead: A General Conclusion', in Schlemmer (2000), pp. 315–29.

Mendelievich, Elías (ed.) (1979) *Children at Work*, Geneva: ILO.

Mendoza, I. (1993) *Trabajo infantil rural en el Perú: la agricultura de esparragos en la Costa Norte (en Valle de Viru)*, Geneva: INTERDEP/CL/1993/2.

Mendoza Gálvez, Carmen (1991) *La escuela productiva. Una alternativa productiva para la región Grau*, Piura and Lima: Instituto de Pedagogía Popular.

Menninger, W. C. (1964) 'The Meaning of Work in Western Society', in Henry Borow (ed.), *Man in a World at Work*, Boston, MA: Houghton Mifflin, pp. xiii–xvii.

Meueler, Erhard (1993) *Die Türen des Käfigs. Wege zum Subjekt in der Erwachsenenbildung*, Stuttgart: Klett-Cotta.

Meyer-Bendrat, Klaus-Peter (1987) *Die Warenförmigkeit kindlicher Spielarbeit. Die Verformung des Spiels im Lichte industrieller Erkenntnisinteressen*, Frankfurt, Berne, New York, Paris: Peter Lang.

Meyers Enzyklopädisches Lexikon, vol. 13, Mannheim, Vienna and Zurich: Bibliographisches Institut.

Middleton, Sue and Julia Loumidis (2001) 'Young People, Poverty and Part-time Work', in Mizen et al. (2001b), pp. 24–36.

Middleton, Sue, Jules Shropshire and Nicola Croden (1998) 'Earning Your Keep? Children's Work and Contributions to Family Budgets', in Pettitt (1998), pp. 41–58.

Mihalic, Sharon Wofford and Delbert Elliott (1997) 'Short- and Long-term Consequences of Adolescent Work', *Youth & Society*, 28(4): 464–98.

Miljesteig, Per (2000) 'Establishing Partnerships with Working Children and Youth. Implications for Research', in Lieten and White (2001), pp. 117–29.

Mizen, Phillip (1992) 'Learning the Hard Way: The Extent and Significance of Child Working in Britain', *British Journal of Education and Work*, 5: 5–17.

Mizen, Phillip, Angela Bolton and Christopher Pole (1998) 'It's Just a Job Really: The Motivations for Paid Work among School Age Children', *Social Policy in Time and Place*, Social Policy Association Annual Conference, University of Humberside and Lincoln, July.

— (1999) 'School Age Workers: The Paid Employment of Children in Britain', *Work, Employment & Society*, 13(3): 423–38.

Mizen, Philip, Christopher Pole and Angela Bolton (2001a) 'Why be a School Age Worker?', in Mizen et al. (2001b), pp. 37–54.

— (eds) (2001b) *Hidden Hands. International Perspectives on Children's Work and Labour*, London and New York: Routledge Falmer.

Molina Barrios, Ramiro and Rafael Rojas Lizarazu (1995) *La niñez campesina. Uso del tiempo y vida cotidiana*, La Paz: UNICEF.

Möller, Carola et al. (1997) *Wirtschaften für das 'gemeine Eigene'. Handbuch zum gemeinwesenorientierten Wirtschaften*, Berlin: trafo.

Moore, Henrietta L. and Megan Vaughan (1994) *Cutting Down Trees. Gender, Nutrition, and Agricultural Change in the Northern Provence of Zambia 1890–1990*, London: James Currey.

Moore, Sally Falk (1986) *Social Facts and Fabrications. 'Customary' law on Kiliman-jaro 1880–1980*, New York: Cambridge University Press.

Morrow, Virginia (1994) 'Responsible Children? Aspects of Children's Work and Employment outside School in Contemporary UK', in Berry Mayall (ed.), *Children's Childhoods Observed and Experienced*, London: Falmer Press, pp. 128–43.

— (1996) 'Rethinking Childhood Dependency: Children's Contributions to the Domestic Economy', *Sociological Review*, 44: 58–77.

— (2000) 'Warum englische Kinder neben der Schule arbeiten', in Hengst and Zeiher (2000), pp. 143–58.

Mortimer, Jeylan T. and Michael D. Finch (eds) (1996) *Adolescents, Work, and Family. An Intergenerational Developmental Analysis*, Thousand Oaks, London and New Delhi: Sage.

Mortimer, Jeylan T. and Monica Kirkpatrick Johnson (1998a) 'Adolescents' Part-time Work and Educational Achievement', in Borman and Schneider (1998), pp. 183–206.

— (1998b) 'New Perspectives on Adolescent Work and the Transition to Adult-hood', in Jessor (1998), pp. 425–96.

Moskowitz, Seymour (2000) 'Child Labor in America: Who's Protecting Our Kids?', *Labor Law Journal*, 51(4): 202–11.

Mull, L. D. (1993) 'Broken Covenant: The Future of Migrant Farmworker Chil-dren and Families in the United States', in *Children who Work – Challenges for the 21st Century*, Washington, DC: Child Labor Coalition of the National Consumers League (mimeo).

Myers, William and Jo Boyden (1998) *Child Labour – Promoting the Best Interests of Working Children*, London: ISCA.

Myers, William E. (1999) 'Considering Child Labour: Changing Terms, Issues and Actors at the International Level', *Childhood*, 6(1): 13–26.

— (2001a) 'Valuing Diverse Approaches to Child Labour', in Lieten and White (2001), pp. 27–48.

— (2001b) 'Can Children's Education and Work be Reconciled?', *International Journal of Educational Policy, Research and Practice*, 2(3): 307–30.

Nasaw, David (1985) *Children of the City: At Work and at Play*, Garden City, NY: Anchor Press/Doubleday.

National Child Labor Committee (1994) *Child Labor in the 90s: How Far Have We Come?*, New York: National Child Labor Committee.

Negt, Oskar (1997) *Kindheit und Schule in einer Welt der Umbrüche*, Göttingen: Steidl.

Nieuwenhuys, Olga (1994) *Children's Lifeworlds. Gender, Welfare and Labour in the Developing World*, London and New York: Routledge.

— (1996) 'The Paradox of Child Labor and Anthropology', *Annual Review of Anthropology*, 25: 237–51.

— (2000a) 'The Household Economy and the Commercial Exploitation of Children's Work: The Case of Kerala', in Schlemmer (2000), pp. 278–91.

— (2000b) '"The Worst Forms of Child Labour" and the Worst for Working Children', *Rethinking Childhood – Working Children's Challenge to the*

Social Sciences, international conference, Institut de Recherche pour le Développement (IRD), Bondy-Paris, 15–17 November, Information Bulletin no. 3, pp. 41–52 (mimeo).

Nunes, Angela (1999) *A sociedade das crianças A'uwê-Xavante. Por uma antropologia da criança*, Lisbon: Instituto de Inovacão Educacional and Ministerio da Educaçao.

O'Donnell, Catherine and Leroy White (1998) *Invisible Hands: Child Employment in North Tyneside*, London: Low Pay Unit.

Ole Saitoti, Tepilit and Carol Beckwith (1981) *Die Massai*, Cologne: DuMont.

Ortiz Rescaniere, Alejandro (1994) *Un estudio sobre los grupos autónomos de niños – a partir de un trabajo de campo en Champaccocha, Andahuaylas*, Proyecto de Inovaciones Pedagógicas No Formales, Documento de Trabajo no. 3, Lima: Fundación Bernard Van Leer and Ministerio de Educación.

Overwien, Bernd (1997) 'Employment-oriented Non-formal Training for Young People in the Informal Sector in Latin America', *Education*, 55/56: 146–57.

— (2001) 'Informal Learning, Social Movements and Acquisition of Competences for Self-determined Working and Living', in Liebel et al. (2001), pp. 247–67.

Oxfam (1999) *Circus in Ethiopia. Report Paper*, Addis Ababa (mimeo).

Paul, Sigrid (1997) 'Die Sozialisationsfunktion von Spielen in traditionellen afrikanischen Gesellschaften', in Renner et al. (1997), pp. 194–206.

PEETI (Plan on the Elimination of Child Labour Exploitation) (2001) *Child Labour in Portugal: Social Characterization of School Age Children and Their Families*, Lisbon: Ministry of Labour and Solidarity.

Penvenne, Jeanne Marie (1995) *African Workers and Colonial Racism. Mozambican Strategies and Struggles in Laurenço Marques, 1877–1962*, London: James Currey.

Peters, Jeanne M. and Virginia A. Haldeman (1987) 'Time Used for Household Work. A Study of School-age Children from Single-parent, Two-parent, One-earner, and Two-earner Families', *Journal of Family Issues*, 8(2): 212–25.

Pettitt, Bridget (ed.) (1998) *Children and Work in the UK. Reassessing the Issues*, London: Save the Children Fund.

Piaget, Jean (1978) *Le jugement et le raisonnement chez l'enfant*, Paris: Delachaux & Niestlé.

Pineda, Gustavo and Bertha Rosa Guerra (1998) *How Children See Their World. An Exploratory Study*, Managua: Redd Barna.

Piotrkowski, Chaya S. and Joanne Carrubba (1999) 'Child Labor and Exploitation' in Barling and Kelloway (1999), pp. 129–57.

Pollack, Susan H., Philip J. Landrigan and David L. Mallino (1990) 'Child Labor in 1990: Prevalence and Health Hazards', *Annual Review of Public Health*, 11: 359–75.

Pond, C. and A. Searle (1991) *A Hidden Army?*, London: Low Pay Unit.

Portocarrero Grados, Ricardo (1998) *El trabajo infantil en el Perú. Apuntes de interpretación histórica*, Lima: Instituto de Formación para Educadores de Jóvenes, Adolescentes y Niños Trabajadores de América Latina y el Caribe.

Postman, Neil (1982) *The Disappearance of Childhood*, New York: Delacorte Press.

Propper, A. M. (1972) 'The Relationship of Maternal Employment to Adolescent Roles, Activities, and Parental Relationships', *Journal of Marriage and the Family*, 34: 417–21.

Quijano, Aníbal (1998) *La economía popular y sus caminos en América Latina*, Lima: Mosca Azul Editores and CEIS-CECOSAM.

Qvortrup, Jens (2000) 'Kolonisiert und verkannt: Schularbeit', in Hengst and Zeiher (2000), pp. 23–44.

— (2001) 'School-work, Paid Work and the Changing Obligations of Childhood', in Mizen et al. (2001b), pp. 91–107.

Ranjan, Priya (1999) 'An Economic Analysis of Child Labor', *Economics Letters*, 64, Department of Economics, University of California, pp. 99–105.

Razeto, Luis (1997) *Los caminos de la economía de solidaridad*, Buenos Aires: Lumen-Humanitas.

Reagan, Timothy (1996) *Non-Western Educational Traditions. Alternative Approaches, Educational Thought and Practice*, Mahwah, NJ.

Recknagel, Albert (2001a) ' "School is no good to me, I prefer to work." Doubts about the Formula "School Rather than Work" and Project Alternatives Linking Education and Work', in Liebel et al. (2001), pp. 233–45.

— (ed.) (2001b) *Bäuerliches Wissen und Pflege der Lebensvielfalt in den Anden. Von der Entwicklungshilfe zur Stärkung der lokalen Kultur*, Frankfurt: IKO.

Rengifo Vásquez, Grimaldo (2001a) 'Niñez y juego en los Andes', in terre des hommes–Alemania (ed.), *'Yo juego como los sapitos.' Niñez y juego en los Andes*, Cochabamba, Bolivia: terre des hommes, pp. 9–21.

— (2001b) 'Die Entwicklung verlernen, um die andine Kultur zu erlernen', in Recknagel (2001b), pp. 45–61.

Renner, Erich (ed.) (1995) *Kinderwelten. Pädagogische, ethnologische und literaturwissenschaftliche Annäherungen*, Weinheim: Deutscher Studienverlag.

— (1997) 'Kinderwelten – Zur ethnographischen Dimension von Kindheit', in W. Köhnlein et al. (eds), *Kinder auf dem Wege zum Verstehen der Welt*, Bad Heilbrunn: Klinkhardt, pp. 180–99.

Renner, Erich, Sabine Riemann, Ilona K. Schneider and Thomas Trautmann (eds) (1997) *Spiele der Kinder. Interdisziplinäre Annäherungen*, Weinheim: Deutscher Studienverlag.

Renner, Erich and Fritz Seidenfaden (eds) (1997) *Kindsein in fremden Kulturen. Selbstzeugnisse*, 2 vols, Weinheim: Deutscher Studienverlag.

Reymann, Engel Christiane (2001) 'Wo Arbeit Lebensbedürfnis ist. Schülerfirmen in Ostdeutschland', *Neues Deutschland*, 30/31 June: 19.

Reynolds, Pamela (1985) 'Children in Zimbabwe. Rights and Power in Relation to Work', *Anthropology Today*, 1(3).

— (1989) *Childhood in Crossroads. Cognition and Society in South Africa*, Cape Town: David Philip.

— (1991) *Dance Civet Cat: Child Labour in the Zambezi Valley*, London, Athens, OH, and Zimbabwe: Zed Books, Ohio University Press and Baobab Books.

Rikowski, G. and M. Neary (1997) 'Working School Children in Britain Today', *Capital and Class*, 63 (autumn): 25–35.

Ritsert, Jürgen (1997) *Gerechtigkeit und Gleichheit*, Münster: Westfälisches Dampfboot.

Robertson, Claire C. and Martin A. Klein (eds) (1983) *Women and Slavery in Africa*, Madison: University of Wisconsin Press.

Rodgers, Gerry and Guy Standing (1981a) 'The Economic Roles of Children: Issues for Analysis', in Rodgers and Standing (1981b), pp. 1–45.

— (eds) (1981) *Child Work, Poverty and Underdevelopment*, Geneva: ILO.

Rodgers, Paula (1997) 'Save the Children's Position', in McCloskey (1997), pp. 105–14.

Rogoff, B. S., S. Oirrota, N. Fox and S. White (1975) 'Age Assignments of Roles and Responsibilities in Children. A Cross-cultural Survey', *Human Development*, 18.

Rostrowrowski, María (1988) *Historia del Tawantinsuyu*, Lima: Instituto de Estudios Peruanos.

Rubin, V. (1983) 'Family Work Patterns and Community Resources: An Analysis of Children's Access to Support and Services Outside School', in C. D. Hayes and S. B. Kameraman (eds), *Children of Working Parents*, Washington, DC: National Academy Press.

Sack, Allen L. (1977): 'Sport: Play or Work?', in Stevens (1977), pp. 186–96.

Salazar, María Cristina (1990) *Niños y jóvenes trabajadores. Buscando un futuro mejor*, Santa Fé de Bogotá: Universidad Nacional de Colombia.

— (1995) 'The Social Significance of Children and Adolescents' Work in Latin America and the Caribbean', in *Children's Work. To be or not to be*, Lima: Rädda Barnen, pp. 61–82.

Salazar, María Cristina and Walter Alarcón Glasínovich (eds) (1996) *Better Schools: Less Child Work. Child Work and Education in Brazil, Colombia, Ecuador, Guatemala and Peru*, Innocenti Essays, no. 7, Florence: UNICEF.

Salguero, Guillermo (1992) 'El proyecto de unidades de producción escolar', in Gallardo et al. (1992), pp. 184–9.

Sander, Uwe and Ralf Vollbrecht (1985) *Zwischen Kindheit und Jugend. Träume, Hoffnungen und Alltag 13 bis 15 jähriger*, Weinheim and Munich: Juventa.

Sanik, Margaret (1981) 'Division of Household Work: A Decade Comparison – 1967–1977', *Home Economic Research Journal*, 10: 175–80.

Sanz, Andrés (1997) 'From Kundapur to Geneva: The International Coordination of Working Children', *NATs – Working Children and Adolescents International Review*, 3(3–4): 11–23.

Sarmento, Manuel Jacinto, Alexandra Bandeira and Raquel Dores (2000) *Trabalho domiciliário infantil – um estudo de caso no Vale do Ave*, Lisbon: Ministério do Trabalho e da Solidaridade.

Save the Children (1998) 'Children's Perspectives on Work', in Pettitt (1998), pp. 58–79.

— (2000) *Big Business, Small Hands. Responsible Approaches to Child Labour*, London: Save the Children Fund.

Schäfer, Wolfgang (1999) 'Zwischen Kartoffelfeld und Fußballplatz. Der Alltag von Arbeiterjungen in den fünfziger Jahren in der Weser-Solling-Region', *SOWI – Sozialwissenschaftliche Informationen*, 28(2): 137–41.

Scherr, Albert (1997) *Subjektorientierte Jugendarbeit. Eine Einführung in die Grundlagen emanzipatorischer Jugendpädagogik*, Weinheim and Munich: Juventa.

Schibotto, Giangi (1990) *Niños trabajadores. Construyendo una identidad*, Lima: MANTHOC.

— (2001) 'Child Work and Cultures of Child Work: Ecosystem, Taboo and Critical Appraisal', in Liebel et al. (2001), pp. 17–29.

Schildkrout, Enid (1978) 'Age and Gender in Hausa Society. Socio-economic Roles of Children in Urban Kano', in Jean S. La Fontaine (ed.), *Sex and Age as Principles of Social Differentation*, London: Academic Press, pp. 109–37; reprinted in *Childhood*, 9(3) (2002): 344–68.

— (1980) 'Children's Work Reconsidered', *International Social Science Journal*, 32(3): 479–89.

— (1981) 'The Employment of Children in Kano (Nigeria)', in Rodgers and Standing (1981b), pp. 81–112.

Schimmel, Kerstin (1993) *Straßenkinder in Bolivien. Darstellung und Problematisierung vorhandener Betreuungsangebote unter besonderer Berücksichtigung der Lebensbedingungen der Straßenkinder in Cochabamba*, Pädagogische Hochschule, Flensburg (mimeo).

Schlemmer, Bernard (ed.) (1996) *L'enfant exploité*, Paris: Editions Karthala – ORSTOM.

— (ed.) (2000) *The Exploited Child*, London and New York: Zed Books.

Schoenhals, Mark, Marta Tienda and Barbara Schneider (1998) 'The Educational and Personal Consequences of Adolescent Enployment', *Social Forces*, 77(2): 723–62.

Schroeder, Joachim (1989) *Arbeit – Selbstbestimmung – Befreiung. Lateinamerikanische Gegenentwürfe zur europäischen Schule*, Frankfurt: IKO.

Schulenberg, John and Jerald G. Bachman (1993) 'Long Hours on the Job? Not So Bad for Some Adolescents in Some Types of Jobs: The Quality of Work and Substance Use, Affect and Stress', paper presented at the Annual Conference of the US Society for Research on Child Development, New Orleans (mimeo).

Schwartz, Rüdiger (1992) *Das Kinderspiel in Western Samoa und Tonga. Eine vergleichende Analyse zur autochthonen Bewegungskultur*, Münster, Hamburg and London: LIT.

Seabrook, Jeremy (2001) *Children of Other Worlds. Exploitation in the Global Market*, London and Sterling, VA: Pluto Press.

Seidenfaden, Fritz (1997) 'Imitation, Identifikation und ironische Distanz – über einige Funktionen des Kinderspiels in traditionellen Gesellschaften', in Renner et al. (1997), pp. 181–93.

Sennett, Richard (1998) *The Corrosion of Character*, New York: W. W. Norton.

Serrano, Vladimir (1999) (ed.) *Economía de solidaridad y cosmovisión indígena*, Quito: Ediciones ABYA-YALA.

Shanahan, Michael J., Glen H. Elder Jr, Margaret Burchinal and Rand D. Gonger (1996) 'Adolescent Earnings and Relationships with Parents', in Mortimer and Finch (1996), pp. 97–128.

Sheffield, James R. and Victor P. Diejomach (1972) Non-formal Education in African Development, New York: African-American Institute.

Sifuentes, Víctor et al. (1991) Escuela de trabajo. Escuela productiva, Lima: Instituto de Pedagogía Popular.

Singh, Kusum (1998) 'Part-time Employment in High School and Its Effects on Academic Achievement', Journal of Educational Research, 91(3): 131–9.

Skarin, K. and B. E. Smoely (1976) 'Altruistic Behavior: An Analysis of Age and Sex Differences', Child Development, 47: 1,159–65.

Solberg, Anne (1996) 'The Challenge in Child Research: From "Being" to "Doing"', in Brannen and O'Brien (1996), pp. 53–65.

— (1997) 'Seeing Children's Work', in Coninck-Smith et al. (1997), pp. 186–209.

— (2001) 'Hidden Sources of Knowledge of Children's Work in Norway', in Mizen et al. (2001b), pp. 108–20.

Song, Miri (1996) '"Helping Out": Children's Labour Participation in Chinese Take-away Business in Britain', in Brannen and O'Brien (1996), pp. 101–13.

— (1999) Helping Out. Children's Labor in Ethnic Businesses, Philadelphia, PA: Temple Press.

— (2001) 'Chinese Children's Work Roles in Immigrant Adaptation', in Mizen et al. (2001b), pp. 55–69.

Spittler, Gerd (1990) 'La notion de travail chez les Kel Ewey', Revue du Monde Musulman et de la Méditerranée, 57(3): 189–98.

Stark-von der Haar, Elke and Heinrich von der Haar (1980) Kinderarbeit in der Bundesrepublik Deutschland und im Deutschen Reich, Berlin: Verlag Die Arbeitswelt.

Steel, Lauri (1991) 'Early Work Experience among White and Non-white Youths. Implications for Subsequent Enrollment and Employment', Youth & Society, 22(4): 419–47.

Steinberg, Laurence D. and Shelli Avenevoli (1998) 'Disengagement from School and Problem Behavior in Adolescence: A Developmental-contextual Analysis of the Influences of Family and Part-time Work', in Jessor (1998), pp. 392–424.

Steinberg, Laurence D. and Elizabeth Cauffman (1995) 'The Impact of Employment on Adolescent Development', Annals of Child Development, 11: 131–66.

Steinberg, Laurence D. and Sanford M. Dornbusch (1991) 'Negative Correlates of Part-time Employment during Adolescence', Developmental Psychology, 27(2): 304–13.

Steinberg, Laurence D., Suzanne Fegley and Sanford M. Dornbusch (1993) 'Negative Impact of Part-time Work on Adolescent Adjustment: Evidence from a Longitudinal Study', Development Psychology, 29(2): 171–80.

Steinberg, Laurence D., Ellen Greenberger, A. Vaux and M. Ruggiero (1981a)

'Early Work Experience: Effects on Adolescent Occupational Socialisation', *Youth & Society*, 12(4): 403–22.

Steinberg, Laurence D., Ellen Greenberger et al. (1981b) 'Early Work Experience: A Partial Antidote for Adolescent Egocentrism', *Journal of Youth and Adolescence*, 10(2).

Steinberg, Laurence D., Ellen Greenberger, L. Garduque and S. McAuliffe (1982) 'High School Students in the Labor Force: Some Costs and Benefits to Schooling and Learning', *Educational Evaluation and Policy Analysis*, 4(3): 363–72.

Stephens, William N. (1979) *Our Children Should be Working*, Springfield, IL: Charles C. Thomas.

Stern, David and Dorothy Eichorn (eds) (1989) *Adolescence and Work: Influences of Social Structure, Labor Markets, and Culture*, Hillsdale, NJ: Lawrence Erlbaum Associates.

Stevens, Constance J., Laura A. Puchtell, Seongryeol Ryu and Jeylan T. Mortimer (1992) 'Adolescent Work and Boys' and Girls' Orientations to the Future', *Sociological Quarterly*, 33(2): 153–69.

Stevens, Phillip (ed.) (1977) *Studies in the Anthropolgy of Play: Papers in Memory of B. Allan Tindall*, West Point, NY: Leisure Press.

Stone III, James R., David Stern, Charles Hopkins and Martin McMillion (1990) 'Adolescents' Perceptions of Their Work: School Supervised and Non-school Supervised', *Journal of Vocational Education Research*, 15(2): 31–49.

Sunter, Deborah (1992) 'Juggling School and Work', *Perspectives on Labour and Income*, 4 (spring): 15–21.

Sutton-Smith, Brian (1973) 'Spiel, das Vermitteln von Neuem', in *Sport in unserer Welt – Chancen und Probleme*, Berlin, Heidelberg and New York: Springer, pp. 607–13.

— (1978) *Die Dialektik des Spiels. Eine Theorie des Spielens, der Spiele und des Sports*, Schorndorf: Hofmann.

— (ed.) (1979) *Play and Learning*, New York: Gardner Press.

— (1983) 'Die Idealisierung des Spiels', in Grupe et al. (1983), pp. 60–75.

Sutton-Smith, Brian and Diana Kelly-Burne (1986) 'The Idealization of Play', in Peter K. Smith (ed.), *Play in Animals and Humans*, Oxford and New York: Blackwell, pp. 305–21.

Swart, Jill (1990) *Malunde: The Street Children of Hillbrow*, Johannesburg: Witwatersrand University Press.

Swift, Anthony (1999) *Working Children Get Organised. An Introduction to Working Children's Organisations*, London: Save the Children Fund.

— (2001) 'India – Tale of Two Working Children's Unions', in Liebel et al. (2001), pp. 181–95.

Talayesva, Don C. (1964) *Sonnenhäuptling Sitzende Rispe. Ein Indianer erzählt sein Leben*, Kassel: Röth.

Talib, Mohammad (1998) 'Educating the Oppressed: Observations from a School in a Working Class Settlement in Delhi', in S. Shukla and R. Kaul (eds), *Education, Development and Underdevelopment*, New Delhi: Sage, pp. 199–209.

— (2000) 'Learning from Labour vs Learning to Labour: Two Experiences from India', *Rethinking Childhood – Working Children's Challenge to the Social Sciences*, international conference, Institut de Recherche pour le Développement, Bondy-Paris, 15–17 November, Information Bulletin no. 3, pp. 53–64 (mimeo).

Tapscott, Don (1998) *Growing Up Digital. The Rise of the Net Generation*, New York: McGraw-Hill.

TAREA-TINKUY (1989) *Impacto de la crisis en la educación y alternativas de respuesta*, Lima: Tarea.

Terenzio, Fabrizio (2001) 'From Projects for Children via Projects with Children to Children's Trade Unions. Description of a Development in Africa', in Liebel et al. (2001), pp. 289–94.

Thomson, Donald and Isabel White (1993) 'Kinder der Traumzeit. Es war einmal in Australien', in Loo and Reinhart (1993), pp. 366–81.

Thrall, C. A. (1978) 'Who Does What? Role Stereotyping, Children's Work, and Continuity between Generations in the Household Division of Labor', *Human Relations*, 31: 249–65.

Thüringen (2000) Thüringer Landesamt für Soziales und Familie (ed.), *Kinderarbeit im Freistaat Thüringen*, Suhl.

Tienda, Marta (1979) 'The Economic Activity of Children in Peru: Labor Force Behavior in Rural and Urban Contexts', *Rural Sociology*, 44(2): 370–91.

Tienda, Marta and Avner Ahituv (1996) 'Ethnic Differences in School Departure: Does Youth Employment Promote or Undermine Educational Attainment?', in *Of Heart and Mind: Social Policy Essays in Honor of Sar A. Levitan*, Kalamazoo, MI: Upjohn Institute, pp. 93–110.

Toffler, Alvin (1980) *The Third Wave*, New York: Morrow.

Tolfree, David (1998) *Old Enough to Work, Old Enough to Have a Say. Different Approaches to Supporting Working Children*, Stockholm: Rädda Barnen.

Touraine, Alain (1994) *Critique of Modernity*, New York (orig. *Critique de la modernité*, Paris: Librairie Arthème Fayard, 1992).

Touré, Marema (1998) 'A Case Study of the Work of Enda in Senegal in Supporting the Association of Child and Young Workers', in Tolfree (1998), pp. 179–200.

Traoré, Mamadou (1940) 'Jeux et jouets des enfants Foula', *IFAN Bulletin*, 2: 5–6.

TUC (1997) *Working Classes: A TUC Report on School Age Labour in England and Wales*, London: Trades Union Congress.

Ulmann, Gisela (1979) 'Hau ab und spiel. Arbeit und Erziehungskrise', in: Neue Gesellschaft für Bildende Kunst e.V. and Staatliche Kunsthalle Berlin (eds), *Die gesellschaftliche Wirklichkeit der Kinder in der bildenden Kunst*, Berlin, pp. 17–46.

'Una Experiencia de Educación y Producción en el C. E. "Madre Admirable" de El Agustino (1989)', in TAREA-TINKUY (1989), pp. 32–4.

UNICEF (1997) *The State of the World's Children 1997*, New York: United Nations Children's Fund.

Van Hear, Nick (1982) 'Child Labour and the Development of Capitalist Agriculture in Ghana', *Development and Change*, 13: 499–514.

Van Onselen, Charles (1976) *Chibaro. African Mine Labour in Southern Rhodesia 1900–1933*, London: Pluto Press.

Viezzer, Moema (1981) *'Wenn man mir erlaubt zu sprechen ...' Zeugnis der Domitila, einer Frau aus den Minen Boliviens*, Bornheim-Merten: Lamuv (7th edn).

Voss, Günther (1998) 'Die Entgrenzung von Arbeit und Arbeitskraft. Eine subjektorientierte Interpretation des Wandels der Arbeit', *Mitteilungen aus der Arbeitsmarkt- und Berufsforschung*, 31(3): 473–87.

Wadel, Cato (1979) 'The Hidden Work of Everyday Life', in Sandra Wallmann (ed.), *Social Anthropology of Work*, London: Academic Press, pp. 365–84.

Wagner, W. and F. Elejabarrieta (1994) 'Representaciones Sociales', in José Francisco Morales et al. (eds), *Psicología Social*, Madrid: McGraw-Hill.

Watson, Lawrence C. (1970) 'Self and Ideal in a Guajiro Life History', *Acta Ethnologica et Linguista*, 21, Vienna.

Weiss, Florence (1981) 'Kinder schildern ihren Alltag. Die Stellung des Kindes im ökonomischen System einer Dorfgemeinschaft in Papua New Guinea', *Basler Beiträge zur Ethnologie*, 21, Basle: Wepf.

— (1993) 'Von der Schwierigkeit, über Kinder zu forschen. Die Iatmul in Papua-Neuguinea', in Loo and Reinhart (1993), pp. 96–153.

— (1995) 'Kinder erhalten das Wort. Aussagen von Kindern in der Ethnologie', in Renner (1995), pp. 133–47.

— (1999) *Vor dem Vulkanausbruch. Eine ethnologische Erzählung*, Frankfurt: Fischer.

Werth, Helmut (1997) 'Spiel – nichts als Arbeit. Spielend erfährt das Kind den Ernst des Lebens', Bolzano, Verein für Kinderspielplätze und Erholung – Associazione Campi Gioco e Ricreazione (not published).

Wetzel, Susanne and Martin Sorge (1999) *Kinder- und Jugendfirmen – eine Chance für eigeninitiatives Lernen und Arbeiten in der offenen Kinder- und Jugendarbeit*, Science of Education thesis, Technical University of Berlin (mimeo).

White, Ben (1994) 'Children, Work and "Child Labour": Changing Responses to the Employment of Children', *Development and Change*, 25(4): 849–78.

— (1996) 'Globalisation and the Child Labour Problem', *Journal of International Development*, 8(6): 829–39.

— (1997) 'Child Labour in the International Context', in McCloskey (1997), pp. 11–28.

— (1999) 'Defining the Intolerable: Child Work, Global Standards and Cultural Relativism', *Childhood*, 6(1): 133–44.

White, Lynn K. and David B. Brinkerhoff (1981a) 'Children's Work in the Family: Its Significance and Meaning', *Journal of Marriage and the Family*, 43: 789–98.

— (1981b) 'The Sexual Division of Labor: Evidence from Childhood', *Social Forces*, 60: 170–81.

WHO (1987) *Children at Work. Special Health Risks*, Technical Report Series no. 756, Geneva: World Health Organization.

Wienold, Hanns (1997) 'Kinderarbeit in Deutschland. Ein Massenphänomen', *Jugendpolitik*, ed. Deutscher Bundesjugendring, 3 (October): 16–18.

Wilhelm, J. H. (1953) 'Die Kung-Buschleute', *Jahrbuch des Museums für Völkerkunde*, vol. 12, Leipzig, pp. 178–81.

Wilk, Valerie A. (1993) 'Health Hazards to Children in Agriculture', *American Journal of Industrial Medicine*, 24: 283–90.

Wintersberger, Helmut (1996) 'The Ambivalence of Modern Childhood. A Plea for a European Strategy for Children', *Children on the Way from Marginality towards Citizenship. Childhood Politics: Conceptual and Practical Issues*, international seminar, Montebello, Canada, 16–20 October 1995 (Eurosocial Report 61/1996), Vienna, pp. 195–211.

— (1998) 'Ökonomie der Kindheit – Wandel der ökonomischen Verhältnisse zwischen den Generationen', in Kränzl-Nagl et al. (1998), pp. 77–103.

— (2000) 'Kinder als ProduzentInnen und als KonsumentInnen. Zur Wahrnehmung der ökonomischen Bedeutung von Kinderaktivitäten', in Hengst and Zeiher (2000), pp. 169–88.

Winters-Smith, C. and M. Larner (1992) 'The Fair Start Program: Outreach to Migrant Farmworker Families', in M. Larner, R. Halpern and O. Harkavy (eds), *Fair Start for Children: Lessons Learned from Seven Demonstration Projects*, New Haven, CT: Yale University Press, pp. 46–67.

Woodhead, Martin (1998) *Children's Perspectives on Their Working Lives: A Participatory Study in Bangladesh, Ethiopia, the Philippines, Guatemala, El Salvador and Nicaragua*, Stockholm: Rädda Barnen.

— (1999) 'Combating Child Labour: Listen to What the Children Say', *Childhood*, 6(1): 27–50.

— (2001) 'The Value of Work and School. A Study of Working Children's Perspectives', in Lieten and White (2001), pp. 103–16.

Wright, Marcia (1993) *Strategies of Slaves and Women. Life Stories from East/Central Africa*, London: James Currey.

Zeiher, Helga (2000) 'Hausarbeit: zur Integration der Kinder in die häusliche Arbeitsteilung', in Hengst and Zeiher (2000), pp. 45–69.

Zeiher, Helga, Peter Büchner and Jürgen Zinnecker (eds) (1996) *Kinder als Außenseiter? Umbrüche in der gesellschaftlichen Wahrnehmung von Kindern*, Weinheim and Munich: Juventa.

Zelizer, Viviana A. (1994) *Pricing the Priceless Child. The Changing Social Value of Children*, Princeton, NJ: Princeton University Press (1st edn New York: Basic Books, 1985).

— (2002) 'Kids and Commerce', *Childhood*, 9(4): 375–96.

Zill, N. and J. L. Peterson (1982) 'Learning to Do Things without Help', in L. M. Loasa and I. E. Sigel (eds), *Families as Learning Environment for Children*, New York: Plenum Press, pp. 343–74.

Zinnecker, Jürgen (1997) 'Metamorphosen im Zeitraffer: Jungsein in der zweiten Hälfte des 20. Jahrhunderts', in Giovanni Levi and Jean-Claude Schmitt (eds), *Geschichte der Jugend. Von der Aufklärung bis zur Gegenwart*, Frankfurt: Fischer, pp. 460–505.

Index